D1518638

Hay and Forage Harvesting

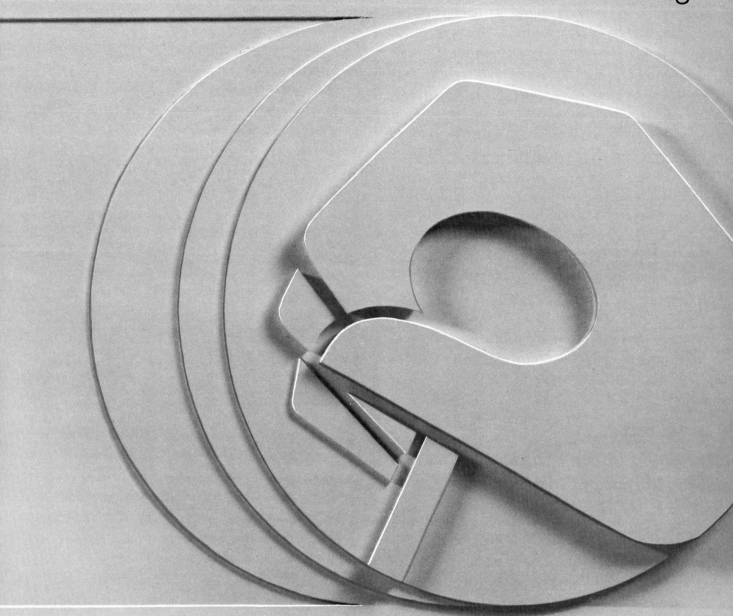

Fundamentals of Machine Operation

JOHN DEERE

PUBLISHER

Fundamentals of Machine Operation (FMO) is a series of manuals created by Deere & Company. Each book in the series is conceived, researched, outlined, edited, and published by Deere & Company. Authors are selected to provide a basic technical manuscript which is edited and rewritten by staff editors.

PUBLISHER: DEERE & COMPANY SERVICE TRAINING, Dept. F, John Deere Road, Moline, Illinois 61265.

JOHN DEERE FUNDAMENTAL WRITING SERVICES EDITORIAL STAFF

Managing Editor: Louis R. Hathaway
Editor: Larry A. Riney
Promotion: Annette M. LaCour

FOR MORE INFORMATION: This text is part of a complete series of texts and visuals on agricultural machinery called Fundamentals of Machine Operation (FMO). For more information, request a free FMO Catalog of Manuals and Visuals. Send your request to John Deere Service Publications, Dept. F., John Deere Road, Moline, Illinois 61265.

AUTHORS: Allen R. Rider, assistant professor of agricultural engineering, Oklahoma State University, has been an agricultural engineer since 1972 and is a machinery specialist for hay and forage harvesting equipment.

Stephen D. Barr, is an agricultural journalism graduate from the University of Missouri. He was an editor for the FMO series of publications and is now a copywriter in the Deere & Company Advertising Department.

CONSULTING EDITORS: Roland F. Espenschied, Ed.D., Professor of Agricultural Engineering and Vocational Agriculture Service, University of Illinois, has written many publications and prepared other types of audio-visual materials in agricultural mechanization during his 27 years as a teacher and teacher-educator. Professor Espenschied has spent 17 years specializing in agricultural mechanics in the Agricultural Engineering Department of the University of Illinois following ten years of teaching vocational agriculture.

Thomas A. Hoerner, Ph.D., Professor and Teacher-Educator in Agricultural Engineering and Agricultural Education at Iowa State University. Dr. Hoerner has 19 years of high school and university teaching experience. He has authored numerous manuals and instructional materials in the agricultural mechanics area.

Keith R. Carlson has 20 years of experience as a high school vocational agricultural instructor. Mr. Carlson is the author of numerous instructor's guides, including the American Oil Company's "Vo-Ag Management Kits."

Many of his aids have been available under the name Vo-Ag Visuals. All instructor's kits for the FMO texts are being prepared by Mr. Carlson.

SPECIAL ACKNOWLEDGEMENTS: The authors and editors wish to thank the following Deere & Company people for their assistance: Robert A. Sohl, Director of Service; Tom W. Myers, Senior Staff Engineer, Technical Center; personnel at John Deere Ottumwa Works, Service and Service Publications Departments; and a host of other John Deere people who gave extra assistance and advice on this project.

CONTRIBUTORS: The publisher is grateful to the following individuals and companies who were helpful in providing some of the photographs used in this text:

Ag Sales Inc., McPherson, Kansas — pp. 205, Fig. 48.

Allis-Chalmers Mfg. Co. — pg. 148, Fig. 1; pg. 150, Fig. 4.

Deweze Mfg. Co., Harper, Kansas — pg. 125, Fig. 4; pg. 175, Fig. 52; pg. 176, Fig. 54.

Farmhand Inc., Hopkins, Minnesota — pg. 79, Fig. 18; pg. 90, Fig. 6; pg. 124, Fig. 2; pg. 159, Fig. 28; pg. 177, Fig. 56; pg. 185, Fig. 5; pg. 188, Fig. 13.

Ford Tractor Operations, Ford Motor Company, Troy , Michigan — pg. 95, Figs. 17, 18, 21.

Foster Mfg. Co., Madras, Oregon — pg. 91, Fig. 7.

Freeman, J.A. & Son, Inc., Portland, Oregon — pg. 128, Fig. 9.

Gehl Co., West Bend, Wisconsin — pg. 158, Fig. 25; pg. 174, Fig. 51; pg. 189, Fig. 14; pg. 205, Fig. 46; pg. 239, Fig. 14; pg. 267, Fig. 8; pg. 268, Fig. 11; pg. 291, Fig. 10.

Graves Mfg. Co., Clinton, Oklahoma — pg. 124, Fig. 1; pg. 173, Fig. 50.

Hawk Bilt Co., Vinton, Iowa — pg. 151, Fig. 8; pg. 152, Fig. 11; pg. 155, Figs. 19, 20 & 21; pg. 156, Figs. 22 & 23.

Haybuster Mfg. Inc., Jamestown, North Dakota — pg. 188, Figs. 11 & 12.

Hesston Corp., Hesston, Kansas — pg. 151, Fig. 9; pg. 204, Fig. 43; pg. 205, Fig. 47.

International Harvester, Chicago, Illinois — pg. 74, Fig. 7; pg. 179, Fig. 62.

Kent Mfg. Co., Tipton, Kansas — pg. 125, Fig. 3.

Massey-Ferguson, Inc., Des Moines, Iowa — pg. 45, Fig. 11; pg. 78, Fig. 17.

Purdue University, Ag Information Dept., Lafayette, Indiana — pg. 40, Fig. 2.

Rider, Allen R. — pg. 92, Fig. 11; pg. 138, Fig. 32; pg. 139, Fig. 33; pg. 157, Fig. 24; pg. 159, Fig. 27; pg. 160, Fig. 29; pg. 164, Fig. 38; pg. 165, Fig. 40; pg. 173, Fig. 49; pg. 176, Fig. 55; pg. 177, Fig. 57; pg. 178, Figs. 58, 59, 60; pg. 179, Fig. 61 & 63; pg. 180, Fig. 64; pg. 192, Fig. 19.

Smith, Kenneth H. — pg. 5, Fig. 6.

Sperry New Holland, New Holland, Pennsylvania — Chapter 7, Figs. 6, 7, 10-15, 19-32, 34; pg. 151, Fig. 7; pg. 155, Fig. 18.

Vermeer Mfg. Co., Pella, Iowa — pg. 75, Fig. 9; pg. 175, Fig. 53.

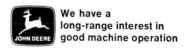

We have a long-range interest in good machine operation

Contents

5
RAKES

6
BALERS

7
BALE HANDLING AND STORAGE

8
ROUND BALERS AND MOVERS

9
STACK WAGONS AND STACK MOVERS

10
HAY CUBERS

11

FORAGE HARVESTERS

12

SELF-UNLOADING FORAGE WAGONS

13

BLOWERS

14

SELECTING EQUIPMENT

APPENDIX

1
Introduction

Fig. 1—The Hay Wain

TIMES CHANGE

When John Constable painted his well-known picture, The Hay Wain (Fig. 1), in rural England early in the 1800s, the Fundamentals of Machine Operation as they applied to Hay and Forage Harvesting were simple, indeed.

The Hay Wain was a wagon for hauling hay, probably made by the local wainwright (wagonmaker). If there had been a Hay Wain Operator's Manual or an FMO book on haymaking, it might have suggested:

"The operator should make sure the wheels of his wain are tight and sound. If inspection shows that spokes have dried and shrunk away from the rims and hubs, drive the wain into a shallow stream, and let the components soak up enough water to make them tighten up. Maintain your power source in good condition; allow horses to rest frequently, and supply them with adequate water for their cooling systems as well as comfort, especially on a hot day. A good manager may combine the two functions — soaking the wheels and watering the horses — before returning the wain to the field where operators of the scythes, hand rakes, and pitchforks may have another wainload ready for transport."

A hundred years later, good managers were still looking for ways to improve hay harvesting and storage efficiency. Round barns (Fig. 2) rose on farmsteads, with the idea that a man could operate his pitchfork most efficiently from the haymow if he could toss hay down to mangers in a circular pattern. Today, descendants of round-barn builders may choose to feed from self-unloading forage wagons (Fig. 2).

Today hay and forage harvesting machines have greatly improved the efficiency of crop handling and storage. What once was a labor intensive part of farming now has become a highly automated science (Fig. 3).

This book is devoted to hay and forage harvesting equipment. It touches only lightly on the how and why of feeding and nutrition and the selection and growing of hay and forage crops.

Good hay and forage management requires a complete understanding of the many machines that handle cereal and legume crops from cutting to storage. It also requires that you preserve as much of the nutritional value in the crop as possible, with the lowest investment of labor and money. The fundamental knowledge you get from this book can help you select specific management targets, then hit the bull's-eye with top efficiency.

Knowledge learned and then applied is the basis of good management. Your accomplishments show up in gratifying financial rewards and personal satisfaction.

Fig. 2—Round Barn Near Irasburg, Vermont

WE REPEAT AND REPEAT

Throughout this book we stress safety, planning, and preparation — safety, planning, and preparation. Safety repetition is good. It's very good. It's for your own good. It's a drumming background that makes you so conscious of the fundamentals of safety that practicing those fundamentals will become automatic. **Think. Then do it.**

WE DON'T HAVE ROOM FOR EVERYTHING

Construction and use of silos isn't detailed in this book. Nor are the specifics of livestock feeding. Such topics are supplemental to hay and forage harvesting machinery.

Fig. 3 — Crop Handling Is A Highly Automated Science.

This book is for today's problems and methods.

Changes are coming in measurements, in the crops grown, and in livestock feeding. Even more changes are coming in machinery you will use in the future.

But the "fundamentals" will always be the same.

MANY CROPS, MANY MACHINES

We'll start with a discussion of hay and forage crops grown in North America. Then we will discuss methods used to cut, cure, package, harvest, and store crops. First, the crops:

- **Hay**
- **Silage**
- **Haylage**

HAY

Hay is produced in every state in the union. Millions of tons of hay are harvested each year. The production volume is second only to corn.

Hay is a green forage crop harvested for livestock feed and stored at low moisture levels so no special storage structures or preservatives are required. Crops harvested for hay:

- **Alfalfa**
- **Clover**
- **Sorghum**
- **Birdsfoot trefoil**
- **Reed canary grass**
- **Smooth bromegrass**
- **Bermuda grass**
- **Wheat grass**
- **Canada wild rye**
- **Timothy**
- **Russian wild rye**
- **Native grasses**
- **Cereal grains such as oats, barley, and wheat**

Alfalfa is the most common hay crop.

With proper management, hay returns a good profit. It is produced by commercial hay growers and by stockmen who feed their own hay. High-quality hay can have nutrient levels nearly equivalent to many concentrates. Hay is one of the least expensive sources of protein for livestock feed.

Also, hay can be grown on rough terrain unsuitable for other crops. Although outside hay storage is acceptable, inside storage helps preserve quality. Hay requires a lot of labor to harvest. However, with good hay equipment, mechanization is possible, from field to feeding (Fig. 5).

Fig. 4—Hay Is Grown In Every State

Many farmers consider hay a second-class crop because it has not matched the production increases of other crops in the last 20 years. However, only a small percentage of farmers have applied the best tillage and fertilization practices to increase production. Even fewer farmers have developed the management skills required to grow and harvest high quality hay. The shortage of reliable farm labor to harvest and handle hay has discouraged some hay growers. Some farmers fear rainy, damp weather that can cause severe quality losses on windrowed hay and square bales left in the field.

Farmers must cure their hay without excessive loss to have an efficient operation.

CURING

Hay is cured in:

- **Field**
- **Barn**
- **Dehydrator**

Field

Field curing is inexpensive, but losses in quality and quantity are greater than barn and dehydrator curing. Timely field operations and good machine performance are needed to minimize losses. Hay is open to damage from bad weather while it is being field cured.

Barn

Barn drying is usually a supplement to field curing. Barn drying is used in humid climates. The hay may be dried with natural air or heated air. At least partial field curing is required for natural air barn drying to prevent spoilage before the hay is completely dry. However, losses, in quality and quantity, are usually less than in field curing due to decreased exposure to weather. But barn curing is not widely practiced because it takes additional labor to stack hay uniformly for even air distribution. And, constructing and operating the drying system costs extra money.

Fig. 5—Hay Harvesting Labor Is Reduced with New Equipment

Fig. 6—Dehydrator Rapidly Removing Moisture from Hay

Dehydrator

A dehydrator uses fuel such as natural gas to heat the hay and evaporate moisture (Fig. 6). A dehydrator can cure direct-cut hay or wilted hay. This method of curing produces the highest quality hay with minimum quantity losses. However, it only pays to dehydrate the highest quality forages, such as alfalfa.

Harvesting or "packaging" field cured hay is an essential part of most haying operations. You have to harvest a lot of hay to pay for a dehydrator.

HARVESTING

Hay packaging equipment:

- **Balers**
- **Round balers**
- **Stackers**

Most of this equipment is covered in detail later, so only a brief discussion follows in this introduction.

Balers

Balers produce a package suitable for both the commercial hay grower and the stockman who feeds his own hay (Fig. 7). Bales are made from field cured hay, but low density bales may be barn dried. There are four sizes of bales weighing from 50 to 2000 pounds.

Round Balers

Big, round balers are well matched to the needs of the stockman. But due to handling problems and bulk of large, round bales, the commercial hay grower needs a nearby market to make them pay off. Round bales (Fig. 8) are usually rolled from field cured windrows, but some round bales are barn-dried.

Fig. 7—Bales Form Convenient Hay Packages

Round balers can be modified to bale silage. A special kit must be used to reduce roll wrappage and crop buildup. Modifications must include roll scrapers and anti-wrap spirals. A deflector can be added to help eject the silage bale.

Pellet Mills

Stationary cubers and pellet mills are specialized packaging machines used at hay processing plants. Some cubers and pellet mills are mounted on trucks, and are moved to hay collection points to reduce hauling hay.

Stationary machines can process bales, stacks, large round bales, and direct-cut, dehydrated hay into cubes or pellets. Alfalfa is generally the crop processed. Only large commercial hay operations or cooperatives can justify ownership of stationary cubers and pellet mills. Because these machines are not used extensively by farmers, a detailed description is not presented in the text.

Whether a hay grower decides to produce bales, stacks, round bales, cubes, or pellets, he must manage carefully. A well managed hay harvesting system has:

- **Timely operations**
- **Properly maintained equipment**
- **Trained, skilled operators**
- **Constantly followed safety precautions**

Intelligent management is the key to consistent, economical harvesting of quality hay.

Fig. 8—Big Round Bales Are Made Fast and Easily

Fig. 9 — Maintain Equipment Properly

Fig. 10 — Baling Silage

STORING

Climate determines the kind of storage you use (Fig. 12). Types of storage commonly used are:

● Barn

● Temporary cover

● Field

These methods are discussed briefly here.

Barn

Barn storage provides the most protection from weather. So it preserves the quality of hay more effectively than other storage methods. However, barn storage is also the most expensive method. Square bales, small round bales, and cubes are best for barn storage. Bales stack easily and efficiently in a barn. Neither small or large round bales stack effectively, but some hay growers are willing to sacrifice some storage efficiency. Cubes are stored inside to prevent deterioration and preserve their quality.

Temporary Covers

Temporary covers are sometimes placed over hay to keep it dry. Temporary covers are usually polyethylene sheets, canvas, or nylon tarpaulins. Although expensive, temporary covers protect hay quality.

Field

Field storage is the least expensive method of hay storage. But, because the hay is exposed to sun, wind, and moisture, quality losses may be excessive. However, thoughtful selection of the storage site can help minimize loss of quality. A proper site has good drainage and protection from wind. Large round bales and loose-hay stacks are often stored outside. Hay stacks with tightly compacted, sloping surfaces resist penetration by rain and wind. Cubes may also be stacked outside for a short period in dry weather.

Fig. 11—Every Harvesting System Needs Good Management for High Quality Hay

Fig. 12—Hay May Be Stored in the Barn or Field

SILAGE AND HAYLAGE

Green forage may also be preserved as silage or haylage. Most silage and haylage is fed to dairy and beef cattle.

Silage is forage converted into succulent livestock feed through fermentation.

Haylage is a low-moisture (40 to 50 percent) hay silage which is normally stored in an oxygen limiting storage unit. However, with excellent management and proper preparation, haylage may be stored in a good conventional silo. Haylage is chopped fine so it will pack down and exclude air.

Some crops that are harvested for silage:

- **Corn**
- **Grain sorghum**
- **Forage sorghum**
- **Sudan grass**
- **Sorghum-sudan hybrids**
- **Oats**
- **Alfalfa**
- **Alfalfa-grass mixtures**

Corn is the most common silage crop (Fig. 13).

QUALITY FEED

Because silage crops are harvested in a high-moisture condition, leaf losses are less than hay harvested and field-cured. Saving leaves increases forage quality. With high-quality forage, a balanced ration can be provided with less supplemental feeding. Also, the effect of weather on quality is minimized because silage can be harvested in damp weather. Properly stored silage can be kept two years or more with little nutrient loss.

The silage fermentation process kills weed seeds and helps reduce weed problems on the farm. In addition, stored silage is less susceptible to fire than barn-stored hay.

LABOR REQUIREMENT

Labor can be saved during silage feeding by using automated equipment. However, a large, competent labor force is needed during harvest to harvest at the right time and to fill the silo quickly.

LIMITATIONS

Even with its many advantages, proper management of the entire silage crop from planting through feeding is needed to assure quality. Management problems encountered with silage are generally associated with harvest and feeding. A silage harvesting operation must be well planned to avoid hauling bulky, heavy, chopped forage long distances from the field to storage. Furthermore, scheduling and hiring the labor crew needed during harvest is frequently difficult. Also, silage must be fed soon after it is removed from storage or it will spoil.

A silo is needed to store silage. If you stop feeding silage, alternative uses of the silo are limited. Also, due to its high moisture content and perishability, there is little flexibility in marketing excess silage. Long-distance transportation is not feasible. A large investment is required for harvesting equipment.

HARVESTING

Two types of silage harvesting operations:

- **Direct-cut**
- **Wilting**

Direct-cut

In direct-cut harvesting, a forage harvester cuts the standing crop, then chops and blows it into a forage wagon or

Fig. 13—Corn Is the Major Crop Grown for Silage

Fig. 14—Direct-Cut Forage Harvesting

truck for transportation to storage (Fig. 14). Harvest losses are minimized because the green crop is fed directly into the forage harvester. Also, harvest labor is reduced with an operation that cuts, chops, and blows forage into a wagon or truck in one operation.

Wilting

The wilting method starts with windrowing green forage. After the windrowed crop has wilted to about 60 to 70 percent moisture, a forage harvester with pickup attachment picks up the windrow and chops and blows the forage into a wagon or truck for transportation to the silo (Fig. 15). Wilting the crop before chopping increases labor and field losses.

Forage crop wilting is required to reduce the moisture content so proper fermentation occurs to produce silage or haylage. Some crops have too much moisture. Excess moisture will increase seepage loss during storage and cause silage to be soggy, sour, and unpalatable. A wilting period reduces the moisture content enough to overcome these problems.

To produce haylage, the crop moisture must be reduced from 70 to 85 percent moisture to between 40 and 50 percent. Curing requires approximately 4 hours in good drying weather.

SILAGE ADDITIVES

Additives are sometimes added to green, chopped forage to aid the ensiling process or to increase feeding value. Additives are:

- Chemical additives
- Feeds
- Nutrients

These are described in the following paragraphs.

Chemical Additives

Chemicals are added to change or maintain the pH level for proper fermentation. Chemicals do not add food value nor reduce the silage moisture content. They are usually organic acids, water soluble salts, or finely-crushed limestone.

Feed Additives

Certain feed additives aid the ensiling process and add food value to the silage. Typical feed additives are molasses or grain. Molasses provides sugar for the ensiling process but does not reduce the moisture content. Grain reduces silage moisture and assists fermentation.

Nutrient Additives

Nutrient additives increase the feeding value. A proper additive mixture can provide a balanced ration for a specific feeding program. Nutrient additives are not intended to aid the ensiling process, and may actually hinder fermentation under some conditions. Nutrient additives reduce or eliminate the need for supplemental feeding. They include mineral supplements, urea, and anhydrous ammonia.

STORING

Green, chopped forage, harvested for silage, is stored in silos classified as:

- Vertical

Oxygen-limiting

Conventional

Fig. 15—Wilted-Forage Harvesting

Fig. 16—Silage and Haylage Are Stored in Vertical Silos

- **Horizontal**

Bunker

Trench

Stack

Vertical Silos

Vertical silos may be classified as *oxygen-limiting* or *conventional* (Fig. 16).

Oxygen-limiting units can reduce storage losses and are used to store haylage and silage. They cost more per cubic foot of storage space than conventional silos. They are usually made of metal with an inner liner of fused glass, but some concrete silos may be satisfactorily sealed with an interior coating or lining.

Conventional silos are constructed from metal, concrete, or tile.

Primary advantages of vertical silos are:

- *Relatively low storage losses*
- *Easy adaptability for automated feeding*
- *No need for extensive packing*
- *They can be located near livestock*

Primary disadvantages are:

- *Need for special equipment to fill and unload*
- *Difficulties in feeding if unloader malfunctions*
- *High cost of storage per ton of dry matter*
- *Acids formed during fermentation may cause deterioration of some silo walls*

Horizontal Silos

Horizontal silos are often classified as *bunkers, trenches,* or *stacks.*

A *bunker silo* is placed above the ground surface and usually has concrete or plank walls and a concrete floor.

A *trench silo* is dug into the ground, usually into the side of a hill. It may have concrete walls and floor, but frequently the soil is used for both sides and floor.

A *stack silo* is merely a compacted pile of silage placed on the ground with no walls. Stack silos should be used only for emergency storage of excess silage. Stack silage should be fed fast, before it spoils.

Primary advantages of horizontal silos are:

- *No special loading and unloading equipment*
- *Easy to build*
- *Adaptable to self feeding*
- *Cost less per cubic foot of capacity, compared to vertical silos (Fig. 17)*

Primary disadvantages of horizontal silos are:

- *Require extensive packing*
- *Not suitable for automated feeding*
- *Well drained locations are not always available*
- *Unless very good management is applied, horizontal silos often incur more spoilage and leaching losses than vertical silos*

PLANNING FOR A FORAGE CROP

Growing, harvesting, storing, selling, and feeding a quality forage crop is difficult. In planning a profitable forage system, a good manager must evaluate many factors and details — always keeping in mind:

The primary reason for incorporating a forage system into a farm enterprise is to earn maximum profits.

Some factors that must be considered are:

● *Suitability of the farming enterprise for incorporating a forage system (soil type and terrain, crop rotation, scheduling harvest operations, etc.)*

● *Managerial abilities and desires*

● *Type and yield of crops suitable for the terrain, soil, and climate*

● *Selecting a forage crop that produces acceptable quality and quantity.*

● *Feeding or selling the forage crop*

● *Agronomic practices required to produce forage (tillage, fertilization, etc.)*

● *Availability of sufficient water*

● *Type of insect and disease controls required*

● *Labor requirement and availability*

● *Selection of an appropriate harvest system*

QUALITY HAY — A MANAGEMENT GOAL

Hay feeding value is perishable. Of the many factors that affect hay quality, timely and efficient harvest is most important. The crop must be cut at the right time, cured properly, and handled with care to produce top quality hay (Fig. 18).

Leaves contain most of the food value in hay, especially in legumes such as alfalfa and clover. Consequently, every field operation must be planned and carried out to minimize leaf loss.

Most field losses occur during cutting and through the time when the hay is picked up for packaging. Field operations and equipment are very important in limiting field loss.

Fig. 17—Horizontal Silos Provide Economical Storage

SUMMARY

Legume and cereal crops are grown throughout the United States for livestock feed and are harvested as hay, silage, or haylage.

Hay is a green forage crop. It includes many varieties. The most common is alfalfa. Hay may be grown on rolling and rough land not suited to other crops. It is a low-cost, high-nutrient livestock feed. And, with the right equipment, hay doesn't require many man hours to harvest.

HAY is usually packaged in square bales, round bales, stacks, cubes, or pellets. It may be cured in the field, in barns, or in dehydrators. Timely cutting and curing are important. Hay must be cured until the moisture content is just right. And weather can damage hay while it is curing. Packaged hay may be stored inside or outside. Outside storage is least expensive, but it subjects the hay to quality loss, especially if the storage site is damp and windy or if the bales or stacks are not properly made.

SILAGE is commonly made from corn. However, other silage crops, such as sorghums, sudan, oats, and alfalfa, are also used. Crops are harvested green and incur less leaf loss than field-cured hay. The high moisture silage produced by cutting or chopping the crop at 60 to 70 percent moisture content is stored in vertical or horizontal silos. Silage is excellent livestock feed.

HAYLAGE is low-moisture silage (40 to 50 percent) which is usually stored in an oxygen limiting silo.

Most silage crops must be windrowed and wilted for a short time to lower moisture content enough for proper fermentation. Slightly longer wilting is required to produce haylage. Additives, including chemicals, feeds, and nutrients, may be mixed with silage as preservatives or to improve food value.

A FORAGE crop with the proper moisture content may be direct-cut with a forage harvester, which chops and blows the forage into a forage wagon or truck. Direct cutting reduces curing losses and labor.

Good management and planning are the keys to any haying or silage operation.

Fig. 18—Time Field Operations Carefully

CHAPTER QUIZ

1. What is the most common crop grown for hay?

2. Name three locations where hay is usually cured.

3. List the different kinds of equipment usually used for packaging hay.

4. What are three major factors that affect hay quality regardless of the equipment used?

5. What is the least expensive method of storing hay?

6. What is the most common crop grown for silage?

7. (True or false.) Haylage is a low-moisture silage which must be finely chopped for better packing.

8. Give two reasons for wilting a crop for silage before chopping.

9. (Fill in blanks.) Silos are classified as either _____ or _____.

10. What factor has been most urgent in the shift to mechanization of hay and forage harvesting?

11. (True or false.) Managerial abilities and desires must be considered when planning for a forage crop.

2
Mowers

Fig. 1—Mowing Hay with a Scythe

Fig. 2—Horse Powered Mower

INTRODUCTION

Crops and grasses have been cut for hay for thousands of years with the sickle and scythe (Fig. 1). While these hand tools are still used in some parts of the world, most man powered hay cutting equipment was replaced by horse drawn mowers in the 1800s (Fig. 2). Now, tractor powered mowers with increased field capacity and reduced labor requirements have replaced nearly all horse powered equipment (Fig. 3).

PURPOSE AND USE OF MOWERS

The function of a mower is to cut standing vegetation. On farms, a mower is used to cut hay and weeds, clip pastures, and to dispose of crop residues. A mower must cut materials from tender grasses to small brush without clogging.

CUTTING METHODS

Hay crops are cut by applying either impact or shearing forces to the standing vegetation. An *impact* occurs when a blade hits a stem (Fig. 4). A corn knife, scythe, rotary mower, and flail mower use impact force to cut plants.

A *rotary mower* has one or more rotating blades and is commonly used to cut weeds, stalks, grass, and brush (Fig. 5). Because they are low and coupled close to the tractor, rotary mowers are frequently used in orchards to trim grass and weeds under trees.

Rotary disc mowers. High speed rotating disks with two replaceable knives cut at a high rpm. Rotary cutters hug the ground for a smooth cut of hay. Rotary action allows the cutter to float over the ground and cut through even wet and tangled hay (Fig. 5).

Flail cutters have flails attached to a rotating horizontal shaft. Flail mowers are good for chopping crop residue

Fig. 3—Tractor Powered Mower

Fig. 4—Cutting Hay with Impact Force

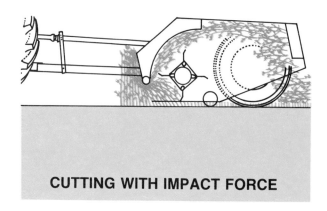

CUTTING WITH IMPACT FORCE

Fig. 5 — Bottom View of Rotary Disc Mower

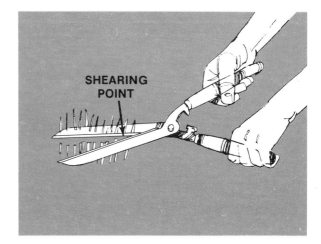

Fig. 7—Shears

such as corn and cotton stalks. Flail cutters are also used to clip grass, weeds, and brush (Fig. 6). Rotary and flail mowers are not used extensively in the United States for cutting hay crops because their chopping action shreds and pulverizes hay.

A *shearing force* is applied to stems when two opposing blades pass each other with little clearance. Ordinary hedge shears are an example. (Fig. 7). Their shearing principle is refined and expanded into a *cutterbar* for efficient, high capacity hay cutting (Fig. 8).

Fig. 6—Flail Mowers Are Used for Clipping Grass and Weeds

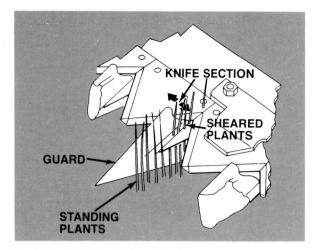

Fig. 8—Shearing Action of Mower Cutterbar

Fig. 9—Cutterbar Mower Cutting Hay

CUTTERBARS

The most commonly used hay cutting device is a cutterbar with a reciprocating knife that shears plant stems (Fig. 9). Cutterbars are used on mowers, windrowers, forage harvesters, and grain combines. All cutterbars have the same basic components, but design variations are available to deal with specific crops. Cutterbars are also called sicklebars or sicklebar mowers.

Mower size is designated by cutterbar length. Lengths are 5, 6, 7, 8, and 9 feet (1.8, 2.1, 2.4, 2.7 m). Most cutterbars are 7 or 9 feet (2.1 or 2.7 m) long.

CUTTERBAR COMPONENTS

A complete understanding of cutterbar components (Fig. 10) and functions is essential. Basic cutterbar components are:

- Knife assembly
- Guards and ledger plates
- The bar
- Inner shoe
- Outer shoe
- Knife clips
- Wear plates
- Grass board and stick
- Yoke (cutterbar hinge)

Fig. 10—Basic Cutterbar Components

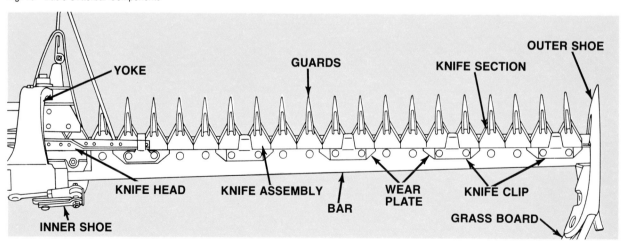

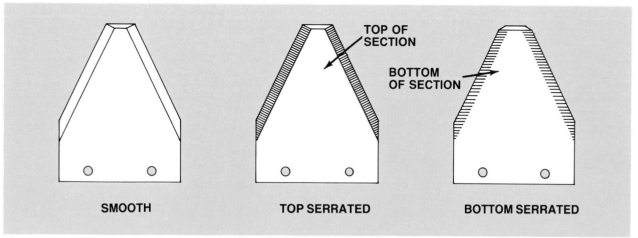

Fig. 11—Common Types of Knife Sections

KNIFE ASSEMBLY

Cutting is done between the knife assembly and the guards. Proper knife and guard adjustment, operation, and maintenance is necessary for efficient mower operation. (The knife is also known as a sickle.)

The *knife head,* at the driven end of the knife, connects the knife and knife drive. The knife head is riveted to the knife back so it can be replaced easily.

The *knife back* is a flat steel bar with the knife sections riveted to it. Knife sections may be replaced if they are broken or badly worn.

A *knife section* is an individual cutting unit matched to specific crop conditions (Fig. 11). Four types of sections are:

- **Smooth**

- **Top-serrated**

- **Bottom-serrated**

Smooth sections are used in fine-stemmed crops, particularly where juices, released during cutting, build up. Chromed sections resist buildup better than plain sections.

Top serrated sections are used in coarse crops such as alfalfa, clover, timothy, straw, and other stiff stemmed crops. The serrations hold crop stems to they can be cut cleanly. Serrated sections retain their cutting ability. Chrome surfacing provides a slick face that reduces plant juice build up.

Bottom serrated sections are used in somewhat the same conditions as top serrated sections. However, with the serrations on the bottom, sections may be sharpened.

GUARDS

Mower guards are usually spaced on 3-inch (75 mm) centers. The most common knife stroke is also approximately 3 inches. However, the stroke varies on mowers from 2½ to 3¾ inches (60 to 90 mm).

Guards have three functions. They protect the knife from solid objects, (Fig. 12) hold the stationary *ledger plates* so the crop is sheared efficiently, and guide the plants into the knife for cutting.

Fig. 12—Guards Protect Knife Sections

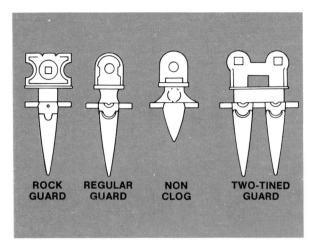

Fig. 13—Major Types of Guards

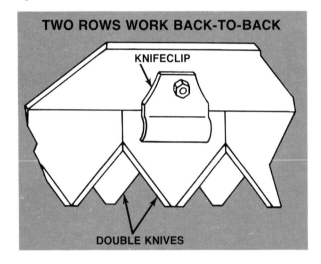

Fig. 14—Double-Knife Cutterbar

Fig. 15—Ledger Plates Are Riveted or Snapped into Position

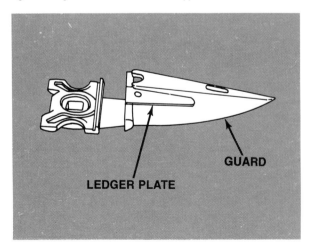

Match guards to field conditions. The major kinds of guards are (Fig. 13):

- **Rock**
- **Regular**
- **Non Clog**
- **Two-tined or double**

Rock guards are usually made of steel and are designed to take the abuse of rough, stony ground.

Regular guards look like rock guards but are made of malleable iron or forged steel.

Lipless guards are designed for crop penetration problems particularly in down, damp, heavy crop. Lipless guards are also called *pea, non-clog,* or *stub guards*. Knife sections ride on top of lipless guards to cut with less choking and plugging. Special knife hold-down clips are required because there are no guard lips or fingers above the knife.

Two-tined or double guards are made and mounted in pairs for strength and are less expensive per set than regular guards. They have a low profile and slim design for good crop penetration. Advanced mowers have a built-in knife support bar that eliminates wear plates.

Double-knife cutterbars are used for cutting dense, matted crops. Two knives, working back-to-back in opposite directions, provide more positive cutting than regular cutterbars (Fig. 14). Because knives move in opposite directions, vibration is almost eliminated. No guards are used on double-knife mowers to reduce resistance as the bar moves through the crop. Proper knife adjustment is very important with double-knife mowers, and the knives wear faster than on conventional cutterbars.

A *ledger plate* is the cutting part of a guard (Fig. 15). A ledger plate may have smooth or serrated edges depending on crop conditions. Ledger plates are attached to guards by riveting or snapping the plates into position. Some guards have sharpened cutting edges instead of ledger plates.

OTHER CUTTERBAR COMPONENTS

The *bar* is the frame the cutting components are attached to.

The *inner* and *outer shoes* are gauging mechanisms which support the cutterbar and maintain the cutting height.

Knife clips hold the knife snugly against the ledger plates for clean cutting (Fig. 16).

Wear plates guide the knife. They keep the knife back in proper position in relation to the ledger plates to shear the hay crop off clean (Fig. 16).

The *grass board* and *grass stick* separate the cut and uncut hay, and provide a clean track for the inner shoe of the cutterbar the next tiime around.

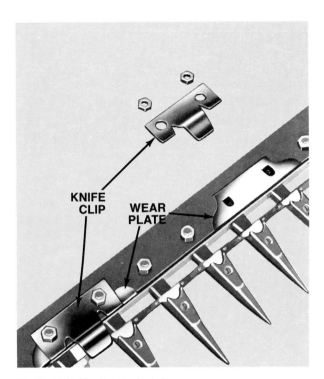

Fig. 16—Knife Clips Hold the Knife Down

Fig. 17—Pitman-Driven Mower

The exact method used to reduce vibration is not significant. More important is the fact that reduced vibration can result in a longer service life for both mower and tractor. Reduced vibration pitmanless drives permit faster knife speed, which results in greater mowing capacity. Normal pitman driven knife speed is 1,600 to 2,000 strokes per minute compared to 1,800 to 2,200 strokes per minute for pitmanless drives (Fig. 19).

The *yoke* supports the inner end of the cutterbar and is the hinge between the mower frame and cutterbar. The balanced head drive on pitmanless mowers is usually an integral part of the yoke.

KNIFE DRIVES

Another method of classifying mowers is by the type of knife drive. For years, the standard knife drive required a pitman to translate rotational motion of a flywheel into linear knife motion (Fig. 17). Dynamically-balanced knife drives have now largely replaced pitman drives (Fig. 18).

Balanced Head Drive

Balanced head knife drives reduce vibration. There are several designs, but the principles are basically the same. Balanced head drives use an opposing, reciprocating weight nearly in line with the knife action. One design attaches the knife to a pitman-driven lever. A second flywheel crank, exactly 180 degrees away, drives another lever with counterweights that move in the opposite direction of the knife to dampen vibration.

Fig. 18—Balanced-Head Knife Drive

BALANCED-HEAD
DRIVE

Fig. 19 — A Powerline Saving Equaling Hitch Reduces Vibration and Provides Power During Sharp Turns.

PRIMARY MOWER COMPONENTS

Shape and strength of the main frame and powertrain design may vary, but the basic mower components are similar (Fig. 20):

- **Main frame**
- **Drag bar**
- **Pull bar**
- **Float spring**
- **Cutterbar**
- **PTO shaft**
- **Drive belt of pitman**

Here are some brief descriptions of these components:

MOWER COMPONENT FUNCTIONS

The *main frame* supports the mower drive and cutterbar mechanism. Frame shape, size, and design depend on how the mower is attached to the tractor.

Fig. 20—Primary Mower Components

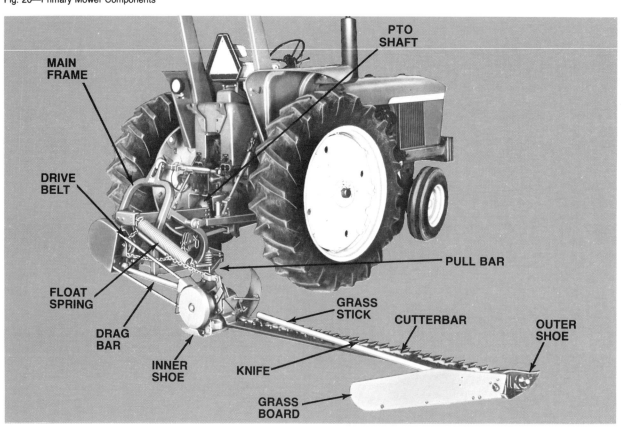

The *drag bar* connects the main frame and yoke. The *yoke* is usually a heavy casting which the cutterbar hinges on. The drag bar is adjustable to maintain proper distance between the flywheel and cutterbar on pitman drives, or between the drive sheave and balanced head drive on pitmanless mowers.

The *pull bar* keeps the cutterbar aligned with the pitman or drive belt for proper operation. The pull bar usually incorporates a *breakaway* feature: A spring-loaded catch which allows the cutterbar to pivot rearward to clear an obstruction in the field without damaging the mower (Fig. 21).

All mowers must be protected from damage when the cutterbar strikes an obstruction. Some semi-mounted mowers have a spring-loaded latch which releases automatically to allow the entire mower to pivot rearward. Side-mounted mowers may have a breakaway feature or a linkage which shuts off the tractor power when the cutterbar hits an obstruction.

The *float spring* helps the cutterbar follow ground contours and helps maintain a uniform stubble height.

The *PTO shaft* delivers power from the tractor to the mower. Power is then transmitted from the main drive line to the knife-head assembly through a *drive belt or pitman.*

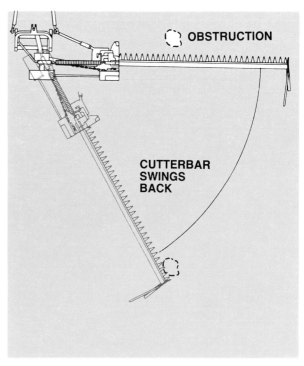

Fig. 21—Cutterbar Pivots Rearward To Clear an Obstruction

Fig. 22—Trailed Mower

CARRYING WHEEL

Fig. 23—Semi-Mounted Mower

Fig. 24—Rear-Mounted Mower

3-POINT HITCH CARRIES MOWER WEIGHT

MOWER ATTACHMENT

Mowers may be attached to the tractor by one of four methods:

- **Trailed**
- **Semi-mounted**
- **Rear-mounted**
- **Side-mounted**

Brief descriptions of these methods:

TRAILED MOWER

A trailed mower has two wheels which carry most of the mower weight. The mower is attached to the tractor drawbar and is driven by the power takeoff (Fig. 22). A trailed mower is easy to attach to a tractor.

SEMI-MOUNTED MOWER

A semi-mounted mower is connected to a tractor's 3-point hitch lower links and is driven by the power takeoff (Fig. 23). One or two trailing caster wheels support part of the mower weight. The 3-point attachment lets the cutterbar follow ground contour. A semi-mounted mower may be attached and detached quickly.

REAR-MOUNTED MOWER

A rear-mounted mower is attached to a tractor's 3-point hitch (Fig. 24) and responds directly to tractor steering changes. All of the mower's weight is carried by the tractor (Fig. 25).

SIDE-MOUNTED MOWER

It is possible to use rear-mounted or towed equipment with a side-mounted mower still attached to the tractor. This is particularly convenient for operating a hay conditioner. A side-mounted mower responds quickly to tractor steering, and you can see the cutterbar.

A side-mounted mower is more difficult to attach and detach than other mowers. A special drive may be required from the rear power takeoff to the mower. Additional mounting kits may be required to transfer the mower to another tractor.

OPERATION AND ADJUSTMENTS

The primary goal of any haying operation is the production of quality hay. Hay must be cut at the proper time. Hay mowed before it has fully matured does not produce its maximum yield. Hay mowed too late is overmature, and quality and palatability are reduced. If hay cut at the proper stage of maturity is rained on before packaging, leaves are

Fig. 25 — Mower mounted on a 3-point hitch

Fig. 26—Count The Blooms

lost and quality is reduced. If hay is mowed at the proper stage of maturity, but packaged too wet, it will spoil. If hay is packaged too dry, leaves are lost, and quality drops. In summary, the factors that affect the quality of harvested hay are:

- **Weather**

- **Timeliness of field operations**

- **Management**

You can't control the weather. But sound management can help minimize losses due to bad weather. The amount of hay mowed each day should not exceed the one-day capacity of the baler, stack wagon, and other packaging machines. Watch the weather carefully before you decide to mow.

Hay must be cut at the proper stage of maturity for maximum quality. A common method of choosing the proper time to cut is related to the stage of bloom. Alfalfa should be cut before 1/10 bloom. Choose a few major stems (culms) at random and count the number with one or more blossoms (Fig. 26). If one out of 10 stems have a blossom, the crop is at about 1/10 bloom stage.

RECOMMENDED STAGES OF MATURITY FOR HARVESTING HAY CROPS

KIND OF HAY	WHEN TO CUT
Alfalfa	**Prebud to 1/10 bloom**
Sweet clover	**First bloom**
Red and alsike clover	**1/4 bloom to 1/2 bloom**
Birdsfoot trefoil	**Early head**
Smooth bromegrass	**Medium head**
Other perennial grasses	**Boot to early head**
Forage sorghums	**First to early head**

PLANNING AND PREPARATION

To get maximum quality, a hay or forage crop must be carefully managed from planting through harvesting. Proper scheduling of other farming operations can ease the management burden during hay harvesting. However, even the best made plans can go wrong. Therefore, the farming operation must be flexible enough to accommodate the unforeseen. When the crop is ready, it must be cut to prevent costly losses. To meet this requirement, the mower and tractor must be in proper operating condition before it is time to mow.

TRACTOR PREPARATION

The tractor must be prepared to accept the mower and to operate efficiently in the field. An unreliable tractor can slow down mowing and cause costly field losses. Do the following before attaching the mower:

- *Service the tractor as recommended in the operator's manual.*

- *Make sure the tractor PTO speed matches the speed required by the mower.*

- *Adjust the drawbar height and length to the standard position for PTO operation as specified in the tractor operator's manual.*

- *For rear-mounted and semi-mounted mowers, adjust the 3-point-hitch draft links so the mower cannot be lowered too close to the ground or lifted too high above the ground (Fig. 27). Proper adjustment prevents excessive strain on the mower PTO shaft.*

- *Adjust the tractor wheel spacing or adjust the main frame to match the tractor wheel setting.*

ADJUST LIFT LINK

Fig. 27—Avoid PTO Strain by Limiting Hitch Movement

Fig. 28—Park Mower on Level Surface for Easier Hookup

MOWER PREPARATION

Each mower model has a different preparation and attachment procedure. A complete discussion of every procedure is beyond the scope of this book. For complete details on each mower, consult the operator's manual.

After preparing the tractor, attach the mower:

1. Always park the mower on a level surface with the cutterbar or mechanical lift in raised or transport position for safer, easier attachment (Fig. 28).

2. Adjust the mower main frame to match tractor wheel spacing.

3. Attach tractor draft links to hitch pins on rear-mounted or semi-mounted mowers. Connect the tractor top link to the main frame on rear-mounted mowers. Or, attach the mower to the drawbar.

4. For a side-mounted mower, attach mounting brackets to the tractor. Drive the tractor to line up brackets with mower attaching points. Couple the mower as directed in the operator's manual.

5. Connect chains or special attaching devices.

6. Level rear-mounted or semi-mounted mowers from side to side by adjusting tractor draft links. Use the center link to level the main frame fore and aft on rear-mounted mowers.

7. Connect the telescoping PTO driveshaft to the tractor powershaft. Install PTO shield.

FINAL INSPECTION

After the mower is attached to the tractor:

1. Check the knife. Is it sharp? Are any sections damaged? Sharpen or replace sections if necessary. For rotary knives, make sure they are not frozen in position. Check for sharpness.

2. Examine guards for damage. Straighten or replace guards which are out of alignment or broken.

3. Replace badly worn or damaged ledger plates, wear plates, and knife holddown clips.

4. Clean the mower completely.

5. Lubricate the mower.

6. Tighten bolts and nuts.

7. If necessary, run the mower to break-in new parts. Follow instructions in operator's manual. Avoid contact with moving parts.

8. Inspect the drive system carefully. Adjust the drive-belt tension if necessary.

9. Review the operator's manual.

PRELIMINARY SETTINGS AND ADJUSTMENTS

Reciprocating mower parts must be adjusted before operation so they won't breakdown in the field. Also, poorly adjusted mowers cut unevenly and inefficiently. Time spent checking and adjusting the mower will help prevent loss of time in the field, where time is precious.

Float Spring

Adjust the float spring so the cutterbar follows the ground contour (Fig. 29). Weak spring tension lets the cutterbar drag on the ground. Too much spring tension makes the cutterbar bounce along and cut unevenly. With the cutterbar in field position, there should be approximately 80 to 100 pounds (36 to 45 kg) of weight on the inner shoe. Check by lifting the inner shoe with a hand scale (Fig. 29).

The outer shoe must also follow ground contour for uniform cutting. About 20 to 35 pounds (9 to 16 kg) is required to lift the outer shoe on a correctly adjusted cutterbar so it won't bounce or drag. Use a scale to check the adjustment. An adjusting bolt sets the tension (Fig. 31) on most machines.

Cutterbar Lift

Some older mowers used a hand lift. Cutterbars on newer mowers are raised by a hydraulic cylinder or the tractor 3-point hitch. Before mowing, check the lift mechanism for smooth operation and sufficient lift. Make linkage or cylinder adjustments if required.

Cutterbar Tilt

Correct cutterbar angle in relation to the ground and direction of travel is necessary for clean cutting. The cutterbar is normally operated parallel to the ground (Fig. 32). When the crop is tangled or down, a downward tilt is recommended so the guard points penetrate and lift the crop before cutting. Tilt up guards in stony fields to reduce damage to the knife and guard.

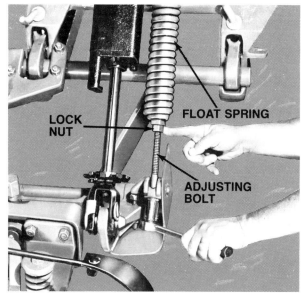

Fig. 29—Float-Spring Tension Adjustment

Fig. 30—Checking Float-Spring Tension with Scale

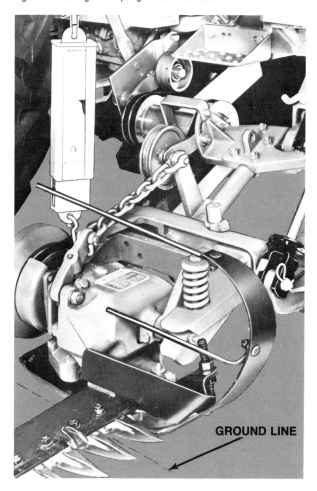

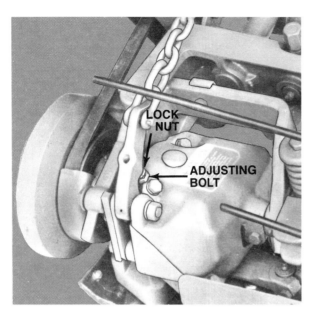

Fig. 31—Adjustment Bolt for Outer-Shoe Float

Cutterbar Lead

During operation the resistance of plants being cut pushes the outer end of the cutterbar to the rear. To compensate for this drag force, position the outer end of the cutterbar slightly ahead of the inner end when the mower is stopped. This is called *cutterbar lead*. With proper lead, the cutterbar is at a right angle to forward motion during operation. Normal lead on most mowers is approximately 1/4 inch per foot (.6 mm per 305 mm) of cutterbar. Therefore, a 7-foot (2.1 m) cutterbar would require 1 3/4 inches (45 mm) of lead.

A simple way to check the lead on pitmanless mowers is the straight board method (Fig. 33). Park the tractor and mower on a level surface. Place the cutterbar flat on the ground. Take up slack by pulling the outer end of the cutterbar to the rear by hand. Place a sturdy, straight board so it touches the front of both rear tractor tires and extends outward. Then measure the distance between the board and the inner and outer ends of the cutterbar knife. The outer-end measurement should be 1/4 inch per foot (.6 mm per 305 mm) of cutterbar length less than the inner measurement (1 3/4 inches on a 7-foot bar) (45 mm on a 2.1 m bar). If the lead is incorrect, adjust it as shown in the operator's manual.

Fig. 32—Typical Cutterbar Tilt Adjustment

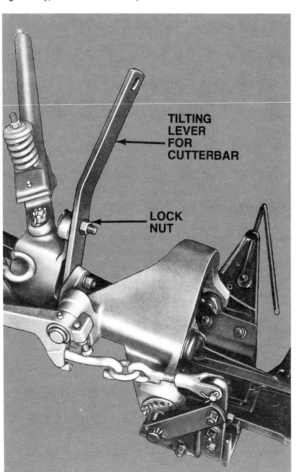

Fig. 33—Straight-Board Method of Checking Cutterbar Lead

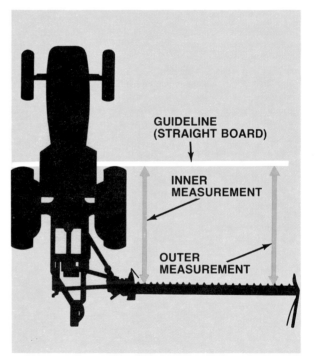

The lead adjustment procedure varies with mower models and makes (Fig. 34). Common methods are:

1. *Shorten the pull bar or front main support.*

2. *Lengthen the drag bar or rear main support.*

3. *Shorten the breakaway linkage.*

4. *Adjust the eccentric bearing in the cutterbar yoke.*

Primary and Secondary Lead

To set cutterbar lead for pitman mowers adjust the *primary lead* (the cutterbar), and the *secondary lead* (the pitman). The pitman must operate at a right angle to the mower's line of travel. Always check secondary lead after setting primary cutterbar lead. Adjust secondary lead by lengthening or shortening the pull bar. See operator's manual.

Knife Register

Knife register must be correct for smooth cutting and minimum side draft. The knife is in register when the knife sections are an equal distance from the centerline of the guards at each end of the stroke (Fig. 35). For those adjustable types, the register should be checked by hand rotating the drive with the cutterbar in a level cutting position. The knife stroke on some mowers is less than the distance between guards. The knife stroke is greater than guard spacing on others.

Knife register does not usually change unless the pitman is damaged or cutterbar lead is changed. Most pitmanless-drive cutterbars remain in register automatically because the reciprocating mechanism is mounted on the cutterbar.

Methods of adjusting knife register may vary according to the mower. However, adjustments are usually made by moving the entire cutterbar in or out with respect to the pitman crankshaft or by changing pitman length.

MOWER CONTROLS

Mower operating controls are the tractor PTO clutch for knife operation and a remote hydraulic cylinder or 3-point hitch control for cutterbar lift. On some models, the cutterbar must be lowered to cutting position manually.

FIELD OPERATION

Before field operation, run a new mower through a break-in procedure as outlined in the operator's manual. Then adjust the cutterbar height and tilt for the crop and field conditions.

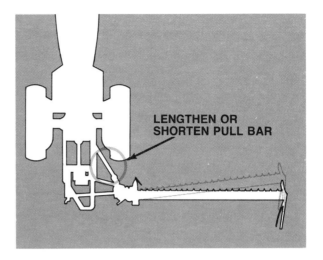

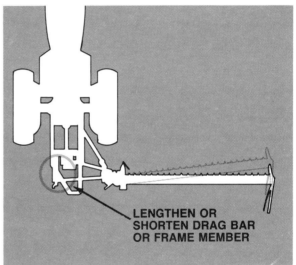

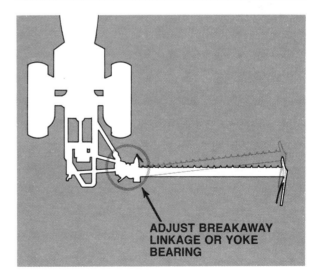

Fig. 34—Some Methods of Adjusting Cutterbar Lead

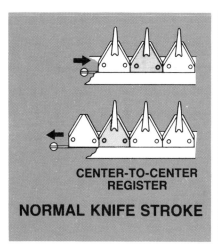 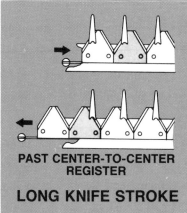 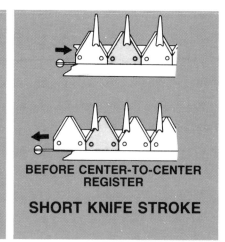

CENTER-TO-CENTER REGISTER

NORMAL KNIFE STROKE

PAST CENTER-TO-CENTER REGISTER

LONG KNIFE STROKE

BEFORE CENTER-TO-CENTER REGISTER

SHORT KNIFE STROKE

Fig. 35—Proper Knife Register

Opening a Field

There are two common methods of opening a field.

To use the first method, first cut the hay next to the fence or border by mowing around the field counterclockwise.

CAUTION: When the mower is turning to the left, the cutterbar will travel much faster than normal. Slow down by shifting to a lower gear when you turn left. Simply reducing engine speed for such a turn will slow the knife too. It could plug.

Fig. 36—After a Field Is Opened, Mow Clockwise

After cutting the first round, mow the remainder of the field by traveling clockwise (Fig. 36).

In the second field-opening method, mow one or two rounds in the normal clockwise direction. Then cut the outside round, or backswath, before continuing to mow the rest of the field. The backswath should be cut about the same time adjacent swaths are mowed, so the hay dries equally and will be ready to package at the same time.

Turning

Most mowers can cut neat, square corners. With proper operation, it is seldom necessary to raise the cutterbar at corners. To make a clean, square corner with a rear-mounted or semi-mounted mower, turn quickly when the right rear tractor wheel reaches the edge of uncut hay. With a side-mounted mower, turn quickly when near the end of the cut. The distance between the cutterbar and tractor wheels, and operator experience, dictates when to start turning with a trailed mower.

See the operator's manual for suggestions about turning. Use the right-wheel brake on the tractor to help make sharp, square turns.

Field Adjustments

Make field adjustments to suit specific crops and field conditions for clean, efficient mowing. Some preliminary adjustments may require changing in the field.

Speed

Select mowing speed to match field conditions. Excessive speed can cause unnecessary breakdowns and a ragged mowing job. Correct speeds usually result in more hay mowed at the end of the day, less wear on equipment, and less operator fatigue. Under most conditions, a mowing speed of 5 to 7 miles per hour (8 to 11 km/h) is most productive.

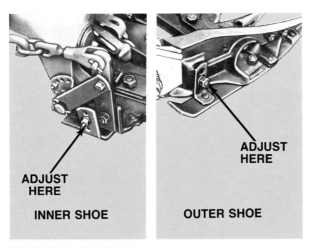

Fig. 37—Height of Cut Adjustments

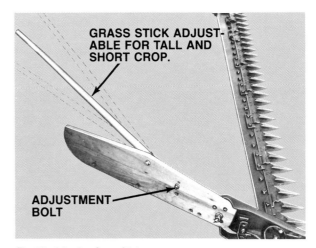

Fig. 38—Adjusting Grass Stick

Knife Selection and Care

Proper knife selection is important to avoid plugging and uneven cutting. Knife selection is usually made before field operation, but the knife may have to be changed after cutting begins. Gumming can be a problem under some conditions. Wash the gum off the cutterbar with water after the mower is stopped and it will last longer. If trash hardens on the cutterbar, parts can break when moving starts again.

CAUTION: Stay clear of moving parts when you wash the cutterbar.

Cutting Height

Cutting height depends on crop and ground conditions. In rocky fields, increase the height so the knife and guard aren't damaged. Adjust the cutting level to suit the crop. Mowers usually have adjustable inner and outer shoes to set cutting height (Fig. 37).

Grass Board and Stick

The grass board and stick divide mowed hay from the standing crop. Dividing provides a clear path for the inner shoe on the next round and permits easier raking. Raise or lower the grass stick, according to crop height, by moving the adjustment bolt on the grass board (Fig. 38).

TRANSPORT

Before transporting a mower, disengage the tractor PTO clutch and raise the cutterbar to the transport position. Always stop the tractor engine and take the key before handling the cutterbar. When raising the cutterbar by hand, keep your fingers away from cutting parts. Your hand could slip, or the knife could drop. With the cutterbar in its highest position, connect the transport latch rod (Fig. 39). Raise a rear-mounted mower to the highest position.

Do not exceed safe tractor speed for the terrain when transporting a mower. Use a lower gear on steep downgrades.

Be sure the tractor is in proper operating condition, with good enough brakes for safe operation with a mower.

When transporting a mower, use a clearly visible SMV emblem and turn on your flashing lights to warn others.

Fig. 39—Securing the Cutterbar with Transport Latch Rod

SAFETY

A mower cutterbar is dangerous. Always disengage the PTO, shut off the engine, and take the key before dismounting from the tractor. Never attempt to clear a clogged cutterbar with the mower operating. Never clean, oil, or adjust the mower when it is running.

Be sure all drive-belt and PTO shields are in good condition and properly secured on the mower before you engage the PTO.

Reduce the risk of personal injury and mower damage. Operate at the correct PTO speed only.

Never allow passengers to ride on a tractor or mower.

Never permit children to play on or near a mower, even if it is parked.

Reduce the danger of injury by covering the cutterbar during storage.

See hydraulics safety message page 334.

TROUBLESHOOTING FIELD PROBLEMS

Most mower operating problems result from improper adjustments or neglect of essential service. The following chart will help you when a problem develops by providing some probable causes and solutions.

TROUBLESHOOTING CHART		
PROBLEM	POSSIBLE CAUSE	POSSIBLE REMEDY
BEARINGS OVERHEAT.	Lack of lubrication.	Lubricate.
	Bearings too tight.	Replace bearings.
WON'T CUT; CUTTERBAR PLUGS.	Guards loose or out of line.	Tighten and align guards.
	Bent guard.	Replace or realign guard.
	Guard lip bent too close to knife.	Reset lips or replace damaged guards.
	Guard points are blunt.	Replace damaged guards or sharpen points.
	Missing or dull ledger plates.	Replace ledger plates.
	Dull or worn knife.	Sharpen or replace knife or sections.
	Wrong knife for crop condition.	Replace knife.
	Drive belt slipping.	Adjust belt tension.
	Mowing too close to ground.	Adjust cutting height at inner and outer shoe.
	Too much cutterbar tilt.	Change tilt angle.
	Cutterbar lead incorrect.	Adjust lead.
	Pitman out of alignment.	Adjust secondary lead.
	Out of register.	Adjust register.
	Knife clips not properly set.	Reset knife clips.
	Wear plates worn out.	Replace.
BAR BREAKS BACK.	Won't cut; cutterbar plugs.	See preceding section for possible causes and remedies.
	Inner shoe too heavy.	Adjust float spring.
	Outer shoe too heavy.	Adjust outer shoe float.
	Breakaway latch too loose.	Adjust spring tension.

PROBLEM	POSSIBLE CAUSE	POSSIBLE REMEDY
PLUGGING AT INNER SHOE.	Swath not properly divided.	Adjust grass board and stick.
	Inner shoe too heavy.	Adjust float spring.
	Cutting too low.	Adjust inner shoe height.
	Excessive gather or bunching.	Adjust deflector or fender rod on inner shoe.
	Material catching on drive parts.	Adjust deflector or fender rod.
PLUGGING AT OUTER SHOE.	Stripper plate improperly adjusted.	Adjust stripper plate.
	Outer shoe out of alignment.	Remove or add shims.
	Crop hangs onto outer shoe.	Install outer shoe divider.
	Outer shoe too heavy.	Adjust outer shoe float.
	Outer shoe ledger plate worn.	Install new ledger plate.
KNIFE BREAKAGE.	Guards loose or out of line.	Tighten and align guards.
	Dull sections and guard plates.	Sharpen or replace.
	Worn knife head pin or bushing.	Replace.
	Nicked or broken sections.	Sharpen or replace.
	Overspeed of PTO.	Operate PTO at rated rpm only.
	Bow in cutterbar.	Check lifting-chain position.
	Crooked knife.	Straighten or replace.
	Wear plates too far forward.	Adjust wear plates.
	Loose rivets.	Replace with new rivets.
KNOCKING AND NOISE IN DRIVE	Check yoke pivot bearing for looseness.	Tighten yoke pivot bolt or replace bearings.
	Check knife head pivot for looseness.	Tighten clamp bolt or replace knife head bushing.
	Wrong PTO speed.	Operate at rated speed.
	Knife too tight.	Loosen knife.
	Loose bolts.	Tighten all bolts.
UNEVEN STUBBLE.	Cutterbar not level.	Check shoe adjustment.
	Outer shoe too light.	Adjust outer shoe float.
	Inner shoe too light.	Adjust float spring.
	Driving too fast.	Reduce mowing speed.
POWERLINE FAILURE.	Improper lubrication.	Keep telescoping shaft well lubricated.
	Improper belt tension.	Adjust belt tension.
FREQUENT PITMAN BREAKAGE.	Loose pitman bolts.	Torque bolts as recommended in operator's manual.
	Secondary lead out of adjustment.	Readjust secondary lead.
	Overspeed of PTO.	Run at proper PTO speed.

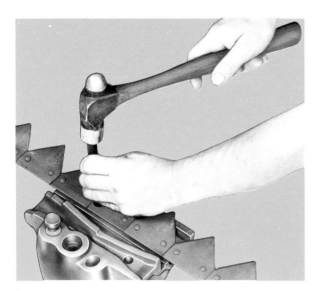

Fig. 40—Replacing Damaged Knife Section

Make sure you are dealing with the real problem, not just the symptom. A thorough understanding of the mower is needed to correct operating problems.

MAINTENANCE

Maintenance of a mower is concentrated mostly on the cutterbar.

Knife

The *knife* must be sharp so it will shear, not tear plants. Replace broken, worn knife sections promptly (Fig. 40). Most knife sections may be resharpened if wear is not too severe. But the original knife cutting angle and bevel must be maintained (Fig. 41). Improper sharpening increases the power requirements and reduces the efficiency.

A bent knife will not move freely in the cutterbar and can break. Remove the bent knife from the cutterbar, clamp the knife in a vise, and straighten it by bending. Be careful during this operation.

Inspect *wear plates, knife clips,* and *knife-head guides* regularly to maintain proper cutting performance. Excessive play in these parts will speed wear, increase the possibility of knives breaking, and result in ragged cutting.

Wear Plates

Badly *worn wear plates* let knives vibration. As wear occurs, move wear plates forward to hold the knives securely (Fig. 42). Slotted holes are provided in the wear plates for adjustment. Do not move the wear plates too far forward, or the knife will not move freely.

Knife Clips

Check *knife clips* regularly. If clips are too loose, the knife can move up and down causing ragged cutting and choking. If clips are too tight, the knife will bind. Two methods used to adjust knife clips are:

1. Add or remove spacers to obtain proper clearance between clips and knife sections.

2. Bend clips with a hammer to obtain proper clearance (Fig. 43).

Knife-head Guides

Excessive wear on *knife-head guides* will cause the knife to slap or hammer. Because of their design, knife-head guides on pitman mowers are more subject to excessive wear than those on pitmanless mowers. Most knife-head guides are adjusted by inserting or removing shims (Fig. 44). The amount of clearance between guides and head is

Fig. 41—Proper Knife Sharpening

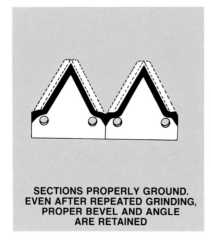

SECTIONS PROPERLY GROUND.
EVEN AFTER REPEATED GRINDING,
PROPER BEVEL AND ANGLE
ARE RETAINED

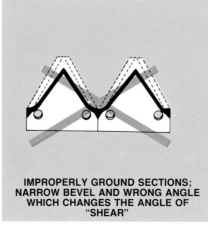

IMPROPERLY GROUND SECTIONS;
NARROW BEVEL AND WRONG ANGLE
WHICH CHANGES THE ANGLE OF
"SHEAR"

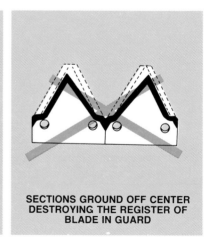

SECTIONS GROUND OFF CENTER
DESTROYING THE REGISTER OF
BLADE IN GUARD

Guards

Guards protect knife sections, hold ledger plates, comb the crop, separate plants, and guide plants into the knife. Guards need frequent maintenance to perform all of their functions properly. Guard maintenance may be divided into three areas:

1. *Conditioning or replacing damaged guards*

2. *Aligning guards*

3. *Adjusting guard lip clearance*

While guards are mounted on the cutterbar, inspect to see if guards are worn, nicked, rusty, bent or broken. Inspect ledger plates for the same problems. Replace broken guards and dull or broken ledger plates. Use a file to remove rust and nicks, and to sharpen guard points. Tighten loose ledger plates.

Align guards so knives will move freely. Remove the knife for guard alignment. Disregard position of guard points.

Use a straightedge to align the guard ledger plates with the inner shoe ledger plate (Fig. 45). Strike the guards gently with a hammer to raise or lower the guard for proper alignment. Avoid bending the guard lip during alignment.

Adjusting guard lip clearance is the final step in guard maintenance. Too little clearance results in plugging and binding the crop. Too much clearance leaves the knife unprotected. Most guards require approximately $^3/_8$ to $^1/_2$ inch (10 to 13 mm) clearance between the rear of the guard lip and ledger plate (Fig. 46). To decrease clearance, tap lightly on the lip with a hammer. To increase clearance, gently wedge the lip upward with a chisel (Fig. 47).

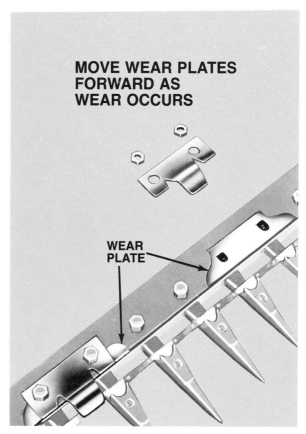

MOVE WEAR PLATES FORWARD AS WEAR OCCURS

WEAR PLATE

Fig. 42—Adjusting Wear Plates

Fig. 43—Setting and Loosening Knife Clip with Hammer

LOOSENING CLIP

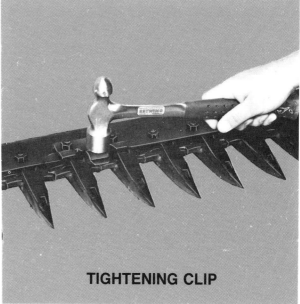

TIGHTENING CLIP

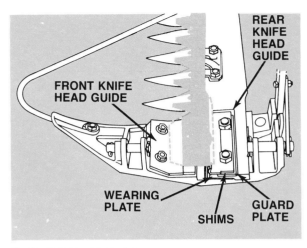

Fig. 44—Knife-Head Guide Adjustment

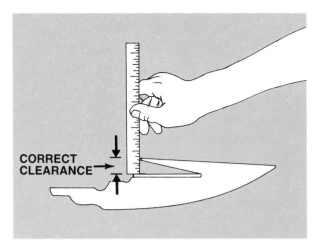

Fig. 46—Checking Guard Lip Clearance

Service; Replacement Parts

Lubricate, inspect, and service bearings, belts, chains, and gears to prevent field breakdowns. If the mower uses hydraulic power, inspect hoses and cylinders regularly, and make repairs promptly.

Have replacement parts available in the field at all times to save time when something breaks.

Most breakdowns happen in the cutting mechanism. Have spare knife sections, ledger plates, and guards on hand to

repair the cutting mechanism. A replacement pitman is recommended for pitman mowers. A spare drive belt is desirable. Replacement wear plates, knife clips, and knife head guides are needed as the mower gets older. Buy other replacement parts as wear is observed.

STORAGE

Proper storage of the mower during the off-season helps reduce maintenance costs and prolongs machine service life. Clean the mower thoroughly. Lubricate as specified in the operator's manual. Repaint worn surfaces. Remove tension from belts, and clean them with a non-flammable cleaning agent to remove grease, oil, and dirt. Place the cutterbar in the transport position, and, if possible, store the mower in a dry shelter.

Finally, make a list of needed repairs, and order replacement parts so they can be installed during the off-season.

SUMMARY

A mower cuts standing vegetation by either shearing or impact. Cutting should be clean and sharp, without clogging.

Rotary and flail mowers cut by impact force. The rotary mower has horizontally rotating blades. Flail mowers have flails or knives mounted vertically on a rotating horizontal shaft. These mowers are not widely used in hay cutting, as they tend to pulverize the crop.

Fig. 45—Checking Guard Alignment with a Straightedge

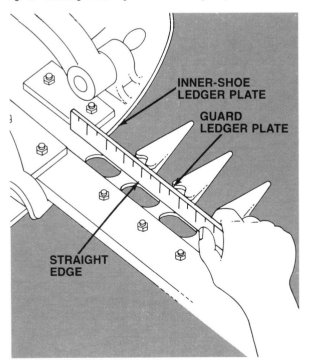

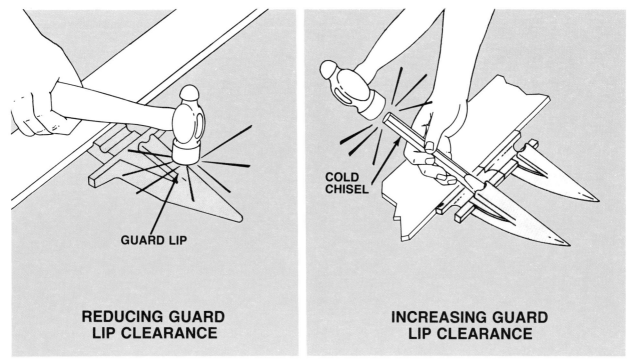

REDUCING GUARD LIP CLEARANCE

INCREASING GUARD LIP CLEARANCE

COLD CHISEL

GUARD LIP

Fig. 47—Adjusting Guard Lip Clearance

Cutterbars, which cut by shearing, are widely used on mowers, windrowers, forage harvesters, and combines. Several kinds of knife sections and guards are available to suit crop and field conditions. Mower cutterbars are usually 7 or 9 feet (2.1 or 2.7 m) long.

Mowers are classified as trailed, semi-mounted, rear-mounted, or side-mounted. They are powered by the tractor PTO or a hydraulic motor. Old time mowers were ground-driven.

Pitmanless balanced-head knife drives have less vibration than pitman drives.

Good management and timely operations are important to avoid bad weather and ensure hay is cut at the proper stage of maturity. The amount of hay cut in a day should not exceed the capacity of the hay packaging equipment.

Ground speed, cutting height, knife selection and register, cutterbar tilt, and lead all affect mower efficiency. Each must be adjusted to match crop and field conditions.

CHAPTER QUIZ

1. (Fill in blanks.) Force to sever vegetation may be either _____ or _____.

2. Name three components of a cutterbar knife.

3. Name four types of cutterbar knife sections.

4. Name at least seven cutterbar components.

5. What are the functions of guards on a cutterbar?

6. (True or false.) A knife is in proper register when sections are centered between the guards at each end of the stroke.

7. What protection does the cutterbar and knife have from stones?

8. What is the function of the grass board and stick?

9. What is generally accepted as the proper amount of cutterbar lead?

10. What is the greatest disadvantage of a pitman drive compared to a balanced-head knife drive?

11. (Fill in blanks.) Under most conditions, a mower should be operated at _____ to _____ miles per hour.

3
Hay Conditioners

Fig. 1—Hay Conditioner

INTRODUCTION

Since farmers can't control the weather, they are always searching for new ways to reduce the time to cure hay — time when the crop is vulnerable to damage by rain and storm. Research in the 1930s led to the development of hay conditioners. Hay conditioners, which speed up the curing process, became available during the 1950s (Fig. 1). These individual hay conditioners are now being replaced by machines which mow, condition, and windrow in one pass. However, the principles of operation are similar for all hay conditioners.

PURPOSE AND USE OF CONDITIONERS

Hay conditioners crack or crush plant stems (Fig. 2). Cracking and crushing permits more rapid moisture loss from inside the stems so they dry faster. Stems and leaves then dry at approximately the same rate.

Conditioning reduces the time needed for field-curing, and so increases the possibility of packaging hay before it can be damaged by rain. Studies show that curing time may be reduced by 30 to 50 percent for conditioned hay compared to unconditioned hay.

Conditioned hay has better quality and palatability than unconditioned hay. Leaf loss from shattering is substantially reduced, because hay is packaged before leaves become brittle. Reduced exposure to bad weather helps the crop retain color, vitamins, and nutrients. Coarse, stiff stems are crushed or cracked, and become more palatable. From one to 4 percent of the potential crop yield may be lost in conditioning, depending on the conditioner and crop conditions. However, the actual quantity of hay harvested may increase because of reduced field losses from handling and exposure to weather.

Conditioning is most effective on coarse-stemmed, leafy hays. Legume hays are particularly well suited to conditioning because their leaves become fragile when dried. However, conditioning fine-stemmed grass hays may be beneficial, especially where weather might damage hay before it can dry naturally.

CONDITIONERS IN THE WORKPLACE

Conditioners are covered as a separate unit in this chapter because they are still in use in many parts of the world. Usually, mower conditioners are used in order to eliminate the separate job of mowing.

Fig. 2—Magnified Comparison of Conditioned and Unconditioned Alfalfa Stems

CONDITIONED ALFALFA STEM

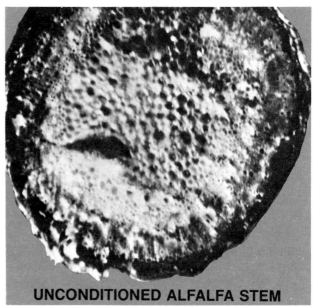

UNCONDITIONED ALFALFA STEM

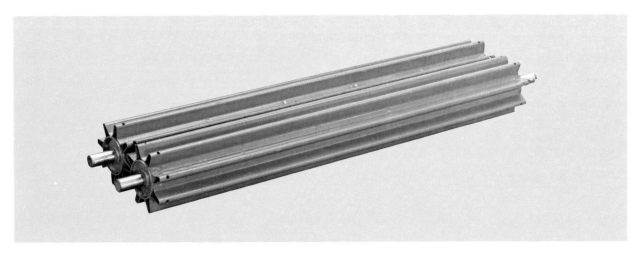

Fig. 3—Crimping Rolls

TYPES AND SIZES

Two kinds of hay conditioners are built:

- **Crimpers**
- **Crushers**

Each conditions hay in a different way.

Crimper

A crimper has two corrugated rolls which mesh like gears (Fig. 3). These steel or rubber rolls bend and crack the stems every 1 to 3 inches (25 to 75 mm) along the length of the plant. Crimping opens the stem for faster drying.

Crusher

A crusher may have two rubber rolls, or one steel roll and one rubber roll. Different roll configurations are available (Fig. 4).

Fig. 4—Crushing Rolls

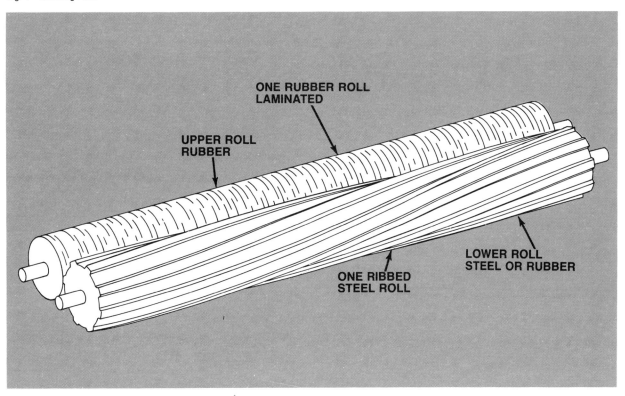

ONE RUBBER ROLL
LAMINATED

UPPER ROLL
RUBBER

LOWER ROLL
STEEL OR RUBBER

ONE RIBBED
STEEL ROLL

Fig. 5—Rubber Crimper and Crusher Rolls

Tests show crushed hay dries faster than crimped hay. To obtain the benefits of both types of conditioners, some manufacturers use molded rubber rolls with wide inter-meshing cleats that provide both crimping and crushing action (Fig. 5).

Conditioner Widths

The conditioner is a simple machine with few working parts. It can be towed and powered by a small tractor, or attached to a mower-conditioner or windrower. Common hay conditioner widths are 7 and 9 feet (2.1 and 2.7 m). These widths match the length of most mower cutterbars to allow conditioning of one complete swath each round. Conditioners integrally mounted on mower-conditioners and windrowers may be shorter — typically 4 to 5 feet (1.2 to 1.5 m) but possibly as long as 9 feet (2.7 m).

The remainder of this chapter is devoted to towed conditioners. However, most adjustments are similar on both types of machines. Specific features and operation of integral conditioners are described in the chapter on *Mower-Conditioners and Windrowers.*

PRIMARY CONDITIONER COMPONENTS

Primary components of a typical hay conditioner are (Fig. 6):

- **PTO driveshaft**
- **Gearcase**
- **Upper- and lower-roll drive chains**
- **Conditioning rolls**
- **Fluffing board**
- **Windrow-forming shields**

Some conditioners use belt drives instead of chains.

Component Functions

Power is transmitted from the tractor to the *conditioning rolls* through the *PTO shaft, gearcase,* and *chain drives.* The lower roll acts as a pickup to lift hay into the conditioning rolls. Conditioner rolls rotate in opposite directions to pull hay between the rollers for conditioning (Fig. 7). The upper roll is set slightly ahead of the lower roll to throw the hay into the air after conditioning.

The thrown hay then contacts the adjustable *fluffing board* which fluffs and distributes the hay evenly in the conditioned swath.

The *windrow-forming shields* may be fully opened to drop the conditioned hay into a swath, or pulled together to place

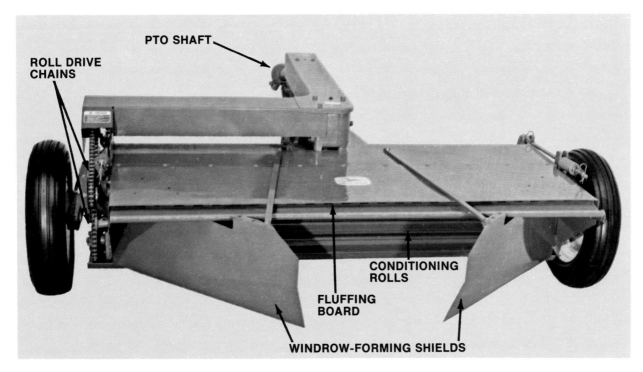

ROLL DRIVE CHAINS

PTO SHAFT

CONDITIONING ROLLS

FLUFFING BOARD

WINDROW-FORMING SHIELDS

Fig. 6—Hay Conditioner Components

hay in a windrow to eliminate raking. By adjusting these shields to match crop conditions, a windrow can be formed with proper width for efficient pickup by the packaging equipment. Proper conditioner adjustment and operation results in a fluffy windrow of conditioned hay that dries fast and is easy to pick up.

OPERATION AND ADJUSTMENTS

Hay conditioning is not required in haymaking. Conditioning is a tool to increase the quality and quantity of hay harvested. Conditioning does not eliminate the hazards of weather damage to cut hay, but it reduces the chance of damage by shortening the field-curing time. Like other haying operations, maximum benefits are obtained by conditioning hay at the proper time. Poor timing may result in inefficient crushing of the stems, increased leaf loss, and reduced machine productivity.

PLANNING AND PREPARATION

Timeliness is essential to an efficient hay conditioning operation. Labor and equipment must be ready. By mowing and conditioning simultaneously (Fig. 8), one man and a tractor can complete the job of two men and two tractors. Simultaneous operation also reduces the problem of mowing too far ahead of conditioning. In either case, the mower and conditioner must have nearly the same field capacity.

Hay conditioners work best in level, clean fields. On uneven fields, the lower roll does not "float." It can dig into high ground or leave unconditioned hay in low areas. Rocks and trash picked up by the conditioner rolls can cause severe damage.

TRACTOR PREPARATION

The conditioner and tractor must be ready to operate when the hay is mowed. Poorly maintained, unreliable equipment causes unnecessary delays during field operation. To prepare the tractor for operation:

Fig. 7—Rolls Discharge Hay

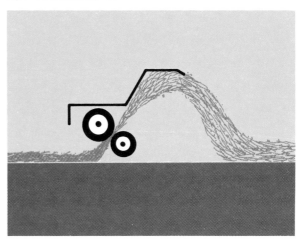

Fig. 8—Mowing and Conditioning Simultaneously

• *Service the tractor as recommended in the operator's manual.*

• *Make sure tractor PTO speed matches the speed required by the conditioner.*

• *Adjust the drawbar to the standard position for PTO operation, or as specified in the hay conditioner operator's manual.*

• *Lock the drawbar parallel with the centerline of the PTO shaft.*

Fig. 9—Properly Timed Crimper Rolls

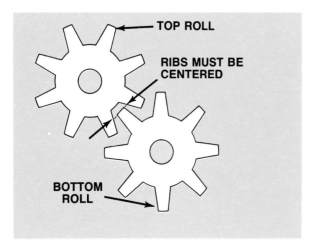

• *Check the hydraulic system; add oil if necessary.*

• *Raise 3-point hitch draft links to highest position.*

Read the operator's manual for specific instructions.

CONDITIONER PREPARATION

After the tractor is ready, review the conditioner operator's manual and prepare the conditioner for the field. Follow these steps:

• *Lubricate as recommended in the conditioner operator's manual.*

• *Clean the conditioner thoroughly.*

• *Tighten all bolts and nuts to specified torque.*

• *Check oil level in the gear case.*

• *Check and adjust tension of bolts and drive chains.*

• *Check and inflate tires if necessary.*

• *Attach the conditioner hitch to the tractor drawbar, or to the special conditioner hitch on the mower.*

• *Connect the telescoping PTO shaft to the tractor powershaft or PTO shaft extension on the mower.*

• *Connect remote-cylinder hydraulic lines.*

PRELIMINARY SETTINGS AND ADJUSTMENTS

Check the PTO shaft slip-clutch before each season. Be sure it will slip when needed and that it has not "seized" during storage. Recheck slip-clutch adjustment periodically throughout the season. If a shear pin is used instead of a slip-clutch, be sure proper pins are used, and have extras on hand in the field.

Crimper rolls must be timed so the ribs on one roll mesh in the center of the gap between the ribs on the opposite roll (Fig. 9). Contact between the meshing rolls during operation can cause rapid roll wear. Serious damage to the roll and drive train may result if rolls are badly out of time and roll ribs are forced against each other as they turn.

If rolls are out of time, hay will not be conditioned uniformly because of reduced space on one side of the rib (A, Fig. 10), and too much space on the other side (B, Fig. 10). If roll clearance is very small, or if ribs actually touch (A, Fig. 10), stems and leaves may be pinched off, resulting in excessive loss of leaves and fine stems. This not only reduces the quantity, but also lowers the quality of what hay is harvested, as leaves and fine stems contain the most nutrients.

Consult the operator's manual for specific instructions for slip-clutch and roll-timing adjustments.

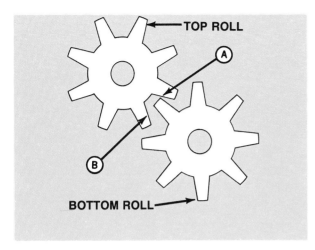

Fig. 10—Improperly Timed Crimper Rolls

Fig. 11—Condition Hay before Wilting Starts

FIELD OPERATION

Hay conditioner controls include the tractor's PTO clutch for roll operation, and a remote hydraulic cylinder control or hand cranks for roll height.

Before field operation, run a new hay conditioner slowly for a short brea-in period. Be certain all parts operate freely and normally. Make adjustments if necessary.

To begin field operation, lower the rolls to within 4 to 7 inches (100 to 175 mm) of the ground. Then, slowly engage the PTO clutch and set the engine speed to get rated PTO speed. Always travel in the same direction the mower traveled. You will get better conditioning and more complete pickup.

Condition Before Hay Wilts

For best results, hay should be conditioned within 15 to 30 minutes after cutting, before wilting begins (Fig. 11). Wilted stems are so flexible they do not split open for rapid drying. Also, wilted hay is more likely to wrap on the conditioner rolls.

Be alert for rocks, sticks, and trash that might damage the conditioner.

Keep in mind: The effect of conditioning does not become visible immediately. Some crops require one to two hours before significant moisture loss can be noticed. Don't make machine adjustments prematurely.

FIELD ADJUSTMENTS

Field adjustments must match specific crop and field conditions. Adjustments include:

- **Ground speed**
- **Roll height**
- **Roll spacing**
- **Roll pressure**
- **Fluffing board position**
- **Windrow-forming shield setting**

Many of these settings are interacting.

Ground Speed

Conditioning rolls are most effective when the speed of the outer surface of the roll exceeds ground speed. Ground speed that is too slow results in excessive plant damage and broken stem and leaf clusters. If ground speed is too fast the rolls can clog. Rough fields may require a slower ground speed than is best for good conditioning. Adjust ground speed by changing gears so the standard PTO speed is maintained. reduced PTO speed usually results in a plugged conditioner.

Roll Height and Spacing

Set the rolls as high as possible, 4 to 7 inches (100 to 175 mm), but low enough to pick up the swath. Raising the rolls reduces the chance of picking up rocks and trash which damage the conditioner. If the operating rolls are too low, hay will wrap on the rolls. If the rolls are too low, the conditioner will scalp high spots in the field. Adjust roll height with a hydraulic cylinder, or by manually turning adjusting cranks (Fig. 12). Some conditioners are designed to automatically spread the conditioner rolls when rolls are raised for transport.

Recommended roll spacing varies with the crop and maturity. If the crop is tender and light and roll spacing is too close, excessive leaf loss and plant damage can occur.

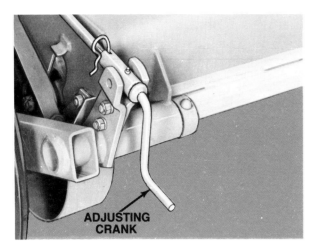

Fig. 12—Adjust Roll Height

Fig. 13—Roll Spacing Adjustment

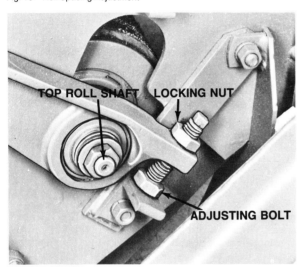

Fig. 14—Roll Pressure Adjustment

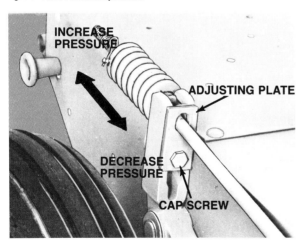

Tough crops require a closer spacing for effective conditioning. If spacing is too wide, the rolls will not crush the stem adequately to allow quick drying.

You can set the roll spacing with an adjustment bolt (Fig. 13). Spacing must be the same at each end of the rolls.

Roll Pressure

Recommended roll pressure varies with the kind of hay, stage of maturity, and the yield. The object of conditioning is to break open the stem, but not to squeeze juice from the plants. A grass hay requires light pressure, a legume-grass mixture usually needs medium pressure, and a legume hay or forage sorghum requires high pressure. Too much roll pressure results in excessive leaf loss and plant damage. Insufficient pressure permits the hay to pass through the rolls without conditioning the stems. Roll pressure is typically adjusted by setting the length of a compression spring which holds down the top roller (Fig. 14). As in roll spacing, roll pressure must be the same on both ends of the rolls. On some machines, a single adjustment changes roll pressure and spacing.

Fluffing-Board Adjustment

Adjust the fluffing board to form a loose, fluffy swath for fast field-curing. If the fluffing board is too low in heavy crops, hay will bunch and feed back into the conditioner.

In light crops, set the fluffing board low for a looser swath or windrow. Always adjust the fluffing board an equal amount on each end of the conditioner for uniform drying and better-shaped windrows (Fig. 15).

Windrow-Forming Shields

Windrow-forming shields can eliminate raking the swath. Adjust shields to form a windrow of suitable width for the packaging equipment. The windrow must be wide enough to allow rapid, uniform curing of the hay. But, if the ground is quite wet, a high, narrow windrow may dry faster. Adjust each shield equally for uniform windrows (Fig. 16).

Fig. 15—Adjust Fluffing Board Equally on Each Side

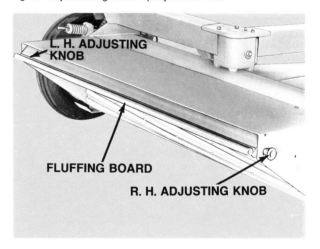

TRANSPORT

To prepare the conditioner for transport, disengage the tractor PTO clutch and raise the rolls to their maximum height so they can pass over bumps without damage (Fig. 17).

Be sure the tractor is in proper operating condition with sufficient braking capacity. Do not travel faster than safe tractor speed for the terrain covered. Use a lower gear on steep downgrades.

Always use a clearly-visible SMV emblem and auxiliary lights to warn operators of other vehicles when you transport a hay conditioner.

SAFETY

See hydraulic safety message page 334.

Hay conditioner rolls operate at very high speed and can throw rocks and objects at high velocity. Keep shields in place to reduce the danger from projectiles. Never let anyone stand behind an operating conditioner.

Make sure everyone is clear before engaging the PTO. Reduce the risk of personal injury and conditioner damage by operating at the correct PTO speed only.

Never clean, oil, or adjust a conditioner while it is in operation. Turn off the tractor engine and take the key before you work on a conditioner.

Disengage the PTO and shut off the tractor before attempting to clean out plugged rolls.

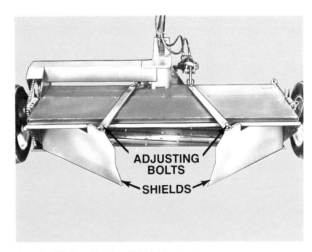

Fig. 16—Windrow-Forming-Shield Adjustment

Never allow any passengers to ride on the conditioner or tractor during operation or transport.

Do not allow children to play on or near a hay conditioner during operation, transport, or storage.

TROUBLESHOOTING FIELD PROBLEMS

Most conditioner problems are caused by improper adjustment or lack of maintenance. The troubleshooting chart will

Fig. 17—Transporting a Conditioner

help you correct problems by suggesting causes and solutions.

Use good judgment when you apply these remedies. Look beyond the immediate trouble area. Find the real source of the problem. There could be more than one cause. A thorough understanding of the conditioner is required to correct operating problems.

TROUBLESHOOTING CHART

PROBLEM	POSSIBLE CAUSE	POSSIBLE REMEDY
NOISE IN POWERLINE	Worn universal joint.	Replace U-joints.
	Bent shielding.	Replace shields.
	Drawbar improperly set.	Readjust drawbar setting.
POWERLINE FAILURE	Improper lubrication.	Repair or replace broken parts; see operator's manual.
	Drawbar improperly set.	Repair or replace broken parts; readjust drawbar.
	Slip clutch too tight.	Readjust slip clutch.
NOISE IN ROLLS.	Roll out of time.	Retime rolls.
	Mud buildup in rolls.	Clean rolls.
	Improper roll spacing.	Increase spacing.
CAN'T KEEP ROLLS IN TIME.	Worn drive parts.	Replace worn drive parts and retime.
ROLLS PLUG.	Improper ground speed.	Shift to lower gear.
	Improper roll spacing.	Increase roll space.
	Improper roll height.	Increase roll height.
	Foreign objects between rolls.	Clean rolls.
	Improper roll pressure.	Decrease roll pressure.
	Loose drive chains or belts.	Readjust chain or belt tension.
	PTO speed too slow.	Operate at standard PTO speed.
EXCESSIVE LEAF LOSS OR STEMS SHREDDING.	Improper roll spacing.	Increase roll spacing.
	Improper roll pressure.	Decrease roll pressure.
	Improper ground speed.	Increase ground speed.
HAY NOT CONDITIONED.	Improper roll spacing.	Decrease roll spacing.
	Improper roll pressure.	Increase roll pressure.
WON'T PICK UP HAY.	Improper roll height.	Reduce roll height.
PICKS UP EXCESSIVE TRASH AND ROCKS.	Improper roll height.	Increase roll height.
TIGHT, BUNCHY SWATH.	Fluffing board out of adjustment.	Raise fluffing board.
WINDROW TOO NARROW.	Windrow-forming shields out of adjustment.	Increase space between windrow-forming shields.
WINDROW TOO WIDE.	Windrow-forming shields out of adjustment.	Decrease space between windrow-forming shields.

MAINTENANCE

A hay conditioner is a simple machine that will last for years with proper maintenance. The conditioning rolls do the work and require the most maintenance. Keep them clean, timed correctly, and repaired.

Careful routine maintenance of bearings, belts, chains, and gears reduces chances breakdowns. Maintain proper slip-clutch adjustment to ensure protection when needed.

Few replacement parts are needed for conditioners. However, spare drive-chain links and belts are useful. Have extra shear pins in the field if the conditioner drive line is protected by a shearpin instead of a slip clutch. When you observe unusual wear on parts, correct the problem immediately and purchase replacement parts to reduce downtime in the future.

STORAGE

Proper storage during the off-season helps reduce maintenance costs and prolongs machine life. Before placing a conditioner in storage:

• *Clean and lubricate the conditioner thoroughly.*

• *Repaint surfaces where paint has worn off.*

• *Clean chains and brush them with heavy oil to prevent corrosion and rust.*

• *Relieve belt tension. Clean belts with a non-flammable agent to remove grease, oil, and dirt.*

• *Store the conditioner in a dry shelter.*

• *Block up the conditioner to remove weight from the tires. Do not deflate tires.*

• *If inside storage is not possible, remove tires and store them in a cool, dark, dry place.*

• *Finally, make a list of repairs needed, and order replacement parts so you can install them during the off-season.*

SUMMARY

Hay conditioners reduce the time required for field curing hay. Reducing the field-curing time in turn reduces the possibilities of weather damage to the crop.

Conditioners crush or crack stems, so they lose moisture fast. Conditioned hay cures faster and more evenly. The result is high quality and more palatable hay.

Conditioners are classified as crimpers or crushers, based on the configuration of the conditioner rolls. Tractor-towed conditioners are usually 7 or 9 feet (2.1 or 2.7 m) wide to match the widths of mower-cutterbars.

Fluffing boards and windrow-forming shields can be used to shape conditioned hay into a fluffy windrow so it dries faster and is easy to pick up.

Proper planning and timeliness are essential for successful hay conditioning. Conditioning must take place soon after plants are cut, before wilting begins. Simultaneous mowing and conditioning saves labor, and reduces the problem of mowing too far ahead of the conditioner.

Crimper rolls must be properly timed and spaced to match crop conditions. Crusher roll pressure must be increased for heavy crops. Too much crimping or crushing can cause excessive leaf loss and reduce hay yield. Too little conditioning wastes operating time and does little to hasten drying.

Conditioner rolls must be operated low enough to pick up all mowed plants, but high enough to miss rocks, sticks, and high spots in the field. Operating the conditioner too fast can plug it. Driving too slow over-conditions hay and increases leaf loss.

CHAPTER QUIZ

1. What is the mechanical function of a hay conditioner?

2. What are the benefits of conditioning hay?

3. Name the two types of hay-conditioning rolls.

4. Why must crimper rolls be properly timed?

5. (True or false.) Hay conditioners may be either towed by a tractor or integrally attached to a mower-conditioner or windrower.

6. What are the common widths of tractor-towed hay conditioners?

7. What is the function of the fluffing board?

8. How do adjustments to windrow-forming shields affect windrow configuration?

9. What are the advantages of mowing and conditioning simultaneously?

10. (True or false.) Hay should be permitted to wilt before it is conditioned.

4
Mower-Conditioners
and Windrowers

Fig. 1—Mower-Conditioners Cut, Condition, and Windrow Hay in One Operation

INTRODUCTION

Faced with a continuing shortage of reliable farm labor, hay growers must search for more efficient and higher-capacity hay harvesting equipment. An effective way of increasing efficiency and cutting manpower needs is to reduce the number of field operations required for harvesting the crop. Mower-conditioners and windrowers help do this by combining three operations into one. They cut, condition, and windrow hay in a single operation (Fig. 1).

PURPOSE AND USE

Mower-conditioners and windrowers essentially combine the functions of a mower and a conditioner, to convert standing crops into properly conditioned windrows. Then, with normal crop and weather conditions, no further hay processing is needed before packaging.

Mower-conditioners do not reduce the need for timely harvest to produce high quality hay. However, they ease the scheduling problems required for three separate field operations: mowing, conditioning, and raking. In addition, mower-conditioners and windrowers help save money and labor. Maintenance and storage costs are confined to one machine. For large acreages, self-propelled units can eliminate the need for a tractor during mowing and conditioning (Fig. 2).

Mower Conditioners

Mower-conditioners are used on small hay acreages which do not require a large, self-propelled windrower. Mower-conditioners are less expensive than self-propelled windrowers and are more maneuverable, which is needed in small, irregular-shaped hay fields.

Self-propelled Windrowers

Windrowers are used on nearly all commercial hay farms, and are widely accepted by farmers who grow hay for their own use. Self-propelled windrowers have more capacity than mower-conditioners, so in areas with a small labor supply, growers prefer windrowers over mower-conditioners. Windrowers may be purchased without conditioners for harvesting grain crops.

TYPES AND SIZES

Look at the difference between mower-conditioners and windrowers.

Most *mower-conditioners* have conditioning rolls that are about as long as the cutterbar. The cut hay is not conveyed laterally on the platform to enter the conditioner. Most mower-conditioners are tractor-powered, but self-propelled models are available.

A *windrower* may be self-propelled or tractor-powered. Most windrowers have a detachable hay conditioner. Some windrowers have integral conditioners and are built strictly for cutting and conditioning hay. Windrowers usu-

Fig. 2—Self-Propelled Windrower

Fig. 3—Full-Width Conditioning Rolls

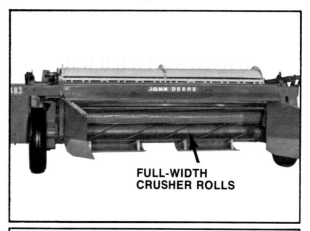

FULL-WIDTH CRUSHER ROLLS

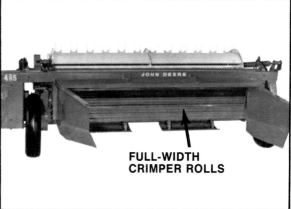

FULL-WIDTH CRIMPER ROLLS

ally have wider platforms than mower-conditioners: 12 to 14 feet (3.6 to 4.27 m).

The main difference between windrowers and mower-conditioners is in windrowers the hay is conveyed laterally on the platform by an auger or draper before entering the conditioning rolls or dropping onto the ground.

However, some equipment manufacturers and customers may use the words "mower-conditioner" and "windrower" interchangeably. Windrowers used primarily for cutting grain are also known as *"swathers"* in some areas.

MOWER-CONDITIONERS

Mower-conditioners are designed to provide efficient conditioning by using full-width conditioning rolls (Fig. 3). Most mower-conditioners use intermeshing rubber rolls that *crimp* and *crush* the hay. Either crushing rolls or crimping rolls are available for some machines.

Pulled mower-conditioners attach to a tractor drawbar and PTO shaft (Fig. 4). Power is transmitted to the mower-conditioner through a PTO shaft, slip clutch, and gearbox. Then, power goes to the reel, cutterbar, and conditioner through belts, chains, and gears. Most pulled mower-conditioners have cutterbar lengths of 7 to 10 feet (2 to 3 m).

Self-propelled mower-conditioners are compact, maneuverable machines that meet the needs of many small to medium acreage hay farms (Fig. 5). One unit has a 9-foot (2.7 m) cutting width.

WINDROWERS

Windrowers may be classified by the type of conveying device on the platform:

- **Auger**
- **Draper**

Auger Platform

The auger platform (Fig. 6) handles all hay, but is particularly effective on crops over 5 feet tall (1.5 m). The auger carries out hay from the cutterbar to the center of the platform, where it is fed into the conditioner or dropped on the ground.

Draper Platform

The draper platform (Fig. 7) cannot efficiently handle tall crops because it is not aggressive enough to bend the long stems. Draper platforms are used on hay-grain farms where one machine handles both crops. Drapers are good for windrowing grain because they handle crops gently, without excessive shattering. However, draper platforms require more maintenance than augers.

Draper platforms have conveyor belts which carry the crop to the center of the platform. Ribs or slats on the conveyor belts help keep the crop moving.

Fig. 4—Pulled Mower-Conditioner

Fig. 5—Self-Propelled Mower-Conditioner

PULLED WINDROWERS

Pulled windrowers may also be classified by type of drive. Most have a mechanical PTO drive. But some use hydraulic drives.

Mechanical PTO drive is similar to the drive used on pulled mower-conditioners. Mechanical PTO drive windrowers have a platform length of 9 to 16 feet (2.7 to 4.8 m). Some grain windrowers have a 20-foot (6.1 m) platform for extra-high capacity.

Hydraulic-driven, pull-type windrowers have a hitch over the platform (Fig. 8). The hydraulic drive allows wide flexibility for turning and maneuvering the windrower, because it is not restricted by a mechanical PTO drive train. Consequently, the hitch may be adjusted hydraulically into a variety of positions for field operation and transport (Fig. 9). Most of these units have 12- or 14-foot (3.6 or 4.3 m) cutting platforms.

SELF-PROPELLED WINDROWERS

Self-propelled windrowers provide the highest capacity for cutting, conditioning, and windrowing hay (Fig. 10). The mounted engine provides power for cutting and conditioning the crop and for ground propulsion. The power train to the drive wheels may be mechanical or hydrostatic. Platforms are usually 10 to 16 feet (3 to 4.8 m) wide for windrowers used in hay. Platforms for some grain windrowers are more than 20 feet (6.1 m) wide.

WINDROWER DRIVE

The windrower's engine is placed in the rear to balance the weight of the cutting platform and to position the operator forward for a good view of the windrower operation. The engine transmits power through separate drive trains for the platform and drive wheels. The platform drive usually consists of belts, chains, and gears that deliver power at the correct operating speeds for reel, auger, and cutterbar.

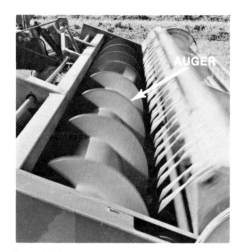

Fig. 6—Auger Platform

Fig. 7—Draper Platform

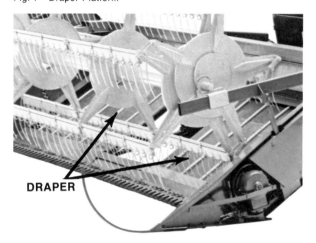

DRAPER

Fig. 8—Hydraulic-Driven Windrower

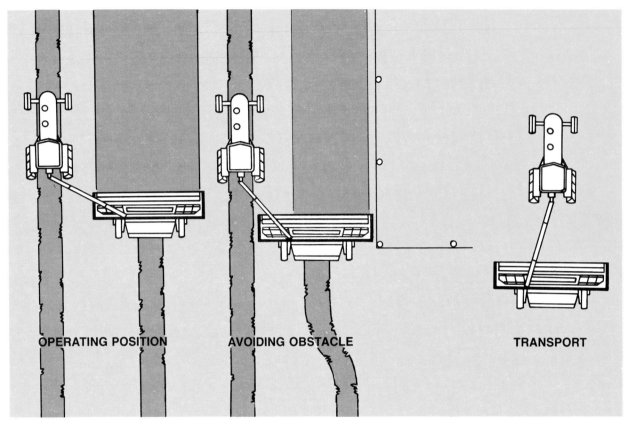

OPERATING POSITION   **AVOIDING OBSTACLE**   **TRANSPORT**

Fig. 9—Variable-Position Hitch on Hydraulic-Driven Windrower

Fig. 10—Self-Propelled Windrower

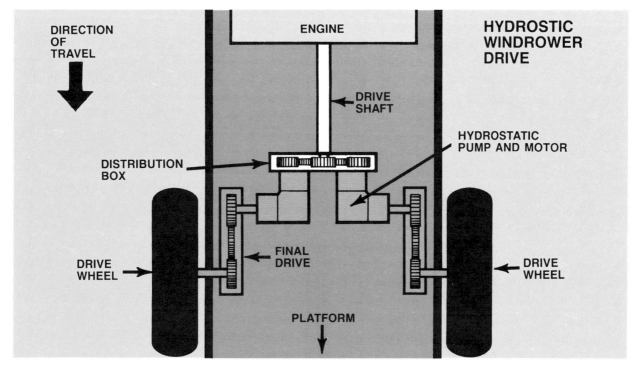

DIRECTION OF TRAVEL

ENGINE

HYDROSTIC WINDROWER DRIVE

DRIVE SHAFT

HYDROSTATIC PUMP AND MOTOR

DISTRIBUTION BOX

DRIVE WHEEL

FINAL DRIVE

DRIVE WHEEL

PLATFORM

Fig. 11—Hydrostatic Drive for Windrower

Fig. 12—Mechanical Drive for Windrower

Hydrostatic Drive

Windrower drive wheels may be powered hydraulically or mechanically. A typical hydrostatic drive system takes power from the engine and delivers it to two hydrostatic pump and motor units; one for each windrower drive wheel (Fig. 11). The variable displacement pumps provide infinitely variable forward and backward ground speeds. This system also controls steering by slowing one drive wheel. It also provides a slow-speed range for field operation and a fast-speed range for transport. Power is transmitted from the hydraulic system to the drive wheels through a spur gear final drive.

Mechanical Drive

On mechanical drive windrowers, power is transmitted with belts and a set of variable sheaves for speed and directional control (Fig. 12). Variable speed sheaves on the engine and main driveshaft control ground speed. Trim-steering sheaves control turning by slowing one drive wheel. Power goes to each drive wheel through a reversing drive for forward and backward control. From the reversing drives, power is transferred through a chain reduction drive.

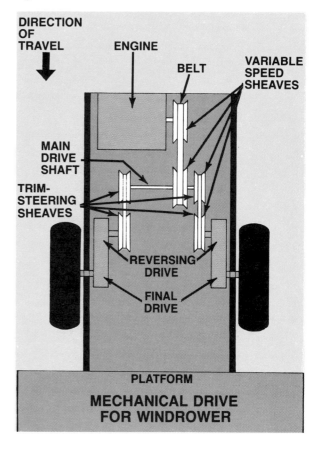

DIRECTION OF TRAVEL

ENGINE

BELT

VARIABLE SPEED SHEAVES

MAIN DRIVE SHAFT

TRIM-STEERING SHEAVES

REVERSING DRIVE

FINAL DRIVE

PLATFORM

MECHANICAL DRIVE FOR WINDROWER

Fig. 13—Windrower Cabs Protect Operators from Dust and Dirt

Operator Protection

On self-propelled windrowers, cabs protect operators so operators can work in a clean, healthful environment (Fig. 13).

MOWER-CONDITIONER AND WINDROWER OPERATION

There are so many different mower-conditioners and windrowers available, that a complete discussion of each is beyond the scope of this text. The rest of this section discusses features of typical PTO-driven mower-conditioners and self-propelled windrowers. For additional information, refer to specific operator's manuals.

The auger platform is more commonly used for windrowing hay than the draper platform.

Fig. 14—Mower-Conditioner

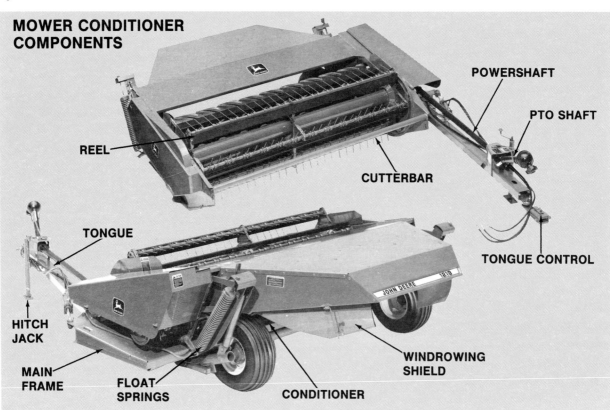

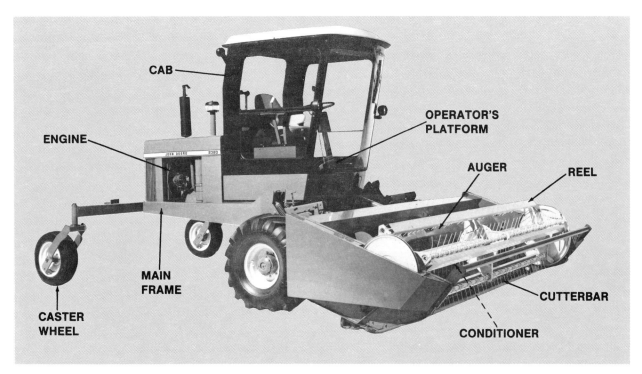

Fig. 15—Windrower

AUGER PLATFORM

PRIMARY COMPONENTS

Primary mower-conditioner components (Fig. 14) are:

- **Reel**
- **Cutterbar**
- **Conditioner**
- **Float spring**
- **Windrow-forming shields**
- **PTO shaft**
- **Main frame with hitch and wheels**

Primary windrower components (Fig. 15) include:

- **Reel**
- **Cutterbar**
- **Auger**
- **Conditioner**
- **Engine and drive train**
- **Main frame with wheels**
- **Operator's platform**

The operator's platform may or may not have a cab.

COMPONENT FUNCTIONS

Some components on mower-conditioners and wind-rowers have similar functions.

Platform

A cam actuated *reel* lifts and pushes the standing hay against the *cutterbar* which cuts the hay. The reel then lifts the cut material onto the *platform*.

For details on cutterbar action, refer to Chapter 2, *Mowers*. As stated previously, mower-conditioners move cut material straight back into the conditioner.

On windrowers, the cut crop is carried by the *auger* to the center. The material then feeds into the *conditioning rolls*, or is dropped on the ground and picked up by the conditioner.

Conditioner operation is explained fully in Chapter 3, *Hay Conditioners*.

Platform Flotation

The *main frame and wheels* carry the load of pulled mower-conditioners and windrowers. *Float springs* permit vertical movement of each end of the cutting platform (Fig. 16). Vertical movement allows the platform to follow ground irregularities for close cutting and to avoid damage to the cutterbar.

The windrower platform is mounted in front of the power unit (Fig. 17). This location permits the platform to move up and down under varying field conditions and for transport. Platform height is controlled with hydraulic cylinders. A set of springs at the lift arms provides platform flotation for uniform cutting over uneven terrain.

Fig. 16—Platform Flotation for Rough Terrain

Conditioner Drive

Conditioners may be driven with chains, belts, or gears. The gear drive does not require maintenance as frequently as belts and chains (Fig. 18). The conditioner is attached to the main frame of the platform.

Windrow-Forming

Conditioned hay is dropped to the ground in a fluffy windrow (Fig. 19). Adjustable *windrow-forming shields* let you set the windrow width for drying and efficient pickup by packaging equipment.

Fig. 17—Lift and Flotation System for a Self-Propelled Windrower Platform

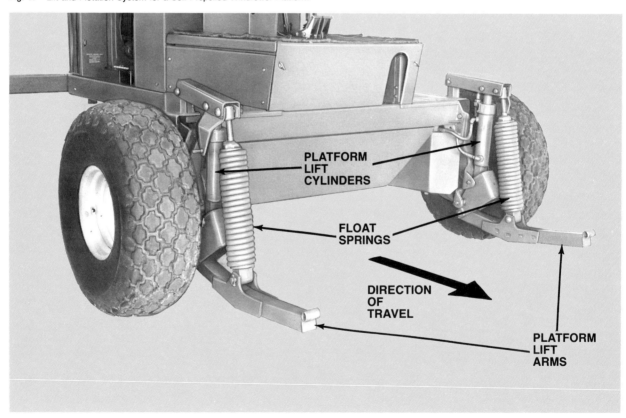

PLATFORM LIFT CYLINDERS

FLOAT SPRINGS

DIRECTION OF TRAVEL

PLATFORM LIFT ARMS

OPERATION AND ADJUSTMENT

Windrower and mower-conditioner operation must be properly managed to harvest quality hay. Weather and cutting time also affect the quality of hay.

Weather can't be controlled, but sound management helps minimize losses due to bad weather. Flexible scheduling and attention to weather forecasts can help you avoid the problem of having hay windrowed during rainy, cool weather.

However, the single most important factor in preserving the quality of mature hay is cutting time. Quality and yield both drop if hay is cut too early. Hay harvested too late loses quality and palatability.

Refer to the guide, *Stages of Maturity to Harvest Various Hay Crops,* in Chapter 2, *Mowers.*

PLANNING AND PREPARATION

Timely hay harvesting is based on good planning, proper operation, and reliable equipment.

Grow a hay crop that is compatible with other parts of the farming enterprise. No other farming operations should interfere with hay harvesting.

Proper operation of mower-conditioners and windrowers increases productivity and reduces loss of time in the field.

Reliable equipment also helps get hay harvested. Keep mower-conditioners and windrowers in top condition with a good service and maintenance schedule.

MOWER-CONDITIONER AND WINDROWER PREPARATION

Inspect and service mower-conditioners or windrowers before operating in the field. The following procedure is recommended before you make preliminary adjustments:

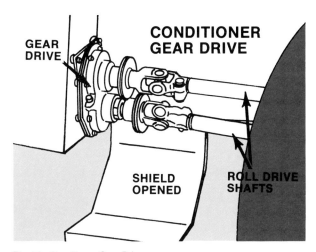

Fig. 18—Conditioner Gear Drive

● *Review the operator's manual.*

● *Lubricate the mower-conditioner or windrower according to the operator's manual (Fig. 20).*

● *Clean the machine.*

● *Check air pressure and inflate tires, if necessary.*

● *Tighten all loose bolts, nuts, and setscrews.*

● *Inspect the drive system carefully.*

● *If any parts have been replaced, run the mower-conditioner or windrower without load for a short break-in period, usually 5 to 30 minutes, or as recommended by the manufacturer. Watch for hot bearings and improperly functioning parts.*

Fig. 19—Good Windrow

Fig. 20—Lubricate Before Starting the Machine

PREPARE SELF-PROPELLED WINDROWER

Check and service the engine, drive train, and hydraulic system. Consult the operator's manual for specific instructions.

PREPARE TRACTOR

Pulled windrowers and mower-conditioners require a tractor for power. Prepare the tractor for field operation as follows, before connecting the mower-conditioner or windrower:

● *Service the tractor according to the operator's manual.*

● *Make sure the tractor PTO speed matches mower-conditioner drive requirements.*

● *Place the drawbar in the standard position for PTO operation, as directed in the mower-conditioner or windrower operator's manual.*

Fig. 21—Connect PTO Shaft

● *Lock the drawbar parallel with the centerline of the PTO shaft.*

● *Check the hydraulic system. Add oil if necessary.*

● *Adjust wheel spacing so you don't drive on windrows.*

ATTACH THE MOWER-CONDITIONER

After the tractor is prepared, follow this sequence to attach the mower-conditioner:

● *Raise or lower the mower-conditioner hitch with the hitch jack to engage the drawbar.*

● *Back the tractor to align holes in the hitch and drawbar, and insert the safety hitch pin.*

● *Place the hitch jack in the transport position.*

● *Attach the powershaft to the tractor PTO shaft (Fig. 21). Install the PTO shield.*

● *Install hydraulic hoses in breakaway couplers.*

● *Attach the tongue-positioning control rope to the tractor, if it is required.*

To detach, reverse the attaching procedure.

PRELIMINARY SETTINGS AND ADJUSTMENTS

A mower-conditioner or windrower will not perform satisfactorily if it is not adjusted properly. To avoid loss of field time, adjust the machine in advance to match conditions. It may be necessary to reset some preliminary adjustments, but an experienced operator can usually predict field and crop conditions and make adjustments accordingly.

BREAK-IN

Before beginning field operation, run a new mower-conditioner or windrower slowly through a break-in period. Observe the machine closely to make sure all parts are operating properly. Make necessary adjustments.

KNIFE SELECTION

Choose the correct knife to avoid plugging and uneven cutting. Refer to Chapter 2, *Mowers,* for information on knife selection.

Fig. 22— Float Spring Adjustment

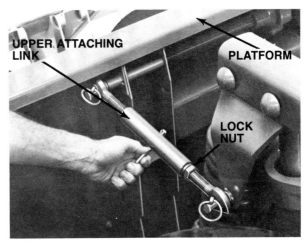

Fig. 23—Cutterbar Tilt Adjustment on a Windrower

PLATFORM FLOTATION

Adjust float springs to level the platform with the ground surface and allow it to follow the ground contour. Improper spring adjustment may cause the platform to bounce, which results in uneven cutting. Or, it may not allow the platform to rise, which causes it to drag heavily on the ground. Adjust flotation by changing the length of float springs (Fig. 22). Springs on both ends of the mower-conditioner, or bolt lift arms on the windrower must be adjusted equally. See the operator's manual for details.

CUTTERBAR TILT

As with mowers, the cutterbar guard angle (or tilt with respect to the ground) must be adjusted on both mower-conditioners and windrowers (Fig. 23). Cutterbar tilt determines how well the guards lift and penetrate the crop.

These adjustments must be equal on both ends of the platform. The operator's manual specifies adjustment procedures for different conditions.

Unlike mowers, cutterbar adjustments are seldom required on mower-conditioners and windrowers. No cutterbar lead adjustment is needed because the cutterbar is supported throughout its length by the platform. Knife register is not usually a problem because most mower-conditioners and windrowers use a pitmanless knife drive.

WINDROWER AUGER

Auger speed must be adjusted to the crops, field conditions, and travel speed. When the crop is heavy, or ground speed is high, increase auger speed. Reduce auger speed in light crops, or when rough fields slow ground speed. The auger should run just fast enough to feed the crop to the conditioner evenly. On most windrowers, the auger speed is adjusted before reel speed is adjusted, because the reel is driven from the auger drive shaft.

Strippers

Strippers clean hay from the turning auger flights so the hay doesn't bind the auger. Both the auger and strippers can be adjusted for different crop conditions. If the auger is too high or strippers are too far from the auger, hay will carry over on the auger, bunch up, and plug. Always set strippers as close to the auger as possible, but don't let the strippers touch the auger flights (Fig. 24).

REEL ADJUSTMENT

Adjust the reel to match crop conditions so the crop feeds evenly.

Reel adjustment consists of selecting the proper horizontal and vertical location and dump position for reel teeth, plus reel speed. These adjustments are similar for mower-conditioners and windrowers.

Fig. 24—Strippers Help Clean the Auger

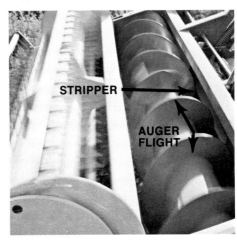

Fig. 25—Adjusting Reel Cam

Operate the reel just low enough to maintain a steady flow of material to the auger or conditioner. For tall, heavy crops adjust the reel forward and upward. For short, light crops, adjust the reel down and back. Equal adjustments on each end of the reel are required for both horizontal and vertical adjustments.

Reel Speed

Adjust the speed of the reel to slightly faster than ground speed (commonly 1.25 times faster) in the standing crop.

Fig. 26—Operator's Platform with Controls

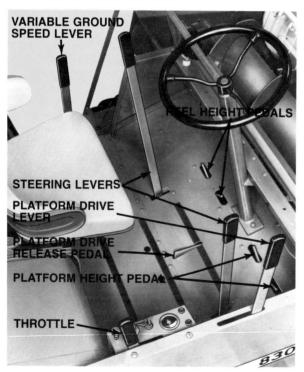

VARIABLE GROUND SPEED LEVER

REEL HEIGHT PEDALS

STEERING LEVERS

PLATFORM DRIVE LEVER

PLATFORM DRIVE RELEASE PEDAL

PLATFORM HEIGHT PEDAL

THROTTLE

830

This allows the reel to push the crop over the cutterbar for clean, efficient cutting. In down or tangled crops, the reel must run even faster to lift the hay before cutting. However, reel speed that's too fast can damage the crop by unnecessary reel batting and heavy material will not have time to drop from the reel teeth. The reel should turn just fast enough to lay the crop well back on the platform as it is cut.

Reel Teeth

Adjust reel teeth to release cut material well ahead of the conditioner rolls. In tall crops an early-release position will provide even feeding. In short crops, a late tooth-release position helps ensure the crop is carried back into the platform for even feeding. Fast reel speed will require earlier material release from the reel teeth than a slower reel speed. Adjustment is made by repositioning cam-adjusting bolts (Fig. 25).

ROLL TIMING

Check and adjust the conditioner crimper roll timing if necessary. This adjustment for mower-conditioners and windrower conditioners is similar to the procedure described in Chapter 3, *Conditioners.*

SLIP CLUTCH

Check and adjust all slip clutches to meet specifications in the operator's manual. A slip clutch is a safety device to prevent excessive damage if a malfunction occurs. An overly tight slip clutch will not slip if it is overloaded. A loose slip clutch permits excessive slippage during operation, which can cause overheating and reduce field efficiency.

FIELD OPERATION

Controls for mower-conditioners and windrowers vary according to model and optional features. Here are basic controls for machines.

PULLED MACHINES

Pulled machines generally require a *PTO clutch* to control platform components and the conditioner, and a *remote hydraulic cylinder* to control platform lift in addition to the usual tractor-operating controls. A *tongue-positioning control rope* may be used on some units.

To begin field operation of a pulled mower-conditioner or windrower, position the hitch, if it is adjustable, or adjust the tractor wheel tread so the tractor will not be driven on the windrow. Then lower the platform into position. Engage the PTO clutch and accelerate the engine to give the rated PTO speed.

SELF-PROPELLED MACHINES

For self-propelled windrowers and mower-conditioners, all controls are mounted on the operator's platform (Fig. 26). Controls are for *steering, propulsion, platform drives,* and *platform lift.*

For steering, some self-propelled units with mechanical drive use lever control instead of a steering wheel (Fig. 27). Another lever controls forward speed. Also, levers are available for left and right trim-steering to make small steering changes.

Some others use levers for sharp turns, and a steering wheel for minor steering corrections (Fig. 27). Experience in using the control levers provides a competent operator complete control of the machine.

OPENING THE FIELD

To open a field, first cut the hay next to the fence by driving around the field counterclockwise. Make left turns slowly on this first round to avoid damage to equipment from hitting fences.

Shift to a lower gear to reduce speed instead of reducing engine speed. Reducing engine speed also slows the cutterbar, reel, auger, and conditioner, and could cause plugging. After the first round, reverse the direction of travel, and harvest the rest of the field in a clockwise direction.

Some operators prefer to open the field by cutting one or two rounds in the normal clockwise direction, then reversing direction to cut the backswath next to the border.

A self-propelled windrower or mower-conditioner operates equally well in clockwise or counterclockwise direction. So opening a field is no problem. In fact, self-propelled machines can cut a field back and forth in adjacent passes rather than going around the field (Fig. 28). Back and forth mowing is commonly used in fields that are flood-irrigated between borders.

Both pulled and self-propelled mower-conditioners and windrowers can cut neat, square corners (Fig. 29). With careful operation, it is seldom necessary to raise the platform at corners.

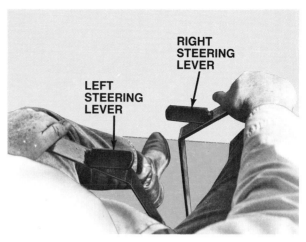
Fig. 27—Lever Controls for Steering.

FIELD ADJUSTMENTS

Frequent field adjustments must be made to ground speed and cutting height to match crop and field conditions. Most adjustments are similar to those needed for mowers and conditioners and are discussed in Chapters 2 and 3. Reel and auger adjustments are discussed under "Preliminary Settings and Adjustments" in this chapter.

Ground Speed

Adjust ground speed to match crop and field conditions. Slow speeds are advisable in down and tangled crops. Fast ground speeds are sometimes acceptable on smooth terrain in a light, scattered crop. However, excessive speeds can result in unnecessary breakdowns. A steady, reasonable speed results in more hay cut, conditioned, and windrowed each day. Under most conditions, a speed of 4 to 6 miles per hour (6.4 to 9.6 km/h) will produce a good windrow and not cause undue machine wear.

Fig. 28—Windrowing a Field Back and Forth

WINDROWING
BACK
AND
FORTH

Fig. 29—Turning a Square Corner with
Hydraulic-Driven Pulled Windrower

Cutting Height

The cutting height depends on crop and terrain conditions. In rocky conditions, the stubble may need to be higher to reduce cutterbar damage. Under ideal conditions, the cutting height is adjusted to suit the crop. Mower-conditioners and windrowers have adjustable gauge shoes to help maintain a uniform cutting height. Adjust them up or down for the right cutting height. Adjust each end of the platform equally for uniform cutting.

Rock Door

On some auger platforms, a removable rock door is available. With the rock door removed, a hole in the bottom center of the platform lets stones fall through, while hay is fed into the hay conditioner. The rock door is removed in stony conditions unless the hay is extremely short. Very short hay will not span the gap and can fall through or plug by catching in the opening.

Fig. 30—Mower-Conditioner in Transport Position

Other Adjustments

Field adjustments for most conditioners concern roll spacing and pressure, and the fluffing board and windrow-forming shields. Refer to Chapter 3, *Conditioners,* for details on these adjustments.

TRANSPORT

On many pulled mower-conditioners and windrowers, an adjustable hitch can be changed from the field-operating to the transport position before the machine is transported. This change lets the unit follow directly behind the tractor (Fig. 30), and cross bridges or go through gates.

A self-propelled windrower or mower-conditioner should be transported under its own power or loaded on a truck. However, if the unit is to be towed, the parking brake and the main power train should be disengaged. Most units have a throwout shaft to disengage the power train for towing.

Always raise the platform so it will clear obstructions.

Transport speed should be adjusted for terrain and surface conditions and not exceed the manufacturer's recommendations. Use a lower gear and slower speed on steep downgrades.

Be sure the brakes are adequate and reliable; especially on hilly terrain.

When transporting a mower-conditioner or windrower always use a clearly visible SMV emblem and turn on flashing accessory lights to warn others.

SAFETY

Since mowers and conditioners are the primary components of mower-conditioners and windrowers, refer to Chapter 2, *Mowers,* and Chapter 3, *Conditioners,* for safety guidelines.

See Hydraulic safety message page 334.

TROUBLESHOOTING

Most operating problems that occur with mower-conditioners and windrowers result from improper adjustments or lack of timely service. The following chart suggests probable causes and recommended solutions to common problems.

Apply these suggested remedies carefully. An incorrect remedy could cause a serious malfunction. A thorough understanding of the mower-conditioner or windrower is a must to correct problems satisfactorily.

This troubleshooting chart is for the platform components. Refer to the operator's manual for field problems in the engine and power train.

TROUBLESHOOTING CHART

PROBLEM	POSSIBLE CAUSE	POSSIBLE REMEDY
EXCESSIVE NOISE.	Rolls too close.	Increase roll spacing.
	Rolls out of time.	Retime rolls.
	Knife or guards bent.	Straighten knife and reset guards.
LEAF DAMAGE OR LEAF LOSS.	Reel speed too fast.	Reduce reel speed.
	Roll spacing too close.	Increase roll spacing.
	Over-crushing.	Increase roll spacing. Decrease roll pressure.
STEMS SHREDDING.	Improper roll spacing.	Increase roll spacing.
ROLLS PLUGGING.	Foreign objects between rolls.	Disengage tractor PTO or platform drive and stop engine. When all moving parts are completely stopped, remove foreign objects.
CUTTERBAR PLUGGING.	Loose cutterbar drive belt.	Adjust belt tension.
	Dull or broken knife sections.	Resharpen or replace, as required.
	Bent or broken guards.	Straighten or replace, as required.
	Improper platform float spring adjustment.	Readjust float springs.
	Improper knife hold-down adjustment.	Readjust hold-downs.
	Improper reel adjustment.	Adjust reel position and cam.
EXCESSIVE BREAKAGE OF KNIFE SECTIONS OR GUARDS.	Cutterbar operating too low in stony field conditions.	Raise cutterbar, using gauge shoes, and check float. Change guard angle.
	Improper platform float spring adjustment.	Readjust float springs.
	Improper guard alignment.	Realign guards.
	Improper knife hold-down adjustment.	Readjust hold-downs.
	Ground speed too fast.	Reduce ground speed.
GUARDS BREAKING AT FRONT OF SLOT.	Reel teeth too low (teeth into knife).	Raise reel or replace damaged teeth.
LEAVING LONG OR UNEVEN STUBBLE.	Excessive ground speed.	Reduce ground speed.
	Worn or damaged cutterbar.	Replace parts or readjust, as necessary.
	Improper platform float spring adjustment.	Readjust float springs.

PROBLEM	POSSIBLE CAUSE	POSSIBLE REMEDY
Continued	Loose cutterbar drive belt.	Readjust belt tension.
	Improper cutting height.	Readjust gauge shoes.
	Dull knife.	Sharpen.
	Guard angle too flat.	Change guard angle.
	Reel not lifting down or tangled crop.	Move reel forward and down.
POORLY FORMED OR BUNCHY WINDROWS.	Reel speed too slow.	Speed up reel.
	Swath board down.	Adjust board up.
	Improper PTO speed.	Correct PTO speed.
	Reel cam set for late tooth release.	Adjust cam.
STRIPS OF UNCUT MATERIAL.	Crowding uncut crop.	Allow enough room for crop to be fed to cutterbar.
	Foreign objects on cutterbar.	Disengage tractor PTO or platform drive and stop engine. After all moving parts are completely stopped, remove foreign objects.
	Broken knife sections.	Replace knife sections as required.
POOR CUTTING ACTION.	Various parts of cutterbar, such as knife sections, guards, wearing plates, etc., are worn, damaged, or broken.	Check and replace all worn and broken parts on cutterbar to obtain an even cutting of crop.
	Bent knife, causing binding of cutting parts.	Straighten a bent knife. Check guard alignment and align if necessary for a smooth cut.
	Ground speed too fast.	Slow down.
	Lips of guard out of adjustment or bent, causing poor shearing action.	Adjust lip of guard.
	Loose cutterbar drive belt.	Adjust drive belt tension.
IMPROPER REEL DELIVERY		
Reel wrapping in tangled and weedy crops.	Incorrect location of reel and improper setting of reel slats.	Place reel well ahead and down.
	Reel speed too fast.	Reduce reel speed to allow crop to fall into platform.
Reel carrying around crop.	Tall grain or nodding varieties of crops catch on reel slats and arms.	Increase width of reel slats with wire screen or canvas for nodding varieties of crops.
	Reel speed too fast.	Reduce reel speed so crop will not carry over top of reel. Reel should turn just enough faster than ground travel so that crop heads are laid well back on cutting platform.
	Reel height too low.	Raise reel height to reduce amount of crop gathered by reel.

MAINTENANCE

Mowers and conditioners are the primary components of mower-conditioners and windrowers. Refer to Chapter 2, *Mowers,* and Chapter 3, *Conditioners,* and the operator's manual for proper maintenance procedures. Also refer to the operator's manual for maintenance and service information on the engine and power train of self-propelled windrowers and mower-conditioners.

SUMMARY

Mower-conditioners and windrowers combine a mower and a conditioner and save manpower and time. They cut, condition, and windrow hay in one operation.

Mower-conditioners are used on small farms because they cost less than self-propelled windrowers and work well in irregular-shaped fields.

Windrowers are used on most commercial hay farms and by farmers who grow their own hay. Self-propelled windrowers usually have more capacity than mower-conditioners.

Mower-conditioners are usually tractor-powered, although self-propelled units are available. The conditioning rolls on a mower-conditioner are about as long as the cutterbar.

On self-propelled and tractor-powered windrowers, the crop is carried across the platform before it is discharged into conditioning rolls or onto the ground. Conditioners on windrowers are usually half the platform width, or less. Grain windrowers do not have a conditioner.

Mower-conditioners are usually 7 to 10 feet (2 to 3 m) wide. Most use intermeshing rolls that both crimp and crush the crop.

Windrowers have draper platforms or auger platforms which are good in tall crops. Windrowers may be pulled or they may be self-propelled. Windrowers may be powered by a mechanical or a hydraulic drive. Platform widths range from 9 to 16 feet (2.7 to 4.8 m) for use in hay.

Reels are used to push standing crop against the cutterbar which cuts the crop. Cutting and conditioning is similar to that of mowers and conditioners.

Selfpropelled windrowers may have hydraulic or mechanical drives. Steering is controlled by levers or a steering wheel.

CHAPTER QUIZ

1. What is the main advantage a windrower or mower-conditioner offers to a hay producer?

2. What three functions do windrowers perform?

3. (True or false.) Strippers must be set at least 3 inches (76 mm) from the auger flights.

4. Does a mower-conditioner or a windrower deliver the most efficient hay conditioning? Why?

5. (True or false.) One of the primary adjustments on a windrower is cutterbar lead.

6. What are the functions of a reel on a mower-conditioner or windrower?

7. (Choose one.) Reel speed should be (increased; decreased) in a down, tangled crop.

8. (True or false.) Adjust the reel rearward and downward for tall, heavy crops.

9. (True or false.) Self-propelled windrowers and mower-conditioners can be used to cut a field "back and forth."

10. What is a rock door on a windrower?

5
Rakes

Fig. 1—Horse Powered Sulky Rake with Hand Dump

Fig. 2—Early Horse Drawn Side-Delivery Rake

INTRODUCTION

Hay had to be raked with crude hand tools until the early 1800s when the horse-drawn sulky rake was developed (Fig. 1).

Although improvements were made, farmers became dissatisfied. In the late 1800s, the horse-drawn side-delivery rake was developed (Fig. 2). The side-delivery rake placed the hay in straighter windrows. Continuing developments have led to tractor powered, side-delivery rakes (Fig. 3).

PURPOSE AND USE

Rakes were developed to gather newly-cut hay into small piles or windrows to make hay collection easier. Rakes lift mowed hay from the swath and place it in a loose, fluffy windrow with the green leaves inside, protected from the sun's rays. The leaves retain their fresh, green color, and the stems cure. Rakes are also used to windrow straw and crop residue for harvest or burning.

Mower-conditioners and windrowers that cut, condition, and windrow in one field operation have not eliminated the need for rakes. Rakes combine windrows in light hay crops. Combining windrows are also combined for high-capacity balers, round balers, stack wagons, and bale wagons that operate best with heavy windrows. Rakes are sometimes used to turn windrows for even exposure to the sun. Turning rain soaked windrows for uniform drying is also a common practice.

TYPES AND SIZES

Side-delivery rakes are classified as:

- **Parallel-bar rakes**
- **Wheel rakes**

PARALLEL-BAR RAKES

Parallel-bar rakes require a power source to drive the rake reel and bars (Fig. 4). They may be ground-, PTO-, or hydraulically-driven.

Parallel-bar rakes may be further classified by the way they are attached to the tractor:

- **Trailed**
- **Rear-mounted**
- **Front-mounted**

Trailed Rakes

Some trailed, parallel-bar rakes have a gauge wheel in front (Fig. 5). This gauge wheel supports part of the rake's weight and provides immediate response by the rake reel to any terrain irregularities.

Other trailed rakes attach directly to the tractor drawbar without a gauge wheel (Fig. 6). Without the front gauge wheel, the tractor drawbar carries part of the rake's weight and response to terrain irregularities is not as fast.

Trailed rakes are usually ground-driven. But hydraulically-driven models are available. Ground-driven rakes are easy to hookup, and have a direct relationship between reel speed and ground speed.

Fig. 3 — Hydraulic Powered Side-Delivery Rake Powered By Tractor
Hydraulic System

Fig. 4—Parallel-Bar Rake

Fig. 5—Ground-Driven, Trailed, Parallel-Bar Rake

Fig. 6—PTO-Driven, Rear-Mounted, Parallel-Bar Rake

REAR-MOUNTED
PTO-DRIVEN RAKE

Rear-Mounted Rakes

Rear-mounted, parallel-bar rakes are connected to a tractor's 3-point hitch (Fig. 6). All of the rake weight is carried by the 3-point hitch during transport, and most of the weight is on the tractor during operation. Caster wheels on the rear help gauge the terrain. These maneuverable rakes are ideal for raking small, irregular-shaped fields. Rear-mounted rakes can be transported easily by raising the 3-point hitch. Rear-mounted, parallel-bar rakes are driven by the PTO.

Front-Mounted Rakes

Front-mounted, parallel-bar rakes can rake while other hay and forage equipment is operated behind the tractor (Fig. 7). Front-mounted rakes usually combine windrows just before baling or stacking hay, or chopping haylage. Front-mounted rakes are driven hydraulically.

RAKE SIZE

A parallel-bar rake may have a 7, 8, or 9 foot raking width (2.1, 2.4, or 2.7 m). Widths match the length of cutterbars on most mowers.

Raking capacity may be increased by using two rakes connected to a tandem hitch (Fig. 8). A twin rake is also available (Fig. 10). Twin rakes are trailed, hydraulic-driven, and have a 21 foot (6.4 m) raking span.

Most tandem hitches can be adjusted to form a single windrow (Top, Fig. 10), or to form two windrows (Lower, Fig. 10).

WHEEL RAKES

Wheel rakes are simpler than parallel-bar rakes because no chains, belts, or gears are needed to drive the wheels (Fig. 11). The raking wheels are turned by the rake teeth on the ground. Rake teeth break because they are always on the ground, and they may rake rocks and brush into the windrow. Wheel rakes tend to make tight, rope-like windrows that dry relatively slow. But individual wheel flotation

Fig. 7—Hydraulic-Driven, Front-Mounted, Parallel-Bar Rake

Fig. 8—Two Rakes with Tandem Hitch Cut Raking Time

Fig. 9—Twin Rake

Fig. 10—Two Rakes and a Tandem Hitch Can Form One or Two Windrows

provides clean raking on rough terrain. Also, wheel-rake teeth travel slower than parallel-bar rake teeth so they are more gentle.

Wheel rakes are *trailed, rear-mounted,* or *front-mounted.* Trailed rakes offer more flexibility for adding extensions. And, trailed rakes are available in larger sizes. But mounted rakes are more maneuverable.

TEDDERS, FLUFFERS

Specialized raking equipment is used to aid drying in damp climates. A *tedder (fluffer)* raises, loosens, and turns hay (Fig. 12). Fluffers are PTO driven or ground driven. The width of a swath is 7 to 12 feet (2.1 to 3.6 m).

RAKE OPERATION

Rakes have few moving parts. Draft is low so a small tractor can pull them.

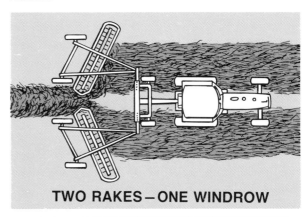

TWO RAKES—ONE WINDROW

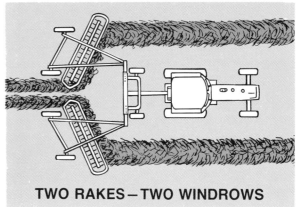

TWO RAKES—TWO WINDROWS

Fig. 11—Wheel Rake

Fig. 12—Hay Tedding Speeds Drying

COMPONENTS

REAR-MOUNTED, PARALLEL-BAR RAKE

Components of a PTO-driven, rear-mounted, parallel-bar rake (Fig. 13):

- **Main frame**
- **PTO shaft**

- **Drive sheave**
- **Front and rear reel ends**
- **Toothbar**
- **Teeth**
- **Stripper rods**
- **Caster wheels**

Fig. 13—Parallel-Bar Rake Components

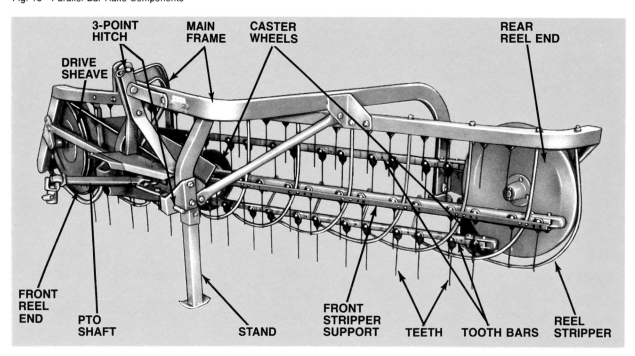

TRAILED WHEEL RAKE COMPONENTS

A typical trailed wheel rake has (Fig. 14):

- **Tongue**
- **Main frame**
- **Raking-wheel beam**
- **Lift crank**
- **Raking wheels**
- **Teeth**
- **Float springs**

COMPONENT FUNCTIONS

REAR-MOUNTED, PARALLEL-BAR RAKE

The PTO-driven, rear-mounted rake is fastened to the tractor 3-point hitch. The rake hitch is connected directly to the *main frame* which supports the rake.

Power to drive the parallel-bar reel comes from the tractor's PTO, through the telescoping *PTO shaft,* to a V-belt *pulley.* A V-belt between this pulley and one on the *front reel end* completes the simple drive.

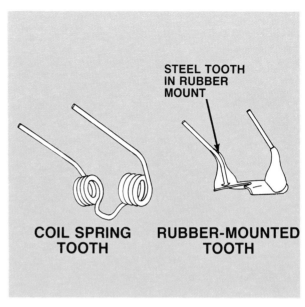

Fig. 15—Coil Spring and Molded Rubber-Mounted Rake Teeth

Teeth

Broken teeth reduce efficiency leaving hay unraked in the swath. Steel teeth have a coil spring or molded rubber mount (Fig. 15) to absorb shock. Rubber-mounted teeth are more expensive than spring mounted teeth, but usually have a much longer life. Also, their ability to flex in any direction is particularly valuable in rough ground.

Fig. 14—Wheel Rake Components

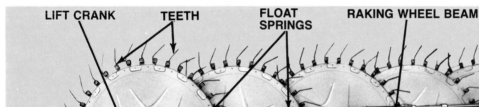

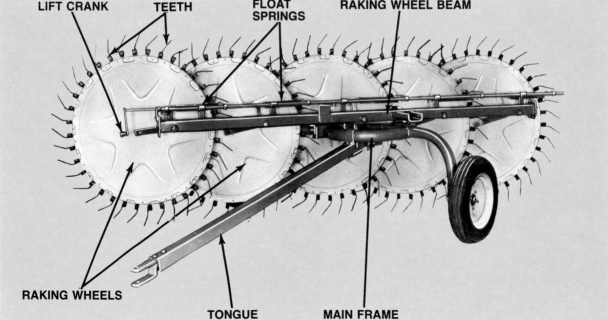

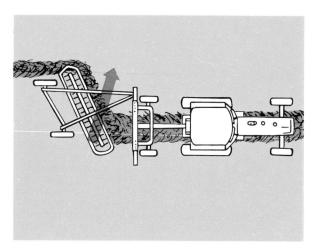

Fig. 16—Movement of Hay During Raking

Toothbars

Toothbars hold the rake teeth which contact the hay. Through a series of strokes by each toothbar, hay is rolled sideways along the front of the reel and off the trailing end of the rake to form the windrow (Fig. 16).

Stripper Rods

Stripper rods help pull hay from the teeth. Without stripper rods, the teeth tend to carry hay up and over the reel.

Caster Wheels

On some rakes, changing caster wheel position changes the angle of the teeth. Tooth pitch determines the fluffiness of the windrow. Caster wheels help gauge rake height, guide the rake over terrain irregularities, and help reduce the possibility of damage to the teeth and toothbars.

WHEEL RAKE

The wheel rake *tongue* is pinned to the tractor's drawbar and is connected to the *main frame* which supports the weight of the rake. The *raking-wheel* beam holds the *rake wheels.*

When the rake is in working position, the bottom teeth on the outer rim of each wheel touch the ground lightly. As the rake is pulled forward, the diagonally-set wheels turn, moving the hay forward and to the side. This roll of hay is kept in front of the rake wheels until it rolls off the trailing end of the rake. As the hay rolls past the end of the rake, the windrow is formed.

Raking Wheel Mounting

Raking wheels are attached individually or in groups to a movable *crank arm.* The wheels are partially supported by a tension or *float spring,* which allows each wheel to follow the ground contour without excessive pressure on the teeth.

Raking Wheel

Two raking wheels are available: *Finger wheels* and *solid disk wheels.*

Finger wheels have teeth radiating from a center hub (Fig. 17). These long teeth flex along their entire length and float around obstructions that could break short, stiff teeth. However, in windy conditions some finger wheels are susceptible to crop tangling and wrapping on the wheels, which results in poorly formed windrows. Severity of the problem is usually related to the diameter of the center hub where teeth are attached. Windshields are available for some finger wheel rakes.

Solid disk wheels are not affected by wind as much as finger wheels (Fig. 18).

Fig. 17—Finger Wheel Rake

Fig. 18—Solid-Disk Wheel Rake

OPERATION, TIMING, AND ADJUSTMENTS

Timely and proper raking can help maintain hay quality.

MOISTURE *IS* IMPORTANT

Timely raking helps reduce leaf loss and helps fast, even drying. Raking wet hay slows drying because the windrow reduces exposure to the sun and wind. Raking dry hay causes leaf shatter. Losing leaves means losing quality. Rake hay when its moisture content is approximately 50 percent. If the moisture content falls much below 50 percent, wait until the dew sets before raking.

PLANNING AND PREPARATION

Planning for raking means: "Be ready when the hay is ready."

The rake and tractor have to be in good operating condition. Breakdowns due to poor maintenance can cause needless delay and severe quality loss. Since a rake does not require much power, it is often used with an old tractor. This is acceptable if the tractor is reliable, or a replacement tractor is available. An hour lost due to a breakdown can cause hay to dry too much for raking.

REAR-MOUNTED RAKE

A hookup and preparation procedure for a PTO-driven, rear-mounted, parallel-bar rake follows: Since specific procedures vary with each make and model of rake, consult the operator's manual for details.

TRACTOR PREPARATION

First, prepare the tractor for field operation as follows:

1. Service the tractor according to the operator's manual.

2. Make sure the tractor's PTO speed matches the rake drive speed.

3. Move the drawbar so it won't interfere with the rake.

4. Check and adjust the 3-point hitch linkage for correct operation.

5. Adjust wheel spacing. Narrower spacing reduces turning radius, but reduces tractor stability.

6. Add ballast to the tractor front end if it is needed for stability.

RAKE PREPARATION

When the tractor is ready, attach the rake as follows:

1. Adjust the hitch-pin locations on the rake main frame to match the tractor's 3-point hitch.

2. Back the tractor into position and lower the draft links until they are approximately in line with the hitch pins. Turn off tractor and take the key.

3. Connect draft links to hitch pins.

4. Attach the tractor's center link to the rake's upper hitch point.

5. Level the rake from side to side using draft links.

6. Adjust the tractor hitch sway chains or stabilizers so the rake won't swing back and forth.

7. Connect the telescoping PTO shaft to the tractor power takeoff.

8. Raise the rake and put the parking stand in its upper position (Fig. 19.

9. Raise and lower the rake with the 3-point hitch to make sure the PTO shaft does not bind. Also check for interference between the rake and tractor wheels and drawbar. Readjust the hitch position if necessary.

Detaching procedure is the reverse of the attaching procedure.

Fig. 19—Hitching the Rake to Tractor Drawbar

FINAL CHECK

After the rake is hitched to the tractor, start the final inspection:

1. Review the operator's manual.

2. Lubricate the rake as recommended in the operator's manual.

3. Clean the rake.

Fig. 20—Tooth Pitch Adjustment for Rear-Mounted Rake

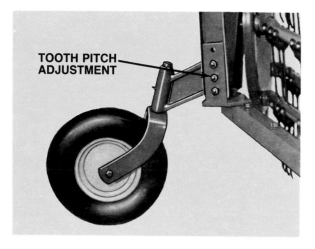

TOOTH PITCH
ADJUSTMENT

4. Tighten bolts and nuts to the recommended torques.

5. Replace damaged teeth.

6. Turn the reel by hand to make sure it moves freely and that the teeth do not strike the stripper rods.

7. Inspect the drive system carefully. Adjust the drive-belt tension if necessary.

TOWED RAKE

The preparation and hookup procedure for towed rakes is much simpler and faster because the rake doesn't use the 3-point hitch or PTO shaft. Extra tractor ballast is not required because the tractor does not carry the rake.

Adjust the tractor drawbar to the recommended position and attach the rake tongue with a safety hitch pin to finish the hookup (Fig. 19). Finally, inspect and service the rake before making preliminary adjustments.

ADJUSTMENTS

Proper settings and adjustments help make the rake work efficiently. Once the proper adjustments are made, a rake is easy to operate.

PARALLEL-BAR RAKES

Set the tooth pitch and add more toothbars if necessary for short crops.

Tooth Pitch

Tooth pitch determines the shape and density of the windrow. Forward tooth pitch has more lift and makes a loose, fluffy windrow. A rearward pitch produces a tighter, more dense windrow which dries slower. Tight windrows are good for hay that will be field-chopped for silage or haylage. For some rear-mounted rakes, the caster wheels are mounted in different holes to change tooth pitch (Fig. 20).

Toothbars

Parallel-bar rakes usually have four or five toothbars. Four bars are adequate for most raking conditions, but raking short, light crops can require additional toothbars and teeth for complete cleanup. Most parallel-bar rakes have extra holes in the reel ends for a fifth toothbar. And some rakes can use six toothbars. Extra teeth can be added on most bars to reduce the space between the teeth and provide better cleanup in short crops (Fig. 21).

WHEEL RAKES

Wheel rakes require more preliminary adjustments for efficient field operation than other rakes:

1. *Level the rake-wheel beam.*

2. *Set the tooth pitch.*

3. *Set the rake-wheel flotation.*

4. *Position the tongue.*

5. *Set the raking width.*

Raking -Wheel Beam

When the rake is hitched to the tractor drawbar, the raking-wheel beam must be level. If the beam is not level, ground contact pressure will vary for each rake wheel. See the operator's manual for leveling instructions.

Tooth Pitch

As with parallel-bar rakes, the tooth pitch is adjusted to determine the shape and density of the windrow. Tilting the bottom ends of the teeth forward (forward pitch) produces a light, fluffy windrow. Backward pitch (tilting tooth points back) produces a tight, dense windrow. Adjust the tooth pitch on a wheel rake as directed in the operator's manual.

Raking Wheel Flotation

To prevent raking wheels from bouncing and missing hay or exerting too much pressure on the ground and breaking teeth, adjust the raking-wheel flotation. Lower the rake into raking position and use a hand scale to measure the force required to lift each wheel (Fig. 22). If the force required to lift the wheel does not meet the manufacturer's recommendations, adjust the flotation spring (Fig. 23) or adjust according to the operator's manual.

Rake Tongue

The rake tongue makes the rake follow directly behind or trail to the side of a tractor. The trail-behind position lets you rake near fences and around obstacles. The side-trailing position keeps tractor wheels from running on unraked hay. Adjust the tongue position by raising the raking wheels and repositioning the tongue.

Raking Width

Adjust raking width to suit the crop conditions. In light crops the maximum raking width may be needed to produce heavier windrows. In heavy crops, a narrow raking width may produce suitable windrows. For extremely fragile

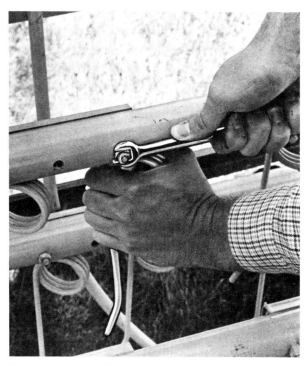

Fig. 21—Add Teeth for Short Hay

crops, the raking width should be narrow to reduce the distance hay travels on the ground during raking. Adjust raking width by repositioning the rake transport wheels (Fig. 24). The wheels must be adjusted equally.

Raking width of some wheel rakes can be changed by adding or removing one or more raking wheels.

Fig. 22—Check Flotation on Rake Wheel

Fig. 23—Adjust Flotation Spring

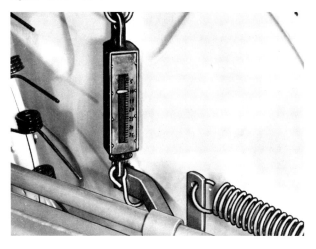

FIELD OPERATION

Raking is an important operation in the haymaking process yet its importance is often neglected. Unless care is exercised in raking, many of the nutrient-rich leaves are lost.

CONTROLS

Operating controls for a rake are different with each model. Every rake has a control to raise and lower the raking reel or raking wheels. A lift crank, a hydraulic cylinder, or the tractor 3-point hitch is used.

Parallel-bar rakes also have a clutch control to engage and disengage power (Fig. 25).

To begin field operation, lower the rake reel or raking wheels into position. Then, if the rake has a power drive, engage it. Select an appropriate forward gear and begin raking.

DIRECTION OF TRAVEL

When the hay has wilted slightly it is ready for raking. If crop moisture falls below 40 percent before raking leaf loss may be excessive.

For the most efficient raking, the rake must travel in the same direction as the mower.

During mowing the plants fall back over the mower cutterbar exposing the leafy heads in an overlapping arrangement. Raking the same way the mower traveled, against the heads of the plants, places most of the leaves inside the windrow. The leaves are shaded from the sun and are cured by air circulation. The exposed stems dry rapidly by exposure to both the sun and wind (Fig. 26).

Fig. 25—Engaging Clutch on a Ground-Driven Rake

ENGAGING RAKE CLUTCH

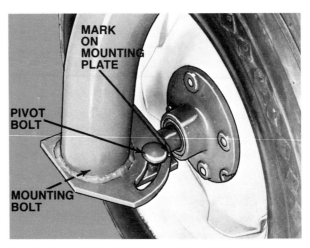

MARK ON MOUNTING PLATE

PIVOT BOLT

MOUNTING BOLT

Fig. 24—Transport Wheel Adjustment To Change Raking Width

Raking in the opposite direction of mower travel reverses plant direction in the windrow. More hay is missed by the rake, and leaf loss during raking is usually higher. With the leaves exposed and the stems shaded, even curing is impossible. The leaves will dry and shatter before the stems are dry enough for packaging.

WINDROW TURNING

To speed up curing use a rake to turn the windrow upside down. Wet windrows will dry faster and more evenly if turned after the top of the windrow has dried. To set a wheel rake for windrow turning raise all except the last two raking wheels off the ground. The front raking wheels do not move hay, and unnecessary wear will occur if they are used. Position the tongue to trail the rake directly behind the tractor.

To turn windrows, travel in the same direction as the previous raking or windrowing operation. Drive with the rear wheel alongside the windrow, and turn the windrow with the trailing end of the rake (Fig. 27).

FIELD ADJUSTMENTS

Make field adjustments to suit specific crop and field conditions. Some preliminary adjustments may have to be changed. The most common field adjustment is selecting the proper ground speed. Tooth height may need adjustment on parallel-bar rakes.

MATCH SPEED TO CONDITIONS

PTO- and hydraulically-driven, parallel-bar rakes have a wider operating range of reel-to-ground speed than ground-driven rakes. Wide range helps match the reel speed to the crop conditions. A high reel-to-ground speed ratio is needed for heavy crops, and a low reel-to-ground speed ratio is best for light crops.

Set the reel-to-ground speed ratio by first selecting a ground speed acceptable to the terrain. Speed usually varies from 2 to 7 miles per hour (3.2 to 11.2 km/h). Under normal conditions, a speed of 5 miles per hour (8 km/h) produces the best windrows. Set the reel-to-ground speed by matching an appropriate tractor gear to the throttle setting for PTO-driven rakes or hydraulic oil flow for hydraulic-driven rakes. It is seldom necessary to operate a tractor at full throttle for raking. One-half to three-quarters throttle usually produces the best windrows. Full-throttle settings also increase noise level, fuel consumption, and leaf shatter.

WHEEL-RAKE SPEED

Most wheel rakes are designed for raking at higher speeds than parallel-bar rakes. Wheel rakes are sometimes towed in the field behind pickup trucks. Some manufacturers make no recommended top operating speed. Ground conditions, crop conditions, plus operator judgment and experience usually dictate the proper speed.

HEIGHT OF TEETH

Parallel-bar rake teeth should clear the ground by 1 to 2 inches (25.4 to 50.8 mm). The teeth usually operate just below the top of the stubble. Setting teeth too low results in a dirty window and increases the possibility of raking foreign objects into the windrow,and can break teeth. Setting teeth too high skips hay.

The method of adjusting tooth height varies with rake model and make. A hand crank lowers the reel on some trailed models. A hydraulic cylinder is used to adjust tooth

Fig. 26—Properly-Formed Windrow with the Stems Exposed and Leaves Shaded

Fig. 27—Windrows Dry Faster if You Turn Them

Fig. 28—Adjust Top Link To Change Tooth Height on Rear-Mounted Rakes

height on others. On rear-mounted parallel-bar rakes, tooth height is adjusted by lengthening or shortening the upper link on the 3-point hitch (Fig. 28).

TRANSPORT

When preparing to transport a parallel-bar rake, disengage the reel drive. Disconnect the ground driveshaft or PTO shaft to prevent accidental engagement during transport.

For both parallel-bar and wheel rakes, raise the teeth as high as possible to reduce the chances of teeth striking a ridge or rock.

Wheel rakes are adjusted easily for trail-behind transport by repositioning the tongue and pivoting the wheels on the main-frame spindle mounting (Fig. 29).

Tow twin rakes and rakes on a tandem hitch behind each other.

Transport speed must be slow enough to maintain complete control over the rake and tractor.

If a tractor is used to tow the rake, the tractor brakes must be strong enough to stop both tractor and rake. Use a lower gear on steep downgrades.

Be especially careful turning. A sharp turn can cause the tractor or truck to contact the rake, bend a raking wheel or reel, and possible damage tires.

During road transport, make sure an SMV emblem is clearly visible to drivers of vehicles approaching from the rear. Use auxiliary lights to warn operators of other vehicles.

SAFETY

The same safety precautions apply to rakes that are used for other hay and forage harvesting equipment. Remember: Never clean, adjust or service equipment that is in motion. Never allow any passengers on the tractor platform or drawbar during operation.

Because raking is done at fairly high speeds, care must be taken to avoid striking stones, stumps, or other obstacles or dropping wheels into holes or ditches. Be especially careful on steep hillsides. The danger of tractor tipping increases as speed goes up.

Fig. 29—Wheel Rake in Transport Position

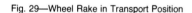

TROUBLESHOOTING

Most operating problems that occur with rakes result from improper adjustments or lack of timely service. The following chart suggests a possible cause and the recommended solution when a problem occurs.

Apply these suggested remedies carefully. An incorrect remedy could cause a severe malfunction or create new problems. Study the operator's manual and understand the rake.

This troubleshooting chart applies to both parallel-bar and wheel rakes.

MAINTENANCE

A rake has few moving parts and will last for years with proper maintenance. Maintenance is concentrated on the raking wheels and teeth of wheel rakes. The reel, toothbars, and teeth of parallel-bar rakes require the most maintenance.

Rake teeth are frequently broken or bent. Repair or replace broken teeth promptly.

The raking wheels and toothbars which support the teeth may also be damaged during raking. Damaged bars and wheels must be repaired or replaced.

Stripper rods on parallel-bar rakes may be bent or broken. To allow smooth real action and prevent throwing hay over the reel, damaged rods must be repaired or replaced.

Rakes are usually operated in dry, dusty conditions. Many hayfields have sandy, abrasive soil which can cause severe wear. Regular lubrication, routine maintenance, and careful service of bearings and drive-train components are needed.

Teeth are the most frequently replaced rake parts. Keep extra teeth available. In unusually rough terrain, an extra raking wheel or toothbar may save time. A spare reel-drive belt should be available for PTO-driven rakes.

TROUBLESHOOTING CHART		
PROBLEM	**POSSIBLE CAUSE**	**POSSIBLE REMEDY**
RAKE MISSING OR SKIPPING HAY.	Broken teeth.	Replace teeth.
	Rake bouncing.	Check tire pressure or reduce ground speed.
	Wheels on wheel rake bouncing.	Improper float-spring adjustment on raking wheels.
	Traveling too fast.	Reduce speed.
EXCESSIVE TOOTH BREAKAGE.	Teeth set too low.	Raise teeth.
	Rusty teeth coils or worn molded-rubber mounts.	Install new teeth.
	Backing up with teeth down.	Raise teeth before backing rake.
	Too much weight carried on raking wheels of wheel rake.	Adjust spring tension to reduce wheel pressure.
	Rocky fields, ditches, washouts, rough terrain.	Reduce speed.
HAY CARRY-OVER.	Bent strippers.	Straighten.
	Mud on teeth.	Too wet to rake. On wheel rakes, adjust float spring tension to reduce wheel pressure.
	Hay caught in coils of teeth; teeth too low.	Raise teeth or adjust float-spring tension on raking wheels of wheel rake.
	Hay catching in finger wheels on wheel rake.	Use wind shield on each raking wheel.

STORAGE

Proper rake storage helps avoid maintenance problems and prolongs machine service life. Store the rake in a shelter. Tires deteriorate rapidly when exposed to sunlight. Protect tires from direct sun.

Clean and lubricate the rake. Paint surfaces where paint has worn off.

For PTO-driven rakes, release drive-belt tension. Clean the belt and remove grease, oil, and dirt. For ground-driven rakes, clean the chains and brush them with heavy oil to prevent corrosion and rust.

Order parts and install them during the off-season.

SUMMARY

Rakes are used to form windrows of mowed hay. Rakes are also used to combine windrows in light hay crops to permit more efficient operation of big-capacity balers, round balers, stack wagons, and bale wagons. Rakes are also used to turn windrows for even exposure to the sun and to help get more uniform drying of rain-soaked windrows.

Side-delivery rakes are the most common. They are parallel-bar or wheel rakes.

Parallel-bar rakes may be ground, PTO-, or hydraulically-driven.

Parallel-bar rakes are trailed, rear-mounted, or front-mounted in relation to the tractor. They are usually 7, 8, or 9 feet (2.1, 2.4, or 2.9 m) wide to match mower cutterbar length. Raking capacity may be increased by using two rakes with a tandem hitch.

Wheel rakes are driven by teeth that contact the ground. Wheel rakes make tight windrows that dry slowly, rake clean on rough ground, and provide a gentle raking action. They may be trailed-, rear-mounted, or front-mounted.

Tedders, sometimes called fluffers, are rakes used in damp climates to raise, loosen, and partially turn hay in the field so the hay will dry faster.

Hay is ready for raking when it is slightly wilted. The rake must travel in the same direction the mower traveled.

Proper ground speed and tooth height are important for efficient raking with parallel-bar rakes.

CHAPTER QUIZ

1. What are the functions of rakes?

2. (Fill in blanks.) The two kinds of side-delivery rakes are _____ and _____.

3. What needs to be done if a rake won't pick up all the hay in a swath?

4. (True or false.) Parallel-bar rake teeth are normally set to just scratch the surface of the ground.

5. How are the wheels driven on a wheel rake?

6. What does a tedder do?

7. What are the advantages of rubber-mounted rake teeth?

8. (Choose one.) For the best raking, hay must be raked in the *same* or *opposite* direction the mower traveled.

9. What is the result of raking hay that is too dry?

10. (True or false.) The proper time to rake hay is when its moisture content is approximately 50 percent.

6
Balers

Fig. 1—Stationary Baler

INTRODUCTION

The U.S. Patent Office recorded a patent for a hand-operated hay baler in 1813. Developments and improvements continued. By 1920, stationary balers were well designed and gaining popularity with farmers, primarily as custom machines. A stationary baler had a rectangular, continuous-baling chamber with a crank-driven baling ram (Fig. 1). Stationary balers required a lot of hand labor. For instance, it took two men just to hand tie the bales.

Fig. 2—PTO-Driven Baler

By 1930 a few companies had converted stationary balers to field balers by adding a pickup attachment. However, the major development in balers came during the 1930s and 40s when automatic twine-tie and wire-tie mechanisms were successfully developed. From these developments evolved the balers used today (Fig. 2).

PURPOSE AND USE

Baling is essentially a "packaging" operation. The materials that can be packaged with a baler range from high-quality hay to crop residues.

The popularity of baling is greater than any other hay-packaging method. Such wide acceptance has come because people like the size, shape, and density of bales. Bales are small enough to be manhandled for stacking and feeding (Fig. 3) and dense enough for efficient inside storage. Loose hay takes twice as much storage space as baled hay. This 10 to 14 pounds per cubic foot (4.54 to 6.3 kg) density is extremely important to commercial hay growers because it makes long distance transportation feasible.

Bailing used to be primarily a custom operation. Now, most hay farmers own balers. Small, lower-priced, PTO powered balers match the needs of many smaller operations. Own-

Fig. 3—Bales Can Be Handled by Hand or Mechanically

Fig. 4—Manual Bale Loading

ing a baler lets a farmer time his own haying operations, which is essential for high-quality hay. Some hay growers with small acreage cannot economically justify ownership of a baler. But custom baling is available for them.

HIGH LABOR REQUIREMENT

The disadvantage of baled hay is the labor required for hauling bales from the field to storage. Handling equipment helps reduce labor, but the cost for equipment is high. Because of the high labor requirement and handling costs, excellent management is needed to bale and store quality hay.

Direct-Loading Bales

To reduce the labor of picking up and hauling bales from the field, auxiliary equipment may be attached to a baler. The simplest method is to add an extension chute to the bale chamber and pull a wagon behind the baler. Men then stack the bales on the wagon bed (Fig. 4).

Bale Ejectors

Automatic bale ejectors eliminate manually loading bales. Field baling and loading becomes a one-man operation (Fig. 5). The ejector attaches to the rear of the bale chamber and throws bales into a trailing wagon. Some ejectors handle bales up to 80 pounds (36 kg) apiece. Smaller bales are normally recommended.

Different ejectors use high-speed rollers, "waffle-tread" belts, and hydraulically-controlled pans to throw bales.

Some are designed to be steered by the tongue of the trailing wagon to keep from losing bales. Other ejectors can be aimed with a remote hydraulic cylinder. Hydraulic aiming prevents bale loss on curves and corners, and keeps bales dropping on-target. A bale "aimer" also aids in placing bales in the right spot on the wagon.

Most bale ejectors also have a way to control the throwing height distance so wagons can be loaded evenly from back to front.

CAUTION: Never stand behind an operating bale ejector. Never allow anyone to ride in the wagon while bales are being loaded with an ejector. People can be seriously injured by a flying bale.

Ejector-loaded bales are normally unloaded into an elevator and stacked at random inside a barn or hay storage shed.

Bale Accumulators

Another method of accumulating bales directly behind the baler is a bale drag. The drag is loaded by stacking bales as they come from the baler and unloaded by sliding the stack off the rear of the drag.

Automatic bale accumulators bunch the bales and drop them in the field (Fig. 6). A tractor with front-end loader and bale-fork attachment can then load the bales on a wagon or truck (Fig. 7). Bale accumulators operate hydraulically or mechanically.

Fig. 5—Bale Ejectors Eliminate Manual Bale Loading

Fig. 6—Bale Accumulators Unload Automatically

BALER TYPES AND SIZES

Balers are classified by:

- **Power source**
- **Size of bale produced**
- **Twine-tie**
- **Wire-tie**

All hay balers produced today are field balers with automatic tying mechanisms.

Tractor drawn balers are powered by the tractor PTO or an auxiliary engine mounted on the baler. Some high capacity balers are self propelled.

PTO-DRIVEN BALERS

A PTO-driven baler requires a tractor for both baler operation and forward propulsion (Fig. 8). A PTO-powered baler is the least expensive. The tractor must be large enough to maintain a constant engine speed during baling and have enough forward speeds to match crop conditions. PTO-driven balers are the most common.

AUXILIARY ENGINES

If a tractor does not have enough power to operate a PTO-driven baler, an auxiliary engine is used (Fig. 9). Auxiliary-engine powered balers cost more because of the engine. But a less expensive tractor can be used to tow the baler. The auxiliary engine is usually in the 20 to 35 horsepower (15 to 26 kw) range.

SELF-PROPELLED BALERS

Self-propelled balers are used on some large hay farms (Fig. 10). Self-propelled balers are more expensive than other pulled balers, but they do not require a tractor. You can see the baler pickup in front and the bale chute behind from the seat.

BALE SIZES

Hay bales are produced in four sizes. Most balers have a 14 × 18-inch (355 × 457 mm) or 16 × 18-inch (406 × 457) bale chamber, and produce bales approximately 36 inches (914 mm) long. These bales usually have two wire or twine wraps per bale (Fig. 11). Some balers produce larger bales about 16 × 24 × 48 inches (406 × 610 × 1,219 mm), tied with 3 wires or twine. The largest bales are 4 × 4 × 8 feet (1.22 × 1.22 × 2.44 m). Each bale is wrapped with six pieces of heavy-duty twine.

Fig 7—Gathering Bales with a Front-End Loader

The weight of a bale depends on baler design, bale dimensions, type of hay, and moisture content. Some bale weights:

BALE SIZE	WEIGHT
14x18x36 inches	50-80 pounds
(355x475x914 mm)	(22.7-36 kg)
16x18x36 inches	70-90 pounds
(406x475x914 mm)	(32-41 kg)
16x24x48 inches	125-150 pounds
(406x610x1,219 mm)	(57-68 kg)
4x4x8 feet	2000 pounds
(1.22x1.22x2.44 m)	(908 kg)

Fig. 8—PTO-Driven Baler

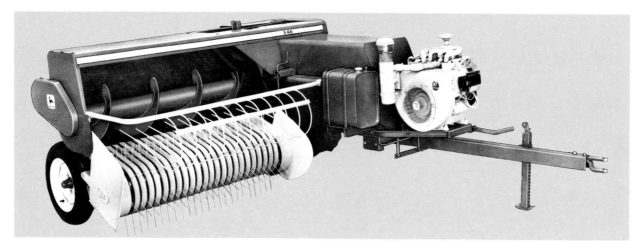

Fig. 9—Auxiliary-Engine Driven Baler

Fig. 10—Self-Propelled Baler

Fig. 11—Two-Wire Bale

Both wire and twine balers are used. Ranchers usually use twine because wire is harmful to their livestock. However, plastic twine is indigestible and should be removed from bales before feeding. Wire-tied bales are stronger than twine-tied bales, so they are preferred for long-distance transportation.

BALER OPERATION

Operating characteristics and principles are similar for PTO-driven, auxiliary-engine driven, and self-propelled balers. PTO-driven balers are the most common.

PRIMARY COMPONENTS

Primary components of a PTO-powered baler (Fig. 12 & 13):

- **Pickup**
- **Auger**
- **Feed tines**
- **PTO shaft**
- **Feeder teeth**
- **Plunger**
- **Hay dogs**
- **Bale chamber**
- **Bale-measuring wheel**
- **Needles**
- **Wire twister or twine knotter**
- **Bale chute**

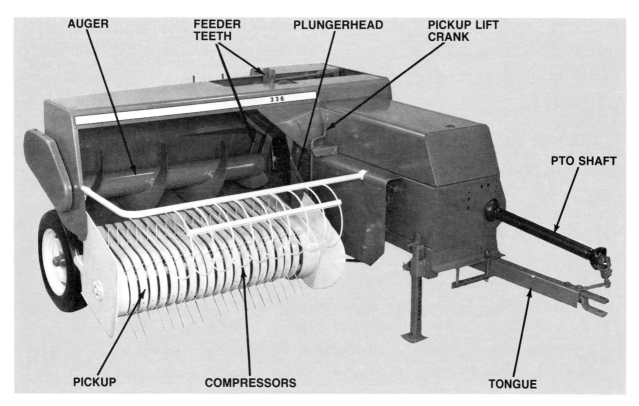

AUGER   FEEDER TEETH   PLUNGERHEAD   PICKUP LIFT CRANK

PTO SHAFT

PICKUP   COMPRESSORS   TONGUE

Fig. 12—Front View of Baler

Fig. 13—Rear View of Baler

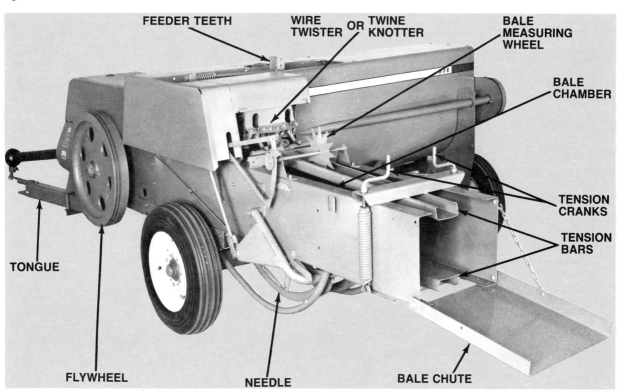

FEEDER TEETH   WIRE TWISTER OR TWINE KNOTTER   BALE MEASURING WHEEL

BALE CHAMBER

TENSION CRANKS

TENSION BARS

TONGUE

FLYWHEEL   NEEDLE   BALE CHUTE

Fig. 14—Pickup Lifting Windrow

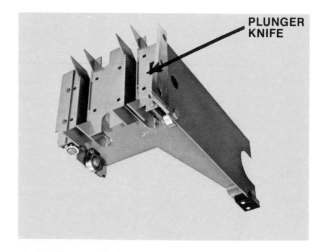

Fig. 16—Plunger Knife Slices Hay

COMPONENT FUNCTIONS

The *pickup* lifts hay from the windrow and carrys it to the auger or feed rake (Fig. 14). *Hay compressors* on the pickup hold hay down for uniform feeding, and keep strong winds from blowing hay out of the pickup.

An *auger, feed rake, or tines* deliver hay to the edge of the *bale chamber. Feeder teeth* then deliver hay into the baling chamber. The feeder teeth are timed to enter the baling

Fig. 15—Hay Movement into the Baling Chamber

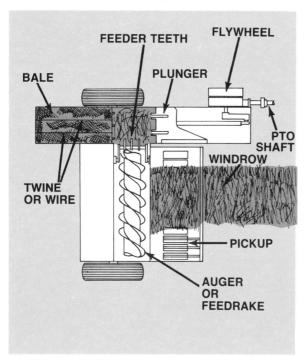

chamber when the plunger is retracted (in the forward position) (Fig. 15).

A crank arm and pitman drive the plunger back and forth in the baling chamber about 80 times per minute. As the plunger moves into the baling chamber, the *plunger* knife (Fig. 16) moves past a *stationary knife* to slice off hay that is outside the chamber. The plunger then compresses the hay in the bale chamber (Fig. 17).

Hay dogs engage the bale to keep the partly-formed bale compressed when the plunger retracts (Fig. 18).

The process of feeding hay into the bale chamber and compressing it with the plunger is repeated until the bale is formed. The density of the bale is determined by adjusting the spring-loaded upper and lower *tension bars* on the bale chamber (Fig. 19). On some models, tension bars are controlled hydraulically.

The *bale-measuring wheel* rotates as the bale moves through the bale chamber (Fig. 20). When the wheel completes a cycle the tying mechanism is tripped. Bale length may be changed by adjusting the bale-measuring cycle.

The *tying mechanism* is timed to synchronize with the plunger movement. When the plunger is at the rear position and hay is fully compressed, *needles* deliver the wire or twine to the tying mechanism (Fig. 21). As the wire or twine is grasped by the tying mechanism the needles retract and the bale is tied.

The process is repeated as each bale passes through the bale chamber and drops out of the baler (Fig. 22).

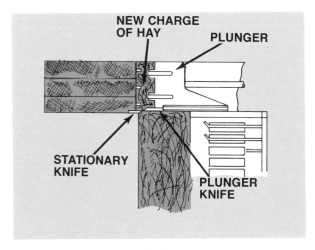

Fig. 17—Hay Is Compressed by the Plunger

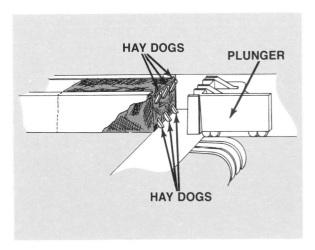

Fig. 18—Hay-Dogs Hold Compressed Hay

TYING MECHANISM

Understand the tying mechanism. Forming proper bales is useless unless the hay is tied.

The measuring wheel cam or bell crank operates a trip rod which starts the tying mechanism. First, the needles pass from one side of the bale chamber to the other, carrying wire or twine. There the knotting or twisting device ties the line. Then the needles withdraw to their "home" position until the metering wheel hits the trip rod again.

Needle Protection

Needles do not penetrate the hay. They go through slots in the plungerhead. The needles are protected by spring action or a shear bolt. They will not enter the chamber if there is an obstruction in the chamber or if the plunger is not in position (Fig. 23). There is a plunger or crank-arm safety stop to protect needles from damage by the plunger if the needles enter the chamber too soon or remain there too long.

Fig. 19—Tension Bars Control Bale Density

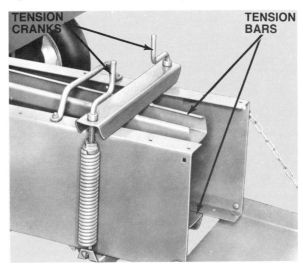

Fig. 20—Bale-Measuring Wheel

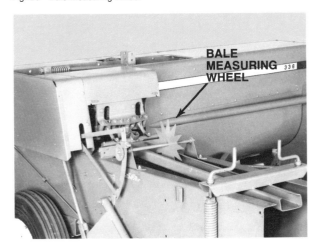

Fig. 21—Bale-Tying Operation

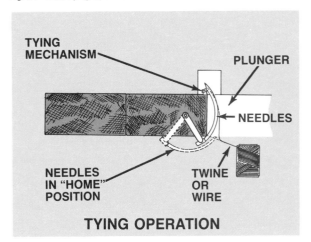

TYING OPERATION

Fig. 22—Bale Dropped on the Ground

Fig. 23—Needle and Knotter Drive

The safety stop automatically enters the chamber (A, Fig. 24) or moves into the path of the crank arm at the same time needles start to enter the bale chamber. The stop remains in position until the needles are fully withdrawn to the "home" position.

The safety stop does not interrupt plunger motion if the plunger is properly positioned when the needles start to move (B, Fig. 24). If the plunger or crank arm is stopped by the safety stop, a shear bolt in the plunger drive is sheared to prevent damage to the baler.

Therefore, if needles and plungerhead are properly timed when the needles go through the bale chamber, there is no needle-to-hay contact. The needles are in the chamber only a fraction of a second while the plunger is at the end of its rearward stroke. The entire tying operation is performed in about 3 seconds—and most of the tying is done in less than one second. You have to "look fast" to see the entire operation.

KNOTTER

The process is completed by tying a knot in the twine, or twisting ends of the wire together. Twiner knotter operation is shown in Figs. 25 through 31. Wire twister operation is covered later.

1. One end of the twine is held firmly in the twine disk by the twine holder (Fig. 25). As the bale is formed, twine is pulled from the twine box and passes around three sides of the bale (Fig. 26).

2. Then the needle brings the twine across the end of the bale, through the guide in the twine knife arm, across the billhook, and into the twine disk (Fig. 27).

3. The twine disk then turns to secure both ends of the twine against the twine holder. The billhook rotates (Fig. 28).

4. As the billhook turns, it loops twine around the hook and the jaw opens to receive the twine (Fig. 29). The knife advances to cut the twine between the billhook and the disk. Notice the needle has started its downward stoke leaving twine in the disk for the next bale.

5. The billhook jaw closes and holds the ends of the twine. The twine is cut and the wiper wipes the looped twine from the billhook. The billhook jaws hold the two cut ends of the twine (Fig. 30).

6. The knot is tied and wiped from the billhook to complete knot (Fig. 31). The same tying cycle is duplicated simultaneously on both sides of each bale.

7. Needles then return to the "home" position, leaving one strand of twine in each knotter twine disk and extending through the bale chamber ready to receive material for the next bale.

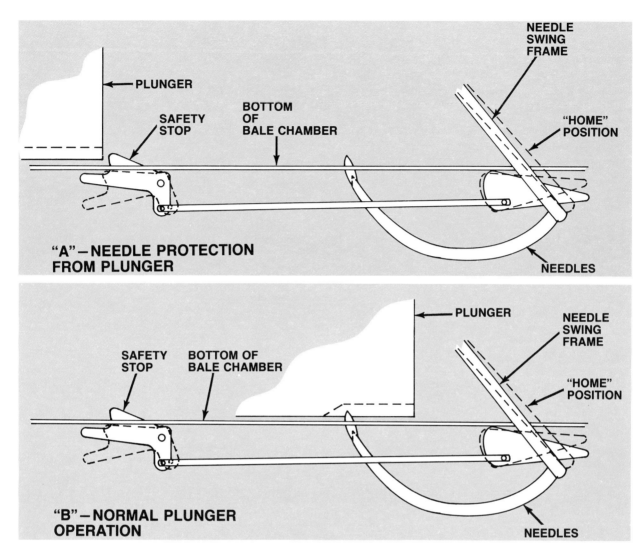

"A" – NEEDLE PROTECTION FROM PLUNGER

PLUNGER

SAFETY STOP

BOTTOM OF BALE CHAMBER

NEEDLE SWING FRAME

"HOME" POSITION

NEEDLES

"B" – NORMAL PLUNGER OPERATION

SAFETY STOP

BOTTOM OF BALE CHAMBER

PLUNGER

NEEDLE SWING FRAME

"HOME" POSITION

NEEDLES

Fig. 24—Plunger Safety Stop Protects Needles

Fig. 25—Twine Held in Twine Disk

Fig. 26—Twine Passes Around the Bale as It Is Formed

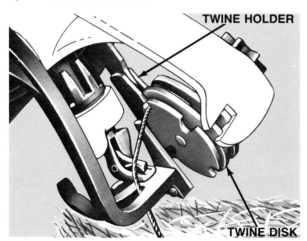

TWINE HOLDER

TWINE DISK

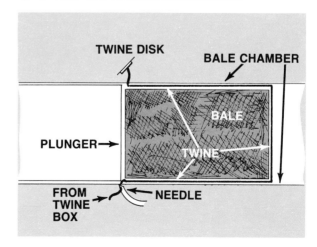

TWINE DISK

BALE CHAMBER

PLUNGER

BALE

TWINE

FROM TWINE BOX

NEEDLE

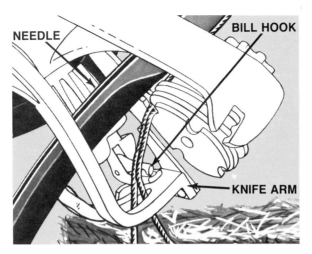

Fig. 27—Start of New Tying Cycle

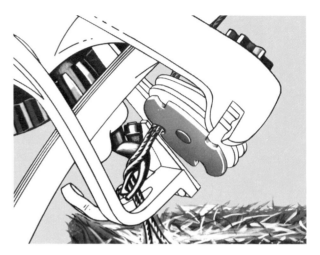

Fig. 28—Billhook Has Started Its Rotation

Fig. 29—Billhook Jaw Has Opened To Receive the Twine

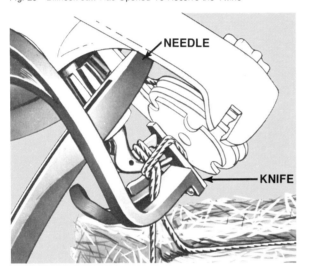

Fig. 30—Billhook Jaw Has Closed

WIRE TWISTER

The wire-twisting operation is triggered by the bale measuring wheel and arm and proceeds as follows:

1. After the needle has been threaded, the end of the wire is anchored by the wire gripper (Fig. 32). As the bale is formed, the wire is pulled around three sides of the bale.

2. When the bale reaches its proper length, the measuring wheel trips the twister drive mechanism. As the needle starts up, it catches the wire at the bottom of the bale and carries it up the front of the bale. The needle continues to rise and positions the wire in the notch in the shear plate on the opposite side of the anchored wire. The twister hook on the twister shaft rotates to begin the twist (Fig. 33). As the twister hook completes one rotation it grasps both strands of wire.

Fig. 31—The Knot Is Tied

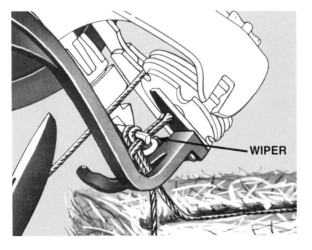

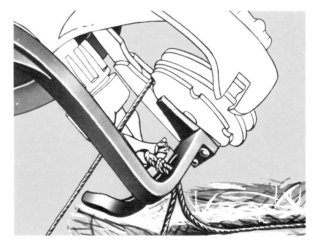

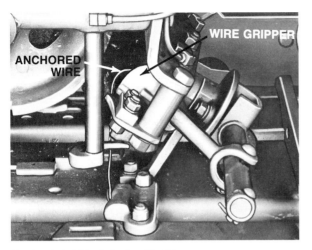

Fig. 32—End of Wire Is Anchored by Gripper

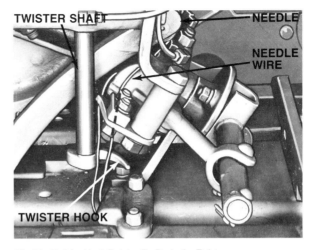

Fig. 33—Twister Hook Rotates To Begin the Twist

3. At this stage, the gripper arm releases the anchored wire. The needle wire is sheared and one end is anchored for the next bale as the gripper moves to the other side. The needle returns "home," and the twister hook makes five or six rotations twisting the wire ends together (Fig. 34).

4. As the completed bale is pushed from the baler it pulls the twisted knot off the twister hook (Fig. 35). Hay for the next bale pulls the anchored wire into position for the next twisting cycle. This entire process is duplicated simultaneously for each wire on the bale.

OPERATION AND ADJUSTMENT

Baler operation depends on the care given the baler. With

experience, the operator can run the baler efficiently for high productivity. He can become adept at making field adjustments to help ensure each bale is properly formed and tied. A skilled operator can also maintain the baler. Good maintenance preserves reliability and lengthens service life.

TIMELY OPERATIONS

Timely field operations and efficient use of labor is essential. An effective manager schedules field work and gets enough labor to ensure quality. Good baling is only one facet of the haying. Quality hay begins with planning and seedbed preparation and does not end until the hay is fed and the livestock reflects the hay quality.

Fig. 34—Wire Has Been Twisted and Needle Returned to "Home"

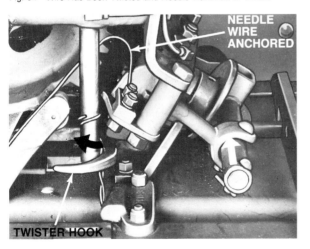

Fig. 35—Twisted Knot Is Pulled off the Twister Hook

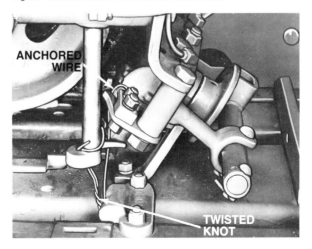

Fig. 36—Dense Bales Are Easier To Handle and Feed

MOISTURE CONTENT

Crop moisture content at baling time affects a baler. Hay baled at proper moisture content yields more nutrition and forms well shaped, solid bales (Fig. 36). Well shaped bales stack and store efficiently. Also, hay baled at proper moisture content maintains high density in storage. And the bales are easier to handle and feed than poorly shaped, loose bales.

When hay is baled too dry, leaves shatter easily. Excessive leaf loss may result in a drastic reduction in quality. Hay baled too dry will not compact tightly; result: loose, poorly formed bales. In addition, the windrow pickup can't lift as much hay.

Wet hay can be baled, but the baler operates under excessive strain. Wet hay is difficult to push through the bale chamber. The baler plunger and other baler parts are overloaded. Also, wet bales are normally heavy; even with the bale tension bars under reduced tension. Wet bales shrink in storage and become loose and sloppy. Bales of wet hay mold. Bales that have heated and molded in storage have lower quality and may even make livestock sick.

Proper hay moisture content for baling depends on type and maturity of crop, weather conditions, and storage life. The effects of each factor must be carefully evaluated. Good managers and operators learn to calculate the best baling moisture content for their needs.

PLANNING AND PREPARATION

Auxiliary haying equipment should be selected to complement the baling operation. Auxiliary equipment includes a mower, mower-conditioner or windrower, rake, and tractor. Of course, handling equipment is also needed to haul bales from field to storage.

Proper planning and field layout will reduce labor.

WINDROW PREPARATION

Good windrow preparation reduces field losses and baling time. Heavy windrows reduce the field travel of a baler and increase daily productivity. However, windrows can be too heavy. Baler ground speed should be relatively fast and the windrow must not be wider than the baler pickup. If windrows are too heavy they plug the pickup.

If conditions prohibit use of a properly sized windrower or mower-conditioner, rake to combine windrows.

A well formed windrow has uniform width and feeds evenly into the baler (Fig. 37). Even feeding helps make bales of uniform density and shape.

Windrows should be loose enough for air to circulate. Conditioning hay as it is cut promotes rapid and even curing, and decreases the chance for weather damage before the hay is baled.

Fig. 37—Properly Formed Windrows Can Be Baled Easily

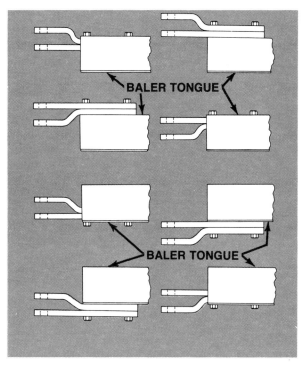

Fig. 38—Adjusting Baler Hitch To Level the Baler

The baler pickup works well in windrows placed on clean-raked stubble. Baler teeth are not designed for raking and will not clean up poorly-constructed windrows or unraked hay.

TRACTOR PREPARATION

Inspect and prepare the tractor and baler before baling starts. Use the tractor and baler operator's manuals. Before you hitch the baler to the tractor:

1. Make sure the tractor PTO speed matches the baler speed if the baler is PTO-driven.

2. Put the tractor drawbar in the recommended position for the baler used.

3. Lock the drawbar parallel with the centerline of the PTO shaft.

ATTACHING THE BALER

After the tractor is prepared, attach the baler:

1. Adjust the baler hitch to keep the baler as level as possible (Fig. 38). Change hitch strap positions if needed.

2. Align the baler hitch and tractor drawbar by adjusting the hitch jack.

3. Back the tractor to align holes and insert safety hitch pin. No one should be between the tractor and baler when the tractor is backing. When holes are aligned shut off the tractor and remove the key so it can not move back and crush someone inserting the pin.

4. Raise the hitch jack to the transport position.

5. Attach the baler PTO shaft to the tractor PTO. Clean the splines so the PTO hooks up easy.

Detach as follows:

1. Install the hitch jack to remove the weight of the baler from the tractor drawbar.

2. Detach the baler PTO shaft from the tractor PTO.

3. Remove the safety hitch pin.

4. Start the tractor and drive forward slowly. Make sure the baler is stable.

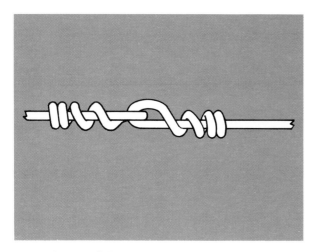

Fig. 39—Good Wire Splice

BALER PREPARATION

With the baler attached to the tractor, make a final inspection and prepare the baler:

1. Remove grease from the knotter mechanism.

2. Remove heavy oil and grease from the bale case and chains.

3. Lubricate the baler as recommended in the operator's manual.

4. Check air pressure in tires.

5. Check and fill gearcase to the proper level.

6. Tighten all bolts, nuts, and screws to the recommended torque.

7. Check and adjust feeder teeth, plunger, and needle timing.

8. Loosen the slip clutch, readjust, and test.

9. Inspect and service the engine as recommended in the operator's manual.

10. Operate the baler several minutes to break-in new parts. Recheck belt and chain tension.

THREADING THE NEEDLES

Load the baler with wire or twine and thread the needles according to instructions in the operator's manual. Procedures for typical balers follow:

Wire-Tie Baler

1. Fill the wire box with the proper size wire.

2. Splice the wire of each coil together as recommended in the operator's manual. Make tight splices so wires will pull through the guides and needles without catching (Fig. 39).

3. When front coils run out of wire, place rear coils forward and add two new cartons of wire in the wire box, and splice.

For typical wire needle threading (Fig. 40):

4. Make sure all wire pulleys turn freely.

5. Thread the wire from the right-hand coil through the guide (1).

6. Continue threading the wire around the front left-hand wire pulley (2).

7. With the needles in home position, thread the wire under the left-hand center wire pulley (3) and over the left-hand needle pulley.

8. Pull the wire back, loop it around the needle frame, and secure it with a twist (4).

9. Thread the left-hand wire through the guide (5), then repeat Steps 2, 3, and 4 through the right-hand pulleys and needle.

When both strands of wire have been properly threaded, trip the bale measuring arm and turn the flywheel counterclockwise by hand. Continue turning the flywheel until the nedles are all the way up, the wire is held by the grippers, and the needles return to the "home" position.

Fig. 40—Threading Needles of a Wire-Tie Baler

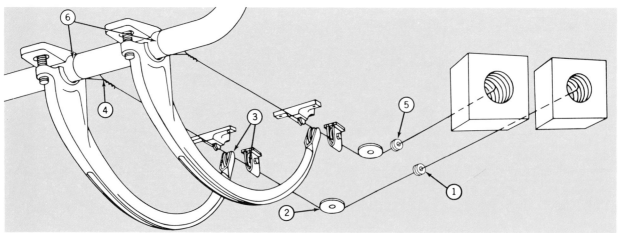

10. Remove the loose wire from the needle frame (6).

Twine-Tie Baler

1. Fill each compartment of the twine box with good-quality twine.

2. Splice the balls of twine together as recommended in the operator's manual. Tie a modified square knot and trim the loose ends of the knot (Fig. 41). The knot must be small enough to pass through the guides and needle eyes.

3. When the first balls run out of twine, shift remaining balls to the first position, add two new balls of twine, and splice.

For typical twine needle threading (Fig. 42):

4. Thread each twine through the guides on the box lid (Fig. 43) and through the twine tension plate (Fig. 44).

5. Thread both ends of twine through the eye on the needle frame (1, Fig. 42). Be sure twine is not crossed.

6. With the needles in home position, run the end of one strand of twine below the needle guard, through the eye beneath the right-hand needle, and through the right-hand needle (2, Fig. 42). Be sure to thread twine OVER the guide on the end of the needle.

7. Run twine back to the needle frame and tie it as shown (3, Fig. 42).

8. Thread the other strand of twine under the needle guard and through the left-hand eye and needle (4, Fig. 42). Tie the end of this twine to the needle frame (3, Fig. 42). When both strands of twine have been properly threaded, trip the bale measuring arm and turn the flywheel counterclockwise by hand. Continue turning the flywheel until needles are all the way up, twine is held in the twine disk, and needles have returned to the home position.

9. Remove the twine which was temporarily secured to the needle frame. The twine is now ready for the baling operation.

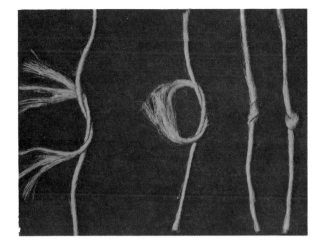

Fig. 41—Proper Twine Knot

Fig. 42—Threading Needles of a Twine-Tie Baler

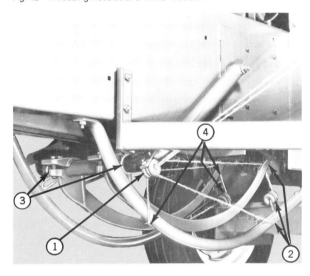

Fig. 43—Use Twine Guides on Twine Box Lid

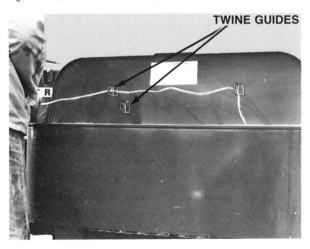

Fig. 44—Thread Twine through Twine Tension Plate

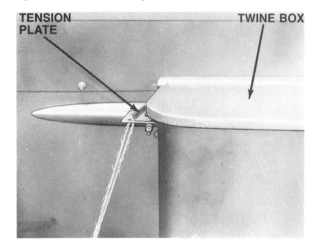

103

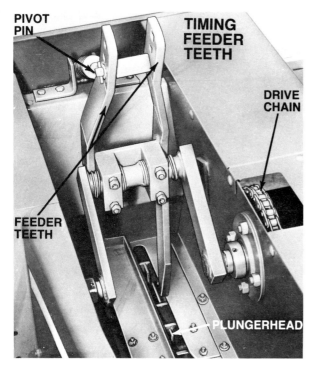

Fig. 45—Feeder Teeth Must Be Properly Timed

PRELIMINARY SETTINGS AND ADJUSTMENTS

Before taking the baler to the field make preliminary adjustments to avoid unnecessary wear or breaking baler components. Make adjustments in the field to match crop and field requirements.

Fig. 46—Check Needle Timing To Avoid Needle Damage

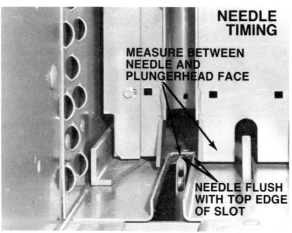

DRIVE-TRAIN PROTECTION

Slip clutches are designed to prevent damage to the baler power train when the baler is overloaded. A properly adjusted slip clutch allows the tractor or engine to transmit power to the baler under normal operating conditions. Adjust the slip clutch according to the manufacturer's recommendations. Excessive slippage results if the clutch is too loose, and wear on the clutch is rapid. Over-tightening the slip clutch eliminates the protection it was designed to furnish the drive train.

Some balers have shear bolts or keys, instead of a slip clutch, for drive-train protection. Use only the shear bolts or keys recommended by the manufacturer.

TIMING FEEDER TEETH

Correct timing allows the feeder teeth and wire or twine needles to enter the bale chamber without being damaged by the plungerhead. Timing is usually controlled by the main drive chain, feeder drive chain, and twister- or knotter-drive gears. If one or more of these parts is removed for service or repair, the baler must be retimed.

Feeder teeth must be timed to leave the bale chamber before the plungerhead passes under the feeder-teeth slots (Fig. 45). Serious damage may result if the feeder teeth fail to clear the bale chamber in time.

TIMING NEEDLES

To protect needles from damage or distortion by contacting hay in the bale chamber, needles must only enter the bale chamber (Fig. 46) when the plungerhead is in position. Needles may be bent or broken and knotters damaged if needle timing is incorrect.

Consult the baler operator's manual for specific feeder-teeth and needle timing instructions.

PLUNGER HEAD AND KNIVES

Proper plungerhead adjustment must be maintained to produce uniform, well shaped bales. The plunger knife and stationary knife must be sharp and adjusted to separate material in the bale chamber from material still in the feeder housing. Worn knives or too much clearance between the knives will let some hay bend over the knife edges instead of being cut. If the knives are sharp and adjusted, less power is required for baler operation and bales will be more uniform.

Plunger

Plunger guides and wear plates must be adjusted periodically to compensate for wear (Fig. 47). If the plunger is out of adjustment knives will not properly shear each charge of hay, and if badly misaligned, the plunger could interfere with needle movement.

Knives

When sharpening stationary or plunger knives, maintain the original bevel and cutting angle on the blade edges to insure efficient cutting. Don't let cutting edges overheat. Overheating reduces blade life and cutting ability.

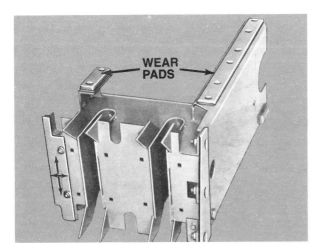

Fig. 47—Plungerhead Wear Pads

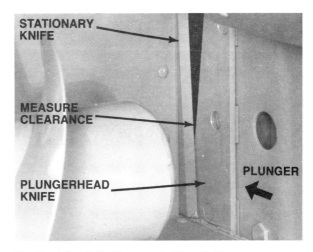

Fig. 48—Adjust Knife Clearance for Clean Cutting

Fig. 49—Stationary Knife Clearance

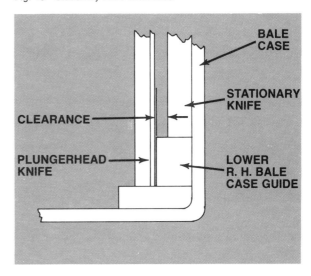

Recommended knife clearance and adjustment procedures vary by baler make and model (Fig. 48). Some manufacturers recommend knife clearance of 0.005 to 0.030
inch (.127 to .762 mm) others specify 0.030 to 0.070 inch
(.762 to 1.78 mm). Always check the operator's manual for
each baler before making knife clearance adjustments.

Stationary knife settings range from 0.020 inch (.508 mm)
inside the edge of the lower right-hand bale case guide
(Fig. 49), to flush or not more than 0.015 inch (.38 mm)
BEYOND the edge of the lower guide assembly. The first
setting keeps knives from locking during the plunger
stroke. On the second baler, the lower end of the plunger
knife is beveled to keep it from catching the stationary
blade as it passes. That bevel must be maintained when
the blade is sharpened.

Set the clearance between knives by adjusting the plunger
guides or tracks inside the bale case or adjusting the rollers
on the plungerhead. Keep track wipers or scrapers
adjusted to keep dirt and crop residue off the plunger tracks
which can throw the plunger out of adjustment. Always
measure knife clearance with a feeler gauge. Set equal
clearance along the full blade length so the blades don't
touch.

After completing knife adjustments, make sure the
plungerhead moves freely throughout a complete cycle by
turning the flywheel by hand.

TWINE TENSION

To maintain uniform twine tension while the bale is being
formed, adjust the tension control on the twine box. Measure the force required at the knotter assembly to pull twine
from the twine box (Fig. 50). The recommended force var-

Fig. 50—Measuring Twine Tension

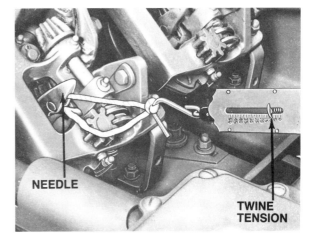

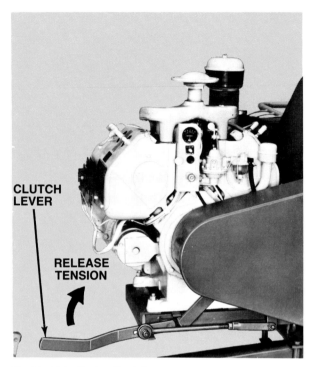

CLUTCH LEVER

RELEASE TENSION

Fig. 51—Baler Engine Clutch Lever

ies from 1 to 2 pounds for plastic twine to as much as 15 pounds for sisal twine. If the tension is not satisfactory adjust the tension control and recheck the tension.

FIELD OPERATION

Run a new baler or a baler with major new mechanical parts empty for several minutes, as specified by the manufacturer, to allow moving parts to seat gradually. After a short run at slow-idle speed, stop the machine and inspect the new parts. Check for hot bearings. Adjust if necessary and resume the slow-idle empty run. During the last half of the break-in period, operate at recommended speed. Inspect the baler frequently during break-in.

For PTO balers, the main operating control is the tractor's PTO clutch. For engine-powered balers, a lever (Fig. 51) operates the drive clutch mounted between the engine and baler powershaft. A self-propelled baler has a baler-drive clutch in addition to the engine and drive-train controls. A good operator becomes familiar with the location and function of both the baler and tractor controls.

BALER OPERATION

When windrows have cured, baling may begin. Bale the driest hay first. For cleaner pickup bale in the same direc-

tion that the windrower or rake traveled. Going in the same direction helps the pickup teeth reach under the windrow and pick up the hay in a "head-first" position.

Before engaging the baler-drive clutch, lower the pickup.

When starting the baler, engage the PTO or engine clutch and bring the engine up to the recommended speed. The plungerhead should be up to normal operating speed before starting to pick up hay.

Drive in a low gear for a short time to be sure the baler is functioning properly. When starting with an empty bale chamber, the first few bales will be light and their length irregular. If hay does not fill the opening in the bale chamber gradually increase ground speed or increase the size of the windrow until good sized charges are fed into the compression chamber without straining the feeding and baling mechanisms.

Balers operate best taking from 12 to 18 charges per bale.

ADJUST TO CONDITIONS

The productivity of a baler depends on crop characteristics, ground conditions, condition of tractor and baler, and the judgment of the operator. Do not crowd the baler. If the feeding mechanism is properly adjusted and still cannot handle the incoming hay the baler is being crowded beyond its capacity and serious damage may result. Reduce ground speed, but maintain recommended PTO speed for proper baler operation. Remember, a good operator is primarily interested in tons per day, not bales per minute.

On rough ground it may be necessary to increase windrow size and reduce ground speed to maintain efficient baler performance and to prevent equipment damage.

Always run the tractor engine fast enough to maintain proper baler operating speed. Disengage the tractor PTO clutch when making sharp turns to avoid excessive vibration.

KEEP BALER CLEAN

Clean accumulated chaff off the twine-or wire-tying mechanism and the plungerhead safety stop. Accumulations of gummy chaff make the trip device function inaccurately resulting in broken parts, long bales, and untied bales.

FIELD ADJUSTMENTS

You can't get top performance unless you understand field adjustment.

When a malfunction occurs, an experienced operator always analyzes the situation before taking action. For example, a baler may occasionally miss tying a bale. Unless a true malfunction pattern is established the condition may be only temporary and require no corrective action.

If you want to rebale bales broken in the field, remove the original wires or twines and spread out the hay so it can be picked up.

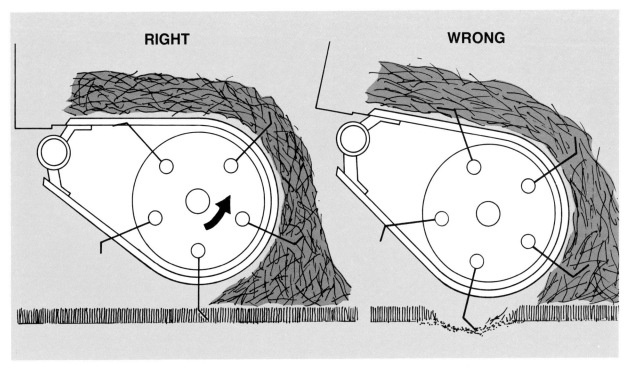

RIGHT   WRONG

Fig. 52—Proper Pickup Height

Do not hand feed broken bales. You can lose an arm in a baler in the blink of an eye.

PICKUP HEIGHT

Adjust the pickup height so you get clean pickup. Normally teeth are set to operate just below the top of the stubble, but not low enough to hit the ground (Fig. 52). If teeth strike the ground they may bend backward. Then, as they recoil, they shatter leaves and mix dirt with the hay. A pickup gauge wheel is available for some balers that prevents such problems and helps the pickup follow the ground contour (Fig. 53).

FEEDER TEETH

Most balers have feeder teeth to move hay from the auger in the pickup into the bale chamber. The teeth may be adjusted to increase or decrease the length of their stroke which alters the distance they move into the bale chamber (Fig. 54). Adjustment lets you make bales of uniform density under different conditions.

If feeder teeth are improperly adjusted more hay will be packed onto one side of the bale than the other. This usually results in one wire or twine being pulled tighter than the other and causes "banana" bales, which are very unstable.

If feeder teeth are set for their longest stroke and material is still not coming far enough into the bale chamber, the baler is probably being underfed. Increase baling speed or combine windrows.

Some balers use a reciprocating rake mechanism with retracting fingers to move hay into the bale chamber instead of an auger and feeder teeth. Refer to the operator's manual for adjustments to those units.

Fig. 53—Pickup Gauge Wheel

GAUGE WHEEL

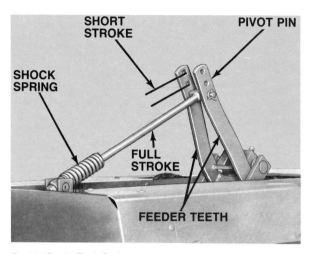

Fig. 54—Feeder Teeth Stroke

BALE WEIGHT

To regulate bale weight, change the tension on the bale chamber by adjusting the two tension cranks on the rear of the chamber (Fig. 55). This pulls upper and lower tension bars closer together and restricts hay passage through the baler. Hydraulic bale-tension control is available for some balers, and can provide on-the-go control of bale weight.

Bale weight is also affected by the size of windrows, moisture content, and the quality of the hay. Since these factors may vary from hour to hour or from windrow to windrow, *bale weight should be checked regularly during operation.*

Bale density may be further increased for baling unusually light windrows and dry, fluffy hay by installing hay resistors in the bale chamber (Fig. 56). Resistors slow the passage of material through the bale chamber and keep it from springing back between plunger strokes. They are particularly helpful for baling slick straw.

When returning to normal hay, and particularly heavy, wet crops, remove resisters to avoid unnecessary strain on the baler caused by the extra resistance.

Loosen bale tension at the end of each day's operation to relieve tension springs and reduce the possibility of bales sticking in the bale chamber. Also, if bales left in the baler are rained on, the material will expand and cause problems when restarting the baler.

Bales that are too tight or too heavy put excessive strain on the baler. They can wear and break parts, twine, and wire.

MEASURING WHEEL

A measuring wheel with prongs projecting into the forming bale rotates as the compressed hay moves rearward (Fig. 57). When the wheel turns a certain distance, the tying mechanism is tripped.

Irregular-length bales come from inconsistent hay density. Make the density more consistent by increasing the ground speed, increasing the size of the windrow, or tightening the bale-tension cracks.

Fig. 55—Bale Weight Control

Fig. 56—Bale Chamber Side Resistors

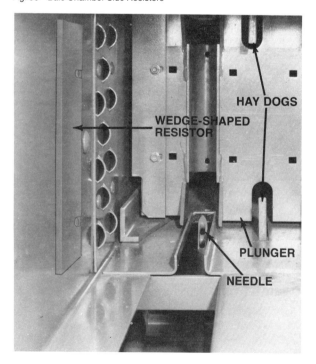

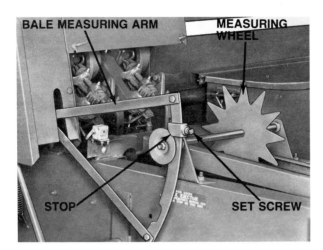

Fig. 57—Bale Length Adjustment

Fig. 58—Flywheel Shear Bolt

FLYWHEEL SHEAR BOLT

The shear bolt in the flywheel will shear if the plunger is blocked. After correcting the block, replace the shear bolt with a new shear bolt (Fig. 58). Use only shear bolts recommended by the manufacturer. Do not replace a shear bolt with a standard bolt. Bolts that are too soft will shear unnecessarily and waste time. Bolts that are too hard may not shear when needed and will not provide protection.

If the needles are in the bale case when the bolt shears return the needles to home position by hand before starting the baler. Turn the flywheel by hand through a complete plunger cycle to be sure all components are functioning and no obstructions are blocking operation.

BALER ATTACHMENTS

Numerous baler attachments are available to adapt balers to special conditions. Some items are optional on some balers and standard or perhaps not available on others. A few of the more important attachments have been described in detail earlier.

Bale ejectors and *bale-chute extensions* with a wagon hitch let you load bales from the baler without letting them drop on the ground.

A *side-drop bale chute* turns bales on edge as they fall from the baler. This places bales in a better position for pickup with an automatic bale wagon or a bale loader. It also keeps twine and wire off the ground.

Plungerhead extensions provide additonal compression needed for baling unusually dry, fluffy hay. *Side hay resistors* restrict material flow through the baler to help manage light, slick materials.

A *pickup gauge wheel* controls pickup height to keep teeth from scratching dirt into the hay. The gauge wheel lets the pickup follow ground contours.

Hydraulic bale tension (density) control provides uniform baling when crop conditions vary around the field. It eliminates manual control of the bale tension ranks.

An *auxiliary engine* helps increase baier efficiency if the tractor lacks power.

Auxiliary lighting kits provide additional light in the pickup and knotter areas for night baling.

A *hydraulic pickup lift* that operates from the tractor hydraulic system provides on-the-go pickup control for crossing ditches and irrigation borders. *Remote control mechanical pickup lifts* provide pickup height control from the tractor.

Dual wheels provide flotation in soft fields and smoother operation over rough places. Dual wheels are available for either right- or left-hand wheels on some balers. *Flotation tires* provide similar advantages.

A heavy, *auxiliary needle guard* provides extra needle protection when the baler is operating over rough ground.

An *automatic bale counter* provides an accurate count of the number of bales produced. Counters are standard equipment on many balers.

Baler safety equipment includes: a *drawbar safety chain* for safer baler transport; *SMV emblem* to warn approaching motorists of a low-moving vehicle; *safety lights* and *reflectors* for protection during road travel.

Other attachments are available for balers to improve performance make them safer to operate and make them easier to service.

Fig. 59—Adjust Tongue To Trail Baler Behind Tractor

TRANSPORT

For transport raise the baler pickup to the highest position so it won't hit the high spots.

Move the baler tongue to transport position so the baler will trail directly behind the tractor (Fig. 59).

Fig. 60—Wait for Flywheel to Stop Before Working on Baler

When transporting the baler on a road turn on the flashing lights. Be sure the SMV emblem is in place to warn operators of other vehicles. Attach the SMV emblem to the left-rear side of the baler for proper light reflection.

SAFETY

The farm can be a safer place to live and work if safe practices are observed. Make the following safety recommendations part of your normal work with a baler:

● Balers should be operated only by responsible people.

● Before servicing or adjusting a baler, removing bales, or hitching a wagon to a baler:

1. Disengage all power.

2. Shut off the engine and take the key.

3. Wait until the baler flywheel has stopped rotating (Fig. 60).

● All rotating sheilds on the PTO drive must turn freely.

● Stand clear of the baler whenever the machine is operating.

● Do not attempt to pull hay from the pickup when the machine is running.

● Be sure the flywheel is not moved when anyone is working on knives.

● Exercise extreme caution when tripping knotters by hand with the baler running. Do not touch the knotter. Stand clear of the needle frame.

● Do not try to remove or pull twine or wire from the bale case or knotter when the machine is running. Your hand can be instantly crushed by the plunger or jerked into the knotter if it is tripped accidentally.

● When knotters malfunction, there may be several bales that must be rebaled. Never kick hay into the pickup or stand close to the pickup and feed hay into the baler by hand. You can be jerked into the machinery if even a thread catches, and it happens so fast you can't pull away.

● Always shut off the engine before refueling.

● Do not smoke or use an oil lantern when refueling.

See Hydraulic Safety message page 334.

TROUBLESHOOTING

Most baler operating problems are caused by improper adjustment or delayed service. This chart is designed to help you when a problem develops by suggesting a probable cause and recommended solution.

Apply these suggested remedies carefully. Make certain you are dealing with the real problem not a symptom. A thorough understanding of the baler is a must to solve operating problems. Refer to the operator's manual for detailed repair procedures.

TROUBLESHOOTING CHART

PROBLEM	POSSIBLE CAUSE	POSSIBLE REMEDY
Knotter Difficulties — Twine Baler		
KNOT IN TWINE OVER BALE	Tucker fingers did not pick up needle twine or move it into tying position properly.	Adjust tucker fingers. Adjust needles or twine disk. Check twine disk and twine-box-tension. Install plungerhead extensions.
	Hay dogs do not hold end of bale.	Free frozen hay dogs. Replace broken hay-dog springs. Reduce feeding rate. Install plungerhead extensions.
TWINE BROKEN IN KNOT	Extreme tension on twine around billhook during tying cycle causes twine to shear or pull apart.	Loosen twine-disk-holder spring. Smooth off all rough surfaces and edges on billhook.
TWINE ENDS FRAYED	Dull twine knife.	Replace twine knife or sharpen cutting edge.
KNOT TOO LOOSE	Worn or damaged billhook tongue.	Replace billhook.
	Bale density too low.	Increase bale case tension
	Excessive twine-holder pressure.	Reduce pressure.
	Normal wear of knotter.	Adjust knife arm.
	Improper adjustment of twine disk.	Adjust twine disk.

PROBLEM	POSSIBLE CAUSE	POSSIBLE REMEDY
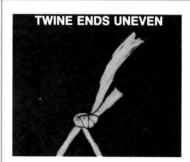 **TWINE ENDS UNEVEN**	Insufficient tension on twine-disk holder. Dull or chipped knife.	Tighten twine-disk-holder spring. Replace twine knife or sharpen cutting edge.
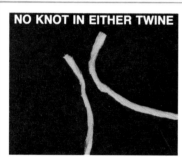 **NO KNOT IN EITHER TWINE**	Twine sheared in twine disks. Billhook not rotating. Billhook tongue fails to open.	Loosen twine holder and/or remove all sharp edges and burrs on twine holder and disks. Check for lost or sheared pin in billhook pinion. Check for lost billhook tongue roller, excessive wear on roller and cam face, or damaged billhook tongue.
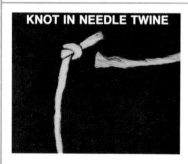 **KNOT IN NEEDLE TWINE**	Twine over bale pulled out of twine disk. (Can be detected by square cut end which has been flattened in disks. This twine will usually be shorter than mating twine tied on opposite side of bale Twine over bale sheared out of twine disks. (Distinguished from above in that twine end will be frayed and torn—not cut squarely by knife.)	Increase tension on twine-holder-disk spring and/or decrease bale tension. Decrease tension on twine-holder-disk spring. Decrease bale tension.
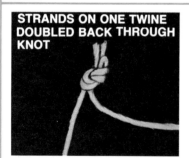 **STRANDS ON ONE TWINE DOUBLED BACK THROUGH KNOT**	Billhook tongue is closing on top of twine.	Model knife arm so groove in knife arm will hold twine over billhook tongue farther to the right. Adjust timing of twine disks.
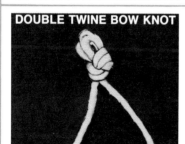 **DOUBLE TWINE BOW KNOT**	Insufficient travel of knife arm past billhook. Billhook-pressure-arm spring too loose.	Model knife arm to obtain more travel past billhook. Tighten adjusting nut on billhook-pressure-arm spring.

PROBLEM	POSSIBLE CAUSE	POSSIBLE REMEDY
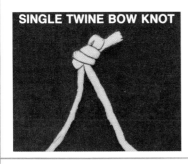 **SINGLE TWINE BOW KNOT**	Insufficient travel of knife arm past billhook.	Model knife arm to obtain more travel past billhook.
	Billhook-pressure-arm spring too loose.	Tighten adjusting nut on billhook-pressure-arm spring.
 **TWINE CUT AND OR FRAYED BEHIND KNOT**	As billhook turns, twine is pinched between billhook and knife arm and twine is damaged below knot.	Bend knife arm so billhook turns freely. Make certain wiper ledge on knife arm contacts back face of billhook.
	Rough knife arm cuts twine.	Smooth rough edge in twine notch of knife arm.
	Extremely high top-twine tension.	Reduce bale weight by loosening bale tension and/or check twine tension.
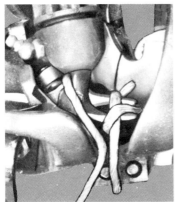 Needle twine over billhook tongue roller.	Needle twine does not enter twine disk.	Adjust needles and/or adjust twine-disk timing.
		Check for sheared or lost pin in twine-disk pinion or in disk worm gear.
		Make certain twine coming from box is going under twine-tension devices on twine box.
	Improper twine tension.	Adjust twine tension.
	Improper twine threading.	See threading needles.
 Needle twine over billhook tongue roller and second knot tied on billhook.	Same as preceding problem; however, operator will usually find this condition rather than the condition described there.	Make corrections as noted before and examine complete knotter for broken or damaged parts.

PROBLEM	POSSIBLE CAUSE	POSSIBLE REMEDY

Needle twine goes under billhook tongue during first quarter of billhook travel.

Tucker finger not carrying twine back to tying position.

Adjust tucker fingers.

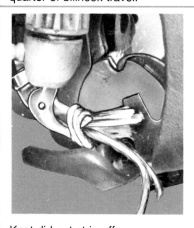

Knot did not strip off billhook.

Excessive billhook tongue tension.	Loosen billhook-pressure-arm spring-adjusted nut.
Knife-arm wiper is not contacting back face of billhook.	Model knife arm so wiper contacts back face of billhook.
Knife-arm lift (or rise) is not sufficient.	Model knife arm to increase movement past end of billhook.
Rough billhook.	Smooth off all rough edges on billhook with emery cloth.
Worn or bent billhook.	Replace billhook.
Bale density too low.	Increase bale-case tension.

Twister-Mechanism Difficulties—Wire Baler

"Tails": One end cut and the other end twisted off.

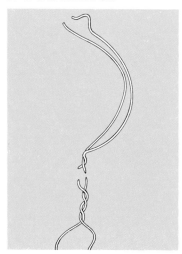

Radius on top of twister hook too sharp.	Polish throat of twister hook.
	Install new twister hook.
	Retard twister hook to specified range.
Excessive wire tension between bale and wire coil during first stage of the tying cycle.	Check all wire pulleys.
	Check for proper wire threading.
	Make sure all of the knock-out disk is removed from the front of wire carton.
	Check for any indication where wire has been catching.
	Check front side of needle for groove or build-up of foreign material that would retard wire flow.

PROBLEM	POSSIBLE CAUSE	POSSIBLE REMEDY
		Check for rough or uneven wire.
		Check top wire guide for grooves deep enough to allow wire to wedge.
	Wire cannot feed down twister-hook slot because of rough twister shaft.	Polish or replace shaft.
Knot consists of one wire twisted around the other.	Excessive wire tension between bale and wire coil.	Check all wire pulleys.
		Check for proper wire threading.
		Make sure all of the knock-out disk is removed from front of wire carton.
		Check for any indication where wire has been catching.
		Check front side of needle for groove or buildup of foreign material that would retard wire flow.
		Check for rough or uneven wire.
		Check top wire guide for grooves deep enough to allow wire to wedge.
	Gripper does not apply equal pressure on each side	Check for loose bolts in entire twister assembly.
		Clean out gripping parts including gripper-drive tube.
		With gripper to the tight side loosen bolts that hold the shear plates to the twister assembly and realign the plates.
		DON'T add washers or coins to the spring in the gripper drive tube!
		DON'T grind material from the cutting edges of the shear blade or plate!
	Twister hook catches needle wire on second revolution instead of first.	Adjust needle closer to gripper.
		Check timing.
		Replace bent needle.
		Install plungerhead extensions.
	Hay dogs not holding end of bale.	Free frozen hay dogs.
		Reduce feeding rate.
		Replace broken hay-dog springs.
		Install plungerhead extensions

PROBLEM	POSSIBLE CAUSE	POSSIBLE REMEDY
"Horse Shoes": Short pieces of wire with both ends cut because wire is caught over nose of the gripper.	Needle adjusted too far sideways.	Adjust the needle.
		Replace needle if it has become damaged.
	Grooves or extreme roughness on nose of gripper.	Grind nose of gripper.
		Replace gripper.
Tension break on top of bale.	Force required to feed wire around bale exceeds the strength of the wire.	Reduce bale density (may be necessary to remove side hay resistors).
		Oil wire coils (light oil or diesel fuel).
		Adjust feeder teeth to put less hay on side where wire is breaking.
		Use proper size wire
		Change wire coils.
	Too much force required to pull wire from wire cartons.	Check all wire pulleys.
		Check for proper wire threading.
		Make sure all of knock-out disk is removed from front of wire cartons.
		Check for any indication where wire has been catching.
		Check front side of needle for groove or buildup of foreign material that would retard wire flow.
		Check for rough or uneven wire.
		Check top wire guide for grooves deep enough to allow wire to wedge.
Tension break on front end of bale.	Wire catches in wire pulleys.	Check wire pulleys and any other place where wire could catch.
Wire breaks at base of knot.	Repeated bending of wire after tying cycle because no hay is entering baler.	Stop baler when no hay is fed into baler.
		Plan windrows to avoid traveling in areas without hay.
		Rake heavier windrows.
		Increase ground speed.

PROBLEM	POSSIBLE CAUSE	POSSIBLE REMEDY
Two successive bales not tied. One long piece of wire with each end twisted but not twisted together.	Bottom strand of wire was missed by the needle.	Remove excessive side movement of needle frame with washers.
		Check for properly shaped needle tip. Replace if necessary.
		Adjust needle.
		Adjust lower-center wire guide.
	Wire not placed in gripper.	Adjust needle.
Wire not cutting clean.	Worn or broken parts.	Replace worn or broken parts.
	Gripper and shear blade assembly not adjusted properly.	Place shims between top of gripper arm and mounting plate.
Wires not twisted together.	Foreign material in twister assembly.	Clean out twister assembly.
	Needles not adjusted properly.	Adjust needles.
	Springs frozen in gripper drive-tube assembly.	Clean out gripper drive tube.
Excessive wear on indexing surfaces of intermittent gear and pinion.	Twister hooks retarded beyond maximum limits.	Advance hooks.

Bale Not of Proper Weight

PROBLEM	POSSIBLE CAUSE	POSSIBLE REMEDY
Bale too light.	Tension cranks too loose.	Tighten tension cranks.
Bale too heavy.	Tension cranks too light.	Loosen tension cranks.
Bale too heavy with tension cranks screwed out.	Hay too wet or too green.	Let hay dry or cure before baling.
	Too many side restrictors or wedges used.	Remove side restrictors.
Bale too long.	Not enough material in top of bale and/or measuring wheel not contacting crop properly.	Incrase bale tension.
Bale too short.	Measuring arm not dropping home.	Adjust bale-measuring control.

Bale Not Uniform

PROBLEM	POSSIBLE CAUSE	POSSIBLE REMEDY
Material not distributed evenly in bale.	Feeder teeth out of adjustment.	Adjust feeder teeth.
	Ground speed of baler too slow and/or windrow too small.	Increase ground speed and/or make larger windrows.
	Bale tension too loose.	Increase bale tension.
	Baling extremely light hay.	Adjust feeder teeth and/or make larger windrows.
Ragged bale.	Dull knives. Plungerhead out of adjustment.	Sharpen knives. Adjust plungerhead.
Irregular bale length.	Measuring arm bounces.	Adjust bale-measuring mechanism.

PROBLEM	POSSIBLE CAUSE	POSSIBLE REMEDY
Pickup Difficulties		
Pickup teeth digging in ground.	Pickup set too low.	Raise pickup.
Not picking up hay clean.	Pickup stays up instead of floating.	Loosen lift spring.
	Pickup teeth set too high.	Lower pickup.
	Ground speed too fast.	Reduce ground speed.
	Hay not all raked.	Turn all hay onto clean stubble.
	Pickup teeth bent or broken.	Straighten or replace teeth.
	Windrows too light.	Rake heavier windrows.
Pickup teeth do not revolve.	Belt slipping, or drive chain broken.	Replace or tighten belt, or repair drive chain.
Feeding Difficulties		
Plungerhead hitting feeder teeth at top of case.	Out of time.	Retime plunger and feeder.
Baler stalls when plungerhead is even with rear side of feed opening.	Dull knives and/or plungerhead out of adjustment.	Sharpen knives and/or adjust plungerhead.
Baler stalls on compression stroke.	Making bales too heavy.	Loosen bale tension.
	Feeding baler too fast.	Reduce ground speed.
	Plungerhead obstructed.	Remove obstruction.
Baler fails to start after being stalled on compression stroke.	Plungerhead obstructed.	Turn flywheel in clockwise direction two or three rotations; then engage clutch on tractor or engine.

CAUTION: Be sure needles are in "home" position before turning flywheel by hand. |
Hay not feeding under auger.	Auger drive V-belt slipping.	Adjust V-belt.
Needles Not Rising		
Trip dog not functioning.	Broken release-arm spring or trip-dog spring lost.	Replace broken or lost spring.
Sheared knotter-drive pin.	(See "Shear bolt difficulties.")	(See "Shear bolt difficulties.")
Power-Drive Difficulties		
PTO slip clutch slips during normal operation.	Slip-clutch bolts loose.	Tighten clutch bolts.
	Shear bolt sheared in flywheel.	Replace shear bolt.
Engine belt slips.	Clutch lever out of adjustment.	Adjust clutch lever.
Shear-Bolt Difficulties		
Flywheel shear bolt sheared.	Dull knives.	Sharpen knives.
	Obstruction in bale chamber.	Remove all obstructions.
	Too much clearance between knives.	Adjust plungerhead.

PROBLEM	POSSIBLE CAUSE	POSSIBLE REMEDY
	Crank arm or plunger safety stop improperly adjusted.	Adjust safety stop.
	Bales too heavy.	Loosen bale tension.
	Needles in bale case.	Place needles in home position, determine cause and correct.
Sheared knotter-and-needle-drive bolt.	Knotter-drive brake too tight.	Loosen knotter-drive brake.
	Needles out of time.	Retime needles.
	Needles hitting obstruction.	Remove all obstructions.
	Obstruction in knotter.	Remove all obstructions.
	Needles out of adjustment.	Adjust needles.
Hydraulic-Pump Difficulties (For balers with engine and hydraulic tension control).		
Pump not delivering oil.	Clogged filter.	Remove, flush, clean filter thoroughly.
	Not enough oil in tank.	Add oil as necessary.
Pump not developing sufficient pressure.	Valving surfaces scored by abrasive matter.	Replace all scored or worn parts.
	Leak in hydraulic-system connections and cylinders.	Eliminate all leaks.
	Oil not of correct weight.	Use correct weight oil.
External leakage.	Faulty shaft oil seal.	Replace shaft oil seal.

MAINTENANCE

Primary maintenance on a baler falls into three areas:

- **Pickup**
- **Plungerhead assembly**
- **Tying mechanism**

Each of these components has parts that wear and break. Inspect these components often to reduce delays during field operation. Perform routine maintenance and lubrication on all baler components.

The *pickup* operates near the ground where abrasion by dust and dirt shortens service life. The most frequent problem with a cylinder pickup is replacing broken or bent pickup teeth. Proper adjustment and clean fields reduce damaged pickup teeth.

The *plungerhead assembly* wears and becomes misaligned. Check and adjust the plungerhead frequently to help ensure free movement. Inspect the plungerhead assembly for damaged parts often.

Most plungerhead maintenance involves keeping the knives sharp and adjusted. A very close tolerance between the stationary and plunger knives is required for clean cutting. This tolerance can only be maintained with frequent adjustments.

Inspect the plungerhead after the first 1,000 bales have gone through a new baler. Thereafter, check the plungerhead according to operating instructions.

The *tying mechanism* has many moving parts which must be properly adjusted and timed. Operating problems are often caused by wear, poor adjustment, and poor-quality twine or the incorrect size wire.

TWINE-TIE BALER

Adjustment	Purpose of Adjustment
Adjust needle lift link.	Allows needle frame to clear main frame when needles are fully raised.
Time baler.	Prevents plunger from breaking needles or feed fingers.
Adjust billhook.	Stops twine from separating billhook jaws.
Adjust twine disk.	Assures catching two strands of twine to be tied.
Adjust knife (wiper) arm.	Cleanly strips knot from billhook.
Adjust twine holder.	Maintains correct pressure to hold twine in twine disk.
Adjust needles.	Allows needles to pass through knotting mechanism.
Adjust tucker fingers.	Catches twine from needle.
Adjust knotter-drive brake.	Eliminates loose, erratic action of knotter mechanism.
Adjust crank arm or plunger safety stop.	Protects needles from breakage if baler is out of time.

WIRE-TIE BALER

Adjustment	Purpose of Adjustment
Adjust needle link.	Allows needle frame to clear main frame when needles are fully raised.
Time baler.	Prevents plunger from breaking needles or feed fingers.
Adjust twister bevel gear and pinion.	Assures proper rotation of twister.
Adjust intermittent-drive-gear clearance.	Prevents gear-tooth breakage.
Adjust wire grippers.	Provides positive shearing action of the wire.
Adjust wire twister hooks.	Assures porper twist on wire.
Adjust needles alignment.	Allows needles to properly pass through knotting mechanism.
Adjust wire guides.	Allows each wire pulley to turn freely.
Adjust knotter-drive brake.	Eliminates loose, erratic action of knotting mechanism.
Adjust crank armor plunger safety stop.	Protects needles from breakage if baler is out of time.

TYING-MECHANISM ADJUSTMENTS

A checklist of common tying-mechanism adjustments and their purpose follows. For specific adjustment details, consult the operator's manual for each baler.

REPLACEMENT PARTS

Good baler maintenance reduces the need for a large stockpile of replacement parts. However, belts, chains, and shear bolts do break. So, keep these parts available in the field to reduce repair time. Always have several replacement pickup teeth on hand. The twine or wire tying mechanism gets very hard use and requires replacement parts. If knife wear is severe or damaging objects are picked up frequently, keep an extra set of knives on hand. Keep an adequate supply of good twine or wire handy in the field.

Give the baler a complete service inspection at the end of each season to prepare for off-season repair work. Make a list of needed repairs and buy parts so you can install them during the off-season.

STORAGE

● Store the baler inside after cleaning it thoroughly. Trash and dirt draw moisture which stimulates rust formation. Block up the baler to remove the load from the tires. Do not deflate the tires. If the baler is stored outside, cover the tires to protect them from deterioration caused by sunlight.

● Lubricate the baler thoroughly. Clean the knotter mechanism and apply a coating of grease. Also, clean all chains by washing them with diesel fuel. Dry them well and coat them with heavy oil.

● Repaint surfaces where paint has worn off. However, do not paint the inside of the bale chamber; instead, brush it with grease.

● If the baler has an engine, consult the operator's manual for proper engine-storage procedure.

SUMMARY

A baler lifts windrowed hay, compacts it into a dense package, and ties wire or twine around the bale. Tightly-bound bales have a box shape, which makes them easy to stack, transport, store, and feed. Most bales are light enough to be handled by one man. They may be stacked inside storage barn.

Balers are also used to "package" crop residues, especially small-grain straw.

Balers are available as tractor-towed or self-propelled units. Towed balers may use the tractor's PTO or have an engine mounted on the baler to drive the baler. Methods of picking up, compacting, and packaging the hay are similar on all balers.

Baling is adaptable to a wide variety of hay and livestock enterprises. The many types and sizes of balers encourage ownership, even on smaller farms. Ownership of a baler permits timely operations essential to harvest high-quality hay. Their size, shape, and density make bales suitable for efficient inside storage and long-distance transportation. Baling usually requires a high amount of labor to haul bales from the field to storage, so the manpower cost can be high.

CHAPTER QUIZ

1. (Fill in blanks.) Bales are held together with either _____ or _____.

2. Name the functions of the plungerhead assembly.

3. Describe the purpose of the bale-measuring wheel.

4. (True or false.) Wet hay is easier to bale than dry hay.

5. What happens if hay is too dry for proper baling?

6. Explain why a baler must be properly "timed."

7. What is the function of baler needles?

8. Why is proper adjustment of twine holders and wire grippers so important?

9. Give two or more reasons why a twine knotter will not tie a knot in either end.

10. Why must needles be aligned properly?

11. (True or false.) To pick up hay efficiently, the baler must travel in the same direction the rake and mower or windrower traveled.

12. List three or more factors that affect baler capacity.

7
Bale Handling
and Storage

Fig. 1—Loading Bales with Bale Loader

INTRODUCTION

The hard work of hauling bales from the field to storage has plagued hay growers for many years. This chapter discusses equipment designed to reduce the labor and time needed.

BALE LOADERS

Many producers use a bale loader and wagon or truck to pick up and haul bales (Fig. 1). A bale loader usually requires one man to drive and another to load the truck.

Fig. 2—Tractor Front-End Loader with Bale Fork

Many loaders can handle 14x16- and 16x18-inch (355x406 mm) and (406x457 mm) bales and small round bales. Some can operate at speeds up to 8 miles per hour (13 km/h).

Some growers use a tractor-mounted front-end loader with a "bale fork" to load accumulated bales in the field and to load and unload wagons or trucks at the storage site (Fig. 2). This system requires at least two men. If hauling long distances, two different tractors, each equipped with a front end loader and bale fork should be used. One for loading in the field and another for unloading at the storage site. This restricts the system to short-distance hauling if only one tractor is available.

SELF-PROPELLED BALE HANDLER

Another machine designed to increase hauling capacity and reduce bale lifting is a self-propelled bale handler (Fig. 3). The bale handler has a drag-chain pickup and delivery chute to carry bales from the ground to the bed of the bale handler. Bales are manually stacked on the handler and then hauled to storage sites. There, the pickup drag-chain conveyor is reversed and the conveyor raised so bales are carried to a stack or barn for storage (Fig. 4). At least three men are required for high-capacity operation.

Fig. 3—Bale Handler in Field

Fig. 4—Bale Handler Unloading Bales into Barn

BALE ELEVATORS AND CONVEYORS

At the storage site, bales may be moved with bale elevators and conveyors (Fig. 5). Many farmers use wide chain-and-slat grain elevators to move bales.

Bale elevators and conveyors close to 100 feet (30.5 m) long may be driven from a single electric motor or small gasoline engine. Additional lengths may be added with power-transfer packages.

An adjustable deflector lets you dump bales at any point to the right or left of the conveyor. Or, bales may be dropped off the end of the elevator.

To reduce labor requirements, bales are usually dropped from the conveyor in a random stack. If labor is plentiful and storage space is at a premium, bales are stacked by hand.

CAUTION: To keep bales from tipping and falling off the elevator, avoid setting elevators at steep angles. Use a longer elevator for extremely high barns or stacks. Poorly formed bales, which tend to bow in the center, are most likely to fall from an elevator.

CAUTION: When positioning elevators do not contact electric power lines. Prevent serious injury or possible death from electric shock.

AUTOMATIC BALE WAGONS

Most automatic bale wagons (Fig. 6) permit one skilled operator to replace the two- or three-man hauling crew required in other systems. The capacity of an automatic bale wagon easily exceeds the productivity of manpower in a hauling crew. This system makes completely mechanized bale handling from field to storage possible.

Fig. 5—Bale Elevators Reduce Labor Compared to Hand Storage

Fig. 6—Automatic Bale Wagon

PURPOSE AND USE

Automatic bale wagons pick up bales from the field and stack them on a load rack (bed) for transportation to storage. The tight weather-resistant stack may be unloaded intact, or unloaded a single bale at a time. The automatic bale wagon can unload the stacks outside or inside if the storage structure is large enough.

High capacity automatic bale wagons help preserve hay quality by hauling hay out of the field fast so weather doesn't damage it.

Removing hay fast also allows quicker irrigation for more rapid growth of the next hay crop. There is increased production per man-hour with automatic bale wagons.

While an automatic bale wagon is best for commercial hay producers, it can also fit many smaller farms. For top efficiency, all field operations must be carefully coordinated. Also, the operator must be skilled enough to use the full capacity of the bale wagon. Commercial hay producers are usually well prepared to manage this mechanized system and willing to hire efficient, skilled labor.

TYPES AND SIZES

There are two types of automatic bale wagons:

- **Towed, tractor-powered**
- **Self-propelled**

The size-rating of a bale wagon is generally based on hauling capacity. The exact capacity depends on several variables including type of hay, moisture content, bale size, and density. However, the maximum allowable load provides a uniform method for rating capacities.

TRACTOR-POWERED BALE WAGONS

Tractor-powered bale wagons are designed to handle "two-wire" or "two-twine" bales (Fig. 7). The smallest bale wagons have a maximum capacity of approximately 2.5 tons. Medium-size wagons are rated for about 3.5 tons, and the large units have rated capacity of about 4.5 tons.

Fig. 7—Tractor-Powered Automatic Bale Wagon

In each case the average load is less than rated — about 1.8 to 4 tons for the three sizes. These bale wagons are designed for smaller acreages.

Tractor-powered bale wagons are built to pick up, transport, and stack bales. Some models can unload single bales onto an elevator for storage on the ground, or into bunkers for feeding (Fig. 8). Some models can retrieve a stack and move it to a new storage or feeding area.

SELF-PROPELLED BALE WAGONS

Self-propelled automatic bale wagons are available to handle either two-wire or three-wire bales (Fig. 6). These large units are designed for commercial hay growers, and have maximum payloads ranging from 5 to 7 tons.

Self-propelled bale wagons are not usually equipped to unload single bales, and retrieving a stack with the bale wagon is not ordinarily required. However, models are available that can retrieve and relocate stacks.

For faster highway transport, truck-mounted stack retrievers are available.

Bale-wagon stacks may be lifted with a squeeze fork and loaded on trucks for long-distance transport (Fig. 9).

Fig. 8—Single-Bale Unloading onto an Elevator

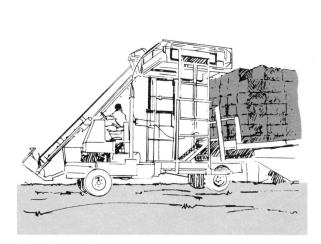

Fig. 9—Squeeze Fork Loads Stack of Bales on a Truck

Fig. 11—Bale Loader Lifting Bale

Fig. 10—Automatic Bale Wagon

BALE-WAGON OPERATION

Bale wagons pick up bales, form a stack on the wagon, transport the stack, and unload the stack.

PRIMARY COMPONENTS

Primary components of an automatic bale wagon (Fig. 10):

- **Controls**
- **Bale loader**
- **First and second bale tables**
- **Load rack**
- **Rolling rack**

Self-propelled automatic bale wagons also have an *operator's platform,* and an *engine* under the second bale table. Bale wagons of each type have a *main frame* and *wheels.*

COMPONENT FUNCTIONS

The *bale loader* has a flanged chute to guide bales into the loading assembly. As a bale is contracted by the bale loader, chain teeth engage the bale and lift it onto the *first table* (Fig. 11). This procedure is repeated until the first table is loaded (two or three bales, depending on the model). When the first table is loaded, a trip arm triggers the automatic tilting action to lift the bales onto the *second table* (Fig. 12).

Another trip arm then actuates the tilting mechanism of the second table so it loads bales on the *load rack* (Fig. 13). This procedure is repeated until the load rack is filled.

Fig. 12—First Table Placing Bales on Second Table

Fig. 13—Second Table Placing Bales on Load Rack

Fig. 14—Stacking Pattern Compared to a Tie Tier on Second Table

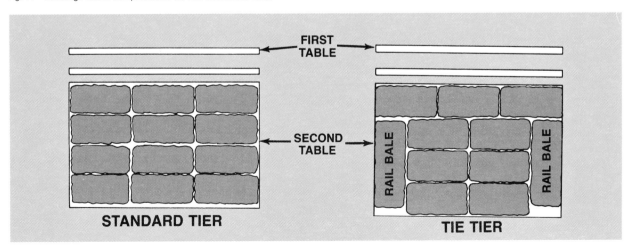

FIRST TABLE

SECOND TABLE

RAIL BALE

RAIL BALE

STANDARD TIER

TIE TIER

Fig. 15—Unloading Stack from Bale Wagon

Tie Tiers

Tie tiers (tiers or layers of bales "tied" in place) have a different stacking pattern on the second table (Fig. 14). Tie tiers improve the stability of the stack. Some bale wagons form the tie tier automatically. On others the bales must be arranged by hand.

Unloading Procedure

After the stack is formed, the operator transports it and unloads it by tilting the load rack until the first tier contacts the ground. The stack is usually unloaded against another stack or a bulkhead so the stack won't topple backwards as the bale wagon is moved away from the stack (Fig. 15).

OPERATION AND ADJUSTMENT

The many advantages of an automatic bale wagon are turned into profit only by applying intelligent management and skilled operation. For efficient performance, these specialized machines must be matched to specific haying operations. Field equipment and storage conditions must be selected to complement the automatic bale wagon.

Proper Baling

The key to success of an automatic bale wagon system is the baling operation (Fig. 16). Problems in using the bale wagon often occur because the bales were not formed properly. Bales must be of uniform density and length to fit on the load rack. A high-density bale is best because it won't deform.

A heavy-duty baler operating under good field conditions provides the best bales.

You can't control weather but in a well-planned haying operation, proper windrowing and raking, timely operations with dependable equipment, and good management can reduce the chance of weather damage.

Fig. 16—Firm, Uniform Bales Improve Automatic-Bale-Wagon Performance

Fig. 17—Combining Windrows with a Set of Tandem Rakes

PLANNING AND PREPARATION

Related haying equipment recommended for an efficient automatic bale wagon system:

- **Mower-conditioner or windrower**
- **A set of tandem rakes**
- **Heavy-duty baler**
- **Tractor**

Match equipment to the automatic bale wagon carefully for proper operation and high productivity. Each machine plays an important part in overall system performance.

PROPER WINDROWING

A mower-conditioner or windrower that can form a heavy windrow under normal conditions is recommended. Frequently, with an automatic bale wagon system, a set of tandem rakes is used to combine windrows (Fig. 17). The result is more uniform windrows for better baling and better efficiency of the bale wagon because bales are dropped closer together. Closely-spaced bales reduce bale-wagon field time.

The field layout time and windrowing pattern also help reduce field time. Smooth fields are best. They permit faster, safer work, and bales are easier to pick up.

EDGE-DROPPING ATTACHMENT

A heavy-duty baler is best. The baler should be equipped with an *edge-drop attachment* so the bale wagon can pick up bales easier (Fig. 18).

TRACTOR REQUIREMENTS

The tractor must match the bale wagon needs. Some bale wagons operate from the tractor's hydraulic system. But usually towed wagons have a separate hydraulic pump driven by the tractor's PTO. Power required by wagons varies depending on terrain, soil, and moisture. However, a 50-horsepower tractor is large enough to handle most tractor-powered automatic bale wagons under good field conditions.

BALE STORAGE

Planning for an automatic bale wagon system is not complete until the bale-storage place has been selected. Bale wagon stacks may be unloaded inside if the storage barn is large enough. The most critical dimension is vertical clearance. A minimum height of 17 feet is required for big bale wagons. The floor must be reasonably level and firm.

Fig. 18—Edge-Drop Attachment on Baler

Fig. 19—Store Bales Near Hay Field

For unloading, the floor should be solid. A slight slope will provide drainage away from the stack. Begin stacking in the low end and progress uphill.

Put the storage site near the hay fields (Fig. 19). Long-distance transportation drastically reduces daily productivity. Don't haul bales more than 4 miles (6.4 km) with tractor-powered, automatic bale wagons. With self-propelled bale wagons, try to limit haul distance to 10 miles (16 km). Trucks and hay-hauling crews are more efficient for long-distance transportation.

OPERATOR SKILL

Proper planning and a skilled operator complement each other. The most proficient bale wagon operators are not only adept at loading and unloading the bale wagon, but also at planning the most efficient loading pattern in the field. If possible, try to start and finish each load near the field exit. Think ahead. Plan the next load while loading and transporting bales. Always watch for poorly-formed and

Fig. 20—Learn the Controls Before Starting the Bale Wagon

flat-dropped bales. Such bales require extra time to load, so most operators leave them in the field to be hand-loaded and hauled in later. The bale wagon is built for continuous high-capacity hauling and stacking. The most efficient operators handle their wagons to deliver that high productivity.

For high efficiency, the bale wagon and tractor must be properly prepared for field operation. Details of preparation depend on the bale wagon model. For specific information, check the operator's manual carefully.

BALE WAGON PREPARATION

Before you operate the bale wagon:

• *Study the entire operator's manual carefully and know the controls (Fig. 20).*

• *Check for loose bolts and nuts. Tighten them to the recommended torque.*

• *Check tension and alignment of chains and belts.*

• *Check tires and inflate them to recommended pressure.*

• *Tighten wheel lug-bolts to manufacturer's recommendation.*

• *Review lubrication chart and lubricate completely.*

• *Inspect and service engine and drive train as recommended in the operator's manual.*

HYDRAULIC SYSTEM CHECKUP

See hydraulic warning page 334.

Proper operation of an automatic bale wagon depends on the hydraulic system. Make a thorough system inspection before going to the field. Before engaging the hydraulic pump, be sure all hydraulic connections are tight, and check for leaks in lines, pipes, and hoses (Fig. 21). Operate each hydraulic component individually and check for proper operation.

If any component malfunctions, recheck the oil level in the hydraulic reservoir and reinspect hoses and lines for leaks.

CAUTION

Use special safety precautions when working with hydraulic lines. Do not use your hands to search for oil leaks. Oil escaping under high pressure can penetrate the skin and cause serious injury. If a leak is suspected but can't be seen, use a piece of cardboard or wood to help find the spray. Always release hydraulic pressure before disconnecting lines. Replace any damaged parts and continue inspection.

TRACTOR PREPARATION

For tractor-powered bale wagons, complete the following tasks before attaching the tractor to the wagon:

• *Make sure tractor PTO speed matches the speed required by the bale wagon drive. (540-rpm PTO speed is most common.)*

• *Place the drawbar in the standard position for PTO operation, or as directed in the bale wagon operator's manual.*

• *Lock the drawbar parallel with the centerline of the PTO shaft.*

• *Raise the 3-point hitch to maximum height.*

• *Check hydraulic oil level and add fluid if necessary.*

• *Add ballast to the tractor front end if necessary for adverse conditions.*

HITCHING THE BALE WAGON

After preparing the tractor, attach the bale wagon following this sequence:

• *Use the hitch jack to align the wagon hitch and tractor drawbar vertically.*

• *Back the tractor to align holes in drawbar and hitch. Shut off the tractor and take the key. If someone is helping you, don't let them get between the tractor and the wagon while you are backing. Put the tractor in forward gear or park. Then insert safety hitch pin.*

• *Place the hitch jack in transport position.*

• *Attach the powershaft to the PTO outlet and attach safety shield.*

• *Install the hydraulic hoses in tractor breakaway couplers, if required.*

• *Make sure operating controls and ropes are in proper position.*

To detach the bale wagon, reverse the foregoing procedure.

SETTINGS AND ADJUSTMENTS

After all bale-wagon and tractor components have been checked and are operating properly, make preliminary adjustments for field operation.

BALE LENGTH

First, determine the size of the bales to be hauled. The bale wagon must be adjusted for the length of bales to be handled, to permit proper loading and stacking. Bales with two ties are usually 14x18 or 16x18 inches (355x457 or 406x457 mm) and of variable lengths. Bale length must be measured before the bale wagon is adjusted.

Fig. 21—Check For Leaks With Cardboard — Not Your Hand!

To determine bale length, select two or three average bales and set them side by side, with ends aligned. Lay a board against the bale ends. Then measure the distance between the boards (Fig. 22). This method allows tufts at the corners of the bale to be included in the length measurement. If there are sizable variations in bale length, or if the length varies more than 2 to 4 inches (50 to 100 mm) from the recommended size, tying the stack together will be difficult, if not impossible.

Fig. 22—Measuring Length of Bales

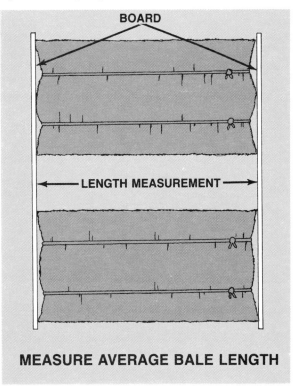

BOARD

LENGTH MEASUREMENT

MEASURE AVERAGE BALE LENGTH

Fig. 23—Bale Loader Lifts Bales to the First Table

ADJUST FOR BALE SIZE

After determining the bale size, adjust the bale wagon according to instructions in the operator's manual. Additional minor changes may be required in the field. After the bale wagon has been adjusted for a specific bale size, most operators prefer to handle only that bale size, to eliminate need for readjustment.

GROUND CLEARANCE

Adjust the bale loader to allow 3½ to 5 inches (89 to 127 mm) of clearance between the ground and the bale-loader skid.

Fig. 24—Center Bales on the Second Table

LOADER SHOE

Set the bale-loader shoes so bales will be held tightly against the loader chain.

BALE DEFLECTOR ROD

The bale deflector rod directs the bale from the bale loader onto the first table. Position the rod just low enough to turn the bale, but high enough to prevent the bale from lodging in the bale loader.

LOADER CHAIN

The loader chain lifts the bale from the ground onto the first table (Fig. 23). To operate properly, the chain must be tight enough to eliminate slack and reduce wear and breakage.

FIRST TABLE

Components of the first table are:

● *First table delay*

● *Trip latch or lock*

● *Trip arm*

● *Return trip control*

● *Tie tier trip arm*

The *first table delay* is controlled by a hydraulic valve that will not permit the first table to rise unless both second table and bale loader are in the low position.

The *trip latch* prevents the first table from lifting before it is fully loaded.

The *trip arm* triggers unloading action when the first table is loaded. If the trip arm is not properly adjusted, bales will not be centered on the second table (Fig. 24).

The *return trip causes the first table to reverse its direction after lifting bales to the second table. Normally, the return trip is engaged when the first table makes a 90-degree angle with the second table. The bales are then loaded on the second table and the first table returns for more bales.*

On models that make tie tiers automatically, the *tie tier trip arm* works when tie tiers are formed. Only two bales (not three) are required on the first table to make the table tilt and unload. These two bales are then replaced and centered on the second table.

SECOND TABLE

Components requiring adjustments are:

● *Table trip*

● *Table trip return*

● *Tie spikes*

The *second table trip* arm actuates the second table lift. The trip arm acts when the second table is loaded.

The *second table trip return* acts when the table has rotated to slightly more than a 90-degree angle to the load rack. This angle helps keep bales from coming back down with the second table.

The *tie spikes,* underneath the second table, hold the outer bales when the tie tier is formed. The spikes penetrate 6 to 8 inches (152 to 203 mm) into the outer ends of the bales. To adjust for different bale lengths, the tie spikes may be placed in different locations.

LOAD RACK

Components requiring adjustment on the load rack are:

- *Side boards*
- *Stabilizer tines*
- *Full-load and tie switches*
- *Rolling rack*

Side boards keep bales from falling off the sides of the load rack and can be adjusted to the length of bales being hauled. Spacing between bale ends and size boards is about 3 to 4 inches (76 to 100 mm) on the bale loader side, and 1 to 2 inches (25 to 50 mm) on the other side.

Stabilizer tines keep bales from falling forward off the load rack onto the second table (Fig. 25). Adjust the stabilizer tine for 14x18-inch and 16x18-inch bales (355x457 and 406x457 mm).

The *full-load* and *tie switches* ring a bell to tell the operator the wagon is loaded or that a tie tier is needed. The switches, under the load rack, are actuated by the rolling rack.

The *rolling rack* on bale wagons that can't unload single bales is spring loaded and controlled by the weight of the bales. On a single-bale unload model, the rolling rack can move the bales forward on the load rack. Hydraulically powered load racks require adjustment of the hydraulic valve stops for single-bale unloading.

FIELD OPERATION

Bale wagon controls vary with the model and optional features. Basic controls regulate the bale loader, second table, and load rack. On self-propelled bale wagons, controls are located on the operator's platform in a convenient console (Fig. 26). Basic controls for tractor-powered bale wagons are on an adjustable control stand close to the tractor seat (Fig. 27).

STARTING OPERATION

Lower the bale loader and check to be sure no one is near the bale wagon. Then engage the hydraulic system.

On tractor-powered units, engage the PTO clutch to start the hydraulic pump.

With the hydraulic system operating, start moving toward the first bale. Adjust forward speed to field conditions. Maximum recommended loading speed is 10 to 15 miles per hour (16 to 24 km/h), depending on bale wagon model and field conditions.

Fig. 25—Stabilizer Tines Hold Bales on Load Rack

LOADING BALES

Load bales by aligning the mouth of the bale loader with the bale (Fig. 28). Flared sides help position the bale for pickup. As the bale enters the loader and engages the chain-loader teeth, start the bale-loader motor and operate it until the bale falls onto the first table. Continue moving the wagon forward during this loading process.

When the first table is loaded it automatically trips and places the bales on the second table. It keeps putting bales on the second table until the second table is loaded. The second table then trips and raises bales to the load rack. This tier of bales is held on the load rack by the side boards, stabilizer tines, and rolling rack. Continue the loading procedure until a tie tier is needed.

TIE TIER

A tie tier helps keep the stack stable. Placement and number of tie tiers depends on bale-wagon model. However, tie tiers can be placed at different levels in the stack. For example, the tie tier is usually lowered one tier in a stack to be used as a bulkhead. Do not use tie tiers in stacks if you want to unload single bales.

With an automatic tie tier, the entire load can be formed non-stop. If the tie tier is formed manually, always shut off the tractor engine before making the tie. Refer to the bale wagon operator's manual for detailed instructions.

After the stack is completely built on the load rack, the second table remains in the raised position. This helps keep the stack stable during transport to the storage site.

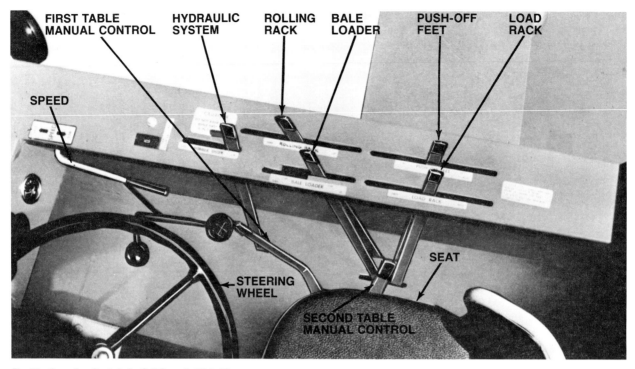

First labels (with arrows pointing to controls):

FIRST TABLE MANUAL CONTROL | **HYDRAULIC SYSTEM** | **ROLLING RACK** | **BALE LOADER** | **PUSH-OFF FEET** | **LOAD RACK**

SPEED

STEERING WHEEL

SEAT

SECOND TABLE MANUAL CONTROL

Fig. 26—Operating Controls for Self-Propelled Bale Wagon

STACK STABILITY

Always place stacks on a solid surface. A few degrees of ground slope is desirable on an outside storage for proper drainage. Build the stack up the slope for best stability. A slight depression in the middle of the stack floor will form a tighter stack, but the depression must not be low enough to hold water.

Start the stack by forming a bulkhead. Form the bulkhead with bales in the first load (Fig. 29), or use a portable bulkhead (Fig. 30). Permanent metal or wooden bulkheads may also be used. Primary bulkhead requirements are stability and a slight backward slant to prevent stacks from tipping (Fig. 30).

Fig. 27—Operating Controls for Tractor-Powered Bale Wagon

Fig. 28—Aligning Bale Loader with a Bale

UNLOADING

For trouble-free unloading, have a solid working surface, a solid bulkhead, and follow these steps:

1. Check behind the bale wagon for people and equipment before backing.

2. Back the wagon into position. The stack, bale wagon, and tractor (if a towed bale wagon is used) should be in a straight line.

3. Lower the second table if it is not directly connected to the load rack.

4. Raise the load rack until the upper end of the rolling rack is about 1½ to 2½ feet (457 to 762 mm) above the ground.

5. Dismount from the operator's platform to make sure the bale wagon is in position and the load rack tilted (Fig. 31). If stack contact is too high, bales on the stack may be broken. If contact is too low, bales may fall off the top of the bale-wagon.

6. Correct the angle of load-rack tilt, if necessary. (Experienced operators may eliminate steps 5 and 6.)

7. Slowly pull forward about 4 to 6 inches (101 to 152 mm).

8. Lower the load rack to extreme position past vertical.

9. Raise the second table about 16 inches (406 mm) above the load if the second table is connected to the load rack.

10. Set stack poles to provide additional stack stability (Fig. 32). Stack hooks on a chain may also be used for support.

11. Extend push-off feet (Fig. 32). On the first load or on soft ground, move the bale wagon forward gently while extending the push-off feet.

12. Pull slightly forward to completely clear the stack.

13. Retract push-off feet.

14. Raise the second table if it is connected to the load rack.

15. Lower the load rack slowly to prevent damage to the load and rolling rack.

16. Return the rolling rack to forward position on hydraulically-controlled rolling racks. Spring-loaded rolling racks return to the forward position automatically.

CHAIN HOLDS STACK TILL NEXT LOAD

Fig. 29—Forming a Bulkhead with Bales

PARTIAL LOADS

If a rough bale count shows less than a full load on the bale wagon, trip the second table manually and be sure the rolling rack is completely rearward before unloading. If only a few bales are on the load rack, they can be unloaded by hand.

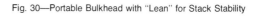

Fig. 30—Portable Bulkhead with "Lean" for Stack Stability

STACK POLES

PORTABLE BULKHEAD

Fig. 31—Keep The Stack Tight

Fig. 32—Push Away From the Stack

AFTER THE LAST LOAD

Unload the bale wagon at the end of each work day to take weight off the wagon, and to make daily maintenance easier. After unloading the day's final load, lower the load rack, second table, and first table. Disengage the hydraulic system and shut off the engine.

FIELD ADJUSTMENTS

To build tight bale stacks, field adjustments may be needed to match bale size and density to field conditions.

Refer to the previous discussions about adjustments for proper settings and methods.

ADJUST BALE SIZE

Modify preliminary settings and adjustments for specific bale sizes if necessary. If bale size and density vary, adjust the automatic trip arms. Hauling bales shortly after baling may reduce the need for field adjustments. If the bales get wet, they will expand and adjustments to the bale wagon will be necessary.

MATCH SPEED TO CONDITIONS

Rough terrain reduces productivity because ground speed must be decreased to keep bales from falling off the load rack and second table. Too much speed may also result in breaking bales at the bale loader because of high impact forces. If ground speed is too slow, poor loading may occur because bales are not held firmly against the loader chain.

Ideal field conditions are dense, uniform bales, closely spaced in long straight rows in a level field. These conditions reduce the need to change speed and direction, and boost daily productivity. The maximum recommended field speed is 10 to 15 miles per hour (16 to 24 km/h).

TRANSPORT

Before transporting a bale wagon, raise the bale loader so it will clear humps in the field and road.

If the bale wagon is loaded, the second table should be locked in the raised position to hold bales on the load rack. If the wagon is not loaded, lower the second table to increase rear visibility.

Because the bale wagon is large and heavy, the tractor brakes or self-propelled bale-wagon brakes must be in good condition. Good brakes are extremely important for travel on roads and hilly terrain.,

CAUTION: THINK SAFETY! Always remember a loaded bale wagon is big and heavy. Watch for narrow passages and low overhead obstructions.

Be sure the Slow Moving Vehicle emblem on the rear of the bale wagon shows up bright and clear before you transport on a road or highway. When transporting a bale wagon use accessory lights to warn operators of other vehicles.

Never exceed recommended maximum safe road transport speed, particularly with a loaded self-propelled automatic bale wagon. Slow down on rolling terrain or if visibility is poor. Maximum road speed for a loaded bale wagon towed with a tractor depends on tractor size and bale-wagon model. Remember, a lightweight tractor cannot control a heavily-loaded bale wagon at high road speeds.

SAFETY

Because a bale wagon is bulky and heavy, the operator must be extremely careful. When the wagon is loaded, the problem of safe operation is compounded by poor visibility to the rear. So, be sure no one is near the bale wagon before backing or engaging the power and hydraulics.

When unloading a bale wagon, check before backing into position. Also, check for overhead clearance, particularly near electrical lines, before raising the load rack.

Keep helpers and watchers a safe distance away from the machine. Never allow passengers on the bale wagon.

Hydraulic System Safety

A hydraulic system is essential for proper bale wagon operation. Be extremely careful with high-pressure hydraulic leaks. Fluid escaping under pressure can penetrate the skin and cause serious injury. If you are injured by escaping hydraulic fluid, stop work and see a doctor immediately. Always disengage the hydraulic system before attempting any service or adjustment procedure.

See hydraulic safety message page 334.

On self-propelled bale wagons, a hydraulic gate automatically shuts off the hydraulic system when the operator prepares to dismount (Fig. 33). Never raise the hydraulic shut-off gate unless you are on the operator's platform.

Additional Safety Precautions

Always shut off the engine and take the key before servicing and adjusting the bale wagon and when manually forming a tie tier. Put the transmission in park and lock the brakes.

HYDRAULIC SHUT-OFF GATE

Fig. 33—Hydraulic Shut-Off Gate Must Be Closed While Operating

Do not attempt to make any adjustments or reach under any of the tables while they are loaded, even though the hydraulic system is disengaged. Always block the tables securely before working under them. Some tables have a support to block the table up (Fig. 34). Never leave a bale wagon unattended while the bale loader or tables are in a raised position.

Fig. 34—Use Table Support For Safety

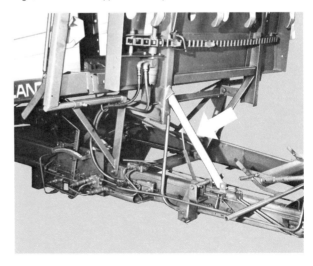

Always maintain safe road and field speeds. Be especially careful when operating on hillsides because humps and gullies will turn over a bale wagon easily. Tipping danger increases as speed goes up.

Add ballast to the tractor for towed bale wagons, as recommended in the tractor operator's manual.

Never allow children to play on or near a bale wagon.

TROUBLESHOOTING FIELD PROBLEMS

Most field problems with bale wagons happen because of poorly-formed bales, hydraulic-system failure, or operator inexperience. This chart was developed to help the operator overcome a wide range of problems. It includes general problems encountered with both self-propelled and towed bale wagons.

TROUBLESHOOTING CHART

PROBLEM	POSSIBLE CAUSE	POSSIBLE REMEDY
Loading		
BALE LOADER FAILS TO PICK UP BALES.	Poor bale weight, density, and shape.	Check and adjust baler.
	Incorrect bale length.	Adjust bale size to length recommended in bale wagon operator's manual.
	Bent or broken pickup chain teeth.	Replace damaged chain teeth.
	Pickup chain too loose.	Tighten chain.
	Bale loader height incorrect.	Set bale loader to recommended height.
BREAKING BALES (BALE LOADER AND FIRST TABLE).	Poor bale weight, density, shape and length.	Check and adjust baler.
	Bales not falling straight on first table.	Adjust bale loader shoe and/or deflector rod.
	Bale loader pickup chain operated before it has contacted bale.	Do not engage bale loader pickup chain until it has firmly contacted the bale.
	Incorrect bale loader height.	Set bale loader to correct height.
BALES SLIDE TOWARD REAR OF SECOND TABLE OR LOAD RACK.	Sudden start.	Start slowly.
BALES FALL FORWARD FROM LOAD RACK.	Sudden stop.	Apply brakes slowly.
	Poor bales.	Adjust baler for better bales.
	Second table return trip set improperly.	See adjustment section in operator's manual.
	Bale stabilizer tines not adjusted.	See adjustment section in operator's manual.
SECOND TABLE TRIPS PREMATURELY.	Bales sliding back.	Install wedge at trip.
BALES FALL BACK ONTO FIRST TABLE FROM SECOND TABLE.	First table not properly adjusted.	See adjustment section in operator's manual.
	Field rough.	Reduce field speed.
	Bales expanded.	Load one less tier on 2nd table.
CANNOT CENTER LOAD ON SIDE HILL.	First-table trip not properly adjusted.	See adjustment section in operator's manual.
	Field rough.	Reduce field speed.

PROBLEM	POSSIBLE CAUSE	POSSIBLE REMEDY
Stacking		
STACK FALLS.	Soft or low-density bales.	Adjust baler to obtain firm, well-shaped bales.
	Wet or green bales.	Hay should be allowed to dry for best operation.
	No tie tier.	Use two tie tiers in every load.
	Improper lean.	Be sure the stack has the correct lean.
	Stacking area is not smooth and level.	Use smooth, level, stacking area.
	Stacking poles or hooks not used.	Use stacking poles or hooks.
	Short bales on bottom of stack.	Bales should be of nearly uniform length (4″ maximum variation).
Loader		
MOTOR WILL NOT RUN OR RUNS SLOWLY.	Control valve not shifting.	Adjust and lubricate linkage.
	Oil pressure too low.	Check priority pressure.
	Orbit motor worn.	Have repaired or replace.
	Foreign material wrapped around sprocket and chain.	Remove foreign material.
Cross Conveyor		
CHAIN STOPS WHEN RUNNING BALE LOADER.	Bale loader control lever not adjusted properly.	See adjustment section in operator's manual.
CROSS-CONVEYOR DOES NOT RUN.	First-table valve spool not shifting properly.	Check first-table trip-linkage adjustment. Clean and lubricate linkage.
	Improper amount of oil flow.	Check flow-divider output. See hydraulic section of operator's manual for correct flow.
First Table		
FIRST TABLE DOES NOT TRIP.	First-table trip lock not releasing.	Lubricate and adjust.
	Trip linkage not over-centering.	Lubricate and adjust.
	Linkage is binding or rusty.	Polish surface and lubricate.
FIRST TABLE WILL NOT RAISE.	Control valve not shifting.	Clean and lubricate external portions of the valve spool.
	Valve hardware too tight.	Loosen and retighten to recommended torque.
	Loader is not completely lowered.	Completely lower the loader.
	First-table delay valve not shifting.	Lubricate and adjust linkage.
	Low hydraulic pressure.	Check the system pressure.

PROBLEM	POSSIBLE CAUSE	POSSIBLE REMEDY
FIRST TABLE DOES NOT RETURN.	Table raising too high.	Adjust first-table return trip.
	Trip linkage not over-centering.	Lubricate and adjust.
	Linkage is binding or rusty.	Polish surface and lubricate.
	Control valve not shifting.	Clean and lubricate external portions of valve spool.
	Breather on cylinder plugged.	Clean or replace.
	Air leakage.	Replace air check or shaft seal.
	Table or cylinder pivot binding.	Repair and lubricate.

Second Table

PROBLEM	POSSIBLE CAUSE	POSSIBLE REMEDY
SECOND TABLE DOES NOT TRIP.	Linkage binding or rusty.	Polish and lubricate surfaces.
	Trip linkage not shifting valve.	Lubricate and adjust.
SECOND TABLE WILL NOT RAISE.	First-table valve not shifted to the rear.	Refer to first table not returning.
	Control valve not shifting.	Clean and lubricate external portions of the valve spool.
	Bales miss trip arm.	Adjust first table trip arm to center bales on the first table.
	Low hydraulic pressure.	Check the main system pressure.
SECOND TABLE DOES NOT RETURN.	Manual control rod in hold position or stop not adjusted.	Check lever and adjust.
	Table raising too high.	Adjust second-table return trip.
	Latch not releasing or linkage is binding or rusty.	Polish surface and lubricate.
	Dampener valve not shifting.	Clean valve spool and adjust linkage.
	Control valve not shifting.	Clean and lubricate external portions of valve spool.
	Breather on cylinder plugged.	Clean or replace.
	Air leakage.	Replace air check or shaft seal.
	Table or cylinder pivots binding. Cylinder shaft bent.	Repair and lubricate.
	Bales wedging between second table and side boards.	Adjust side boards. Keep bale variation to recommendation.

Load Rack

PROBLEM	POSSIBLE CAUSE	POSSIBLE REMEDY
LOAD RACK WILL NOT RAISE OR RAISES SLOWLY.	Push-off feet are extended.	Retract the push-off feet.
	Low hydraulic pressure.	Check main-system pressure and the load-rack push-off auto tie valve-relief pressure.

PROBLEM	POSSIBLE CAUSE	POSSIBLE REMEDY
	The load rack is over-loaded.	Reduce the load.
	Control valve not shifting.	Adjust and lubricate manual control.
	Load rack cylinder seals leaking.	Internal leakage. Replace piston "O" ring and back-up washers and make sure piston is tight on shaft.
Push-off Feet PUSH-OFF FEET WILL NOT MOVE.	Control valve not shifting.	Adjust and lubricate manual control.
	Push-off cylinder seals leaking.	Internal leakage. Replace piston "O" ring and back-up washers and make sure piston is tight on shaft.
PUSH-OFF FEET CREEP OUT.	Valve spool not centered.	Adjust and lubricate the manual control. Clean and lubricate the external portions of the valve spool.
Automatic Tie RAIL BALES ROLL OFF SPIKE.	Poor bale weight, density and shape.	Check and adjust baler.
	Spikes set too far in for length of bales.	Adjust spikes.
RAIL BALES FALL FROM SECOND TABLE WHILE SECOND TABLE IS DELIVERING BALES.	Two-bale trip arm not adjusted properly. Spikes set too far out.	Adjust two-bale trip arm to center bales between the spikes. Adjust spikes so rail bales turn until they are parallel with the sides of the second table.
TWO-BALE TRIP ARM WILL NOT LOWER.	Engine speed too high.	Reduce engine speed while disengaging the auto tie.
	Piston cup swollen.	Replace piston cup.
Single-Bale Unloading SINGLE-BALE UNLOADING MECHANISM WILL NOT OPERATE.	Second-table manual control not in lock position.	Place manual control handle in lock position.
	Second-table manual control not adjusted correctly.	See operator's manual concerning adjustment of the second-table manual control.
BALES ROLL OVER ON SECOND TABLE WHEN SINGLE-BALE UNLOADING.	Bales are wet.	Allow bales to dry.
	Bales are sticking to the table.	Coat the table with teflon spray.
Brakes BRAKES DO NOT SELF-ADJUST.	Adjusting screw sticking.	Clean and free up, lubricate with thin coat of high-temperature grease.

MAINTENANCE

While detailed procedures vary with the model, basic maintenance of bale wagons is the same:

- **Bale-loader assembly maintenance**
- **First table maintenance**
- **Hydraulic system maintenance**

These components receive the most wear so require the most maintenance. Of course, all components should receive regular routine maintenance.

Maintain the engine and drive train for self-propelled wagons according to the operator's manual. This text does not cover engine and tractor maintenance. Refer to the operator's manual for them.

Bale Loader

The bale loader assembly operates near the ground. Abrasion by dust, dirt, and trash shortens the service life of the loader chain, sprockets, and drive system. Always maintain proper chain tension. Replace chain, sprockets, and chainloader teeth when you see excessive wear or breaks.

Because the bale loader absorbs the impact from each bale loaded, it must be checked regularly and carefully for loose bolts, bent metal, and broken welds. Any of these problems can lead to serious field breakdown if not repaired immediately.

First Table Conveyor

Keep the first table cross-chain conveyor tight. Adjust chain tension by moving the idler pulley. This chain moves every bale, so it must be checked frequently, and broken teeth and worn parts must be replaced to prevent field delays.

Controls

All controls must work correctly for maximum automatic bale wagon efficiency and productivity. As both manual and hydraulic controls are used frequently in field operation, wear occurs and the levers must be regularly adjusted to ensure proper seating and operation. For example, even a slight fault in a hydraulic valve spool can change operation drastically.

Hydraulic System

A well-maintained hydraulic system is essential, because most bale-wagon components are operated, at least in part, by hydraulic pressure. Always keep oil in the hydraulic reservoir at the proper level and keep the oil clean. Clean all check valves and breathers regularly to prevent malfunctions. Cleanliness is an important factor in maintaining a hydraulic system.

Replacement Parts

A good supply of replacement parts can reduce loss of time during breakdowns. Belts, chains, and chain teeth break now and then. So spare belts, chain links, and teeth should

be available in the field. For repairing the all important hydraulic system, keep spare couplers, hoses, and lines on hand. As the bale wagon ages, other hydraulic components may require replacement. Watch for wear, and buy replacements before parts break or wear out.

STORAGE

Proper off-season storage of the bale wagon helps prolong machine reliability and service life.

- If possible, store the bale wagon in a shelter; blocked up to remove the load from the tires. Do not deflate the tires. However, if the machine must be stored outside, remove the tires and store them in a cool, dark, dry place.

- Clean the bale wagon thoroughly. Dirt and trash draw moisture which increases rust formation. Touch up bare metal with paint, with some exceptions. The bale loader, first table, second table, and load rack all lose paint on the wear surfaces, but should not be repainted. These surfaces must remain slick for best operation. Cover them with light oil to prevent rusting.

- Lower the bale loader, first table, second table, and load rack to relieve the hydraulic pressure during storage. Inspect the hydraulic system, change oil (if required), and clean check valves and breathers.

- Release tension on all belts and clean belts with a nonflammable cleaning agent to remove dirt, grease and oil.

- Clean chains and brush them with heavy oil to prevent corrosion and rust.

- Grease threads on all belt adjustments.

- Lubricate the bale wagon.

- Prepare a list of repairs and buy or order replacement parts for installation during the off-season.

SUMMARY

Bale wagons help reduce the cost and labor of handling bales from the field to storage. These automatic bale wagons can pick up, haul, and store bales without manual labor. Bale wagons are available in either tractor-powered or self-propelled models.

The high productivity of automatic bale wagons helps maintain high hay quality because the bales are usually removed from the field before weather damage occurs. This high. quality can be preserved when the bales are properly stored. However, large structures with ample vertical clearance are required for the bale wagon to unload.

Excellent management is needed to harvest the highest-quality hay and operate a bale-wagon system at maximum efficiency. Proper matching of windrowers, rakes, balers, etc., timely and efficient field operations, and good planning are all essential.

Operator skill and baler operation also affect the efficiency of a bale-wagon system. The bale-wagon operator must be skilled to produce maximum output. However, even a skilled operator cannot achieve high productivity unless the bales are properly formed. Bales must have a near-uniform density and length to be handled effectively with a bale wagon.

CHAPTER QUIZ

1. List four advantages of bale wagons compared to hand-loading and hauling bales.

2. (Fill in blanks.) Bale wagons are powered by either a _____ or _____.

3. Describe the purpose of the bale-loader chain.

4. Explain why the bailing operation is critical for an automatic bale wagon.

5. (True or false.) Closely-spaced bales in the field are undesirable for an automatic bale wagon.

6. (Fill in blanks.) The first-table delay prevents the first table from lifting when the _____ _____ or _____ _____ is raised.

7. Explain the purpose of a tie tier.

8. (True or false.) A bale-wagon stack should be started at the top of a slope for best stability.

9. How do you keep bales from falling forward from the second table onto the first table in rough fields?

10. (True or false.) Never attempt to make adjustments or reach under the tables while they are loaded, even though the hydraulic system is disengaged.

8
Round Balers
and Movers

Fig. 1—Round Baler Producing Small Bales

SMALL AND LARGE ROUND BALES

Machines that produced "round bales" of hay were first marketed during the 1940s and '50s (Fig. 1). These round balers turned out cylindrical bales weighing 40 to 80 pounds (18 to 36 kg), that could be left in the field or picked up and stored. The concept of weather-resistant bales that could be stored outside appealed to hay growers, particularly those with cow-calf operations. This "all-weather storage" feature coupled with the search for ways to reduce labor brought about the most recent developments in round balers and movers. Now, round, or roll, balers (Fig. 2) produce large cylindrical bales weighing up to 1500 pounds (681 kg), that maintain hay quality well in outside storage and can be handled by machine.

SECTION 1:
ROUND BALERS

INTRODUCTION

For several years, hay growers have been confronted with a severe shortage of reliable farm labor. To cope with this problem, they are turning to hay equipment that requires less manpower from harvest to feeding. Round balers require only about one-third to one-half as much labor as the conventional baling system that requires hand hauling bales to storage. Since hand hauling is eliminated, a round-baling system makes one-man haying from harvest to feeding feasible on many livestock farms. Primarily because of labor savings, costs for harvesting, storing, and feeding large round bales are lower than the costs for conventional square bales.

A large round bale weighs 6 to 13 pounds (32 to 36 kg) per cubic foot. Most of them are about 70 to 80 percent as dense as the traditional 2-wire bale. Bale size varies depending on the model of baler. Most large round bales are 5 to 7 feet (1.5 to 2.1 m) in diameter and 4 to 7 feet (1.2 to 2.1 m) long. Such density, shape, and size make it impractical to store large round bales inside or transport them long distances. However, some hay growers do store large round bales in barns and hay sheds, and in some places they are transported considerable distances between the hayfield and feeding site.

Round bales may be formed from many different crops. High-quality hay, alfalfa, forage sorghums, and grasses will roll into weather-resistant bales. Crop residues, especially small-grain straws and corn stalks, may also be packaged with round balers.

Fig. 2—Round Baler that Produces Large Bales

All of these crops can be stored outside in round bales. The round shape resists water penetration and wind damage (Fig. 3). A few days after baling, round bales form a protective crust over the outside which sheds precipitation. Water follows plant stems around the surface of the bale to the ground instead of soaking in. This crust on well formed bales of good hay is seldom more than 3 to 6 inches (76 to 152 mm) thick and can be eaten by animals.

However, to reduce spoilage on the bottom and prevent damage to the crop stand, large round bales should be removed from the field for storage. The storage area should be well drained and be near the feeding place for convenience.

Storage losses from large round bales stored outside range from about 10 to 50 percent, depending on the type of hay, moisture content at baling, bale density, length of storage, and the amount of precipitation during storage. With good management, losses can be held to 10 or 15 percent, or about equal to the cost of storage facilities.

A major advantage of round bales is that baling may be continued in spite of bad weather. There is no need to rush completed bales into storage before they get wet.

Fig. 3—Round Bales Shed Water

REAR GATE

UPPER BELTS

Fig. 6—Belt-Type Bale Chamber

Fig. 4—Round Baler Rolling "Small" Bales

Round bales become more stable if allowed to settle in the field for a few days, or even a few weeks, before being moved to storage.

Some operators leave large round bales in the field where they were baled, and let animals eat the hay. This can result in excessive waste, as animals open a number of bales, eat some, and use the remainder for bedding. To avoid waste, don't give animals access to more bales than they will clean up in one or two days.

TYPES AND SIZES

Round balers are generally classified by the size of bale, "small" or "large," and the method of rolling the bale.

Fig. 5—Round Baler Producing 1,200-Pound Bale

One round baler (Fig. 4), makes "small" round bales 3 feet (1 m) long with a maximum diameter of 22 inches (559 mm). Weight usually ranges from 40 to 80 pounds (18 to 36 kg). The bales can be twine-wrapped for stability or made without twine if they are fed in the field where they were baled. Waste can be high if you leave untied bales in a field for feed, but labor is extremely low.

Most round balers produce "large" bales weighing 800 to 3,000 pounds (363 to 1362 kg) (Fig. 5). Baler design, type of material baled, and moisture content determine bale weight.

DIFFERENCES IN BALERS

Many features are available on large, round balers. Some balers have a mechanical drive from the tractor's PTO shaft. Others are hydraulically driven. The twine-wrapping mechanism is controlled hydraulically on some models, and manually on others. Some models have an optional twine-wrapping attachment. However, the most distinctive difference between models is the baling chamber.

BALE FORMATION

Most large, round balers carry the bale in a bale chamber as it is formed. Others simply roll the growing bale on the ground and lift the forming mechanism over the bale when the bale is finished.

Carried Bales

The most common kind of baling chamber has *lower and upper belts* (Fig. 6). The lower-platform belt moves inward to hold the bale as it is being formed.

Fig. 7—Bale Chamber with Steel Floor, Chains and Slats

Fig. 8—Ground-Rolling Baler with Chains and Slats

The upper belts also move inward and apply pressure to the bale. Pressure comes from tension applied to the belts with springs and hydraulic cylinders. Pressure is needed to form a tight bale. One model uses *rotating steel rollers* instead of a belt to carry the bale. Another model uses a *steel floor and revolving floor chains* to hold the bale, plus chains with steel slats to apply pressure to the bale during its formation (Fig. 7). With either a belt or chain assembly, the windrow is lifted from the ground and rolled in the bale chamber. The round-baling method is called *chamber rolling*.

Ground-Rolled Bales

The upper portion of ground-rolled bales is confined with *revolving chains and slats,* (Fig. 8), or with a *metal bale-forming grid and revolving belts* (Fig. 9). The chains and belts have pickup tines to clean up the windrow. Springs maintain tension on the upper chains and slats or grid. Tension is necessary to provide the proper bale density. With this type of bale chamber, the windrow is rolled up on the ground to form a bale. This method is referred to as *ground rolling*. Ground-rolled bales are normally less dense than chamber-rolled bales, depending upon hay type, moisture content, and baler adjustment.

ROUND-BALER OPERATION

The round baler packages cured windrows into firm, round bales. After the bale is formed, it may be wrapped with twine for stability. Compact, weather-resistant bales are then stored outside or in sheds until they are fed or ground into rations.

PRIMARY COMPONENTS

Primary parts of a chamber-rolling baler (Fig. 10):

- **Pickup**
- **Twine assembly**
- **Upper belts or chains and slats**
- **Lower platform (belt, chains, or rollers)**
- **Gate**

Fig. 9—Ground-Rolling Bale Chamber with Metal Forming Grid and Belts

151

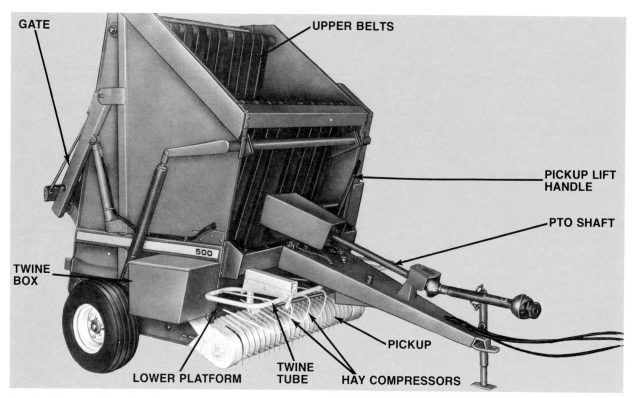

Fig. 10—Chamber-Rolling Baler Components

Fig. 11—Ground-Rolling Baler Components

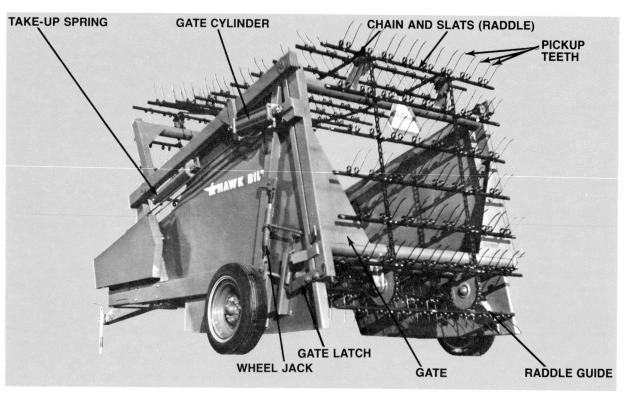

152

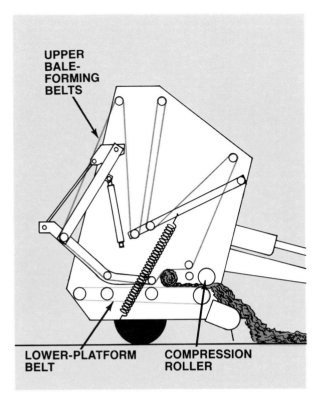

Fig. 12—Starting a Bale

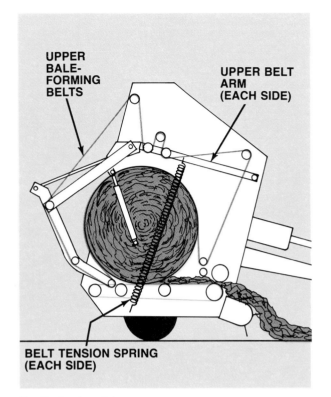

Fig. 13—Forming a Bale

Fig. 14—Completing a Bale

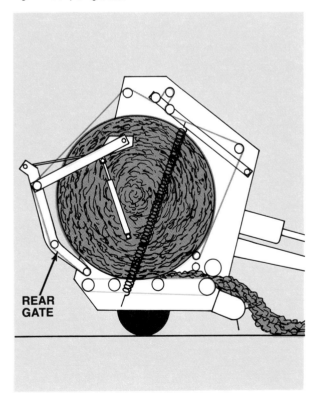

The primary parts of a ground-rolling baler (Fig. 11):

- **Twine assembly (optional)**
- **Chains and slats (raddle) or belts with pickup tines**
- **Gate**

Ground-rolling balers have fewer parts then chamber-rolling balers.

COMPONENT FUNCTIONS

Chamber-Rolling with Belts

The pickup lifts hay from the windrow and carries it between a steel *compression roller* and the lower belt (Fig. 12). This flattened hay then moves onto the full-width *lower-platform belt*. To aid in starting the bale, tension on the upper *bale-forming belts* is reduced.

As the bale is rolled, the *upper belt arms* extend the *tension springs* and tension increases in the *upper belts* to squeeze the bale (Fig. 13).

When the belt springs have completely extended, the hydraulic cylinder on the *rear gate* puts tension on the belts. As the bale diameter continues to grow, a pressure-relief value on the gate cylinder opens and triggers the gate bottom to move to the rear until the maximum bale diameter is reached (Fig. 14).

153

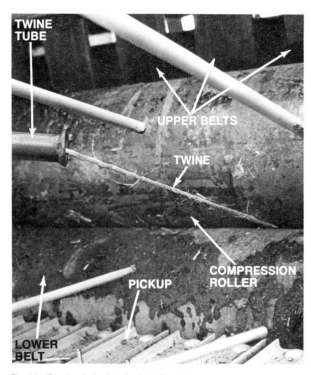

Fig. 15—Feeding Twine into the Bale Chamber

When the bale has reached the full diameter, twine is fed into the bale chamber with the hay (Fig. 15). Immediately after twine reaches the compression rollers, forward travel is stopped. The bale is then twine-wrapped by manual or hydraulic control of the movable *twine tube*. After wrapping, the twine is cut off (Fig. 16).

Finally, the hydraulically-controlled gate is raised and the bale (Fig. 17) is discharged. On some balers, the upper belts are automatically stopped when the rear gate opens to unload a bale.

Fig. 16—Automatic Twine Cutter

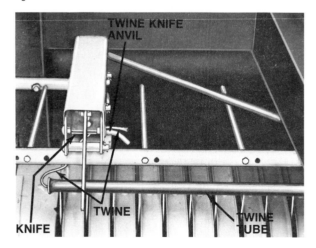

Fig. 17—Discharging a Bale

Chamber-Rolling with Chains and Slats

Baling procedure is similar to balers with chamber belts, except for three differences:

1. The windrow is not flattened between compression rollers before entering the bale chamber.

2. Tension on the upper chains and slats is maintained by springs. The rear gate does not move as the bale diameter increases.

3. A *retractable cam idler* prevents the chains and slats from compacting the hay while the core is forming (Fig. 18).

Ground-Rolling with Chain and Slats

Revolving chains and slats *(power raddle)* with pickup tines begin lifting and rolling up the windrow at the rear of the baling chamber (Fig. 19). In the starting position, the chains and slats ride on cams to keep pressure off the bale while the core is forming (Fig. 20). The chains move approximately 25 percent faster than ground speed to keep the bale in the bale chamber. As the bale diameter increases, a spring-loaded *takeup arm* keeps tension on the chains (Fig. 21).

154

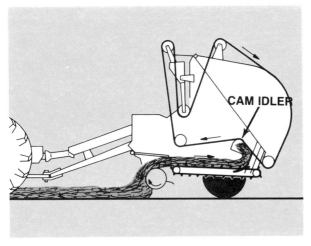

Fig. 18—Cam Idler Keeps Chain and Slats From Compacting Bale Core

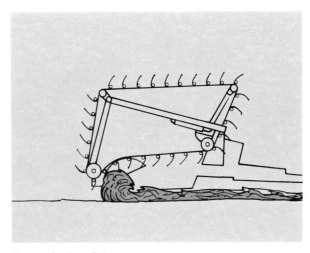

Fig. 19—Starting a Bale

A *twine-wrapping attachment* is optional, and twine on these bales is not tied. As the bale nears full diameter, up to four strands of twine are dropped on the ground and wrapped around the bale as the last hay is added. The baler is then pulled off the windrow, twine completely circles the bale, and the twine is cut. The ends of the twine are left under the bale, untied.

After the bale is formed and tied, the gate is raised and the tractor moves the baler away from the bale (Fig. 22). If the bale was tied, the operator may then circle back to the same windrow, or save time by crossing to the next windrow and starting a new bale (Fig. 23).

Fig. 20—A Cam Keeps Tension off the Bale During Core Formation

Fig. 21—Takeup Arm Retracts as Bale Diameter Increases

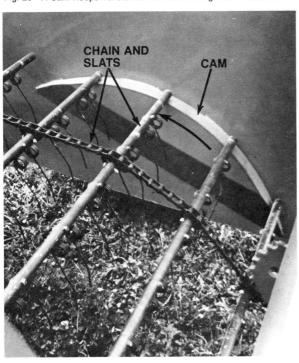

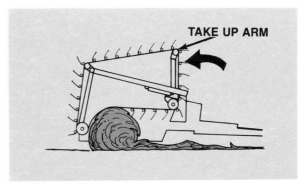

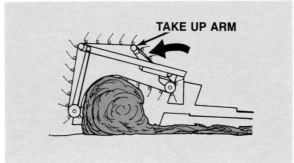

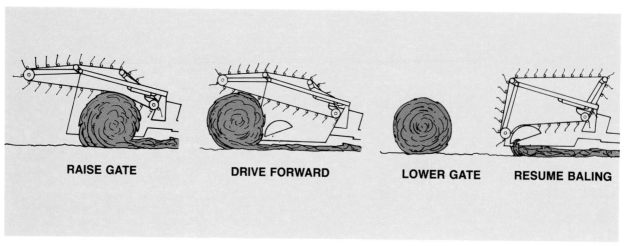

RAISE GATE DRIVE FORWARD LOWER GATE RESUME BALING

Fig. 22—Releasing Bale from Bale Chamber

Fig. 23—Baling Pattern When Twine Bales are Tied

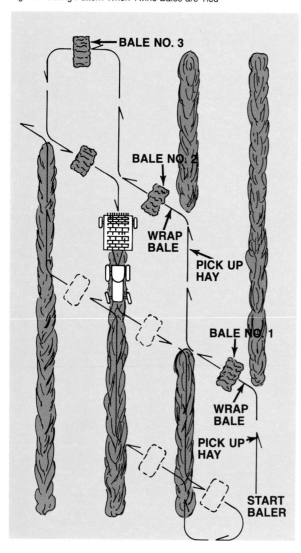

BALE NO. 3

BALE NO. 2

WRAP
BALE

PICK UP
HAY

BALE NO. 1

WRAP
BALE

PICK UP
HAY

START
BALER

Ground-Rolling with Grid and Belts

The baling procedure with this model is similar to ground-rolling with chain and slats, except for three differences:

1. A *metal grid* keeps pressure off the bale while the core is forming.

2. The metal forming grid later applies pressure to the top of the bale by extending springs.

3. Only one strand of twine is lowered into the windrow and is wound across the width of the bale.

The rest of this chapter will concentrate on chamber-rolling balers with belts. Similar operation, transport, safety, and maintenance principles apply to all models. For specific details on a particular model, refer to the operator's manual.

OPERATION AND ADJUSTMENT

Most problems are the result of inexperience. With experience, an operator can produce excellent bales.

EXPERIENCE CUTS LOSSES

An inexperienced operator often produces poorly-formed bales (Fig. 24). Two common problems are insufficient or unevenly-distributed twine on bales, and improper baler adjustment. These conditions lead to problems because bales will not store properly and can't be fed efficiently. Poorly-shaped, low-density bales absorb moisture and spoil during storage. Inexperienced operators may not realize that the bales are poorly constructed.

Harvesting hay during early stages of maturity is very important. Early-cut hay makes bales that have lower storage losses than late-cut hay.

Fig. 24—Cone Shaped Bale

GOOD MANAGEMENT IS ESSENTIAL

- **Review the operator's manual carefully.**
- **Attend training sessions.**
- **Talk with the baler dealer.**
- **Visit with experienced operators.**
- **Study the results *and* mistakes of others.**
- **Learn the correct operating techniques for the round baler being used.**

Managers can overlook problems with new equipment. A manager cannot gain the full advantages of the lower labor requirement and reduced operating cost if hay is baled without proper curing or is stored improperly.

Even with low labor and reduced-cost hay systems, the quality of hay at feeding time can never be higher than the quality of hay baled. The highest-quality hay is possible only with timely field operations. The entire haying enterprise must be carefully planned and equipment must be matched.

WATCH MOISTURE CONTENT

Because most round bales are stored outside or in open-front sheds, some managers believe the hay can be baled considerably wetter than with conventional balers. A tight, round bale will weather well, but it will not continue to dry rapidly after baling. If the hay is too wet when it's baled, heating and spoiling will occur.

Partial Exception. Operators of some ground-rolling balers have found that the less dense bales made by ground rolling machines will dry some after baling. People can bale at slightly higher moisture levels with ground rolling balers than with conventional baling. But, until the operator is thoroughly experienced with round-baler operation it is best to bale hay when the moisture content has dropped to 20 to 25 percent.

If the moisture content of hay is too low, leaf shatter and field losses will be high. In addition, dry hay will not compact to form a good form bale. Sometimes, dry, round bales "explode" after they are ejected from the baler if the twine is loose.

The proper moisture content of hay for round baling depends on type of hay, weather conditions, and the storage method. Bales will dry more in the field exposed to sun and wind than in a shed. Experience is the best guide for determining the proper moisture content. But as a rule of thumb *bale at a moisture content acceptable for conventional baling.*

If hay wraps around the belt rolls, moisture content is too high. When hay moisture content is too high, the potential for spoilage increases, and belts and rollers can be damaged.

PROPER STORAGE PAYS OFF

To have high quality hay at feeding time round bales must be stored properly. The concept of "all-weather bales" may lead the farm manager to think he doesn't have to be concerned with storage conditions. However, without proper drainage, bales soak up water from the bottom and spoil. Round bales should be picked up and moved to a slightly sloping, well-drained stackyard. Store the bales on a bed of gravel to reduce surface-moisture accumulation. Gravel also makes it easier to move the bales to the feeding area during inclement weather.

To further reduce spoilage losses, leave at least one foot between bales in the stackyard (Fig. 25). Space allows free drainage and air circulation. Do not store bales outside on end. Water will soak down through them. Do not stack bales outside. Moisture will be trapped between the bales. Wherever moisture is trapped spoilage occurs.

Fig. 25—Stackyard for Round Bales

If bales are stored in a barn or shed they are often stacked on end to use space better. How bales are stacked inside depends on the equipment and the height at the entrance and roof. Stacking on end reduces the strain on building sidewalls.

Put the stackyard near your feeding place. This reduces travel and transport time for feeding. Remember, most hay is fed in winter, during inclement weather.

Fig. 26—Well Formed Windrow

Fig. 27—Barrel Shaped Bale

PLANNING AND PREPARATION

One of the keys to success for round bales is proper selection of auxiliary equipment such as:

- **Mower-conditioner or windrower**

- **Rake**

- Bale mover

- Tractor

CONDITIONING AND WINDROWING

A *mower-conditioner* or *windrower* cuts, conditions, and puts hay in a windrow for baling (Fig. 26). Hay should be uniformly distributed across the windrow. Conditioned hay dries rapidly and evenly, and reduces the time between windrowing and baling. Conditioning also improves the baling characteristics of hay, particularly coarse-stemmed forage sorghums.

A uniform distribution of hay across the width of the windrow eases the task of forming a good round bale. The recommended windrow width is just under bale length. If the width is too narrow, barrel-shaped bales are formed (Fig. 27). If the windrow is too wide, outer edges of the windrow will not feed into the bale chamber.

RAKING

Raking is not usually required for round baling if the windrow dries evenly and is the proper width. However, if the hay is heavy, raking may be required to turn the hay for faster drying. Rake windrows if rain wets the hay between cutting and baling. Combine sparce windrows into one good, dense batch.

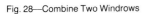

Fig. 28—Combine Two Windrows

WITH TWINE

WITHOUT TWINE

Fig. 29—Bales with and Without Twine after long Storage

BALE MOVERS

Match the *bale mover* to the needs of the specific haying enterprise. Use multi-bale movers if road transportation exceeds 5 miles. Single-bale movers are less expensive and suit the needs of many small hay producers.

TRACTOR PREPARATION

Match the tractor to the round baler and mover. The tractor must have adequate power and hydraulics. Some round balers require dual remote hydraulic valves. One large round baler is driven by a hydraulic motor which is powered by a PTO-driven hydraulic pump. Don't forget moving the bales when matching the tractor and baler. More power and stability are needed to move bales than to power the baler. A 50-to-60-horsepower (37.3 to 45 kw) tractor should do for a round-baling system. Ground-rolling balers require only 35 to 45 horsepower (26 to 34 kw) because the bale weight is not carried on the baler.

Before starting to bale, inspect and service both the tractor and baler. Review the tractor and baler operator's manuals, and before attaching the round baler:

1. Make sure the tractor PTO speed matches the speed required by the baler, usually 540 rpm.

2. Position the drawbar for PTO operation as recommended.

3. Lock the drawbar parallel with the centerline of the PTO shaft.

4. Set out the front and rear wheels to avoid driving on windrows.

5. Check the tractor hydraulic system and add oil, if necessary.

6. Raise the draft links or remove 3-point hitch components if necessary.

ATTACHING THE BALER

After preparing the tractor, attach the round baler. The proper sequence is:

1. Raise or lower the baler hitch jack to engage the tractor drawbar.

2. Back the tractor to align holes. Shut off the tractor and take the key. Insert the safety hitch pin. If someone is helping you, don't let them between tractor and baler while you are backing or even while in reverse gear.

3. Attach the baler powershaft to the PTO outlet.

4. Install hydraulic hoses in tractor breakaway couplers.

5. Attach ropes to the tractor for the manually-controlled twine assembly, if necessary.

6. Replace all shields removed during hookup.

7. Lower the hitch jack and place it in the transport position.

To detach the baler, reverse the attaching procedure.

FINAL INSPECTION

After the baler is attached to the tractor, perform the following daily inspection and maintenance routine:

1. Shut off the tractor and disengage all drives.

2. Lubricate as recommended in the operator's manual.

3. Inspect and adjust drive chains for proper tension.

4. Check and tighten loose bolts and connections to recommended torque.

5. Check tire pressure. Inflate, if necessary.

6. Remove dirt, weeds, vines, and other foreign material from chains, rollers, and near bearings and other moving components.

7. Inspect and service the tractor as recommended in the operator's manual.

8. Check the complete hydraulic system as outlined below.

160

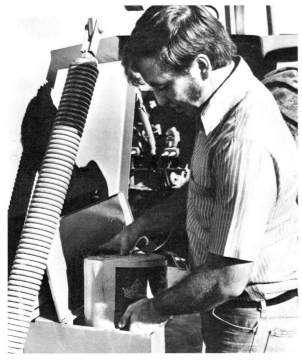

Fig. 30—Fill the Twine Box

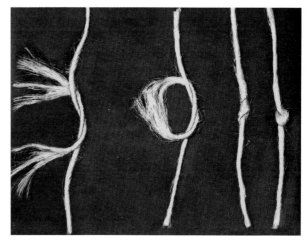

Fig. 31—Tye Sisal Twine Together

9. Operate the baler for several minutes. Check the tracking alignment on upper belts.

10. Stop baler operation. Shut off the tractor and check adjustments.

CHECKING HYDRAULIC SYSTEM

After attaching the baler, recheck hydraulic connections and inspect all hoses for damage before engaging the hydraulic system. Then operate the gate and other hydraulic components several times. If the levers function in reverse, exchange the hose connections in the tractor breakaway couplers. Move the tractor remote-control levers to the operating position through one full cycle to purge the hydraulic system of air.

On most round balers, the hydraulic system is essential to make dense bales. If the hydraulic system is not operating properly, check the fluid level and add oil, if necessary. Inspect hoses and cylinders for leaks. But be careful! Never use your hands to search for oil leaks. Oil escaping under high pressure penetrates skin and causes serious injury. If you suspect leaks, but can't see them, use a piece of cardboard to find the leak. If you find a leak release the hydraulic pressure, and replace the leaking item.

PREPARE TWINE SYSTEM

Before operating, load and thread the twine system. Analyze the storage and handling system. Twine-wrapped bales retain a more rounded shape during storage. But unwrapped bales tend to flatten and settle more on the bottom side (Fig. 29). Twine helps reduce forage loss if bales are exposed to high winds. Also, twine-wrapped bales are more durable during transport.

Selecting the proper twine is important. Both sisal and plastic twine work in round balers. Sisal twine is less expensive but will deteriorate during storage, particularly on the bale bottom. Plastic twine does not deteriorate, but it is indigestible, so it must be removed from bales before feeding.

Remove the twine as bales are fed to prevent later problems of twine wrapping on manure spreaders.

If you expect to store the bales a long time and handle them several times, use plastic twine. Always choose twine that's strong enough to restrain the bale.

Loading Twine

Here's how you load and thread twine:

1. Fill the twine box with good-quality twine (Fig. 30).

2. Use the ball nearest the twine tube to thread the twine-wrapping assembly.

3. Splice the balls of twine together. Tie a modified square knot in sisal twine and trim the loose ends (Fig. 31). Tie a sheet bend knot in plastic twine and trim the ends (Fig. 32). The knots must be small enough to pass through the guides.

4. When you add a new ball, move the partly-used ball to the compartment nearest the twine tube and splice the twine ends.

161

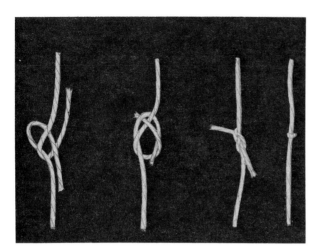

Fig. 32—Tye Plastic Twine Together

Threading the Baler

Round balers have no needles or knotters, so threading and twine-wrapping are much simpler than on conventional balers. See the threading procedure in the operator manual for the baler.

Use a wire to pull twine through the twine tubes (Fig. 33), and be certain the twine passes through each twine guide in the proper sequence and direction. (Keep a piece of wire

Fig. 33—Pull Twine Through Twine Tubes with a Wire

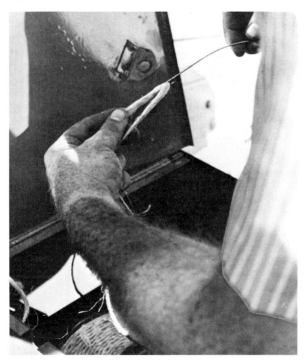

in the tractor toolbox in case the baler must be rethreaded in the field.) After threading is completed, secure the end of the twine in the knife or cut-off assembly as instructed in the operator's manual.

PRELIMINARY SETTINGS AND ADJUSTMENTS

Round balers are built to handle a wide range of crops and conditions. Because field conditions vary, be familiar with the baler adjustments and their effect on baler performance. But familiarity with the machine is not enough. Adjustments must be made as conditions change to maintain proper performance.

A properly-adjusted baler has higher field productivity and fewer breakdowns than a poorly-adjusted baler. Make preliminary adjustments to match the expected conditions. Then make further adjustments during operation in actual field conditions.

PICKUP ADJUSTMENTS

Set pickup teeth as high as possible to reduce the chance for damage yet low enough to ensure complete windrow cleanup.

The pickup float spring functions as a shock absorber and provides a floating effect when the baler works on rough, hilly ground. Change the spring tension to adjust flotation.

A separate pickup is not required on ground-rolling balers. Inspect the belts or raddle regularly, and replace damaged, broken, or missing pickup teeth.

COMPRESSION ROLLER

Adjust the clearance of the compression roller so hay will feed properly onto the lower platform. On some balers, the compression roll is seated firmly near the front of the lower belt. Compression-roll springs provide force needed to flatten hay as it passes under the compression roller.

Fig. 34—Slip-Clutch Adjustment

CLUTCH SPRINGS

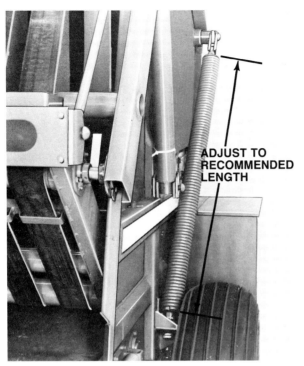

ADJUST TO RECOMMENDED LENGTH

Fig. 35—Adjust Upper Belt Tension Spring

REAR ROLLER SHAFT

Fig. 36—Adjust Lower Belt Tension Spring

SLIP CLUTCH

The slip clutch prevents damage if the baler power train is overloaded. A properly-adjusted slip clutch lets power go from the tractor to the baler under normal operating conditions. To adjust a slip clutch, loosen or tighten the compression springs (Fig. 34). Over-tightening the slip-clutch eliminates the protection it gives the drive train.

If the springs aren't compressed the clutch slips too much.

UPPER-BELT DRIVE

The upper-belt drive on some balers has a clutch which is disengaged when the gate is raised to eject a bale. Adjust this clutch so the clutch is reengaged when the gate is down.

TENSION SPRINGS

Tension springs on the upper belts compress the bale during the rolling process (Fig. 35). If the springs are not properly adjusted, the bale will not have the correct density.

The lower belt has tension springs to keep the belt from slipping. After adjusting these springs, measure the distance from the rear belt roller to the preceding lower-belt roller, on each side of the baler (Fig. 36). If these two measurements differ more than 1/4 inch (6.3 mm), readjust the springs. The lower belt will be damaged due to improper tracking if the rear lower-belt roller is not parallel to the other rollers.

SCRAPERS

To keep hay from wrapping up on the lower drive roll and upper belt shaft, set the scrapers so they just clear the drive roll and shaft (Fig. 37).

TWINE ASSEMBLY

Several adjustments may be needed on the twine assembly, depending on baler model. The operator's manual for each model describes the details for adjustments. Follow the directions given for your baler. Adjustments are commonly required on:

- **Twine**
- **Tension**
- **Automatic twine cutter**
- **Hydraulically or manually controlled twine tube.**

Fig. 37—Properly Adjusted Drive Roll Scrapers

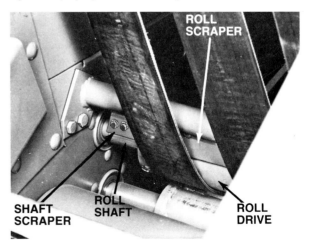

ROLL SCRAPER

SHAFT SCRAPER

ROLL SHAFT

ROLL DRIVE

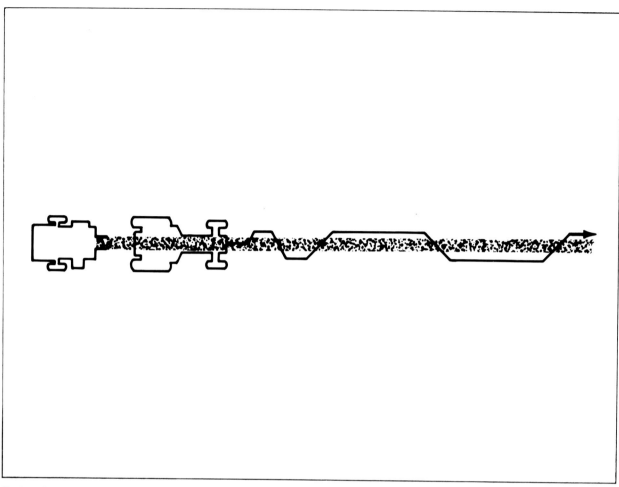

Fig. 38 — Recommended Driving Pattern

Most round balers do not have a twine tension control. However, on balers with this feature the twine tension control adjusts the tightness of the twine-wrap on the bale. Enough tension is applied to make a tight wrap without breaking the twine.

An automatic twine cutter speeds wrapping. When the wrapping is finished the twine is cut before the bale stops rolling in the bale chamber. Adjust the components that hold and cut the twine as recommended in the operator's manual.

The hydraulically-controlled twine tube on some balers controls the number of twine wraps per bale. The faster the twine tube moves, the fewer the wraps of twine around each bale. To control the twine-tube speed, adjust the hydraulic flow control valve on the twine-control cylinder.

FIELD OPERATION

Operating controls for a round baler are the tractor PTO clutch, remote hydraulic cylinder levers, and, on some models, manual control for the twine system. These controls are operated from the tractor platform. A proficient operator knows the exact location and use of all baler and tractor controls.

Baling can start when the windrows are properly cured. For cleaner pickup, run the baler in the same direction the windrower or rake traveled. This helps the pickup teeth reach under the windrow and pick up hay "head-first."

Before engaging the PTO clutch, lower the pickup.

Fig. 39—Bale Size Indicator

STARTING THE BALE

Starting a bale is extremely important. Make the core carefully. To start the bale, set the tractor at $3/4$ throttle and start feeding hay into the middle of the pickup. As the core begins to form, weave across the windrow to get an even core (Fig. 38). After the bale is about 2 feet (609 mm) in diameter do not weave as often. Crossing the windrow too often makes a "barrel shaped" bale. Always drive to the extreme sides and cross over as quickly as possible so the ends of the bale will be flat.

If the windrow is equal to the width of the bale chamber, weaving on the windrow is not required to start or form a well shaped bale. Instead, drive straight down the windrow to bale the windrow.

When the bale reaches full diameter, a bale size indicator warns the operator not to add any more hay (Fig. 39). Hay must stop entering the bale chamber as soon as twine has been fed into the compression rolls.

CAUTION: *Over filling the bale chamber can damage the baler.*

WRAPPING WITH TWINE

When the bale reaches full diameter, it is ready to wrap. Most balers can wrap a bale with twine any time after the diameter is 2 to 2$1/2$ feet (609 to 762 mm) or larger. Twine wrapping procedure:

When ready to wrap a bale:

1. Continue feeding hay into the center of the bale chamber.

2. Move the twine tube over the windrow and allow twine to feed into the compression rolls.

3. Stop forward travel.

4. Move the twine tube to the side of the bale opposite the knife; hold a few seconds to allow one full turn of twine to go around the end of the bale.

Fig. 40—Well Spaced Twine Wraps on Bale

5. Move the twine tube slowly back across the bale chamber. Depending on the crop and expected handling conditions, some manufacturers recommend spacing the twine wraps 6 to 10 inches (152 to 254 mm) apart (Fig. 40).

6. After the twine tube reaches the opposite end of the bale, the twine is cut off automatically. Or the PTO is disengaged, the tractor engine throttled to idle speed, and you cut off the twine.

7. Disengage the PTO and throttle the engine to idle, if twine was cut automatically.

UNLOADING

After the bale is twine-wrapped, discharge it from the bale chamber. Here is a typical unloading procedure:

1. Back the tractor and baler about 8 to 10 feet (2.4 to 3 m) from the last hay in the windrow.

2. Raise the gate (Fig. 41).

3. Engage the power takeoff with the engine at idle speed, and the bale will fall to the ground (Fig. 42).

CAUTION: Don't let people stand near the rear of the baler when a bale is being discharged. Unload the bale on level ground so it can't roll. A large, heavy bale can seriously injure or kill someone if it rolls over them.

4. Move the tractor and baler forward about 8 feet (2.4 m) so the gate won't hit the bale as it closes.

5. Lower the rear gate (Fig. 43) and start baling again.

Fig. 41—Raise the Gate To Discharge

Fig. 42—Drop the Bale on the Ground

FIELD ADJUSTMENTS

Some preliminary adjustments, particularly to the pickup and twine-wrapping assembly, may need changing to match field conditions.

Match ground speed to field and crop conditions. When windrows are properly formed and sized, operating speed may average 4 to 6 miles per hour (6.4 to 9.6 km/h). If windrows are light, you can go faster. More speed will prevent excessive bale rolling in the bale chamber. Operate the engine at full throttle so the pickup can get everything in the windrow.

Excess bale rolling in the bale chamber increases leaf loss. Less agitation and rolling makes a well shaped bale, less hay wrappage, and longer bale storage life. The amount of rolling depends on the windrow. With uniform proper sized windrows, the PTO speed can be reduced and you can drive the tractor faster. Under these conditions, operate the tractor at about ³/₄ throttle. In the ³/₄ throttle range, the PTO-driven pickup gathers the windrow into the baler without agitating the crop.

TRANSPORT

For safe transporting:

● Raise the pickup to clear humps and obstacles.

● Lower the gate to reduce the chance of damage. An SMV emblem is mounted on the gate, and is not visible to approaching motorists when the gate is raised (Fig. 44).

● Do not make sharp turns. With tractor wheels set out wide to straddle windrows, rear tires could strike the baler tongue in a sharp turn.

● Do not exceed safe tractor speed for the terrain.

Most manufacturers recommend limiting towing speed to 10 miles per hour (16 km/h) if a bale is in the bale chamber to prevent baler damage.

● Use a lower gear on steep downgrades.

● Be sure the brakes are safe and dependable. They must stop both tractor and baler.

● Don't let people ride on the baler.

● When transporting the round baler use a clearly visible SMV emblem and turn on the blinking warning lights.

Fig. 43—Rear Gate is Lowered Hydraulically

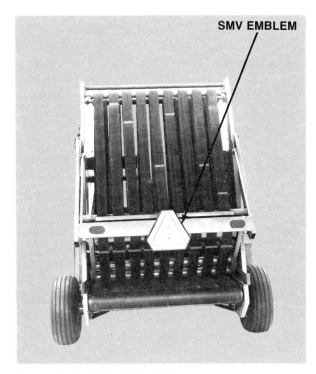

Fig. 44—Use Slow Moving Vehicle Emblem

Fig. 45 — THINK SAFETY AT ALL TIMES

SAFETY

• You can't see around a big baler. Be especially watchful when backing the baler.

• Be sure no one is near the rear gate when it is raised or lowered. Keep everyone clear of the rear of the baler during unloading. Large round bales can roll after discharge.

• Before servicing, cleaning, or adjusting a round baler (Fig. 45) disengage the tractor PTO, shut off the engine, and take the key. The moving belts and chains forming the bale chamber can catch a man and pull him in. *Never pull hay or twine from an operating baler!*

• Always shift the tractor transmission into park and lock the brakes, or block the baler wheels before working on the baler.

• Block up the gate before working under it. Some models have a safety lock pin for the baler gate (Fig. 46), or safety stops for the gate lift cylinders.

• During operation, stay seated on the tractor seat so you won't fall off into the path of the baler. Never allow passengers on the baler or tractor.

• Be extremely cautious when operating a baler on hilly ground. Balers can tip sideways. Balers can drop a downhill wheel in a hole and tip over in a split second.

LOCKING PIN

Fig. 46—Lock Gate up with Pin

TROUBLESHOOTING

Most round baler problems are traced to improper adjustment or lack of service. This chart will help you overcome problems. Apply the suggested remedies with judgment and caution. An incorrect "remedy" could cause a severe malfunction. Have a thorough understanding of the round baler so you can correct operating problems.

Although this troubleshooting chart is primarily for a baler with chamber-rolling belts, in many cases it also applies to other balers.

TROUBLESHOOTING CHART		
PROBLEM	**POSSIBLE CAUSE**	**POSSIBLE REMEDY**
HAY WRAPS AROUND ROLLERS.	Windrows light or short hay.	Make windrows larger and reduce tractor engine speed.
	Moisture content too high, or wet "slugs" in bottom of windrows.	Allow hay to dry more. Turning the windrows may help.
	Scraper not adjusted properly on bottom drive roller.	Adjust scraper.
TOP BELTS NOT TURNING.	Anti-slip tape worn off top drive roll.	Replace anti-slip tape.
	Belt tension is too low.	Adjust belt tension.
TOP BELTS NOT TRACKING PROPERLY.	Belts have changed length.	Remove and repair belts to within 2 inches of each other in length.
	Top rollers were bent by foreign objects, or bale is made too large.	Remove rollers and straighten or replace.
		Keep rollers clean and make smaller-diameter bales.
	Belt not cut squarely.	Check splices.
BROKEN TOP BELT.	Wet material causes hay to build up on rollers.	Allow hay to dry more. Turning windrows may help.
	Not "weaving" properly when starting to bale, causing the end belts to go under the bale.	Weave back and forth rapidly to start bale.
	Belt splice is worn.	Repair belt.
BOTTOM BELT NOT TURNING.	Anti-slip tape worn on drive roll.	Replace anti-slip tape.
	Insufficient belt tension.	Adjust lower belt-tension springs.

PROBLEM	POSSIBLE CAUSE	POSSIBLE REMEDY
	Belt rubbing at edges.	Adjust lower belt-tension springs.
	Rear belt roller not free to slide in guides.	Clean or repair guides.
	Crop residue between rollers and belt.	Clean out foreign material.
DRIVE SLIP CLUTCH SLIPS DURING NORMAL OPERATION.	Slip clutch bolts loose.	Adjust slip clutch bolts.
	Other baler parts malfunctioning, causing overload.	Locate problem and correct.
HAY PASSES THROUGH BALER.	Gate is not all the way down, or is not adjusted properly.	Adjust gate
	Cylinder relief pressure is too low.	Adjust or replace pressure relief valve.
	Top or bottom belts not turning.	Replace worn anti-slip tape or increase belt tension.
PICKUP NOT RUNNING.	Pickup belt broken.	Replace belt.
	Pickup belt loose.	Increase belt tension.
	Cam followers worn or damaged, causing belt to slip.	Replace damaged and severely-worn parts.
	Windrows too large to feed into baler.	Reduce ground speed; prepare lighter windrows.
	Pickup set too close to the ground.	Adjust pickup.
HAY WILL NOT ENTER BALE CHAMBER.	Belts slipping.	Adjust belt tension.
	Compression rolls are out of adjustment.	Adjust compression-roll clearance.
	Hay too wet.	Allow hay to dry.
	Heavy windrows.	Remove the compressor rods over the pickup.
BALE WILL NOT START.	Tailgate not closed.	Close gate; adjust if necessary.
	Belts loose.	Adjust belt tension.
	Feeding hay butt first.	Pick up windrow in same direction as mower-conditioner or windrower and rake traveled.
BALE DOES NOT TURN IN BALE CHAMBER.	Bale chamber over-filled.	Make smaller-diameter bales.
	Upper belts loose.	Adjust tension on belts.
	Drive rollers not operating.	Check drive chain, sprockets, and rollers.
	Idler rollers jammed.	Free rollers and replace bearings if necessary.

PROBLEM	POSSIBLE CAUSE	POSSIBLE REMEDY
BALE WILL NOT EJECT.	Bale too large.	Make smaller-diameter bales.
	Lower belt slipping.	Adjust lower-belt tension.
	Slip clutch slipping.	Check for other power-drive malfunctions; if none, then adjust slip clutch.
"BARREL"-SHAPED BALE.	Windrow too narrow, or too wide.	Prepare windrow properly.
	Weaving too often and baling more hay in center of bale.	Reduce weaving after starting bale core.
"CONE"-SHAPED BALE.	Not baling enough hay on small end of cone.	Weave on windrow for even distribution.
	Compression-roll spring broken on one end.	Replace compression-roll spring.
ENDS OF BALE NOT SQUARE.	Not crowding hay into sides of pickup when baling.	Drive to extreme edge of windrow.
BALE DENSITY TOO LOW.	Malfunction of cylinder relief valve.	Adjust or replace pressure-relief valve.
	Compression-roll springs broken.	Replace compression-roll springs.
	Hay is too dry.	Begin baling sooner, or wait until hay becomes tougher with dew in the evening.
TWINE NOT GOING AROUND BALE.	Twine not threaded properly.	Check baler for proper threading.
	No hay to pick up twine.	Move forward in windrow until the twine catches.
	Twine not being fed in with hay.	Continue feeding hay until twine goes between compression rolls; or pull more twine from twine tube.
	Buildup of hay residue on top compression roll.	Roll scraper not cleaning properly; adjust scraper.
NOT ENOUGH TWINE ON BALE.	Twine tube moves too rapidly.	Manual—Allow more wrapping time.
		Hydraulic—Adjust flow-control valve.
	Oil-filter screen (for hydraulic twine control) plugged.	Clean or replace oil filter.
TWINE CUTTER NOT CUTTING.	Automatic twine cutter out of adjustment.	Adjust twine cutter; sharpen knife.
	Manual twine cutter does not work freely.	Clean twine cutter.

MAINTENANCE

A properly serviced, well maintained round baler will operate efficiently and reliably. Careful maintenance of the belts that form the bale chamber is very important. On round balers with chains and slats forming the bale chamber, give special attention to the chains, slats, and drive assembly. The pickup and hydraulic systems also require regular maintenance, and there are many small components that require routine service.

CHAIN AND SLATS

Keep chains and gears in good condition. If you find excessive wear, determine the cause and correct it to prevent breakdowns.

Inspect the baler drive system often to avoid losing valuable time in the field.

PICKUP TEETH

Because the pickup operates near the ground, abrasion by dust, dirt, and other foreign material can often shorten its service life. Pickup teeth break or bend. Watch for and either repair or replace damaged teeth as quickly as possible.

Hydraulic System

A well maintained hydraulic system is essential to forming high density , properly shaped round bales. Hydraulic pressure is required on most round balers to control the gate for both bale density and discharge.

Hydraulic system maintenance on round balers is worthwhile only if the tractor hydraulic system is also properly maintained. Many hydraulic system failures are caused by lack of oil in the hydraulic reservoir. But correct maintenance of a tractor hydraulic system involves much more than merely adding oil. Refer to the tractor operator's manual and to the FMO Manuals *Tractors,* and *Hydraulics* for details.

Hydraulic-system maintenance for the round baler is mainly repairing or replacing leaky hoses and connections. The pressure relief bypass valve must also function properly. Maintain and repair hydraulic cylinders to prevent oil leaking out the cylinder rams. Remember this: On all hydraulic components, the most important maintenance factor is cleanliness (Fig. 47). Dirt and other foreign material causes most hydraulic system malfunctions.

KEEP REPLACEMENT PARTS ON HAND

To reduce lost time during breakdowns, keep essential replacement parts handy. A belt lacing kit, replacement belt hooks, and a supply of belting are must items for round balers with belts for the bale chamber. With a chain and slat chamber, spare chain links are required. Extra slats are needed to replace worn slats and for adverse baling condi-tions that break slats. Other parts that should be available in the field are spare chain links and belts for the power train and replacement fingers for the pickup. Repair parts for the hydraulic system become more essential as the round baler gets older.

BELTS

Most round baler belts are constructed of high tensile, low stretch, synthetic fabric with a rubber bonding and covering material. The belts are weatherproof, but proper maintenance will prolong their service life considerably. Proper care requires that the belts be:

1. Kept clean

2. Protected from cuts and bruises

3. Not kept under tension during inactive periods of one month or more

4. Stored on the baler in a clean, dry shelter during the off-season

5. Kept properly adjusted during operation

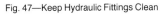
Fig. 47—Keep Hydraulic Fittings Clean

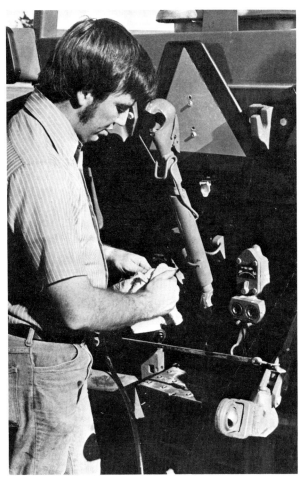

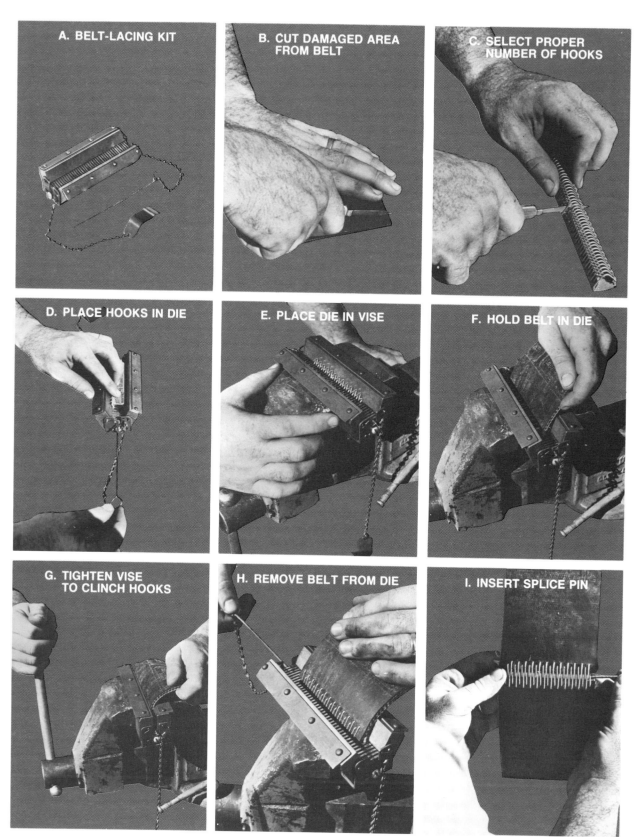

Fig. 48—Belt-Splicing Procedure

Belts may fray or warp, making it appear that repair is needed. If so, trim the frayed edges during daily service inspection. Trimming reduces the chances of the frayed ends being caught as bales are formed and possibly causing additional fraying or serious belt damage.

Belts may break or tear, particularly under adverse operating conditions. Sharp metal objects, glass, and other foreign material conveyed into the bale chamber can cut or damage belts. Maintenance problems can be reduced by keeping hayfields clean and by careful baler operation.

Splicing Belts

Broken belts can be repaired by splicing them with a belt-lacing kit (Fig. 48-A), replacement belts, hooks, and a vise. A general procedure follows:

1. Remove the belt from the baler.

2. Remove the damaged area by cutting the belt off square with the belt edge (Fig. 48-B). Repeat the procedure on the other end of the belt.

3. Select the splice width (Fig. 48-C). See operator's manual for number of belt hooks required.

4. Place the hooks in the belt-lacing die (Fig. 48-D).

5. Place the belt-lacing die in a vise (Fig. 48-E).

6. Visually align the belt in the center of the hooks, and hold it in the die (Fig. 48-F).

7. Tighten the vise to clinch the hooks (Fig.48-G).

8. Remove the belt from the belt-lacing die (Fig. 48-H).

9. Repeat Steps 2 through 8 for the other end.

10. Replace the belt in the baler and insert the splice pin through belt hooks (Fig. 48-I). Be sure the proper side of the belt is turned out.

To shorten upper belts, repeat the foregoing procedure. The upper belts may be shortened several times, but the belts must be very nearly equal in length to apply pressure evenly over the entire length of the bale.

The lower belt usually cannot be repaired successfully after damage, the best preventive maintenance is to keep the belt lacing secure and avoid picking up sharp objects with the windrow.

Proper belt maintenance on some balers includes keeping anti-slip tape on the drive rolls. This anti-slip tape helps keep belts from slipping, and maintains the "tracking" qualities of the belts.

STORAGE

Proper storage of a round baler during the off-season helps reduce maintenance work and prolongs machine service life. If possible, store a round baler in a dry, sheltered shed. Block it up to remove weight from the tires. Direct sunlight causes deterioration of rubber. Cover tires, rubber belts, and hydraulic hoses to protect them from light, weather, grease, and oil. But do not deflate the tires.

Fig. 49—Three-Point Hitch Mounted Bale Mover

Fig. 50—High Lift Bale Mover

Fig. 51—Front Loader Attachment For Hauling Round Bales

Clean the baler thoroughly. Dirt and trash draw moisture which stimulates the formation of rust and speeds deterioration of rubberized belts. Clean and lightly oil the twine assembly. Paint surfaces where paint has worn off.

Give the baler a complete lubrication. Clean all chains with diesel fuel and coat them with heavy oil. Apply a thin layer of grease to the threads of adjustment bolts.

Reduce the tension on bale chamber belts during storage by releasing spring tension. Close the gate during storage.

List repairs and buy replacement parts so you can install them during the off-season.

SECTION 2: ROUND-BALE MOVERS

INTRODUCTION

A round-bale mover is an integral component in a round-bale system. Options are available to match the needs of each baling operation. Functions of the bale mover vary, depending on the distance from the field to storage and feeding areas. Some bale movers lift, haul, and unload bales. Others are used to lift and load bales on trucks, wagons, and feeders.

TYPES AND USES

Round-bale movers are generally classified as:

● **Mounted**

● **Towed**

Towed bale movers may be further divided into *single bale* or *multi-bale* type.

Fig. 52—Truck-Mounted Round-Bale Mover

MOUNTED BALE MOVERS

Mounted bale movers are attached either to tractors or to pickup trucks. The most used round-bale mover is mounted on the 3-point hitch of a tractor (Fig. 49). Some of these bale forks can only unload on or near the ground. Other forks can unload bales onto a truck and stack bales (Fig. 50).

CAUTION: Do not transport bales with the front loader raised high. Keep the loader as low as possible. Carrying a bale high can easily upset a tractor.

Front Loaders with bale clamps are used to move big round bales (Fig. 51). The clamp secures the bale so it does not fall or worse, roll back onto an operator. Tractor mounted round-bale movers are restricted by economics and time. They are used for short distance hauling or loading trucks for longer hauls.

Truck mounted round bale movers generally load bales with a fork (Fig. 52). The fork frame is secured to the truck bed. The operator raises the fork to load the bale on the truck using power from a hydrualic cylinder or an electric winch. A truck mounted bale mover is extremely useful for moving and feeding on the farm. If weight limits are exceeded the truck can be difficult to control.

TOWED BALE MOVERS

Most towed round-bale movers can be attached to a tractor or truck. This allows the towed bale carrier to operate under field conditions that require tractor power, and on roads or highways for faster transportation. Round-bale movers lift, haul, and unload round bales.

Small tractors pull single-bale movers. A small tractor may not be heavy enough to handle a large bale with a mounted bale mover, but it can manipulate the bale on a towed mover.

Fig. 53—MultiBale Mover Towed by Tractor

Fig. 54—Multi-Bale Mover Towed by Truck

Single bale carriers towed by pickup trucks are an alternative to mounted bale movers. Towed bale carriers are usually loaded by raising the bale to transport position with a hydraulic cylinder or electric winch. Towed bale movers can be connected and disconnected easily to free the pickup for other uses.

Multi-bale movers carry a heavier payload. Most can haul at least 3 tons of round bales. A tractor-towed multi-bale mover is best for moving bales from the field to the storage area on short-distance hauls (Fig. 53). A truck-towed multi-bale mover is better for longer road hauls (Fig. 54). In either case, the operator has the convenience of loading and unloading bales with a hydraulic system. Self-contained hydraulic systems are available for pickup trucks and tractors.

Integrally mounted and tilt bed loose hay stack movers are also used to move round bales. Information on these mov-

ers is included in Chapter 9, *Stack Wagons and Stack Movers,* of this book.

BASIC ROUND-BALE MOVER OPERATION

Most round bales are handled in the field with tractor-powered single bale movers, mounted on the 3-point hitch or front loader. Towed bale forks are also popular on small beef cattle operations.

BALE FORKS

A bale fork has one, two, three, or more tines on a frame (Fig. 55). The main frame is constructed to match the 3-point hitch, front-end loader, or wheeled carrier frame. Some bale movers have a hydraulically controlled clamp or grapple to hold the bale securely on the fork.

The tines on a bale fork lift the bale. Two-tined forks slide under the bale and cradle it. One- and three-tined forks "spear" the bale. Spearing is not particularly effective for long distance transportation, but the bales may be unloaded and stacked fast because the tines do not contact the ground or other support under the bale.

Front loader-mounted bale movers hold a bale so it won't fall. Serious injury may result if a 1,200-pound (545 kg) bale falls on someone. A grapple (Fig. 56), or a safety frame is required on all front loader movers to keep bales from falling or rolling down the raised loader arms onto the operator.

TOWED BALE CARRIERS

Towed bale carriers require a bale-lifting device such as a hydraulic cylinder or an electric winch. However, on some models the operator locks the mover brakes and drives the tractor forward, which raises the bale up over the axle into transport position. When the bale reaches transport position, the brakes release and the bale carrier tows freely. Good traction is required for the locked-brake loading. For convenience and all-weather use, most towed bale movers use the tractor's hydraulic system to lift bales.

Fig. 55—Three-Point-Hitch-Mounted Bale Mover

Fig. 56—Front Loader Bale Mover with Grapple

Fig. 57—Adjust Pitch on Upper Link of Fork Tines

PLANNING AND PREPARATION

Proper planning for moving and storage is the key to success in any round bale handling operation. Such factors as selection of twine and bale storage site affect the operation an efficiency of a round-bale mover. As discussed, plastic twine is recommended if extended storage and frequent handling is necessary. Bales that are poorly wrapped or have deteriorating twine may start to fall apart during transport on a fork mover. The bottom layers of a large round bale with deteriorating twine are particularly susceptible to loss during moving.

A good bale storage site can keep twine from deteriorating. A good site provides traction for the tractor.

SPEED CAUSES PROBLEMS

Operation of the round-bale fork mover is simple. An operator needs only limited experience. The most common problem is haste. Fast transport over rough ground can loosen the bale and increase losses. Fast transport also increases maintenance required on both the round-bale mover and the tractor. And, rapid speeds endanger the operator and others. For example, a large round bale can be bounced off a bale mover and roll, causing injury to people nearby, or damage to vehicles or equipment. Also, the very heavy weight on rear mounted movers can lift the tractor front wheels off the ground temporarily when the tractor bounces over rough ground. Consequently, exercise extreme caution at all times when handling large round bales.

TRACTOR PREPARATION

Follow the operator's manual hints for checking and preparing the tractor for a round-bale mover.

Before connecting a *rear mounted bale mover* to the tractor:

● Adjust the tractor drawbar fully forward and pin it in place.

● *Provide sufficient front-end weight to stabilize the tractor at all times, and especially when it is to be operated on hills or rough terrain.*

● Adjust wheel spacing for maximum stability.

● Check air pressure in front and rear tires and adjust as necessary.

● Make sure the 3-point hitch operates properly.

● Check the oil level in the tractors's hydraulic system.

Make minor modifications of this procedure as required for different types of bale movers. For a *towed bale mover,* adjust the drawbar as follows:

● Set the height at 13 to 17 inches (330 to 432 mm) above ground.

● Move the drawbar to locate the hitch-pin hole correctly to permit safe turns without having wheels strike the mover hitch or frame.

● Pin near the centerline of the tractor so the bale mover tows directly behind the tractor.

The *front-end loader-mounted bale mover* requires a properly mounted, correctly adjusted loader in good operating condition.

Fig. 58—Aligning Tractor and Mover with Bale

Fig. 59—Position Bale Fork

ATTACHING THE REAR-MOUNTED MOVER

The sequence for attaching a rear-mounted bale mover follows:

• Back the tractor to within 6 inches (152 mm) of the bale mover's 3-point hitch.

• Connect hydraulic hoses to the tractor hydraulic system, if required.

• Adjust lower arms on the 3-point hitch to the proper height.

• Connect the bale mover to the 3-point hitch.

• Adjust the upper-link length to get the right pitch on fork tines (Fig. 57).

To detach the rear-mounted bale mover, reverse the attaching procedure.

Fig. 60—Lower Fork

OTHER MODELS AND TYPES

Because of differences in each model and type, the exact procedure for connecting each type of bale mover to the tractor is beyond the scope of this text. Consult the operator's manual for specific details.

However, the basic difference between hookups for towed and mounted movers is the use of the tractor drawbar instead of the 3-point hitch. And, of course, the front-end loader-mounted bale mover requires a sturdy front-end loader to maneuver the bale fork.

PREPARING THE BALE MOVER

A final check of the bale mover is essential before field operation. First, review the operator's manual carefully.

Lubricate the bale mover as recommended. For towed movers inspect the ties and check the tires. Make sure the lift system is operating properly. For most round-bale movers, inspecting and preparing the lift system means checking the hydraulic system. However, some bale movers use an electric winch to lift the bales.

BASIC CONTROLS

The controls to operate a round-bale mover vary with the model and the bale-lift system. Basically they consist of hydraulic or electric lift and tractor-propulsion controls. These controls are all located on the tractor operator's platform.

OPERATION

Round-bale fork movers are easy to control. Follow these steps for efficient loading and unloading.

Fig. 61—Backing Into Bale

LOADING

1. Align the tractor, mover, and bale in a straight line. For twine-wrapped bales, the fork mover usually approaches a flat end of the bale (Fig. 58).

2. Move the tractor forward if it has a front-mounted loader, or backward if it has a rear-mounted or towed bale mover, until the bale fork is about one foot from the bale (Fig. 59).

3. Lower the mover into position to accept the bale. If is has a 2-tined fork, lower the bale carrier to the ground (Fig. 60). With 1- and 3-tined forks, lower the mover until the primary load-carrying tine can "stab" the bale near the center.

4. Move the tractor either forward or backward as required to load the bale on the mover (Fig. 61). Stop movement when the bale contacts the main frame of the fork.

5. Tighten the bale clamp (if the mover is so equipped; then raise bale mover into transport position (Fig. 62).

UNLOADING

1. Maneuver the tractor and mover into the desired unloading location (Fig. 63). Leave at least one foot of space between bales as a precaution against spoilage. Make sure the tractor and the towed mover are in a straight line.

2. Lower the bale mover slowly until the bale contacts the ground. Always position bales with the same flat side down the way they were sitting before. This avoids additional spoilage from placing different hay on the ground, and maintains the water-shedding curvature established in the earlier position.

3. Loosen the bale clamp or grapple and drive the tractor forward or backward, as required, to unload the bale.

4. Raise the bale mover from the ground.

FIELD ADJUSTMENTS

Round-bale fork movers require only minor field adjustments, such as setting the proper pitch on the tines. Of course, transport speed must be adjusted to match field conditions.

TRANSPORT

Transporting bales is dangerous.

● Position bales so you can see front and rear. Especially with front loader-mounted movers that can block forward vision.

● Be sure the mover is raised high enough to clear humps and obstructions in the field or road. But remember a bale raised too high makes it easier for a tractor to tip over.

● Match ground speed to field and road conditions. Never exceed the speed recommended by the manufacturer.

● Drive on the far right side of the road (Fig. 64).

● Check tractor brakes. Be sure they operate.

Fig. 62—Moving A Bale

Fig. 63—Position Bales In Storage Yard

Fig. 64—Transporting a Round Bale

SAFETY

Safe operation of bale movers is essential to prevent serious accidents. Do not operate bale movers near bystanders. Only the operator should be on the tractor during operation. Never ride or let others ride on a bale mover.

Block up the mover before working under raised tines. Never adjust, clean, or lubricate a bale mover while it is operating. Set the brakes and block the tractor wheels before working on a round-bale mover or when parking. Never leave a bale in the raised position.

Always provide enough weight to stablize a tractor front end.

Be especially careful with front loader-mounted bale movers. A raised bale makes a tractor top-heavy. A large, round bale can crush someone if it falls. A grapple is required for the front loader-mounted bale movers.

● *See hydraulic safety message page 334.*

TROUBLESHOOTING

Most field problems encountered with a bale mover have obvious causes. To become more proficient in solving problems, study the troubleshooting chart.

MAINTENANCE

Maintenance of a bale mover centers primarily on the hydraulic system. The most important factor is *Keep the system clean and free of foreign material.* Dirt and dust in the hydraulic system cause malfunctions and increase wear.

Proper lubrication of moving parts on the bale mover reduces friction and wear.

Because a round-bale mover is used all year, it may not be stored during an off-season. But proper storage, even for short periods, can help preserve reliability and hold down maintenance costs for the bale mover. Tips for storage:

● Use a safety chain on towed bale movers, especially behind trucks.

● Be sure an SMV emblem is clearly displayed on the rear when operating on roads.

● Attach the SMV emblem to the bale if necessary to make the emblem visible to approaching traffic from the rear (Fig. 64). Bales are dull-colored and can be easily overlooked by approaching motorists.

TROUBLESHOOTING CHART		
PROBLEM	POSSIBLE CAUSE	POSSIBLE REMEDY
BALES SLIP OFF TINES.	Fork tines not level.	Adjust tines to proper position during transport.
	Bent or broken fork tines.	Repair or replace tines.

PROBLEM	POSSIBLE CAUSE	POSSIBLE REMEDY
	Ground speed too fast.	Reduce speed.
	Tractor draft links not levelled laterally.	Level draft links.
BALES SLIDE ON GROUND INSTEAD OF MOUNTING FORK.	Fork tines not level.	Adjust top link on bale mover.
	Mover not properly positioned.	Raise or lower mover as needed.
	Bales have flattened out.	Use better-quality twine.
BALES FALL APART DURING TRANSPORT.	Poor twine wrap.	Make a better twine wrap during baling.
	Twine has deteriorated during storage.	Use better-quality twine or use plastic twine. Select better storage site.
	Ground speed too fast.	Reduce Speed.
LIFT WILL NOT RAISE BALE.	Bale frozen to ground.	Select better storage site.
		Move bales in warmer weather.
	Hydraulic- or electric-lift system not operating properly.	Repair and maintain lift system.
TRACTOR WHEELS SLIP.	Poor traction.	Select better storage site. Move bales when ground conditions are better.

- Store in a dry place, if possible.

- Clean off dirt and trash to slow rust formation.

- Repaint worn surfaces, with this exception: Apply a coat of heavy oil to the polished fork tines.

- Block up a towed mover, to take weight off the tires. Cover tires for protection from sunlight, but do not deflate them.

- Lubricate as specified in the operator's manual.

- Replace worn parts while the mover is stored.

SUMMARY

A round-bale system permits one-man haymaking from harvest to feeding. It lowers costs for harvesting, storing, and feeding hay, by reducing manpower requirements and by permitting outside bale storage.

The major disadvantage of a round-bale system is the problem of long-distance transportation. Round bales do not stack efficiently. This generally restricts the use of round balers on commercial hay farms to operators who have a nearby market.

The primary function of a round baler is to roll windrowed hay into weather-resistant round bales. The exact operating procedure varies with different makes and models. The most common method of producing round bales is to pick up the hay and roll it in a compression chamber formed by belts. When the bale reaches the correct diameter, twine is usually wrapped around the bale. After it is wrapped, the bale is discharged in the field. Then, on most farms, a bale mover takes the bales to a nearby storage place. Then animals are brought to the hay, the hay is moved to the animals, or the hay is sold.

A round-bale system can be mechanized from field to feeding. As in other hay-packaging systems, operator experience and intelligent management pay big dividends in the quality of hay.

CHAPTER QUIZ

1. List four or more advantages of a large round baler over a conventional baler.

2. (True or false.) Round bales are formed by either picking up hay and rolling it in a chamber or by rolling up hay on the ground.

3. Name at least three characteristics you want in an outside round-bale stackyard.

4. What is the proper width of a windrow for a round baler?

5. What is the purpose of twine-wrapping round bales?

6. (True or false.) A barrel shaped bale can be made because of too much weaving on a windrow during baling.

7. Primary maintenance of a chamber rolling round-baler with belts is concentrated on the _____.

8. Which bale mover requires the highest horsepower tractor, towed or mounted?

9. What is the purpose of the tines on a bale fork?

10. Front end loader-mounted bale movers must have a _____ to secure a raised bale.

9
Stack Wagons
Stack Movers

Fig. 1—Horse Powered Stacker

Fig. 3—Making Hay The Hard Way

INTRODUCTION

The scythe, the rake, and the pitchfork put calluses on hard-working hands for generations as farmers cut hay and built it into "loose" stacks the hard way.

Then horse-powered stackers (Fig. 1) took part of the hard work away from men's muscles to put those essential stacks of livestock feed on the rural landscape. On smaller farms, in more humid areas, or where higher-quality hay was needed, loose hay was loaded in the field (Fig. 2), hauled to the barn, and stored loose in the barn (Fig. 3). Even with a hay loader (Fig. 2) and grapple fork (Fig. 3), much of the hay movement required human muscle.

Engine power came, and with it, tractor-mounted stackers on front-end loaders. These work savers sweep hay from the windrow (Fig. 4), carry the hay, and stack it (Fig. 5).

Then came the tractor-powered loose-hay stack wagon (Fig. 6). The stacks are different than those of great-grandpa's day. Stacks are more dense, more uniform, more weather resistant, and more portable.

Fig. 2—Ground Driven Hay Loader

Fig. 4—Tractor Mounted Stacker Gathering Hay

Fig. 5—Loose Hay Stack

SECTION 1:
STACK WAGONS

Although stack wagons have been replaced in most operations with round balers, this chapter gives a historical perspective of this procedure.

PURPOSE AND USE

Stack wagons pick up windrowed hay or stover from the field and form compressed, weather-resistant stacks (Fig. 7). Stacks have a firm, sloping top to shed water. Dense, interlocked material in a well-constructed stack resists damage by wind and water. A crust forms over the surface a few days after stacking. The crust seals out moisture and helps bind the hay together. Stack wagon stacks are usually less susceptible to spoilage than hand-built stacks.

Stack wagon stacks don't need to be covered. But to reduce spoilage on the bottom of a stack, the ground should slope. Stacks should be separated by two or three feet of space so water can drain. Face the narrow end of each stack toward the prevailing wind to help reduce wind damage. Stacks are often placed in rows close to livestock.

Fig. 6—Loose Hay Stack Wagon

Fig. 7—Weather Resistant Stack

A typical stack of hay weighs 5.5 to 7 pounds (2.5 to 3.1 kg) per cubic foot. It is about 50 to 70 percent as dense as a typical 2-wire bale.

RANGE OF STACK SIZES

Stack size depends on the kind and model of stack wagon. Most rectangular stacks are 7 to 15 feet (2.1-4.5 m) wide, 10 to 24 feet (3-7.3 m) long, and 8 to 11 feet (2.4 to 3.3 m) high. Round stacks are usually 11 to 18 feet (3.3-5.5 m) in diameter and 10 to 12 feet (3 to 3.6 m) high.

Fig. 8—Lifting and Conveying Hay into a Covered Stack Wagon

While the relatively low density and large size of most stacks make it impractical to transport them long distances, stack wagons offer many benefits to cattlemen feeding their own hay, and to commercial hay growers close to their markets.

LOW LABOR REQUIREMENT

Harvesting, packaging, storing, and feeding hay stacks requires only about 15 to 35 percent of the labor needed to do the same job with baled hay. Cost savings are significant. The stack wagon and accessory field equipment deliver these labor and cost savings. In many operations, one person can harvest, store, and feed the crop.

HANDLES MANY KINDS OF CROPS

The versatile stack wagon can stack many kinds of crops for outside storage: alfalfa, forage sorghum, grasses small-grain straw corn, and milo stover. Many of these crop residues were not used in the past because of harvesting and feeding problems. Now they may be saved by the versatile stack wagon for use as feed or bedding because of the low labor and operating costs.

STACK-WAGON ECONOMICS

University of Oklahoma studies show that small stack wagons require about one hour of labor per ton of hay harvested and fed, compared to about 1.2 man-hours per ton for large round bales and 2.5 hours per ton for a square bale system. Large stack wagons require only about 0.4 hours of labor per ton of hay harvested and fed.

Purdue University studies show, that compared to conventional baling, stack wagons may be cheaper per ton of hay harvested and fed if more than 50 tons are harvested annually. Oklahoma reports indicate that a one ton stack-wagon system can break even compared to a 2-wire baled hay system at 75 tons per year.

Large stack wagons may harvest 8 tons per hour or more, compared to 4 to 6 tons per hour for a conventional baler, or up to 8 tons for a heavy-duty baler making rectangular bales. Only one man is required for stacking hay and stacks can be left in the field, uncovered. Several men are needed to haul and store bales after harvest to prevent weather damage.

TYPES AND SIZES

Stack wagons are classified according to the method used to compact the stacks:

- **Mechanically-compressed**
- **Air-packed**

With proper operation, both methods form solid stacks with rounded, uniform tops.

MECHANICAL-PRESS STACKERS

Mechanical-press stackers of different produce *rectangular* and *round* stacks.

Rectangular Stacks

The most common stack wagon uses a windrow or flair pickup to lift material and convey it into an enclosed, rectangular wagon (Fig. 8). When the wagon is filled, the operator stops the tractor's forward motion and lowers the canopy hydraulically to compress the stack (Fig. 9). Compression compacts the hay or stover and molds the top of the stack into the rounded shape of the canopy. The number of compression cycles per stack depends on the type and moisture content of the material and the density needed.

Fig. 9—Compacting Hay by Lowering the Canopy

Fig. 10—1-, 2-, and 3-Ton Stack Wagons

187

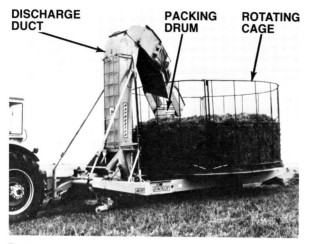

DISCHARGE DUCT   **PACKING DRUM**   **ROTATING CAGE**

Fig. 11—Round Stack Wagon

Fig. 12—Unload Circular Stack

Fig. 13—Air-Pack Stack Wagon

Other methods are used to compact the crop. One uses a series of press arms fastened along the top of the stack chamber. To compact the stack, hydraulically-operated fingers pivot from the sides into the center of the stack forcing the hay downward.

Another model has a false front gate that is pushed to the rear hydraulically to compact the load. The compaction is similar to the canopy-compaction wagon except the stack is compacted front to rear instead of top to bottom.

Mechanical-press stack wagons form rectangular stacks. The size of the stack depends on the wagon. Wagons come in three sizes: 1-, 2-, and 3-ton (Fig. 10).

Round Stacks

Another type of stack wagon lifts the hay or stover and carries it into a circular rotating cage. The loose hay is compacted with a packer drum that rolls on top of the stack as the cage rotates (Fig. 11). The packer drum is controlled hydraulically to exert force on the loose hay. The cage opens and the bed tilts so the stack slides out (Fig. 12). Stack sizes built with these circular stack wagons are about 2-, 4-, 6-, or 8-tons.

AIR-PACK STACKERS

Most air-pack, loose-hay stack wagons lift the windrow (or use a flair pickup in stalks), chop the material, and blow it into a stack chamber (Fig. 13). Chopping hay reduces the stem length to attain greater density in the stack. The *length of chop* in loose-hay stacks may vary from 6 inches (152 mm) down to 3/4 inch (19 mm). An automatic oscillating filler spout or a manually-directed blower spout loads the wagon uniformly. This loading and air-packing process eliminates the need for stopping and compressing the stacks.

Some air-pack stack wagons have an integral chopper and blower (Fig. 13). Others are trail-type stack formers, used behind a special or standard forage harvester (Fig. 14). The size of stack formed by air-pack units depends on the particular model and make. They are generally classified as 3-, 6-, 8-, and 10-ton wagons.

STACK-WAGON FUNDAMENTALS

Every stack wagon requires an auxiliary power source. Most wagons are towed behind and use power from the tractor's PTO shaft. Some air-pack stackers are towed by self-propelled forage harvesters. Forage harvesters are discussed in Chapter 11 of this text. Because most of the features of air-pack stackers are similar to those of mechanical-press stackers, the rest of this chapter is on mechanical-press stackers.

The stack wagon is a packaging machine. It lifts cured hay windrows, straw, or stover, and forms stacks. Usually these stacks are deposited wherever they are completed or near the edge of the field. These compact, weather-resistant stacks are then stored outside until they are needed for feeding or grinding into mixed rations.

Fig. 14—Stack Wagon Loaded by a Forage Harvester

Fig. 15—Stack Wagon

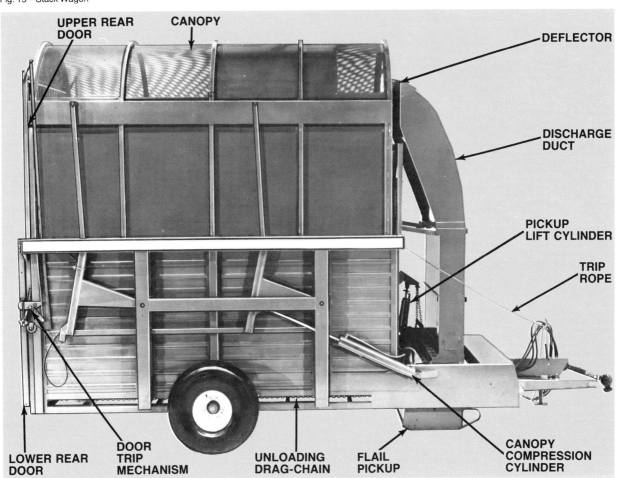

UPPER REAR DOOR

CANOPY

DEFLECTOR

DISCHARGE DUCT

PICKUP LIFT CYLINDER

TRIP ROPE

LOWER REAR DOOR

DOOR TRIP MECHANISM

UNLOADING DRAG-CHAIN

FLAIL PICKUP

CANOPY COMPRESSION CYLINDER

CANOPY (LOWERED POSITION)   DEFLECTOR   DISCHARGE DUCT

Fig. 16—Adjustable Deflector on Discharge Duct

STACK WAGON COMPONENTS

The primary components of a stack wagon are (Fig. 15):

- **Pickup (flail or cylinder)**
- **Discharge duct and deflector**
- **Compression chamber**
- **Chain-slat floor conveyor**
- **Rear doors**

A main frame with wheels supports the hay stack wagon.

Functions of components

A flail pickup can lift windrowed hay and straw or harvest stover. The *cylinder pickup* available on some models also lifts windrowed hay and straw. Cylinder pickup is recommended for alfalfa and other leafy crops because it is gentle and cuts leaf loss.

Either pickup lifts the material and delivers it to the *discharge duct.* It is then forced upward through the discharge duct by an airstream from the flail pickup or an auxiliary blower on cylinder pickups.

As material is blown from the discharge duct, the *deflector* directs it into the *compression chamber* Fig. 16).

Field Use

Here's the operating sequence in field use: When the compression chamber is filled, stop the tractor's forward motion and lower the canopy. This compacts the stack and forms a rounded top (Fig. 17). Repeat this procedure of filling and compacting until the stack has good density and shape.

Fig. 17—Canopy Lowered To Compact and Form A Stack

CANOPY DOWN

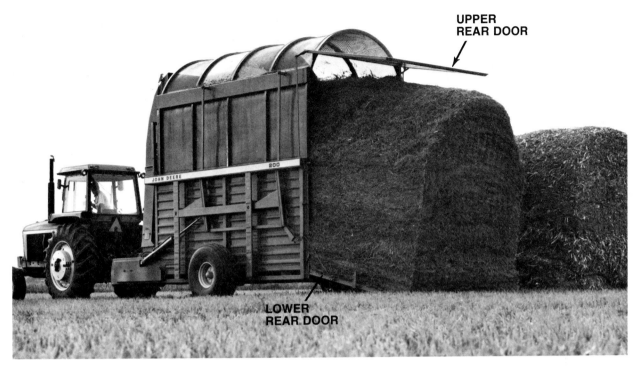

Fig. 18—Unloading Stack

After the stack is formed, open the *rear doors* and push the stack out with the *chain-slat floor conveyor* (Fig. 18). Tilt the bed to the ground or use an unloading conveyor to guide the stack to the ground.

OPERATION AND ADJUSTMENTS

General Information

Operators will do better if they study the operator's manual. The quality of hay at feeding time depends on the quality of hay in the field and on proper operation of the stack wagon. It is particularly important to fill the wagon evenly to produce a stack with uniform density and a sloping canopy.

Remember—quality deteriorates rapidly during storage if the stack is cracked open or loosened. Cracks let in water. Cracks and loosening can happen during unloading if the tractor moves too fast.

Stack wagons are well suited to packaging lower-quality hay and stover too. But even low-quality material requires good management and proper stack-wagon operation to build weather-resistant stacks.

Selecting Proper Moisture Content

The generally-recommended moisture content for wind-rowed hay at stacking time is about the same as that for producing bales. However, some manufacturers and operators suggest stacking at higher moisture content.

Hay with high moisture content does not pack properly in the wagon. An improperly packed stack shrinks during storage. Shrinking results in depressions in the stack (Fig. 19). Water collects in depressions and leaks into the stack.

Fig. 19—Depressions

Stacking hay at a moisture content significantly below the optimum increases field losses. Dry hay does not pack well. A dry stack is particularly susceptible to wind damage before the crust forms. Extra compaction helps reduce problems, but is not a substitute for stacking at the proper moisture content. Until you are thoroughly experienced with stack-wagon operation and stack storage feeding, follow this rule of thumb: *Do not stack hay unless its moisture content is within two or three points of the optimum moisture content for baling.*

Stover stacks are formed at higher moisture content because cooler fall weather conditions and the slow field-curing of corn and milo stalks. However, stacked stover with more than 40 percent moisture content may heat and spoil, even in normal fall weather. Stacking within the proper moisture range provides two major benefits:

1. Hay and stover store well at these moisture contents.

2. Stacks are compacted and formed easily.

PLANNING AND PREPARATION

Other equipment for hay-stacking operations:

- **Mower, mower-conditioner or windrower**
- **Rake**
- **Stack mover**
- **Tractor**

Stover-stacking usually requires only a *stackwagon, stack mover,* and *tractor.*

Matching auxiliary equipment to the stack wagon is essential for an efficient operation.

Mowers are seldom used with stack wagons because of their low field capacity and the need for separate condition-

Fig. 20—Well Formed Windrow

ing (if used) and raking. If hay is mowed, two or more swaths are usually raked together to form adequate-sized windrows.

A *mower-conditioner* or *windrower* should form a uniform windrow nearly as wide as the stack-wagon pickup (Fig. 20). A wide windrow aids in distributing the hay evenly across the compression chamber.

A *rake* is seldom used in the stacking operation, but may be required to turn slow-drying hay or wet hay. Also, a rake may be used to combine light windrows, increasing field efficiency during stacking.

The *stack mover* lifts stacks and moves them from the field.

The *tractor* must have adequate engine power and a dual hydraulic system.

Specific tractor horsepower and hydraulic-system capacity are dictated by the stack wagon.

Fig. 21—Installing Remote Hydraulic Cylinder for Pickup Lift

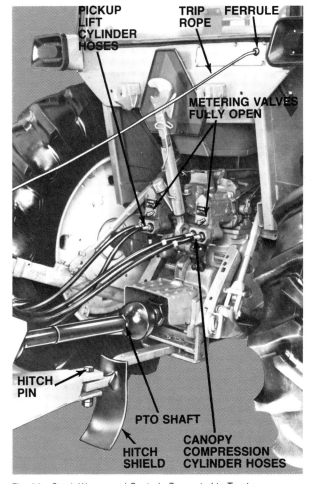

Fig. 22—Stack Wagon and Controls Connected to Tractor

CROP INFLUENCES PLANNING

Coarse-stemmed and broadleaf forages need to be conditioned and field-cured. Conditioning improves both the stacking and drying characteristics of these forages. Fresh wheat or oat straw should be stacked early in the morning or late at night when moisture content is higher. Often these slick materials are not cohesive enough to form a stable stack without high humidity or dew on the windrow. Stover stacking may be restricted by poor traction in wet fields. Timely field operations are essential to success.

TRACTOR PREPARTION

Check a tractor and stack wagon before starting to the field. Follow the operator's manual for preparing the tractor. Before attaching the stack wagon:

- Spread the tractor wheels so they straddle windrows without running on hay.

- Make sure the tractor PTO speed matches the stack-wagon drive requirement.

- Put the drawbar in the recommended position for PTO operation.

- Lock the drawbar parallel with the centerline of the PTO shaft.

- Add ballast on the front end of the tractor if necessary.

- Check the hydraulic oil level and add fluid if necessary.

- Set the hydraulic metering valves in the open position.

- Raise the draft links or remove the 3-point-hitch components.

193

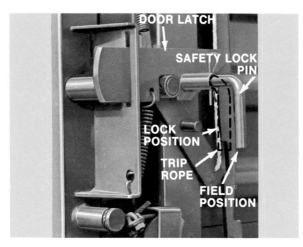

Fig. 23—Safety Pin on Rear Door

Fig. 24—Keep the Number of Flails Balanced

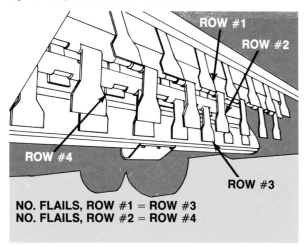

NO. FLAILS, ROW #1 = ROW #3
NO. FLAILS, ROW #2 = ROW #4

ATTACHING STACK WAGON

When the tractor preparation is complete, follow this sequence to attach the stack wagon:

1. Install a remote hydraulic cylinder, if needed for pickup lift (Fig. 21).

2. Raise or lower the stack-wagon hitch with the hitch jack to engage the tractor drawbar.

3. Back the tractor to align holes. Put the tractor in park, shut off the engine, and take the key if working alone. Insert the safety hitch pin. If someone is helping hitch, put the tractor in park or forward before they step in and insert the pin.

4. Attach the PTO shaft to the tractor PTO.

5. Install hydraulic hoses to tractor breakaway couplers.

6. Thread the rear-door trip rope through the ferrule in the back panel of the tractor cab. Allow sufficient slack for turning.

7. Place lowered hitch jack in transport position.

8. Recheck all connections, such as remote cylinders coupled to proper outlets, and PTO shaft locked in position (Fig. 22).

FINAL CHECK

With the stack wagon attached to the tractor, begin final inspection and preparation. Before operating the PTO shaft and hydraulic system:

1. Inspect installation and condition of the trip rope for the rear door.

2. Place the pickup-lift safety lock pin in the field-storage position (Fig. 21).

3. Move the rear-door safety lock pin to the field position (Fig. 23).

Fig. 25—When Exchanging Worn Flails, Keep the Flails on the Same Shaft

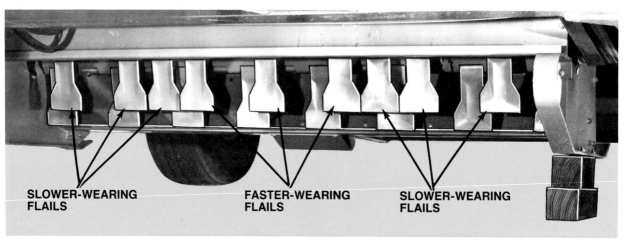

SLOWER-WEARING FLAILS FASTER-WEARING FLAILS SLOWER-WEARING FLAILS

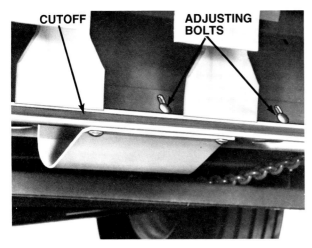

Fig. 26—Pickup-Cutoff Adjustment

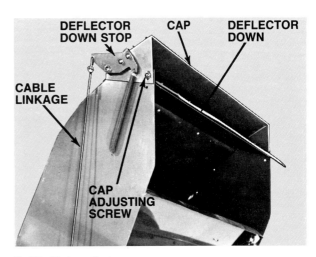

Fig. 27—Discharge Duct

During transport and storage keep the safety pin in the safety position.

Hydraulic System

Inspect the hydraulic system thoroughly after completing the hookup. Before engaging the hydraulic pump recheck the hydraulic system. Be sure all connections are tight and no lines, pipes, or hoses are damaged. Then start the engine and actuate the hydraulic system. Let the pump operate in relief mode for a few seconds to eliminate air, which might cause a cylinder malfunction. Then extend and retract the pickup and compression cylinders several times. If they do not operate properly, shut off the engine and relieve hydraulic pressure in the system. Check the level of oil in the tractor hydraulic reservoir and inspect hoses and lines for leaks. Always release hydraulic pressure before disconnecting lines. Replace any damaged hydraulic parts and continue inspection.

PREPARING THE STACK WAGON

Get the stack wagon ready:

1. Review the operator's manual.

2. Shut off the tractor engine and disengage all drives.

3. Lubricate the stack wagon as recommended in the operator's manual.

4. Inspect and adjust belt and chain tension.

5. Check bolts and tighten all loose bolts to the recommended torque.

6. Replace wheels, if removed, and check tire inflation.

7. Remove foreign matter from the wagon, particularly from moving components.

8. Clean and check the slip clutch.

9. Inspect and service the tractor as recommended in the operator's manual.

10. Operate the wagon for several minutes and recheck belts and chains.

PRELIMINARY SETTINGS AND ADJUSTMENTS

Before starting field operation, check these items:

FLAIL PICKUP

Prepare the flail pickup to match crop and field conditions. First, select the right flail arrangement. The standard arrangement is suitable for most hay and stover. However, for dry, light hay where less-aggressive action may be better, remove some flails. To maintain rotor balance, remove the same number of flails from opposite sides of the flail shaft (Fig. 24).

Exchanging Flails

Most hay enters near the center of a pickup, which causes center flails to wear faster. In stover harvesting, the flails directly over the rows wear faster. To lengthen service life, exchange the worn flails with less worn flails. However, to maintain rotor balance, keep the exchanged flails on the same flail shaft (Fig. 25). If new flails are added, keep the rotor in balance by putting the same number of new flails in opposite positions. On some machines, hardened flails may be installed for stover harvesting.

When changing flail arrangement or exchanging flails, place the wagon on level ground, support the front end, and block the wheels. Put blocks under the pickup to support it safely.

PICKUP CUTOFF

The pickup cutoff requires occasional adjustment. To cleanup windrows or stover, cutoff clearance must be uniform across the pickup (Fig. 26). To adjust the clearance, loosen adjusting bolts, slide the cutoff up or down to get the proper clearance, and tighten the bolts.

Fig. 28—Maintain Proper Conveyor-Chain Tension

DISCHARGE DEFLECTOR

When properly adjusted, the deflector can move far enough to load the compression chamber evenly from front to back. The deflector down stop must be adjusted to control deflector angle for loading the front of the compression chamber. When the canopy is fully raised, the deflector cable must pull the deflector against the discharge-duct cap to fill the rear of the wagon. To adjust, put tension on the cable spring. Field adjustment may be necessary.

UNLOADING MECHANISM

Unloading mechanism adjustment reduces broken parts and malfunctions during unloading. Adjust the conveyor chains so each has equal tension (Fig. 28). To adjust conveyor chains, refer to the operator's manual for recommended chain tension and procedure.

The unloading-drive clutch should be adjusted so it engages and disengages. Adjust the clutch and clutch linkage so they operate smoothly. Refer to the operator's manual for details.

DISCHARGE-DUCT CAP

The discharge-duct cap and deflector must be adjusted to loading the compression chamber evenly (Fig. 27). The discharge-duct cap limits deflector travel upward and should be set so you can load the front and rear of the chamber from the top.

FIELD OPERATION

Stack Wagon controls:

- **Tractor PTO Clutch lever**
- **Remote hydraulic cylinder controls**
- **Trip rope for rear doors**

Fig. 29—Pickup Centered over Windrow

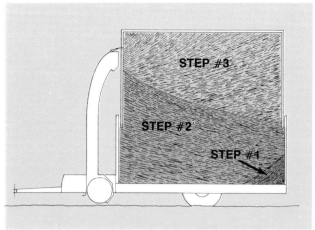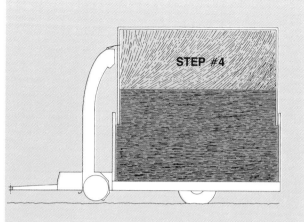

Fig. 30—Compression Chamber Loading

A thorough understanding of controls and tractor operating procedures is essential.

Begin field operation by lowering the pickup enough to pick up hay or stover. Flail tips should touch the tops of the stubble lightly. For stover, set flails low enough to pick up stalks and husks but high enough to miss the ground.

Raise the canopy to its highest position.

Make sure no one is near the stack wagon, then engage the PTO clutch. Throttle the tractor engine up to the rated engine speed. Select a gear to provide the proper speed for field and crop conditions. Begin forward motion with the tractor centered over the windrow (fig. 29).

LOADING COMPRESSION CHAMBER

To build high-density, well shaped stacks, the compression chamber must be loaded according to the manufacturer's recommendations. The following loading procedure for a stack wagon is satisfactory for most hay and stover, but minor modifications may be needed for some crop and field conditions.

Step 1. Begin loading with the canopy raised fully, and continue until the material fills the opening between the floor and the rear door (1, Fig. 30).

Step 2. Lower the canopy until the deflector directs material down to load the front of the compression chamber. Continue until material reaches the bottom of the discharge-duct outlet (2, Fig. 30).

Step 3. Raise the canopy and fill the compression chamber just short of plugging the discharge-duct outlet (3, Fig. 30). Stop forward motion, but maintain engine and PTO speed. Then compress the material by lowering the canopy (Fig. 31).

Step 4. Raise the canopy, resume forward motion, and fill the compression chamber (4, Fig. 30). Compress the material again. Repeat Steps 3 and 4 until:

(a) Tractor hydraulic-relief pressure will not fully retract the canopy cylinders. The last compression must lower the canopy to within 8 or 10 inches (203 to 254 mm) of the fully lowered position so the rear door latches will work (Fig. 32).

or (b) The top of the compressed material springs back up near the top of the rear door.

Fig. 31—Canopy Lowered To Compress Stack

CANOPY DOWN

COMPRESSION CYLINDER

Fig. 32—Canopy Must Be Down To Operate Door Latches

Number of Compactions Varies

With experience, an operator can recognize when a stack is completed. The number of compactions required varies with crop type and condition. Usually three or four compactions are suitable for cured hay. Don't reduce the number of compactions to save stacking time. The hay won't be dense enough and storage problems will result.

After the final compression keep the canopy in the lowered position until you are ready to unload. If the stack is transported to the edge of the field or nearby stackyard, the canopy keeps the stack compressed tightly. This is particularly important on rough ground.

STACK STORAGE

The unloading spot should be level and well drained. The surface must be firm, even in bad weather, if you want to retrieve and feed hay during the winter. Arrange stacks to reduce snow drifting, which can restrict access to stacks.

Avoid spoilage. Do not stack hay where water can stand around the stack bottoms. To reduce wind damage, unload stacks with one end facing the prevailing winds. Leave a 2- or-3-foot (609 or 914 mm) space between stacks for inspection and reloading, and for better curing, and drainage (Fig. 33). Stacks that touch each other trap surface water.

Fig. 33—Well-Planned Stack Yard

Fig. 34—Rear Doors Open for Stack Unloading

1. DRAINAGE   3. SPACE BETWEEN STACKS
2. FIRM SURFACE   4. NEAR FEED AREA

198

Fig. 35—Drive Forward When Stack Contacts Ground

Fig. 36—Rear Door Closing after Unloading

UNLOADING

The following procedure is recommended for unloading:

1. Select the exact location for the stack. Allow enough space for the rear doors to open.

2. Align the tractor and stack wagon in a straight line.

3. Make certain nobody is near the rear of the stack wagon and use the trip rope to open the door (Fig. 34).

4. Disengage the PTO.

5. With the tractor engine idling, put the gear-selector level in low. Do not engage the main clutch. Slowly engage the PTO clutch to move the stack rearward.

6. Watch the stack move. When the rear of the stack contacts the ground, gently engage the tractor main clutch. Move the tractor and stack wagon forward slowly. Inch ahead to let the emerging stack settle gently to the ground so it doesn't break (Fig. 35).

8. Check rear-door latch engagement.

END-GATE CONVEYOR

An optional end-gate conveyor on stack wagons with an upper and lower rear door helps move a stack from the compression chamber to the ground (Fig. 37). Use it with stover that does not interweave well enough to build a stable stack. Step 6 of the unloading process is made easier with the powered end-gate conveyor.

END-OF-DAY ROUTINE

At the end of each work day unload the compression chamber. Hay or stover left in the compression chamber overnight may settle and be difficult to unload later, especially if it gets wet. After unloading, keep the canopy and the pickup fully lowered. Disengage the tractor PTO clutch and shut off the engine. The stack wagon and tractor are then ready for maintenance and inspection before the next day's work.

FIELD ADJUSTMENTS

Some field adjustments may be needed to build properly-compacted, well shaped stacks. Adjust to match the crop and field conditions.

Fig. 37—End-Gate Conveyor Helps Unload Stover

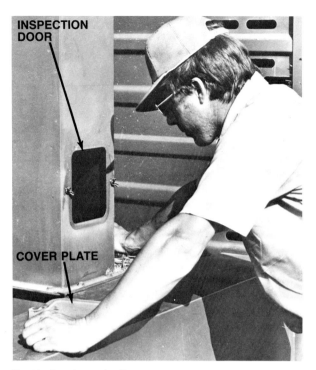

Fig. 38—Duct Inspection Door

Fig. 39—Weaving Across Windrow for Even Distribution of Hay in Wagon

PICKUP-LIFT CYLINDER

Set the stop on the pickup-left cylinder to maintain correct pickup height. With the stop set, the pickup can be raised and easily returned to the same operating height.

GROUND SPEED

Match ground speed to crop and field conditions by using the proper tractor gears. Slow ground speed chops hay, increases field losses, decreases stacking capacity, and causes excessive wear on the pickup. Too-much speed also increases field losses, and often plugs the pickup.

CLEANING PICKUP

If the pickup plugs, stop the tractor, disengage the PTO clutch, back the tractor, and gently "bounce" the pickup with the lift cylinder. Then engage the tractor PTO slowly. If the duct is still plugged, lift the pickup, shut off the tractor engine, remove the duct inspection doors (Fig. 38), and clean out the pickup. Use a stick to loosen loaded material. Never use your hand! Always keep rotor housing air-intake holes clean so the rotor will work.

EVEN DISTRIBUTION OF HAY

In light windrows, the discharge duct may not distribute material evenly across the width of the compression chamber. The result is a lopsided stack. If windrows cannot be raked together, weave the tractor back and forth across the windrow to help distribute hay evenly from side to side in the compression chamber (Fig. 39). Keep the perforated metal in the canopy clean so air can escape from the discharge duct.

TRANSPORT

Stack wagons are bulky. To lower the center of gravity, transport a stack wagon with the canopy lowered.

Raise the pickup to maximum height to clear bumps. Place the pickup lock pin in safety position and the rear door safety lock pin in transport position.

The tractor must have good enough brakes to stop both the tractor and wagon on hills.

When transporting a stack wagon (Fig. 40), be sure the Slow Moving Vehicle enblem on the rear door is clean and visible to others and the flashing yellow warning lights are on.

Do not exceed the manufacturer's recommended speed. Always use a lower gear on steep downgrades.

SAFETY

• *Be extremely observant at all times.* Vision is limited directly behind a bulky stack wagon. Always make certain there are no people behind a wagon before backing.

• Make sure no one is near the rear doors before opening them to unload.

• Never allow anyone to ride on a stack wagon. Only the operator rides on the tractor.

• Do not let children play near a stack wagon during operation, transport, or even storage.

• A stack wagon has high-pressure hydraulics. Be extremely careful with high-pressure hydraulic leaks. Small streams of fluid may be almost invisible. Escaping fluid under pressure can penetrate the skin and cause serious injury.

Hydraulics safety message page 334.

If injured by escaping fluid, stop work, and see a doctor immediately.

• Never lubricate, adjust, or clean a stack wagon while it is operating.

• Always block the wheels if anyone is working on, under,

Fig. 40—Transport Safely

Fig. 41—Poorly-Formed Stacks

or around a stack wagon. Use a sturdy, dependable safety support if any wheel is removed.

• Lower the pickup when a stack wagon is not in use. Block the raised pickup if anyone must work underneath. Also, place the pickup lock in safety position.

• Add ballast to the front of the tractor for stability, and to rear wheels as needed for traction and safe braking.

TROUBLESHOOTING

Field problems are usually improper crop pickup or poorly formed stacks (Fig. 41). Both problems are usually caused by operator inexperience. This chart will help you diagnose problems and correct them. Refer to the stack wagon operator's manual for specific adjustments and additional operating suggestions.

TROUBLESHOOTING CHART

PROBLEM	POSSIBLE CAUSE	POSSIBLE REMEDY
PLUGGED PICKUP.	Ground speed too fast.	Reduce ground speed.
	Material too wet.	Allow material to dry.
	Cutoff improperly adjusted.	Adjust cutoff.
	Belt slipping.	Adjust belt tension.
UNLOADING CLUTCH DOES NOT DISENGAGE WHEN CANOPY IS LOWERED.	Doors not latching.	Adjust door cables.
	Control cable out of adjustment.	Adjust unloading drive clutch.
CANOPY LOWER ON ONE SIDE.	Air in hydraulic system.	Slowly raise canopy to highest position. Hold lever in "up" position for a few seconds, allowing the air to be purged from the system.
REAR DOOR NOT LATCHING.	Door cables out of adjustment.	Adjust door cables.
STACK LOW IN FRONT.	Not putting enough material into wagon during step two (2) of loading cycle.	Review and follow recommended procedure.
	Deflector not adjusted properly.	Make sure the deflector is moving down against the stop as the canopy is lowered.
		Adjust deflector cable and/or stop as necessary.
STACK LOW IN REAR.	Material too wet.	Allow material to dry.
	Rotor speed too low.	Operate tractor at rated PTO speed.
	Rotor speed too low.	Check rotor drive-belt tension.
	Deflector not properly adjusted.	Adjust duct cap and deflector as recommended.
STACK LOPSIDED.	Cutoff improperly adjusted.	Adjust cutoff.
	Poor loading technique.	Review and follow recommended procedure.

PROBLEM	POSSIBLE CAUSE	POSSIBLE REMEDY
	Not driving over center of windrow.	Drive over center of windrow.
	Inlet holes on rotor housing plugged.	Clean air inlet holes.
	Uneven dirt buildup around cutoff.	Clean off built-up dirt.
UNEVEN STACK DENSITY.	Poor loading technique.	Review and follow recommended procedure.
DIRT IN STACK.	Running pickup too low.	Raise pickup, adjust lift cylinder down-stop.
PLUGGED DISCHARGE DUCT.	Filling compression chamber too full.	Stop over-filling compression chamber.

MAINTENANCE

Maintenance is needed on the pickup assembly and the hydraulic system. The main frame and wheels, discharge duct and deflector, compression chamber, and unloading system usually aren't subjected to heavy wear.

PICKUP ASSEMBLY

The pickup system is near the ground where dust and dirt wear the flails (Fig. 42). To get full service from the flails, exchange the worn ones with those less worn. (Refer to the exchange procedure described previously in this chapter and in the stack wagon operator's manual.) When flails wear out completely, replace them with new ones. Flails work more efficiently and last longer if the pickup height is controlled properly.

Cylinder pickups do not need as much maintenance as flail pickups. Repair or replace bent and broken teeth.

HYDRAULIC SYSTEM

A well maintained hydraulic system is essential for high field efficiency and well formed stacks. High pressure is required for canopy compaction force. Otherwise, stacks will not be formed and compacted properly.

Hydraulic system maintenance on a stack wagon is fruitless unless the tractor hydraulic system is also well maintained. While the most common tractor-hydraulic system failures result from lack of oil in the reservoir, maintenance is more complex than just adding oil. The pump and control valves must be in proper operating condition.

Stack-wagon hydraulic system maintenance consists of repairing hoses, lines, pipes, and fittings that are damaged or deteriorating. Keep hydraulic components in good working condition to prevent high pressure fluid leaks. Maintain and repair hydraulic cylinders to reduce the chance of an oil leak.

Maintenance of the tractor hydraulic system is beyond the scope of this book. Refer to the FMO Manuals, *Hydraulics* and *Tractors*, and the tractor operator's manual for details.

REPLACEMENT PARTS

Keep replacement parts on hand so you can fix the machine fast if it breaks down. Belts and chains break, so carry spare chain links and belts in the field. Due to the abrasive conditions at a flail pickup, spare flails are needed, particularly in stony fields. If a stack wagon has a cylinder pickup keep extra pickup teeth. Repair parts for the hydraulic system become more essential as the stack wagon ages.

Fig. 42—Abrasive Conditions at the Pickup

Fig. 43—Integrally Mounted Stack Mover

Fig. 45—Tilt-Bed Trailer Stack Mover

STORAGE

Proper stack wagon storage during the off-season helps reduce maintenance and lengthens service life. Store a stack wagon in a shelter and block it up to take the weight off the tires. Do not deflate the tires. Remove the tires and store them in a cool, dark, dry place if inside storage is not possible.

Clean the stack wagon thoroughly, inside and out. Dirt and trash draw moisture which stimulates rust. Put a light coat of oil on unpainted surfaces to suppress rust. Use paint to touch up surfaces where paint has worn off.

Release the tension on belts. Then clean them with a non-flammable cleaning agent. Clean chains and brush them with heavy oil to prevent corrosion and rust. Grease the threads on adjusting bolts. Give the stack wagon a complete lubrication.

Prepare a list of repairs you need and buy parts so you can make repairs during the off-season.

SECTION 2: STACK MOVERS

INTRODUCTION

A stack mover is an integral part of most stack-wagon operations. Various stack movers are available to match specific needs. However, the functional requirements are similar for all stack movers. A stack mover lifts, hauls, and unloads stacks.

Fig. 44—Integral Stack Mover with Caster Wheels

Fig. 46—Stack Wagon Converted to Stack Mover

Fig. 47—Towed Highway Stack Mover

Fig. 48—Truck-Mounted Stack Mover

Fig. 49—Integral Stack Mover

Stack movers are classified as:

- **Farm and ranch**
- **Towed highway**
- **Truck mounted**

The farm-and-ranch stack mover is pulled by a tractor and is designed to move stacks from the field to the stack yard, or from the stack yard to the feeding area.

The smallest stack movers are designed to handle 1- to 1 1/2-ton stacks, and are integrally mounted on the tractor 3-point hitch (Fig. 43). Most fork movers have caster wheels to help carry the load and eliminate the need for heavy front-end tractor ballast (Fig. 44).

An integrally-mounted mover cannot lift larger stacks. *Tilt-bed trailers* with powered drag chains (Fig. 45) are used to lift stacks weighing 2 tons or more. The drag chains are powered with a hydraulic motor or direct PTO drive, as designed by the manufacturer. Flotation tires are used on most of these movers to allow travel on soft, wet ground. Some stack wagons may be converted to stack movers by removing the stack chamber.

TOWED HIGHWAY; TRUCK-MOUNTED MOVERS

Towed highway (Fig. 47) and *truck-mounted* (Fig. 48) stack movers are used primarily for transporting stacks on the road. Time saved in long-distance hauling is the main advantage of these higher-speed movers.

Stacks are conveyed onto or off of the bed with drag chains, similar to the farm-and-ranch models. These units are designed for the hay grower or buyer who handles large volumes of hay which must be transported long distances; they are built to haul at least 6 tons of hay per load. A detailed discussion of highway stack movers is beyond the scope of this text. The rest of the discussion in this chapter will concentrate on farm-and-ranch stack movers.

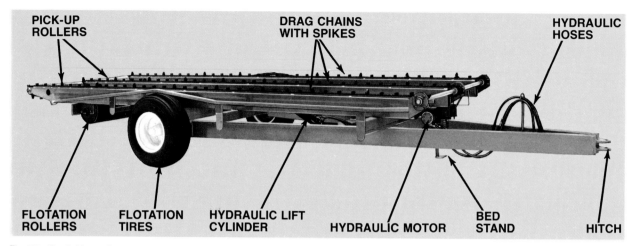

PICK-UP
ROLLERS

DRAG CHAINS
WITH SPIKES

HYDRAULIC
HOSES

FLOTATION
ROLLERS

FLOTATION
TIRES

HYDRAULIC LIFT
CYLINDER

HYDRAULIC MOTOR

BED
STAND

HITCH

Fig. 50—Stack-Mover Components

STACK-MOVER OPERATION

Integrally-mounted stack movers are simple machines with a 3-, 4-, or 5-tined fork, caster wheels, 3-point hitch, and hydraulic cylinders. Fork tines slide under a stack (Fig. 49) and support the stack during moving. Caster wheels carry part of the load during transport. Some movers do not have caster wheels, but require the tractor to support the entire weight of the stack. This requires additional tractor front-end ballast to prevent the tractor from tipping backward. Also, some movers have a hydraulic clamp to hold the stack firmly on the forks (Fig. 43).

PRIMARY COMPONENTS

Primary components of a tilt-bed trailer stack mover are (Fig. 50):

- **Tilt bed with hydraulic lift cylinder**
- **Drag chains with hydraulic-motor or PTO drive**
- **Flotation rollers**
- **Main frame and wheels**

Some manufacturers use a *direct PTO drive* instead of a hydraulic motor on the drag chains. Also, a few manufacturers use skid shoes or crawler tracks instead of flotation rollers.

The *hydraulic cylinder* tilts the bed of the trailer until the *flotation rollers* contact the ground. Flotation rollers prevent the rear end of the bed from sinking into the ground as the stack mover is backed under the stack. They also keep the pick-up rollers or chain sprockets from digging into the ground beneath the stack, or from chewing into the bottom of the stack. The *drag chains* carry the stack from the ground to the tilted bed as the stack mover is backed. The *main frame* and flotation tires support the mover and stack during loading, transporting, and unloading. Depending on

the stack-mover's size, wheels may be single, dual, or tandem. Some large units have tandem duals on walking-beam axles for maximum flotation and load-carrying ability.

OPERATION AND ADJUSTMENT

As in stack-wagon operation, experience pays dividends during stack moving. The most common problem encountered with stack movers is too much haste in loading and unloading. To increase hauling capacity, the operator may try to load and unload too rapidly, causing stacks to split open so water can penetrate the stack core. Fast transportation over rough ground may shake the stack loose and lift the upper layers of hay.

ALLOW STACKS TIME TO SETTLE

All stacks tend to come apart if they are moved too soon after the stack is unloaded from the wagon. Wait at least 48 hours before hauling stacks out of the field with a stack mover. This delay allows the stack to settle and become more tightly knit before it is moved. Unloading stacks near the road or one end of the field requires more stacking time, but reduces moving time later.

TRACTOR PREPARATION

Both the tractor and stack mover must be checked and prepared before operation. Before attaching the stack mover to the tractor, follow recommendations in the operator's manual and:

1. Set the tractor drawbar to the recommended position for the stack mover.

2. Pin the drawbar directly below the center line of the tractor PTO shaft for towed movers.

3. Add weight to stablize the tractor under all terrain conditions. Weight is particularly important with mounted stack movers and when operating on hillsides. Consult the tractor operator's manual for the proper amounts of front end and rear wheel ballast.

4. Adjust wheel spacing for stability.

5. Check air pressure in front and rear tires, and inflate if necessary.

6. Make sure the 3-point hitch operates properly if it is used with a mounted stack mover.

7. Check the tractor hydraulic oil level.

ATTACHING TOWED MOVER

Follow this sequence for attaching a towed stack mover to the tractor:

1. Back the tractor to within 6 inches (152 mm) of the stackmover hitch, shut off the engine and take the key.

2. Connect hydraulic hoses to the tractor and set the stack mover hitch at the proper height.

3. Align hitch-pin holes, insert the safety hitch pin, and attach the safety chain. Never insert or let a helper insert the pin if the tractor is in reverse gear and running.

4. For a PTO-driven stack mover, make sure the tractor PTO speed matches the stack-mover drive requirement, then connect the PTO shaft.

5. Put the bed stand or hitch jack in the transport position after attaching the mover to the tractor.

To detach the towed stack mover, reverse the attaching procedure.

ATTACHING MOUNTED MOVER

To attach a mounted stack mover:

1. Move the tractor drawbar forward and pin it securely.

2. Back the tractor to within 6 inches (152 mm) of the stack mover's 3-point hitch.

3. Connect hydraulic hoses to the tractor. Adjust the height of lower pins on the 3-point hitch.

4. Connect the stack mover to the 3-point hitch.

Detach the stack mover by reversing this procedure.

FINAL CHECKUP

Final preparation of the stack mover is required before field operation starts.

First: Review the operator's manual carefully.

The stack mover should be completely lubricated as outlined in the manual. Inspect all tires and inflate them to the recommended pressure.

For tilt-bed stack movers, check tension in each drag chain (Fig. 51). If chains are not adjusted properly, correct the tension adjustment.

Check all bolts, and tighten to recommended torque.

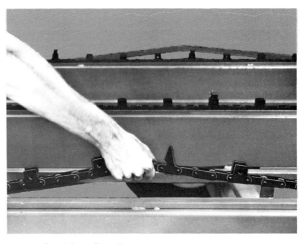

Fig. 51—Check Drag-Chain Tension

Another important step in preparing the stack mover is to make sure all hydraulic systems are operating properly. If a malfunction is found, make repairs. Inspect hoses and lines for leaks. Be especially careful checking for leaks. Prevent serious injury from high-pressure oil leaks by releasing the pressure before disconnecting hydraulic lines or hoses and by using a card to check for leaks.

FIELD OPERATION

OPERATING CONTROLS

Controls to operate stack movers vary with each type and make. They normally include hydraulic-system controls, possibly the PTO clutch, and basic tractor controls. A general operating procedure for mounted and tilt-bed-trailer stack movers follows. For specific details regarding each mover, study the operator's manual.

REAR-MOUNTED MOVER

To easily and efficiently load and unload a rear-mounted stack mover, follow these steps:

Loading

1. Back toward the stack. If possible, approach the end where traction will be best. Stop when the rear of the stack mover is about one foot from the stack. Be sure the tractor, stack mover, and stack are in a straight line.

2. Lower the fork until the tines are level and touching the ground (Fig. 52).

3. Back the tractor until the stack contacts the front frame of the stack mover.

4. Stop the tractor and lift the stack slowly (Fig. 53).

Fig. 52—Stack Mover Ready To Back under Stack

Fig. 53—Ready for Transport

Unloading

1. Move the tractor to the unloading position.

2. Lower the stack mover and stack to the ground.

3. Drive the tractor forward until the mover clears the stack.

4. Raise the stack mover.

TILT-BED MOVER

The following procedure is for loading stacks with a tilt-bed stack mover:

Loading

1. Back toward the stack. Approach the end where traction is best. Stop when the rear of the stack mover is about one foot from the stack. Make sure the tractor, stack mover, and haystack are all in a straight line.

Fig. 54—Tilt Bed Ready To Load

FLOTATION
ROLLERS

Fig. 55—Backing Under Stack

2. Tilt the mover bed until the flotation rollers contact the ground (Fig. 54).

3. With drag chains moving toward the tractor, back the stack mover under the hay stack (Fig. 55). Match the ground speed of the tractor to the drag chain speed and the mover will crawl under the stack.

4. As the stack approaches the front end of the tilted bed, stop the drag-chain movement and the backward motion of the tractor and stack mover (Fig. 56).

5. Slowly tilt the front of the bed downward (Fig. 57). Lowering the bed too fast can damage the stack mover.

Experience will make it easier for the operator to judge the proper ground speed and control the tractor's hydraulic, steering, and propulsion systems simultaneously.

Unloading

Unloading steps for tilt-bed stack movers:

1. Line up the tractor and stack mover.

2. Slowly tilt the bed until flotation rollers touch the ground.

3. Start slow rearward movement of the drag chains and

Fig. 56—Stack Loaded on Tilt-Bed

READY TO TILT

STACK PICK-UP ROLLERS

Fig. 57—Ready for Transport

forward movement of the tractor simultaneously. Match drag-chain speed and tractor speed and the mover will crawl out from under the stack.

4. After driving clear of the stack, stop the drag chains and tractor.

5. Return the bed to the horizontal position.

Fig. 58—Flotation Roller Positions

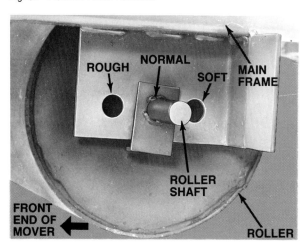

FIELD ADJUSTMENTS

Field adjustments of a tilt-bed stack mover usually involve proper positioning of the flotation rollers or skid shoes, and adjusting the torque of the hydraulic motor that powers the drag chains.

Flotation rollers on a mover may be used in three different positions, which are determined by shaft holes. Position the flotation rollers in the front hole (1, Fig. 58) for uneven ground conditions. Hole 2 is for normal ground conditions. Hole 3 is for soft, sandy conditions. Proper flotation roller position keeps the end of the tilt bed from sinking into the ground or digging into the stack. If the flotation rollers are in the right position, the pickup rollers and chains won't dig into the ground when the mover is tilted.

The regular *drive sprocket* on the drag chains hydraulic motor may be replaced with a smaller-diameter sprocket to increase power to the chains. You may need more power for work on icy, muddy fields or because of extreme stack density and moisture content. Reducing sprocket size for more power also reduces drag chain speed for a given hydraulic flow rate.

TRANSPORT

Proper transporting is safe transporting. Before transporting the stack mover:

1. Raise the bed stand or hitch jack and secure it in the transport position.

2. When transporting under load, be sure the tilt bed is positioned properly. For a mounted stack mover, avoid obstacles and be sure the mover clears rough ground.

3. Always transport with stack mover within the speed range recommended by the manufacturer. Never exceed safe tractor speed for the terrain covered. On a public road keep as far to the right as possible.

4. When the stack mover is unloaded, keep a clearly visible SMV emblem on the tractor to alert motorists approaching from the rear. When loaded, attach an SMV emblem to the stack or rear of the stack mover.

SAFETY

● Be extremely alert at all times. A bulky stack restricts vision. Before operating a stack mover make sure no one is nearby.

● Make sure only one person — the operator — is on the tractor during operation of transport.

● Never ride or permit others to ride on the tractor fender, drawbar or hitch, the stack mover, or the loaded stack.

● Never use the bed stand to support loaded movers.

● Never use the bed stand to support a loaded stack mover.

● Block the wheels before leaving the stack mover on a sloping surface.

● Put on enough weight to stablize the tractor, especially when it is operated on hillsides.

● Be careful with high-pressure hydraulic systems.

● Never adjust, clean, or lubricate the stack mover while it is operating.

TROUBLESHOOTING

Most field problems encountered with a stack mover have simple solutions. The hard part is figuring out which solution to use. This chart will help.

TROUBLESHOOTING CHART		
PROBLEM	POSSIBLE CAUSE	POSSIBLE REMEDY
PICK-UP CHAIN WILL NOT MOVE.	Air in hydraulic system.	Bleed system by cycling hydraulic motor.
	No lubrication.	Lubricate.
	Hydraulic motor damaged.	See your stack-mover dealer.
	Hydraulic system in tractor not working.	Check tractor operator's manual.
	Debris blocking chain or sprockets.	Check for blockage and remove.
	Chain too tight.	Loosen chain tightener.
BED WILL NOT TILT.	Air in hydraulic system.	Bleed system by cycling remote hydraulic cylinder.
	Remote hydraulic cylinder damaged.	See your stack-mover dealer.
	Hydraulic system in tractor not working.	Check tractor operator's manual.
	Debris blocking bed.	Remove debris.
HYDRAULIC MOTOR STALLS.	Wrong hydraulic motor sprocket arrangement.	Remove 16-tooth sprocket, and replace with 13-tooth sprocket on hydraulic motor drive shaft.
	Chain too tight.	Loosen chain tightener.

PROBLEM	POSSIBLE CAUSE	POSSIBLE REMEDY
STACKS FALL APART DURING UNLOADING.	Ground speed too fast during unloading.	Reduce ground speed.
	Transporting on rough ground is shaking stacks apart.	Reduce ground speed.

MAINTENANCE

Maintenance needs depend on the model of stack mover. An integrally-mounted stack mover has few moving parts, so most maintenance involves the hydraulic system.

Most important in hydraulic-system maintenance is keeping dirt out of the system (Fig. 59). Foreign objects in the hydraulic system cause malfunctions and increase wear.

The drag chains operate in abrasive dust and dirt, where excessive wear can occur. They require regular inspection

Fig. 59—Keep Hydraulic Fittings Clean

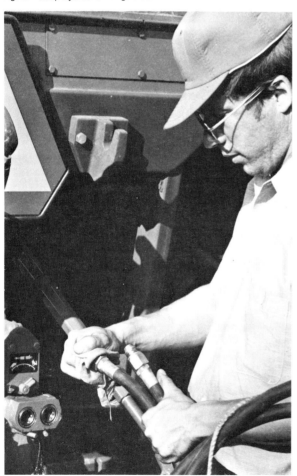

and must be repaired right away when they show wear. Proper maintenance of high-wear parts helps avert major breakdowns.

STORAGE

Proper storage of the stack mover during the off-season helps maintain stack-moving efficiency. Because the stack wagon and stack mover have many similar components and operate in similar field conditions, storage and preparation techniques are similar. Refer to the discussion on stack-wagon storage for details that also apply to stack movers.

SUMMARY

Tractor-powered stack wagons are used to package hay and stover. Stack-wagons can stack a wide variety of crops without a lot of labor and at lower operating cost than other haying systems. These advantages are particularly important for one-man operations where hay or stover is grown, harvested, and fed on the farm.

Commercial hay growers can use stack-wagon systems too if the hay market is nearby. However, low density and large stack sizes prohibit economical long-distance transportation.

A stack wagon lifts a windrow or stover and blows the material into a canopy-covered wagon. The stack is formed by a mechanical press or air-packing. After the stack is compacted, it is discharged with a chain-slat floor conveyor through the rear doors. A properly-formed stack has a thatched, sloping, weather-resistant top.

Stack movers are used to transport stacks from the field to stack yard, feedlot, or market.

Although the stack-wagon system provides mechanization from field to feeding with great savings in labor, proper field management and operating procedures are essential for top benefits. A well planned hay program reflects good judgment in the timeliness and predicted outcome of each field operation and their effect on stacking. For lowest field and storage losses, the material must be stacked at the proper moisture content. To continuously form well shaped, uniform, high density stacks that store well, the stack wagon operator must understand the recommended operating procedure and develop excellent skills. Lack of operator skill and experience can result in poor-quality hay for feeding.

CHAPTER QUIZ

1. (Fill in blanks.) The two methods used to compact stacks in a stack wagon are _____ and _____.

2. Give two reasons why stacks are not suited for long-distance transportation.

3. (Fill in blanks.) Flail pickups may be used to lift _____ or _____ or harvest _____.

4. Describe the problems encountered if hay is stacked when its moisture content is too high.

5. (True or false.) Filling a stack wagon properly begins with loading the lower back of the compression chamber.

6. List two or more operating faults that can cause a stack to be lopsided.

7. (True or false.) Stacks in storage should be butted together to reduce spoilage losses.

8. Name three kinds of stack movers.

9. Describe the function of flotation rollers on tilt-bed stack movers.

10. (True or false.) A tilt-bed stack mover requires two people on the tractor to control the tractor hydraulic, steering, and propulsion systems simultaneously.

10
Hay Cubers

Fig. 1—Cube Handling Is Easily Mechanized

INTRODUCTION

The interest in field cubers is steadily declining. Field cubers are not manufactured today, however, existing machines are used worldwide. Stationary cubers have continued to be somewhat popular and are being manufactured today.

PURPOSE AND USE

Besides lower labor costs and mechanized handling, cubes offer many advantages. Feeding trials indicate less hay is wasted with cubes, compared to bales. Cattle can consume more pounds of cubes than pounds of hay from bales. Consequently, a faster rate of gain for beef cattle and greater milk production from dairy cows may be realized when feeding cubes. Cubes also mix well with silage and concentrates to provide a complete ration. It is possible to produce cubes with hay and grain or mineral additives incorporated. Such "complete-ration" cubes help ensure balanced nutrition for cattle and cut feeding labor (Fig. 2).

The bulk density of cubes is more than double the bulk density of baled hay. So the storage space required for cubes is less than half that required for an equivalent weight of bales. Trucks may be loaded with cubes to the weight limit without exceeding height and width limitations. Also, high cube density makes cubes less likely to catch fire accidentally.

Fig. 2—Mechanized Feeding

Fig. 3—Field Cuber

LIMITATIONS

Some limitations restrict the use of cubers. Field cubing with mobile units is limited to legume crops and to climates that permit hay to dry quickly in the windrow to a moisture-content of 10 to 12 percent. Field cubing alfalfa is an accepted practice in dry climates in the west.

Stationary cubing plants offer a wide range of cube production. Artificially-dried hay, rectangular and large round bales, or even loose-hay stacks may be cubed at a stationary plant. Binders may be incorporated with the forage to permit cubing non-legume crops. Stationary cubing plants can also produce complete-ration cubes.

TYPES AND SIZES

There are two types of cubers:

- **Field**
- **Stationary**

FIELD CUBER

The field cuber lifts hay from the windrow, forms cubes, and conveys the cubes into a towed wagon (Fig. 3). The self-propelled field cuber is used where the climate is dry enough for field curing hay. Cubes are usually collected in high-dump wagons trailed behind the cuber. When loaded, the dump wagon bed is hydraulically lifted and rotated to dump the entire load into a truck for transport to storage or feeding. High-dump wagons are discussed in Chapter 12, *Self-Unloading Forage Wagons.*

PRIMARY COMPONENTS

Primary components of a field cuber are (Fig. 4):

- **Cylinder pickup**
- **Water-spray nozzles**
- **Loose-hay conveyors**
- **Cylinder cutterhead**
- **Press wheel and dies**
- **Cube conveyor**
- **Cube elevator**

A diesel engine supplies power.

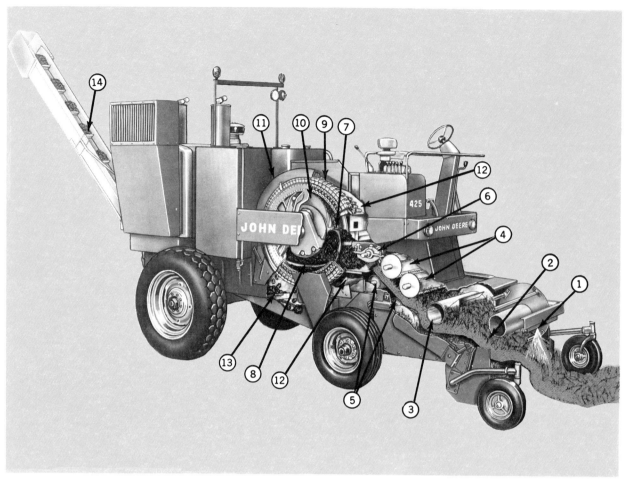

Fig. 4—Field Cuber

COMPONENT FUNCTIONS

Hay flow through the cuber is explained below. Numbers in parentheses refer to cuber components (Fig. 4). Windrowed alfalfa is ready for cubing after it has field-cured to 10 or 12 percent moisture. The hay is sprayed with water (1) as it is lifted by the *cylinder pickup* (2). The pickup conveys hay to an *auger* (3) behind the pickup feeder. The auger centerfeeds the alfalfa to the first of two identical sets of *feed rolls.* The feed rolls (4 and 5) compress and deliver hay to the *cutterhead* or chopper. The cutterhead (6) chops and mixes the hay to help provide even distribution of the water applied earlier.

The water activates the natural adhesive on legume plants. This "glue" helps bond the cube.

A large-diameter *auger* (7), and *spiral bars* (8), on the inside of the auger housing, move the chopped alfalfa uniformly to all openings in the *die ring* (9). As the material leaves the auger flight, a heavy *press wheel* (10) forces the alfalfa into and through the die openings in the ring. The natural legume glue, high pressure of the press wheel, and heat generated by forcing hay through the dies bonds the cubes.

An adjustable deflector (11) around the outside of the die ring breaks off cubes in lengths from 2 to 3 inches (50 to 75 mm). Sheet-metal chutes (12) channel the cubes to a conveyor (13) beneath the die ring. The conveyor carries the cubes to an elevator (14) which delivers them to a towed wagon.

STATIONARY CUBER

The stationary cuber is more versatile than the field cuber (Fig. 5). It is frequently used in areas where climate makes field cubing impractical. The stationary cuber also makes it possible to stockpile hay and extend the cubing season beyond the hay growing season. Stockpiling hay also permits cubing on days when weather is not suitable for field cubing.

The stationary cuber is the heart of a cubing plant (Fig. 6); it is usually mounted on a concrete pad and powered with an electric motor. Accessory equipment to meter hay, spray water on the chopped hay, and blend the ingredients, is usually mounted with the stationary cuber. Cube conveyors move the finished product directly to a cooling pad or to trucks.

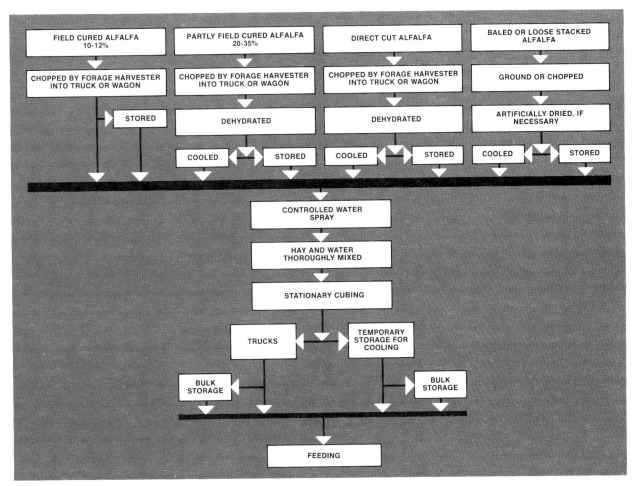

Fig. 5—Flow Chart for Stationary Cubing

Fig. 6—Stationary Cuber and Accessory Equipment

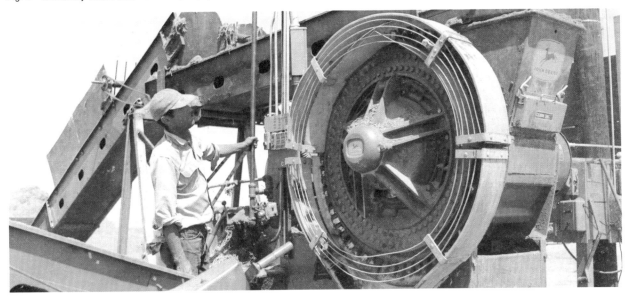

Fig. 7—Unloading Cubes

ADDITIONAL EQUIPMENT

Some stationary cubing operations have additional equipment. Drying drums let you cut alfalfa and cube it immediately or cube hay in wetter climates. Grinders chop baled or loose stacked hay. Holding bins and metering conveyors are used to add grain or mineral supplements to produce complete-ration cubes.

A stationary cuber may be mounted on a trailer with accessory equipment to form a portable cubing system. The equipment is moved from one hay stockpile to another to reduce the hauling distance for the chopped, baled, or loose stacked hay. Some portable stationary cubing systems may also be used to cube cotton-gin trash.

HAY CUBER OPERATION

The self-propelled field cuber is a complete hay-processing machine that picks up windrowed hay and forms hay cubes. The hay cubes are a finished product ready for transport, storage, and feeding.

Legumes are field cubed because they contain a natural, soluble adhesive that helps bind the cubes together.

The remaining discussion of cubing is limited to alfalfa, the only legume grown in commercial quantities that is practical for field cubing.

OPERATION AND
FIELD ADJUSTMENTS

Success of a field-cubing operation depends upon the farm manager and the cuber operator, who may or may not be the same person. Without effective management and a skilled operator, who may or may not be the same person. Without effective management and a skilled operator, a field-cubing operation will not produce high-quality cubes in quantities required for economic success.

The manager's responsibilities extend beyond the actual cubing operation. He must be responsible for crop and field management, as well as machine management. To produce the highest quality cubes, a fine-stemmed alfalfa variety cut at the bud stage is desirable. The influence of weather conditions must be considered. Planning the field operation to ensure cutting at the proper stage and achieving full use of the cuber is not always easy. Acceptable cubes can only be formed if the alfalfa contains less than 10 percent grass, and the grass is evenly distributed throughout the crop.

A skilled operator is more than a self-propelled field cuber driver. He must recognize quality cubes, and adjust the cuber to produce the highest quality cubes from the alfalfa available. He must also perform maintenance and do minor repair work to keep the cuber in top operating condition.

PLANNING AND PREPARATION

Planning for a cubing operation starts with selecting auxiliary equipment to support the field cuber. A combination water-and-fuel truck is needed to replenish water and fuel. Water is applied to the hay at a rate of 20 to 25 gallons (68 to 86 L/t) per ton of hay, and fuel is consumed at about 5 to 7$\frac{1}{2}$ gallons per hour (19 to 28L). In addition, a well-equipped service truck is required to minimize downtime. This support equipment can be used with more than one cuber and many cubing operations have more than one machine to help reduce overhead costs per cuber and per ton of cubes.

Hauling

Trucks must be available to receive cubes from the trailing wagons (Fig. 7). The number and size of trucks required depends on the haul distance and number of cubers. Single-axle trucks are usually used for short hauls, and large trucks with one or two trailers are used for long-distance hauling.

Hay Preparation

Proper equipment is also required to prepare the crop for cubing. Normal procedure is to cut, windrow, and condition the alfalfa in one operation. Conditioning breaks the stems, causing faster, more uniform drying. Adjusting windrow-

forming shields to form the widest possible windrow also aids fast, even drying (Fig. 8). In addition, water may be sprayed more uniformly on a wide windrow than on a narrow one.

If possible, avoid raking to reduce harvesting costs and to save more alfalfa leaves. If the windrowed hay is rained on, it is sometimes necessary to turn the windrow onto dry ground to hasten drying. However, to prevent excessive leaf loss, rake the windrow in the morning when dew is on the alfalfa.

CUBER CHECKUP

At the beginning of each season, give the field cuber a final inspection before going to the field. Follow instructions in the operator's manual to make the following checks and adjustments to help avoid costly breakdowns during the cubing season:

- *Review the operator's manual.*

- *Clean the cuber thoroughly inside and outside.*

- *Make sure all bolts are tight and cotter pins are in place.*

- *Check and adjust the tension of all drive belts and chains.*

- *Check the condition of cutterhead knives. Sharpen and adjust clearance, if necessary.*

- *Check the condition of the die-ring cross-auger and spiral-bar wear pads. Replace if needed.*

- *Check tire inflation.*

- *Thoroughly clean the engine air-cleaner, filter element and precleaner.*

- *Check the the battery electrolyte level.*

- *Check the engine coolant level.*

- *Check the oil level in gearcases, engine crankcase and hydraulic reservoir.*

Fig. 8—Wide Windrows Dry Faster

- *Clean fuel strainers.*

- *Fill the fuel tank.*

- *Lubricate the cuber completely, then run at half-speed for about an hour. Check bearings for overheating or excessive looseness.*

- *Check water tank, pump, lines, and nozzles for leaks and obstructions.*

PRELIMINARY SETTINGS AND ADJUSTMENTS

Each day, before operating the field cuber, give it a preventive-maintenance inspection and service as recommended in the operator's manual. This daily routine helps prevent major breakdowns and assures the operator that the cuber is in proper operating condition. During the inspection, make adjustments needed on the engine and cuber.

PICKUP HEIGHT

Before cubing, adjust the height of the pickup gauge wheels, as necessary. Under normal operating conditions, pickup teeth should clear the ground by 1 to 2 inches (25 to 50 mm). You may need to raise the teeth to avoid picking up green alfalfa leaves.

SPRAYING SYSTEM

Adjust the water-spraying system so you don't waste water (Fig. 9). Nozzles should cover the entire width of the pickup. A nozzle selector on the operator's console can direct water on the windrow only if needed. Plug some nozzles if the nozzle selector does not provide the right width control.

Nozzle tips on the spray bar are used to supply enough water to form a durable cube. Generally, the amount of water required is 5 to 30 gallons per ton (4 to 102L). This wide range reflects the variation in moisture content of the alfalfa. To select the proper nozzle tip size, determine the moisture content of the hay and refer to the operator's manual for recommendations. Experience will help make this decision.

FIELD OPERATION

Controls and instruments for a field cuber are within reach of the operator (Fig. 10). Study and understand the operation and function of each control and instrument before operating the cuber.

After becoming familiar with the controls and instruments, review the operator's manual for instructions covering break-in procedures, operation, lubrication, and maintenance of the cuber and engine.

STARTING THE ENGINE

Field operation begins with starting the cuber engine. Follow the procedure in the operator's manual. If the engine fails to start promptly, let the starter motor cool for one minute, then repeat the procedure.

After starting, allow the engine to warm up to recommended operating temperature before operating under load.

OPERATE AT FULL THROTTLE

When it is properly warmed up, run the engine at full throttle and engage the main clutch to operate the pickup, feeder, and press wheel. Check to see that all components are running freely.

Fig. 9—Spray Entire Windrow

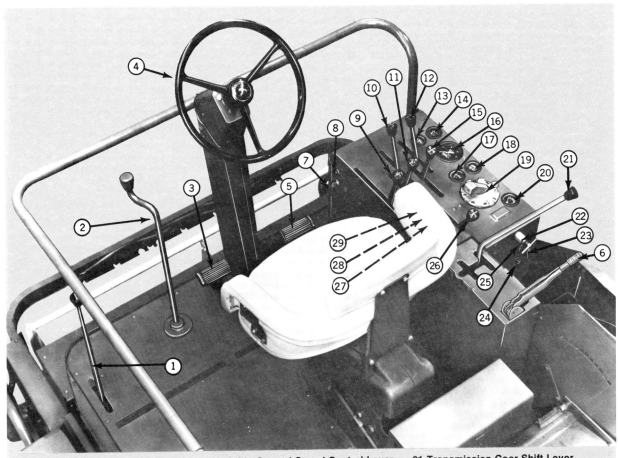

1-Main Cluth Lever (CLUTCH)	11-Variable Ground Speed Control Lever	21-Transmission Gear Shift Lever
2-Pickup Variable Speed Control	12-Wagon Bin Dump Lever (BIN DUMP)	22-Water Pressure Regulator
3-Transmission Clutch Pedal	13-Ammeter	23-15-Amp Light Fuse
4-Steering Wheel	14-Oil Pressure Gauge	24-30-Amp Light Fuse
5-Brake Pedal	15-Elevator Lift Lever (ELEVATOR)	25-Light Switch
6-Parking Brake Lever	16-Tachometer-Hour Meter	26-Conveyor Clutch Lever (CONVEYOR)
7-Key Switch	17-Fuel Gauge	27-Emergency Engine Stop Knob
8-Starter Button	18-Water Temperature Gauge (Engine)	28-Horn Button
9-Throttle Lever (THROTTLE)	19-Nozzle Selector Valve Control Lever	29-Engine Stop Knob
10-Platform Lift Lever (PLAT LIFT)	20-Water Pressure Gauge	

Fig. 10—Field Cuber Controls And Instruments

Failure to run the engine at full throttle before engaging the clutch may result in stalling the cutterhead and damaging the cutterhead belt. Continue to run the engine at full throttle when cubing hay.

Engage the conveyor clutch to start the conveyor and elevator.

Select a low ground speed (first or second gear) that will not overload the machine. Lower the pickup and move into the windrow. Adjust the pickup speed to match ground speed (Fig. 11). Travel the same direction as the windrower travelled when the crop was cut.

Keep the spraying system water tank filled. Spray a small amount of water on the windrow if the die openings are empty. If the die openings are full, do not spray any water on the windrow until cubes start to move out of all the die openings.

DIE RING HEAT-UP

Friction caused by material moving through the dies causes the die ring to heat to about 175 degrees (97.3), the normal operating temperature of most cubers. Heat-up takes 5 or 10 minutes, depending on crop conditions and air temperature. Do not make final spray settings until the die has reached operating temperature. During the warm-up period, a buildup may occur in the dies. This buildup will

Fig. 11—Adjust the Pickup Speed As Required

move out faster and easier if the alfalfa is dry. Some "fines" can be expected during the warm-up period (Fig. 12).

END OF WINDROW

After ending each windrow, shut off the nozzle-selector valve and disengage the conveyor clutch. This prevents wasting water and losing cubes while turning.

As the cuber enters the next windrow, start the spray on the first hay to enter the pickup. Engage the conveyor clutch when the trailing wagon is in line with the cuber and under the elevator hood.

If the operator forgets to engage the conveyor clutch, a horn will sound when cubes are accumulated in the conveyor under the die ring.

At the end of each day, shut off the nozzle-selector valve to stop the spray about 50 feet (15 m) from the end of the final windrow. The dies will fill with dry hay, which can be easily pushed out of the dies when operation is resumed.

STOPPING THE ENGINE

To stop the engine, disengage the main (cuber) clutch and transmission clutch and place the gearshift lever in neutral. Reduce the engine speed and let the engine idle 4 or 5 minutes before stopping the engine. This permits the engine to cool down before stopping and prolongs engine life.

FIELD ADJUSTMENTS

The two primary field adjustments during operation are: controlling the amount of water sprayed on the windrow; and selecting the rate alfalfa enters the cuber.

When the die ring has reached operating temperature, adjust the spray so the cuber can form hard, dense, durable cubes. Properly formed cubes break off cleanly when they contact the cube deflector.

Check cube quality by examining the cubes as they emerge from the die ring (Fig. 13).

REGULATE WATER SPRAY

Wet cubes tend to curve out from the deflector instead of separating. Wet cubes may mold during storage unless they are piled outside on a slab to cool and dry. Cubes that flake off into "fines" before contacting the deflector need more water. Cubes made without enough water are more likely to disintegrate during handling and storage.

GROUND SPEED

The rate alfalfa enters the cuber is controlled by ground speed. Always run the engine at full throttle while cubing. Control ground speed by using the variable-speed-drive and the different transmission speeds. Select transmission speed range; then, with the variable-speed-control lever, adjust ground speed to match field conditions. Proper width windrows permit the cuber to work at an optimum speed of 3 to 4 miles per hour (4.8 to 6 km/h). Within this speed range, the pickup lifts the windrow into the machine without agitating the alfalfa.

Fig. 12—Good Cubes and "Fines"

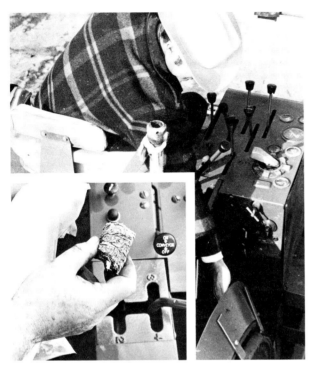

Fig. 13—Operator Examining Cube Quality

TRANSPORT

The field cuber is normally transported from field to field under its own power and requires no special adjustments for road transport (Fig. 14). Raise the pickup to its highest position, disengage the main (cuber) clutch and lower the elevator when a wagon is not hitched.

During road transport, all safety devices including lights and Slow Moving Vehicle emblem should be prominently displayed to warn operators of other vehicles.

For long-distance transportation, field cubers are usually loaded and hauled on a lowboy truck.

SAFETY

A qualified and responsible operator always follows proper safety procedures. Wear clothing that is fairly tight and belted; loose clothing may become entangled in moving parts. Use handrails. Don't fall off a cuber.

Use care and good judgment when operating a field cuber. Before starting the cuber, disengage the main (cuber) clutch and shift the transmission into neutral. Then check to be sure everyone is clear of the cuber before completing the starting cycle. A person standing near the cuber could be injured by moving parts or caught in a drive belt or chain.

TAKE EXTRA CARE ON HILLS

Make sure the field cuber is in gear when traveling down-hill. Be extremely alert and watchful on hillsides because cubers can tip sideways.

Prevent accidents. Keep the cuber in proper operating condition. Replace worn belts before they break. Keep the brakes adjusted properly. Make sure all safety shields and guards are in place before operating the cuber (Fig. 15).

REMOVE THE HAND CRANK

After repairing and servicing the cuber, collect your tools, equipment, and extra parts. These objects could become "flying missiles" when the cuber is restarted. The hand crank used to turn the die ring input shaft or cutterhead shaft when the machine is plugged *must* be removed before starting the engine (Fig. 16). And — this is very important — never clean, oil, attempt to clear obstructions, or adjust the cuber while the engine is running.

Fig. 14—Transporting a Field Cuber

Fig. 15—Keep The Safety Shield in Place

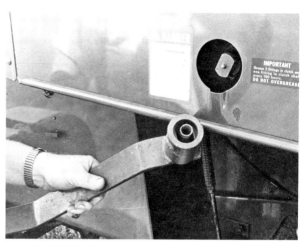

Fig. 16—You Must Remove the Hand Crank before Starting an Engine

BEWARE: HOT WATER

Be very careful while working on the engine, particularly if it is hot. Hot water will scald you if the radiator cap is removed rapidly from a hot engine. The engine has a pressure cooling system, so, to safely remove the radiator cap, cautiously turn it on notch so the steam can escape through the overflow pipe. After pressure is released, remove the cap. Fill the radiator only when the engine is stopped or idling slowly. To avoid possible engine damage, never pour cold water into a hot engine.

AVOID FIRE HAZARDS

Fire is an ever-present hazard with farm equipment. A clean engine is less susceptible to fire, so remove chaff and straw. Refuel only when the engine has been shut off. Do not smoke or have any flames or sparks nearby during refueling.

TROUBLESHOOTING

Most operating problems with a field cuber result from improper adjustments, failure to give timely service, or unsatisfactory crop conditions. This chart will help you find trouble sources and solve problems. However, the suggested solutions should be applied with caution. An apparent problem may be due to another malfunction elsewhere on the cuber. A thoroughly trained and skilled operator must develop the know-how to quickly determine and correct the source of operating problems.

TROUBLESHOOTING CHART		
PROBLEM	POSSIBLE CAUSE	POSSIBLE REMEDY
POOR CUBE QUALITY.	Hay in windrow too wet.	Allow additional drying time. IMPORTANT: Follow recommended hay preparation methods.
	Application of too much water.	Reduce water pressure and size and number of nozzles.

PROBLEM	POSSIBLE CAUSE	POSSIBLE REMEDY
	Worn die blocks or press wheel.	Replace or reverse die blocks or replace press wheel.
	General crop condition not satisfactory:	
	(A) Crop rank; stems too coarse.	Cut crop in bud or pre-bloom stage.
	(B) Too many weeds or grasses.	Use improved cultural practices.
	(C) Too much regrowth stripped by pickup.	Raise pickup to reduce volume of green material going into machine.
POOR PRODUCT SHAPE.	Foreign material in die openings.	Clean die ring of all wire and other foreign matter.
CUBES TOO LONG.	Breaker not working satisfactorily.	Check for damaged or distorted breaker and incorrect installation.
PRESS WHEEL PLUGGED.	Wet slug entered machine.	Using hand crank, back off press wheel and re-engage clutch rapidly. If machine doesn't clear, remove access doors in right-hand die ring casting and clean out.
DIE RING VIBRATING EXCESSIVELY.	Bolts loose between die ring and auger housing.	Tighten bolts to recommended torque.
MAIN CLUTCH SLIPPING.	Clutch facings worn or out of adjustment.	Adjust or replace clutch facings.
CANNOT APPLY ENOUGH WATER.	Nozzles too small or plugged or inadequate pressure.	Change to larger nozzles; service water line strainer; check for obstructions in water lines; check pump drive.
APPLYING TOO MUCH WATER.	Nozzles too large or too many nozzles being used.	Change to smaller nozzles; spray with a single nozzle by adding disk in one nozzle.
NOT PICKING UP CLEANLY.	Pickup too high.	Lower pickup.
	Traveling too fast.	Reduce ground speed or increase pickup speed.
	Pickup speed too fast or too slow.	Match pickup speed to ground speed.
	Pickup teeth bent or broken.	Repair or replace teeth.
	Windrows too light.	Rake heavier windrows.
MAIN DRIVE BELT SLIPPING (SQUEALING).	Belt too loose.	Adjust to correct tension.

227

PROBLEM	POSSIBLE CAUSE	POSSIBLE REMEDY
PICKUP AND FEEDER NOT RUNNING WHEN CLUTCH ENGAGED.	Shear bolt failed.	Replace shear bolt.
	Pickup drive belt broken or slipping.	Replace or adjust.
CONVEYOR-ELEVATOR NOT RUNNING WHEN CLUTCH ENGAGED.	Shear bolt failed.	Replace shear bolt.
FEED ROLLS NOT INTRODUCING MATERIAL TO CUTTERHEAD.	Shear bolt failed.	Replace shear bolt.
HAY BUILDUP IN DUES.	Die ring not "warmed-up" Too much water added.	Reduce volume of water being added and continue to operate for several more minutes until die ring is up to temperature.
DIE-RING END-CAP HEATING EXCESSIVELY (AND SMOKING).	Hay crop too "tough" or wet slug has entered machine.	Remove cleanout door and remove material from right-hand die-ring end-cap housing.
	Auger-tube extension not properly adjusted.	Adjust auger-tube extension.

MAINTENANCE

Cuber maintenance involves these basic components:

- **Engine**
- **Drive train and ground-propulsion system**
- **Pickup and feed assembly**
- **Cutterhead assembly**
- **Cubing assembly**
- **Cube-conveying system**

For details refer to the operator's manual.

CUBING ASSEMBLY

The cubing assembly has a large-diameter auger, die ring, press wheel, and die-ring deflector. The auger, and specifically the auger-flight wear pads, should be inspected every 50 hours of operation and replaced if worn. Check condition of the die ring, die blocks, and press wheel every 100 hours of operation and repair or replace parts. Inspect and service the die-ring deflector frequently. After each 500 hours of operation, remove the entire die ring as a unit and remove, inspect and service the press wheel (Fig. 17). Also, thoroughly inspect and repair the spiral bars and auger flights.

AUGER WEAR PADS

For routine inspection, check auger wear pads through the inspection and clean-out doors on the die-ring casting (Fig. 18), or through the two doors underneath the cutterhead. A special wear pad on the tip of the flight has a hardened surface. Other hard-surfaced wear pads are located along the auger flight. Replace wear pads when their edges are worn away. Pads must be replaced before they wear into the wear-pad backing surface. When the inspection door is open, check the spiral-bar wear pads (Fig. 19). Replace these heat-treated pads before they wear into the wear-pad backing angle.

PRESS WHEEL

Press wheel maintenance consists of rotating the bearings for longer life and gauging the press-wheel edge (Fig. 20). If one edge is serviceable, install the press wheel with the worn edge facing outward. When both edges are worn out, rebuild or replace the press wheel. If one edge is worn excessively, the press wheel should not be used. Excessive loading will occur on the usable edge and make the die ring hot.

DIE BLOCKS

When the die ring is removed, inspect the die blocks carefully. Remove each die block, thoroughly clean it, and

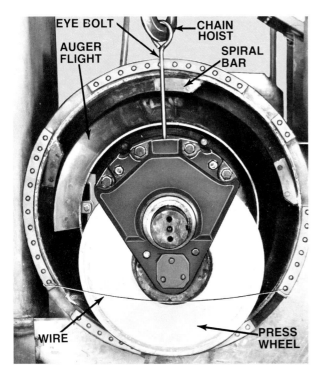

Fig. 17—Remove and Service the Press Wheel Every 500 Hours of Operation

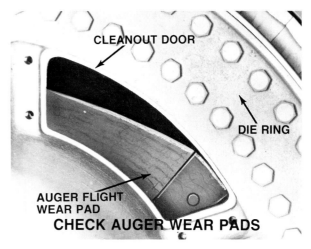

Fig. 18—Inspection and Clean-Out Door

Fig. 19—Spiral-Bar Wear Pad

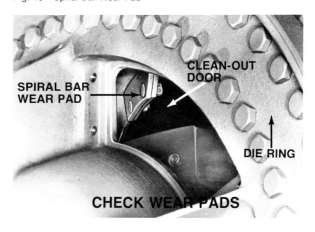

Fig. 20—Gauging Press Wheel Edge

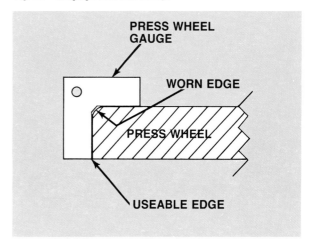

check for cracks and uneven wear. Replace a die block if it is cracked or if more than $\frac{1}{8}$ inch (3 mm) is worn from the shearing edge. Reverse usable die blocks for longer wear life and a new shear edge to the press wheel (Fig. 21). Also, rotate the blocks around the die ring to move blocks originally located next to the spiral bars to positions between the ends of the spiral bars.

Die blocks which apparently require early replacement should be placed in the top section of the die ring. The operator can easily see the cubes from these die blocks and determine when replacement is necessary. Also, the 12 blocks in the top section can be replaced without removing the entire die ring.

SPARE PARTS

It's good management to keep spare parts on hand to reduce loss of time if a breakdown occurs. Breakdowns usually involve drive chains or belts, so keep extra chain links and belts handy. The pickup fingers work near the ground in conditions which can cause rapid wear or break the fingers. So keep extra pickup fingers in the service truck.

Some components get extra-hard wear. It is wise to have replacements for high-wear parts in the service truck. High-wear parts in the cutterhead assembly are the rotating knives and the stationary knife. The wear pads, die blocks, and press wheel are all high-wear parts in the cubing assembly.

229

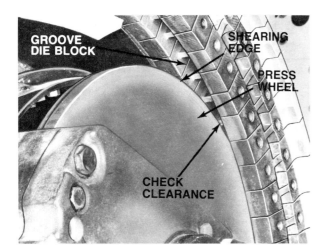

Fig. 21—Press Wheel and Die Blocks Installed

STORAGE

Proper storage of a field cuber during the off-season is essential to keep maintenance costs low and to prolong machine service life. If possible, store the machine in a shelter, and blocked up to remove weight from the tires. Do not deflate the tires. If inside storage is not possible remove the tires and store them in a cool, dark, dry building for maximum tire life.

CLEAN AND LUBRICATE

Thoroughly clean the cuber and engine before storage. Chaff and dirt draw moisture which stimulates rust formation. A light coat of oil on unpainted surfaces will reduce rust formation. Paint touch-up is recommended for surfaces where paint has worn off.

Remove belts. Clean, label, and wrap them in burlap and store them in a cool, dark, dry area. Clean and oil chains. Give the cuber a complete lubrication as recommended in the operator's manual. Grease threads on all bolts used to make adjustments, and the exposed surface of the variable-speed drive hub.

Thoroughly clean the main clutch facings and housing to keep the clutch from sticking during disuse. Place the main cuber clutch lever in the disengaged position. Block the transmission clutch pedal in disengaged position to prevent damage to the clutch plates during storage.

Drain and clean the water-spray supply tank, water pump, and strainer before storage.

ENGINE

To help ensure top performance the following season prepare the engine for storage as recommended in the operator's manual. Drain and refill the crankcase with fresh oil. Install a new oil-filter element. Then idle the engine 15 to 20 minutes to ensure complete oil coverage within the engine.

Seal Engine Openings

Clean the precleaner and air cleaner. Install a new air filter to keep moisture, insects and other foreign material out of the engine. Seal all openings with tape including the exhaust pipe, crankcase breather, and hydraulic oil reservoir breather.

Drain the radiator and engine block if antifreeze is not used. Clean the radiator screen and core with air or water pressure. Drain the fuel tank, filter, and strainer.

If the cuber is stored outside, remove the battery, and store it in a cool, dry shelter where the temperature will stay about freezing. Check the battery and recharge it monthly to prevent damage to plates.

Finally, prepare a list of repairs and buy replacement parts to be installed during the off-season, and avoid delays at harvest time.

SUMMARY

Cubing has many advantages for the hay producer and consumer. Cubes require less harvest labor and storage space, can be transported more efficiently, and can be fed with less waste than other forms of hay. They also fit into mechanized feeding systems better than other types of hay packages. Stationary cubers can produce complete-ration cubes that contain the proper amounts of concentrates and minerals for a balanced ration.

Field cubing requires dry (10 to 12 percent moisture) legume hay, which essentially limits its use to alfalfa. Stationary cubing also requires dry hay, but is not restricted to legumes, because binders can be added. Cubing also requires high initial investment and high power input.

The field cuber lifts the windrow, chops the hay, and delivers it to a set of dies. A press wheel pushes the hay through the dies to form the cubes. Cubes can be handled with special or conventional conveyors and elevators, from the field, to storage, to feeding.

CHAPTER QUIZ

1. List five advantages cubes have over baled hay.

2. (Fill in blanks) Two types of cubers are the _____ cuber and _____ cuber.

3. (True or false.) Field cubing requires the moisture content of alfalfa hay to be eight percent or less.

4. Why is water sprayed on dry legume hay just before cubing?

5. (True or false.) The engine should always be run at full throttle while cubing.

6. What are the primary field adjustments for operating a field cuber?

7. What causes the press wheel to plug?

8. What happens if you don't use enough water during cubing?

9. What happens if cubes are made too wet?

10. (True or false.) Cube density is usually about half that of baled hay.

11
Forage Harvesters

Fig. 1—Forage Harvesters Fit Into Many Hay and Forage Systems

INTRODUCTION

Chopped forage is an established alternative to hay and stover. Forage harvesters are usually one part of a system that permits complete mechanization of harvesting, silage production, and feeding.

Most forage harvesters can harvest several different types of crops (Fig. 1). Pickups are used to gather windrowed crops. Cutting heads are available for direct-cut silage production. Direct-cut row-crop heads are used for whole-plant harvesting of corn and sorghum, and there are attachments for harvesting corn and sorghum stover after grain harvest. Some forage harvesters can use combine ear corn snapping heads to make ear corn silage.

Chopped forage may be stored in upright, trench, or pit silos, or may be fed directly to livestock. Chopped dry hay is usually stored in barns or sheds, but is not widely used because of dust and feeding problems. It is relatively easy to mechanize the handling and feeding of silage or haylage but it is generally not economical to transport the material long distances. Chopping forage can reduce the market-ability of a crop if the market is far away (Fig. 2).

FORAGE HARVESTERS

Forage harvesters fall into three distinct types, depending upon the method of chopping the forage and discharging chopped material:

- **Cut-and-throw**
- **Cut-and-blow**
- **Flail**

Fig. 2—Most Silage Is Fed Near the Field

CUT-AND-THROW VS CUT-AND-BLOW

On **cut-and-throw** harvesters, the cutterhead or flywheel does all the cutting and delivers the crop to a wagon or truck (Fig. 3). **Cut-and-blow** harvesters have a separate blower mounted behind or to the side of the cutterhead to deliver the crop to a wagon or truck. Material may be thrown directly into the fan by the cutterhead (Fig. 4) or carried from the cutterhead or flails to the fan by an auger (Fig.5). Some flail harvesters are also cut-and-blow types, but most use flails to cut and throw material directly into the wagon or truck.

FLAILS

Flail harvesters cut and chop standing forage in a single operation and can also harvest windrowed crops and stover. Flail harvester cutting width is usually 5 to 6 feet (1.5 to 1.8 m). The basic element of a flail forage harvester or chopper is the rotor (a horizontal shaft with flails or knives attached to it). As the shaft rotates, the flails produce a shearing impact on the crop stems. As material is carried around the outer circumference of the flail under the rotor housing, it is pounded, cut, and shattered into small pieces.

Fig. 3—Cut-and-Throw Forage Harvester

Fig. 4—Direct Cutterhead-to-Fan Material Flow (Cut-and-Blow)

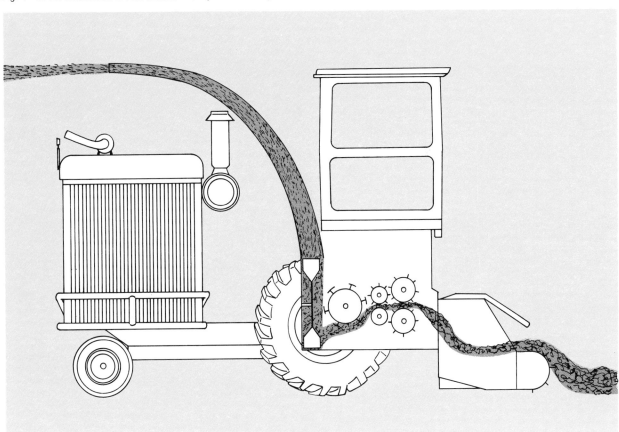

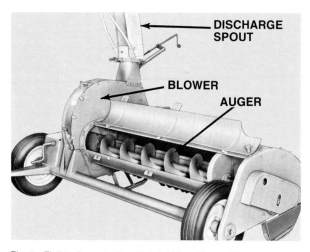

Fig. 5—Flail-to-Auger-to-Fan Material Flow (Cut-and-Blow)

Flails are normally flexible-mounted on the rotor shaft, but centrifugal force keeps them extended straight out during operation. If a flail strikes an obstruction, it will normally deflect around the object with little or no damage.

The length of flail-chopped material varies from about one-inch (25 mm) pieces to nearly uncut material, depending upon machine and the relationship of the crop to the direction of travel (standing or lodged), and the ratio of flail speed to the forward speed of the machine.

MECHANICAL FUNCTIONS

Although forage harvesters are available in many types and sizes, basic machine operation is much the same (Fig. 6). A forage head picks up windrowed material or cuts a standing crop. Material is then carried to a cutting mechanism (the cutterhead) and chopped or shredded into short pieces.

The length-of-cut is usually adjustable. Screens may be used on some cut-and-blow harvesters for better control of length-of-cut. Chopped material is then delivered into a wagon or truck by the cutterhead or flails, or by a separate fan.

CUT-AND-THROW HARVESTERS

Cut-and-throw machines use knives to cut forage to desired lengths (Fig. 7). The rotating blades throw material from the cutterhead to a wagon or truck. Forage is cut between the rotating knives and a stationary knife or shear bar as material is fed into the cutterhead. Controlling the rate forage is fed over the shear bar regulates length-of-cut.

Many early forage harvesters used a cut-and-throw flywheel cutterhead (Fig. 8). Forage was fed over a stationary knife into the side of the flywheel for cutting. Adjusting the feed rate controlled length of cut. Separate impeller blades on the flywheel threw forage into the wagon or truck.

Fig. 6—Basic Forage Harvester Operation

LOAD FORAGE INTO
WAGON OR TRUCK

CHOP CROP INTO
UNIFORM PIECES

LIFT OR CUT OFF CROP

Fig. 7—Cut-and-Throw Cutterhead

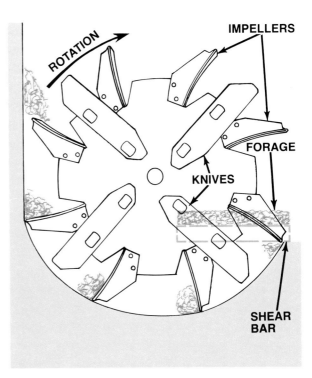

Fig. 8—Cut-and-Throw Cutterhead

CUT-AND-BLOW HARVESTERS

Most forage harvesters use knives mounted on a rotating reel and a stationary shear bar to chop forage as it is fed into the cutterhead (Fig. 9). Length-of-cut is varied by changing the feed rate or on some machines, by changing the number of rotating knives. Reducing the number of knives, or using a larger-diameter cutterhead provides more space for forage to enter the cutterhead, thus increasing capacity.

Recutter screens help provide a finer cut for better forage packing, which produces better silage. The number and size of the holes in the screen determines the cutting capacity of the screen.

FLAIL HARVESTERS

Flail harvesters are pulled behind a tractor and are PTO-driven. Two wheels, mounted behind or on the sides, support the machine and gauge the operating height of the flails.

On some models the wheel on the uncut-crop side may be positioned behind the chopper to avoid running over unchopped crop, or at the outer end of the flail for more accurate gauging of cutting height in rough terrain and when picking up stover.

The tractor PTO delivers power to the rotor, and in the case of some machines, to the auger and blower through shafts, sprockets, chains, or V-belts. The powerline usually has a slip clutch or shear bolt to protect the drive and other components if the machine is overloaded or strikes a large obstruction.

Height of cut or pick-up is controlled by moving the rotor and housing up or down, thereby raising or lowering the "arc" cut by the flails (Fig. 10).

Many flail choppers can be used for mowing grass or weeds by simply leaving the auger door open during operation or blowing material back on the ground. In extremely heavy growth or adverse conditions it may be good to remove the auger and auger housing.

DIRECT-THROW FLAIL HARVESTERS

Direct-throw harvesters use wide, cup-shaped flails to cut, chop, and throw material through a spout into a wagon or truck (Fig. 11). A shear bar may be mounted on the front edge of the flail hood to increase cutting and laceration of the crop.

AUGER-BLOWER FLAIL HARVESTERS

Auger-blower flail machines use curved or L-shaped knives to cut forage and throw it into a cross auger which conveys material to a blower for loading (Fig. 12). Some additional cutting may be done by knives on the blower on some harvesters of this type.

FORAGE HARVESTER CLASSIFICATION

Forage Harvesters may also be classified as:

- **Mounted**
- **Pulled**
- **Self-propelled**

Self-propelled forage harvesters usually have the highest capacity, followed by pulled units and then mounted harvesters.

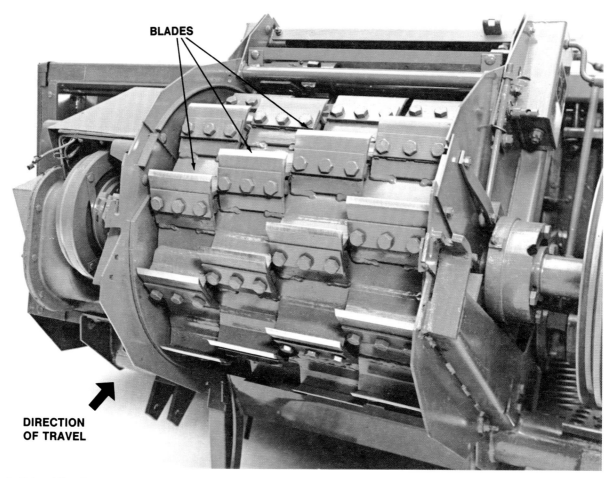

BLADES

DIRECTION
OF TRAVEL

Fig. 9—Cut-and-Blow Cutterhead

MOUNTED FORAGE HARVESTERS

Tractor-mounted forage harvesters have long been popular in Europe, and have recently become more popular here in the United States/Canada. Most mounted forage harvesters are the cut-and-throw type.

Fig. 10—Flail Harvester Height Adjustment

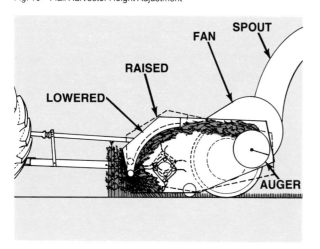

SPOUT

FAN

RAISED

LOWERED

AUGER

Fig. 11—Direct-Throw Flails

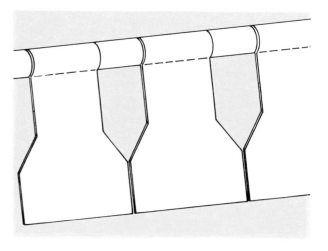

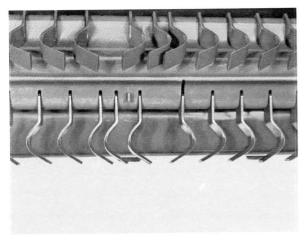

Fig. 12—Curved Flails on Cut-Auger-and-Blow Flail Harvester

Fig. 14—Front-Mounted Forage Harvester.

Mounted- or integral-forage harvesters attach to the tractor 3-point hitch and are usually equipped with a single-row, row-crop head or a windrow pickup head. Because of its limited capacity, the mounted harvester is commonly used on small-acreage farms with crop and livestock operations.

Mounted forage harvesters are highly maneuverable (Fig. 13), and because power is not lost pulling the forage harvester through the field, these machines usually have high productivity with smaller-horsepower tractors. The weight of the mounted forage harvester on the rear tractor wheels aids traction.

Fig. 13—Mounted Forage Harvesters Are Highly Maneuverable

Front-mounted forage harvesters are also available (Fig. 14). The traction advantage is eliminated but front-mounted harvesters are available in double-row, row-crop heads.

PULLED FORAGE HARVESTERS

Pulled forage harvesters are available in sizes that match most tractors (Fig. 15). Pulled harvesters have a wide variety of forage heads (Fig. 16).

- **Direct-cut head**
- **Windrow pickup**
- **One- to three-row, row-crop heads**
- **Ear corn snapper head**

Pulled harvesters may be either the cut-and-throw or cut-and-blow type.

Fig. 15—Pulled Forage Harvester

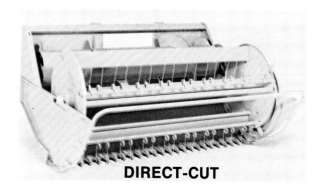

DIRECT-CUT

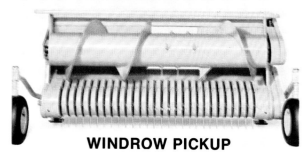

WINDROW PICKUP

ROW CROP

EAR CORN SNAPPER

Fig. 16—Four Types of Forage Heads for Pulled Harvesters

Fig. 17—Forage Harvesters Have Many Advantages

SELF-PROPELLED FORAGE HARVESTERS

Self-propelled forage harvesters generally offer high capacity, good maneuverability, and many operator conveniences. Self-propelled forage harvesters provide the high capacity and productivity needed by large feeding operations and by custom operators (Fig. 17). They can also work in adverse field conditions, especially if equipped with 4-wheel drive which is optional on some units.

Most self-propelled forage harvesters are available with forage heads similar to those offered for pulled harvesters, but in larger sizes, plus some additional units such as flail and stover-pickup heads.

Flail and stover pickup heads retrieve a large percentage of the remaining material after corn or sorghum harvest (Fig. 18). Stover harvesting heads may also be used to make whole-plant corn or sorghum silage.

Types of self-propelled forage harvester heads will be discussed in detail later in this chapter.

BASIC FORAGE HARVESTER COMPONENTS

Most components and their functions are fairly common to different makes of forage harvesters. The primary components include (Fig. 19):

- **Drive train**
- **Forage Heads**
- **Feed Rolls**
- **Cutterhead**
- **Stationary Knife**
- **Recutter screen (cut-and-blow only)**
- **Knife sharpener or grinder**

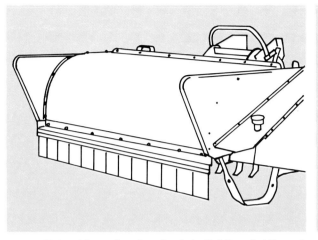 

Fig. 18—Flail and Stover Row-Crop Heads for Self-Propelled Harvesters

All components must function together effectively for efficient operation.

DRIVE TRAIN

Basic forage harvester drive systems fall into two categories:

- **PTO-driven**
- **Self-Propelled**

Each system offers certain advantages.

Fig. 19—Forage Harvester

PTO-DRIVEN FORAGE HARVESTERS

PTO-driven forage harvesters may be:

- **Mounted**
- **Pulled**

Both mounted and pulled forage harvesters are PTO-driven. Tractor power is transmitted from the tractor PTO, through the harvester PTO shaft, to the main gearbox. From the gearbox power is transferred to the forage head, feed rolls, cutterhead, and on cut-and-blow machines, to the blower-fan system and auger, if used.

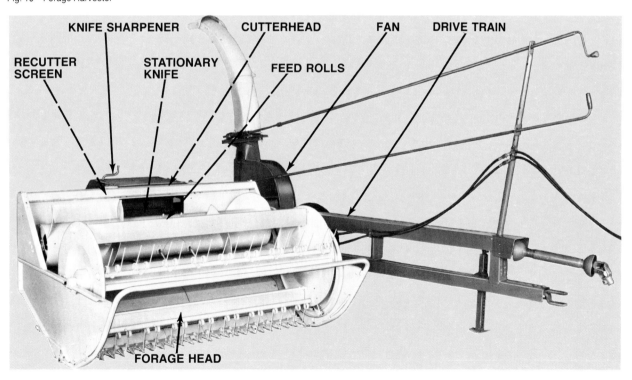

KNIFE SHARPENER — CUTTERHEAD — FAN — DRIVE TRAIN

RECUTTER SCREEN — STATIONARY KNIFE — FEED ROLLS

FORAGE HEAD

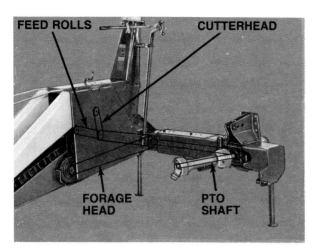

Fig. 20—Drive Train Pattern for a Mounted Forage Harvester

Fig. 22—Direct-Cut Head in Operation

The drive train pattern for a typical mounted forage harvester is simple (Fig. 20).

The drive train pattern for pulled harvesters depends on the cutting delivery system used: cut-and-throw, cut-and-blow, or cut-auger-and-blow (Fig. 21).

SELF-PROPELLED HARVESTER DRIVE TRAIN

Self-propelled forage harvesters may have two- or four-wheel drive with either mechanical or hydrostatic transmissions and power trains. Engine flywheel horsepower is generally 160 to 250 horsepower (119 to 186 kw).

This chapter is mainly concerned with the drive train arrangement for the harvesting components, especially the cutterhead and blower fan used on some models.

The cutterhead assembly and forage heads on self-propelled harvesters are usually belt-driven by the engine, instead of being PTO-driven.

FORAGE HEADS

Forage heads for forage harvesters:

- **Direct-cut or mower bar**
- **Windrow-pickup**
- **Row-crop; one to four rows**
- **Ear-corn-snapper**
- **Stover-pickup**
- **Flail**

Each head is especially adapted to particular crop and field conditions.

Fig. 21—Drive Train Pattern for Three Types of Pulled Forage Harvesters

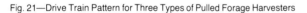

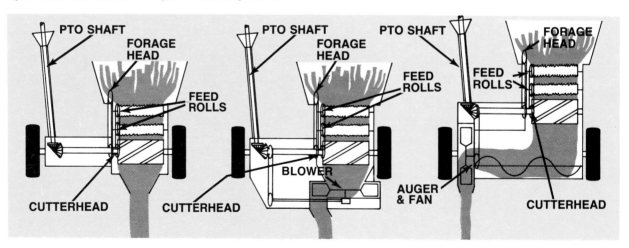

Fig. 23—Windrow-Pickup Head in Operation

DIRECT-CUT HEAD

Mower bars for direct-cutting hay or broadcast forage crops are available for most pulled and self-propelled forage harvesters (Fig. 22). Width of cut may vary from 6 to 12 feet (1.8 to 3.6 m), depending on forage harvester capacity. The direct-cut head uses a reel to gather crop into an auger as it is cut by the sickle bar. The auger feeds material into the feed rolls.

WINDROW-PICKUP HEAD

Windrow-pickups are used on all three forage harvesters for silage, haylage, and dry hay (Fig. 23). Various pickup widths are available to match harvester capacity and windrow size. Retractable fingers and auger-flight extensions feed forage into the feed rolls. Adjustable skid shoes or gauge wheels may be used to regulate pickup working height.

ROW-CROP HEAD

Row-crop heads are available for forage harvesters in one-to four-row sizes and with different row widths. A row-crop head is usually used to harvest corn or sorghum and sorghum-sudan cross silage (Fig. 24).

Gathering guides push the crop forward so the bottom is fed into the cutterhead first. After the crop is cut, gathering chains or belts grab the stalks and feed them into the feed rolls or directly into the cutterhead.

EAR-CORN-SNAPPER

Snapper heads operate the same as snapper heads manufactured for combines. Snapper head equipped harvesters

Fig. 24—Row-Crop Head in Operation

pick and chop ear corn in the field and are available in two-to four-row models.

As the forage harvester moves forward, snapping rolls pull stalks through snapping bars under the gathering chains and snap off ears. Gathering chains carry the ears back to a cross auger, which carries corn to the cutterhead for chopping (Fig.25).

Fig. 25—Ear Snapper Head

Fig. 26—Stover and Whole-Plant Silage Head

Fig. 27—Flail Head for Self-Propelled Harvester

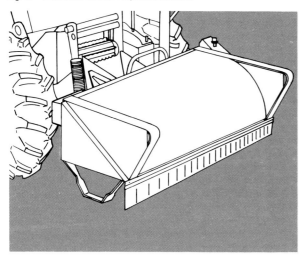

Fig. 28—Front Feed Rolls

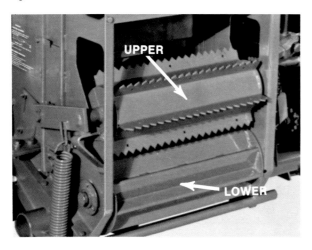

STOVER HEAD

This forage head is designed to pick up stover after grain harvest or for whole-plant silage. Low-profile gathering points pick up downed stalks and guide them to gathering belts (Fig. 26). The belts hold stalks while an oscillating knife cuts the stalks a few inches above the ground. The gathering belts then carry the stalks to an auger which pulls material from the belts and conveys it to the feed rolls.

FLAIL HEAD

Flail attachments are also available for some self-propelled forage harvesters (Fig. 27). Rows of flails revolve under the hood to cut and push material into the cutter head. Flail heads are usually used to harvest stover.

FEED ROLLS

Feed rolls gather material from the forage head and feed it in a uniform layer to the cutterhead. Feed rolls differ in design, according to their functions. The front feed rolls gather forage from the head, and feed the rear rolls. Rear rolls hold and meter material into the cutterhead.

LOWER FEED ROLLS

The lower-front feed rolls generally have deep flutes to aggressively pull in material (Fig. 28). The lower-rear feed roll is not stripped by another feed roll or by the cutterhead, so it is usually smooth. If this roll were fluted, some crops might catch on the flutes be carried past the cutterhead, and dropped on the ground. A scraper on the smooth lower rear roll prevents buildup of gum and dirt on the roll.

UPPER FEED ROLLS

Upper feed rolls must be aggressive to grip the crop mat firmly at all times. The front and rear upper rolls are spring-loaded against the lower feed rolls to keep the rolls as close as possible so the mat is compressed and positively metered into the cutterhead.

FEED-ROLL SPEED CONTROLS LENGTH-OF-CUT

Changing feed-roll speed or adding or removing knives from the cutterhead, controls the length-of-cut. With equal cutterhead speed, a higher feed-roll speed provides a longer length-of-cut because forage moves further between knife cuts. Higher roll speed also provides a thinner mat, which is easier to cut and requires less power. Roll speed is usually varied by changing sprockets or shifting gears.

FEED-ROLL DRIVE

The feed-roll drive may be protected from overload by a shear bolt, which is usually most economical, or by a slip clutch (Fig. 29). However, if frequent overloads or obstructions are encountered, excessive time may be required to replace shear bolts and increase overall operating costs. A jaw-type slip clutch provides roll protection without requiring a stop for repairs if a minor overload is encountered. A jaw-type slip clutch also gives an audible signal when overloaded so that the operator can reduce the feed rate if necessary.

CLEARING FEED-ROLL OBSTRUCTIONS

Some feed rolls are designed to allow forward, neutral, and reverse operation so that an obstruction or material overload in the rolls may be backed out. On some smaller harvesters, rolls are rotated with a wrench provided with the harvester.

The feed roll reverse is often coupled with the forage head drive so that both components are reversed simultaneously. If the auger on a windrow-pickup, for example, is not reversible and continued to feed material in at the same time feed rolls are reversed, a large amount of material could build up between the feed rolls, which are reversing, and the pickup auger, which is continuing to feed material. The surplus forage would then have to be removed by hand before restarting the harvester, and the risk of plugging or damaging the feed rolls and cutterhead increases.

CUTTERHEAD

The heart of any forage harvester is the cutterhead (Fig. 30). Each cutterhead must provide:

- **Uniformity of cut.**
- **Quality of cut.**
- **Capacity.**
- **Efficiency.**

These terms may be defined and explained as follows:

UNIFORMITY OF CUT

The length-of-cut must be consistent. Most of the particles should be very close to the theoretical length-of-cut set on the feed-roll drive. A small amount of "longs" will appear, due primarily to material being fed at an angle through the cutterhead.

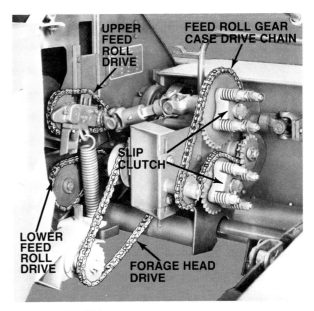

Fig. 29—Feed-Roll Drive

QUALITY OF CUT

Quality is determined by the appearance of the ends of each cut forage particle. Each cut should be smooth and cut squarely. Ends should not be ragged or ripped. Quality of cut depends primarily on the operator's constant attention to cutterhead maintenance (Fig. 31).

CAPACITY

Capacity is the maximum possible amount of forage that can go through the cutterhead.

Fig. 30—Cut-and-Blow Cutterhead

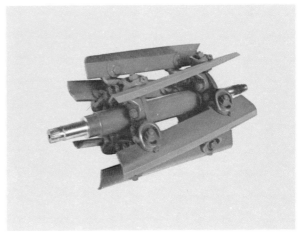

Fig. 31—Quality of Cut Depends on Cutterhead Maintenance.

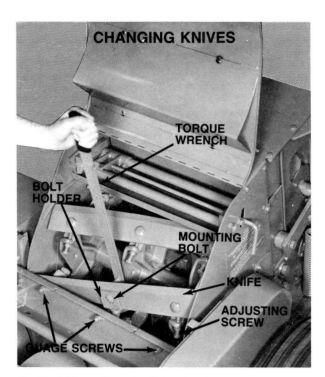

Fig. 32—Adding or Removing Knives Can Change Length-of-Cut on Some Forage Harvesters

EFFICIENCY

Efficiency is the ability to cut forage with minimum horsepower.

Cutterhead performance depends mainly on the:

- **Rotating knives**

- **Stationary knife or shear bar**

Cutting components must be maintained for uniformity and quality of cut, high machine capacity, and good efficiency.

ROTATING KNIVES

Many factors are involved in cutterhead design. For instance, the most significant features of the rotating knives are:

- **Number**

- **Speed**

- **Shape**

- **Angle**

Successful forage harvester operation depends on how well these factors are combined in the design and how well the knives are cared for by the operator.

Number Of Knives

The number of knives on a cutterhead determines the amount of space between knives.

The space between the knives is set so that only one knife is in the mat at a time. The flow of incoming material would be hampered if two rotating knives were attempting to penetrate the mat at the same time. In most cases, one knife would be cutting and the other restricting mat flow. A space between knives also makes it easy to reach knife-mounting hardware.

You can have a problem if you don't have enough knives. With only one, two, or three knives, the mat must be quite thick or the cutterhead very wide to achieve significant capacity. Also, with fewer knives and a thicker mat rotating knives tend to force the mat toward the feed rolls instead of cutting it off.

Length-of-cut may be changed on some forage harvesters by changing the number of cutterhead knives (Fig. 32). Cutterhead speed may also be changed on some harvesters to alter length-of-cut, but this is not a common practice on current machines. Always consult the harvester operator's manual for the correct procedure for changing cutterhead speed or number of knives. Remember: The number and position of the knives on the cutterhead must be such that the cutterhead remains in balance. For instance, on one forage harvester which can be operated with only one rotating knife, a special counterweight must be mounted on the opposite side of the cutterhead.

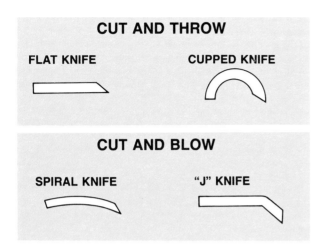

Fig. 33—Knife Shapes

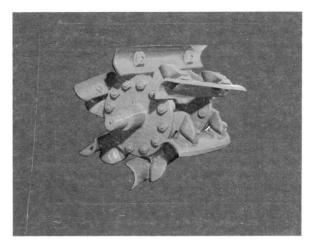

Fig. 34—Cut-and-Throw Cutterhead with Cupped Knives

KNIFE SPEED

Cutterhead speed is very important to harvester operation and is usually a compromise between maximum capacity and high efficiency. The slower the cutterhead speed, the higher the efficiency. Increasing speed provides more capacity, unless speed is so fast that material doesn't have time to leave the cutterhead between knife cuts and is carried around inside the cutterhead. This is most likely to occur with very dry, fluffy material.

Cutterhead speed is particularly important with cut-and-throw machines (and is usually higher than on cut-and-blow models) because material is delivered to a wagon or truck by the cutterhead.

KNIFE SHAPE

Uniformity of cut and cutting efficiency depend upon the shape of the rotating knives. Specially-shaped knives are required for the two basic types of forage harvester—cut-and-throw, and cut-and-blow (Fig. 33).

As explained earlier, knives on *cut-and-throw* harvesters cut the material and deliver it to a wagon or truck. Two types of knives may be used. Cupped knives are more efficient at cutting and throwing material (Fig. 34), but flat knives cost less.

Knives on *cut-and-blow* harvesters cut the material, and a separate fan blows it into a wagon or truck. Most cut-and-blow harvesters use either spiral knives or J-shaped knives (Fig. 35). The J-knife is stiffer and more efficient than spiral knives when used with a recutter screen because the flat rear portion of the knife does a better job of delivering material through the screen. Cutterheads can be operated with one to 12 knives, depending on machine design, crop, and expected capacity.

Knife Angle

The cutting angle and helical angle are important design factors in knife shape. The *cutting angle* is defined as the angle between the beveled edge of the knife which meets the crop entering the cutterhead, and the inside surface of the knife (Fig. 36). A smaller cutting angle gives a more uniform cut, but a larger angle increases knife strength. A compromise angle of 30 to 45 degrees is usually used.

Fig. 35—J-Knife, Cut-and-Blow Cutterhead

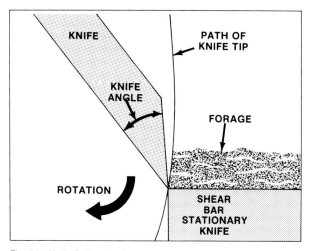

Fig. 36—Knife Cutting Angle

Stationary knives vary in design, but the vertical edge of the knife does the cutting in all cases. Some knives have tungsten carbide on two horizontal edges and can be reversed for more use before replacement. One manufacturer uses knives with tungsten carbide on one vertical edge, and one manufacturer applies tungsten carbide to both the horizontal and vertical cutting edge for maximum wear. Other stationary knives have no tungsten carbide edges, but may be turned two to four times to renew the cutting edge as each side wears.

RECUTTER SCREENS

Recutter screens are useful for custom-cutting crops to the best length or fineness for different types of handling and feeding systems.

Screens can only be used on cut-and-blow forage harvesters and are fitted behind the cutterhead, where they act as several more stationary knives (Fig. 38). Each row of slots in a screen (Fig. 39) acts as a shear bar, and requires extra power per ton of forage. Usually a minimum of 15 percent more power is required with a screen. The amount of extra power depends on the kind of material being chopped, moisture content, and the type and size of screen used. In most hay and silage crops, small-opening screens require more horsepower than large-opening screens. In dry crops and ear corn a small-opening screen is recommended for finer cutting and better packing in storage. These crops also cut easier and require less horsepower per ton for chopping.

KNIFE SHARPENERS

Most forage harvesters are equipped with knife sharpeners such as the following:

The *helical angle* of a rotating knife is the angle between the stationary knife or shear bar and the cutting edge of the knife (Fig. 37). This angle is designed to provide smooth, efficient flow of material and more uniform power requirement throughout the cutting cycle of each blade. A helical angle of 8 to 20 degrees is common and greatly reduces impact loads on the shear bar, cutterhead and drive train compared to cutting with the rotating knife parallel to the shear bar.

STATIONARY KNIFE

The stationary knife and the rotating knives are equally important to good cutting action. The stationary knife cuts as much material as all of the rotating knives combined, so it must be properly maintained and adjusted at all times for efficient performance.

Fig. 37—Knife Helical Angle

Fig. 38—Recutter Screens Fit Behind the Cutterhead of Cut-and-Blow Harvesters

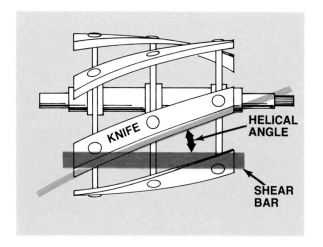

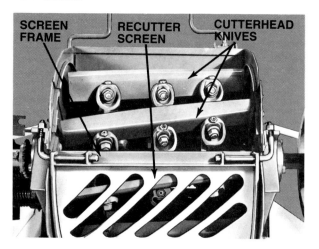

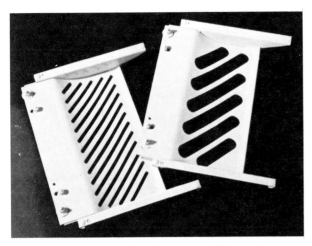

Fig. 39—Recutter Screens Have Openings of Different Shapes and Sizes to Match Crop Conditions

- **Cutting edge touch-up stone**

- **Integral electric grinder**

These sharpeners sharpen knives without removing the knives or cutterhead from the machine.

Cutting Edge Touch-Up Stone

A cutting edge touch-up stone is used to sharpen cutterhead knives as they rotate (Fig. 40). A crank is used to raise and lower the grinding stone to the knives as the cut-

Fig. 40—Cutting Edge Touch-Up Stone in Operation

terhead rotates. The cutterhead may rotate forward or reverse while sharpening, depending on the sharpener design. Reverse grinding maintains knife bevel at more nearly the original cutting angle for closer fit and more efficient cutting between rotating knives and shear bar.

With the cutterhead turning, the operator lowers the stone and moves it back and forth along the length of the knives to grind a uniform cutting edge. The stationary knife must always be readjusted after rotating knives are sharpened because grinding increases the clearance between the rotating and stationary knives. If the stationary knife is not adjusted, all knives will wear more rapidly, power requirements will increase, and forage will be ragged and frayed on the ends. The cutterhead is also more apt to plug as forage tends to wedge between rotating knives and the shear bar instead of being cut off.

Integral Electric or Hydraulic Grinders

Optional integral electric or hydraulic grinders are available to sharpen and rebevel knives in some machines. Cutterhead knives are not rotated during sharpening with an electric grinder. However, as with the touch-up stone, the stationary knife must always be adjusted after the rotating knives are sharpened.

HARVESTING FORAGE

In any forage harvesting operation, speed and forage quality depend largely on the operator. Proper preparation and advance planning, plus careful maintenance and correct operation of the forage harvester help make the job go smoother and faster.

Consideration must also be given to the type of crop and how fine it must be chopped for storage. Finer-cut particles pack better and leave fewer air spaces where spoilage can

Fig. 41—Harvest at the Right Time

start. Because of the relatively high moisture content, haylage and silage can spoil rapidly if exposed to air. Therefore, storage facilities must be in excellent condition and the forage must be well packed to prevent spoilage.

Plan for handling and feeding. Some silo unloaders do not perform well if forage is cut too long. Animals may reject long pieces of forage.

Harvesting at the right stage of crop maturity is important for maximum forage quality and yield (Fig. 41). Adequate machine capacity for the acreage to be harvested helps avoid many harvesting problems and delays.

Basic forage harvesting steps:

- **Machine preparation**
- **Preliminary settings and adjustments**
- **Field operation and adjustments**
- **Transport**
- **Safety**
- **Maintenance**
- **Troubleshooting**

Satisfactory forage harvester operation depends on your thoroughness in preparation, operation, and storage.

MACHINE PREPARATION

Prepare a forage harvester for field operation by following the steps given in the operator's manual. Some common checkpoints are:

- Check the oil in all gearcases. Drain, flush, and refill the gearcases with proper oil at recommended intervals.
- Lubricate grease points shown in the operator's manual.
- Check bolts and tighten them to recommended torque.
- Make sure shields are in place and that rotating shields are free to turn.
- Inspect flails and the cutterhead assembly for proper clearance and operation. Replace damaged or missing parts.
- Check slip clutches for proper slippage under load. Be sure the recommended shear bolts are used to avoid damage because a bolt didn't shear.
- Inspect the forage head and attachments for proper operation.
- Check and adjust the wheel spacing to match row width.
- Follow the instructions in the operator's manual for preparing the engine on self-propelled harvesters.
- Check the tractor for proper PTO speed, tire inflation, wheel tread, category of 3-point hitch and sway blocks (if required), drawbar positions, hydraulic system, and front-end or rear-wheel weights that might be needed.

NOTE: Hitch and PTO Shaft. When attaching a mounted or pulled harvester, remember 3-point hitch settings or drawbar adjustments are critical to universal joints and telescoping PTO shafts . . . and for safe operation of the equipment.

ATTACHING PULLED HARVESTERS

Follow these steps to hitch a pulled forage harvester.

1. Adjust the tractor drawbar to the standard position for PTO operation.

2. Use the hitch jack to raise or lower the hitch to the height of the tractor drawbar.

3. Attach the harvester to the tractor drawbar with a safety hitch pin.

4. Secure the hitch jack in the transport position.

5. Slide the PTO shaft universal joint on the tractor PTO shaft until it is secured by the locking mechanism.

Fig. 42—Set Controls Within Easy Reach

ADJUST CONTROLS FOR EASY REACH

6. Clean the couplings and connect the hydraulic hoses to the tractor breakaway couplings for forage head lift, spout control, etc.

7. Adjust the operating controls for the spout direction, deflector cap, feed roll reverse, etc. so they can be easily reached from the tractor seat (Fig. 42) or connect the remote controls inside tractor cab, if used (Fig. 43).

ATTACHING MOUNTED HARVESTERS

Follow these steps to attach a rear-mounted forage harvester to a tractor:

1. Adjust the forage harvester frame to conform with the overall width of the tractor.

2. Adjust the tractor sway blocks or chains, draft links, and hitch pins to take up as much side play as possible. If there is too much side play the harvester will rub against the rear tractor tire.

Fig. 43—Use Remote Controls for Tractors with Cab

DISCHARGE SPOUT CONTROL

FEED ROLL CONTROL

3. Adjust the tractor center link (top) to the recommended length for leveling the harvester fore and aft. Adjust the draft links to level the harvester from side to side.

4. Raise or lower the harvester until the tractor PTO shaft and harvester gearcase shaft are level.

5. Measure the distance between the tractor PTO shaft and the harvester gearcase shaft. Refer to the operator's manual for the proper distance, and install the PTO shaft or adjust the hitch if needed.

CAUTION: Telescoping sections of the PTO shaft must have a minimum overlap of 4 inches (100 mm) (or as recommended by the manufacturer) in the RAISED position to keep the shaft from separating during machine operation.

6. Adjust the down stop on the tractor 3-point hitch to control cutting height.

IMPORTANT: It is also necessary to adjust the 3-point hitch height stop to limit the transport height of the harvester, to avoid extreme universal joint angles, and to prevent separation of the PTO shaft sections.

PRELIMINARY SETTINGS AND ADJUSTMENTS

LENGTH-OF-CUT

The theoretical length-of-cut of a forage harvester is the distance which the forage mat moves into the cutterhead between knife cuts. The actual length-of-cut will be close to the theoretical cut when straight crops such as corn are fed directly into the cutterhead. However, with non-oriented material, such as windrowed hay, the actual length may average twice as long as the theoretical length.

Minimum theoretical length-of-cut for different forage harvesters is about 1/8 to 1/4 inch (3.1 to 6.3 mm). Maximum lengths range from 1 to 3 1/2 inches (25.4 to 89 mm). However, cutting material any finer than necessary for proper storage or feeding wastes time and power, reduces harvester capacity, and does not improve feed quality.

A theoretical length of 1/4 inch (6.3 mm) is generally recommended for haylage, and from 1/4 to 1 inch (6.3 to 25.4 mm) for high-moisture grass or legume silage. Corn silage should usually be cut from 1/4 to 1/2 inch (6.3 to 12 mm) in length for the best packing and fermentation. Dry hay may be cut considerably longer, from 2 to 3 inches (50 to 75 mm).

Change the feed rate to get a specific length-of-cut at a slower cutterhead speed, rather than remove knives to get the same cut at a higher speed.

To set the length-of-cut:

1. Determine the length for the forage you want.

2. Refer to the operator's manual for the recommended method of changing cutting length.

3. Change feed roll drive sprockets or shift gears on the feed roll drive to change the feed rate.

4. Add or remove cutterhead knives to match the feed rate for the length-of-cut.

5. Adjust the stationary knife after rearranging the cutterhead knives.

ADJUSTING THE CUTTERHEAD AND STATIONARY KNIFE

The cutterhead and shear bar (stationary knife) depend on each other for correct cutting. Proper cutterhead preparation and maintenance results in:

● *Higher quality silage with more uniform length-of-cut*

● *Reduced power requirement*

● *Fewer breakdowns*

The forage harvester cutterhead can do its job well only if rotating knives are kept sharp and the stationary knife is properly adjusted. Reset the stationary knife at least once a day during heavy operation, and every time the rotating knives are sharpened. Rotating knives will stay sharp much longer and shear bar wear will be reduced.

Stationary Knife Setting

Always set the stationary knife to the minimum recommended clearance. For example, if the operator's manual recommended 0.005 to 0.015 inch (.127 to .381 mm) of

Fig. 44—Use a Feeler Gauge to Measure Knife Clearance

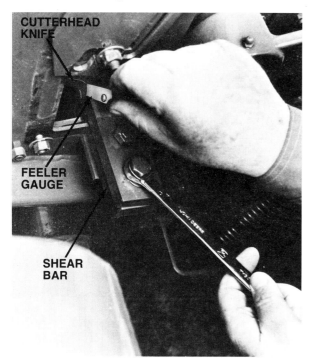

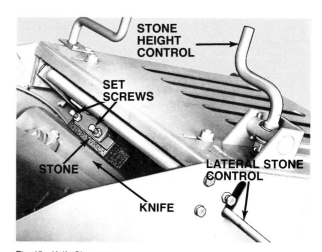

Fig. 45—Knife Sharpener

clearance, and knife clearance exceeds 0.015 inch (.381 mm), adjust the clearance to 0.005 inch (.127 mm). Clearance will increase as the harvester is used. Always use a feeler gauge to set knife clearance (Fig. 44).

Check the edges of rotating knives for sharpness and nicks daily. Sharpen dull knives (Fig. 45) according to the operator's manual. But do not oversharpen the knives. Oversharpening shortens knife life and wastes time.

Rebeveling Cutterhead Knives

The rotating knives on harvesters without reverse grinders require occasional rebeveling. Rebeveling is necessary when the knife "heel" protrudes farther than the cutting edge (Fig.46).

Cutterhead Housing Clearance

The rotating cutterhead blades on cut-and-throw harvesters must have the correct relationship to the cut-

Fig. 46—Knife "Heel" with Correct and Incorrect Bevel

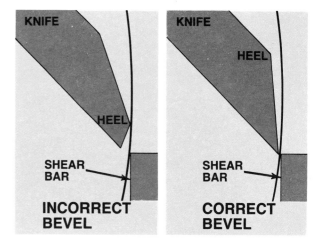

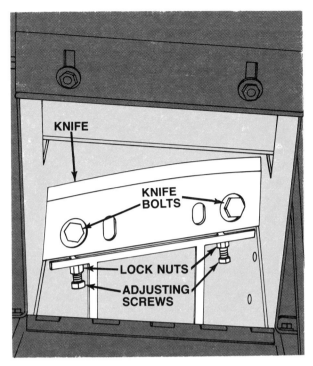

Fig. 47—Adjust Rotating Knives or Cutterhead Housing on Cut-and-Throw Machines

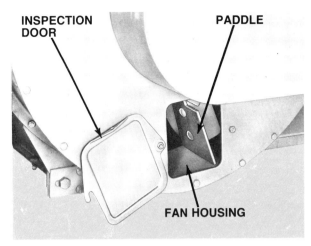

Fig. 48—Adjust Fan-Paddle Clearance for "Throw"

terhead housing to maintain adequate "throw" to deliver chopped material to a wagon or truck. On most harvesters, the cutterhead band or housing can be adjusted to the proper clearance between knives and housing, or knives must be adjusted individually on the cutterhead (Fig. 47). After setting the cutterhead-to-housing clearance, reset the stationary knife in relation to the rotating knives.

Rotating knives on cut-and-blow harvesters must be repositioned when stationary knife adjustments have been made.

Fan-Paddle Clearance

Proper clearance must be maintained between blower-fan paddles and the fan housing (Fig. 48). To reduce material velocity, for instance when loading to the side of the forage harvester, increase paddle clearance. To increase velocity or capacity, reduce paddle clearance. All paddles must be adjusted equally and set according to the manufacturer's recommendations.

Recutter Screen

If a recutter screen is used, it must also be adjusted to minimum clearance between the screen and cutterhead knives. Use a feeler gauge to check the clearance (Fig. 49), and adjust the screen according to instructions in the operator's manual.

FIELD OPERATION AND ADJUSTMENTS

Operating procedures vary with different kinds of crops, and for each type of forage harvester. For example, a self-propelled harvester with a direct-cut or row crop head can start into a field anywhere without knocking down some of the crop like a mounted or pulled machine would. In some cases, a self-propelled combine or picker may be used to open a corn field for a mounted or pulled forage harvester to save grain.

When opening a hay field with a direct-cut head or flail harvester, cut in the opposite direction on the return trip across the field to pick up material that was run down by the tractor and harvester on the first pass.

For best results when chopping stover with a flail or stover head, travel in the opposite direction to that traveled by the combine or corn picker.

Fig. 49—Gauge Recutter Screen Clearance Each Time Screen or Knives are Adjusted

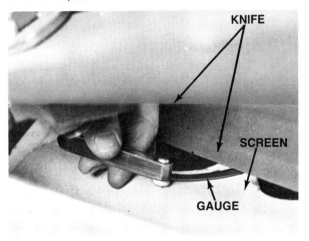

Fig. 50—"Ease" into the Crop

Always service and inspect a forage harvester before operation according to instructions in the operator's manual.

ENGINE SPEED

Start the tractor or self-propelled harvester engine and set the throttle at low rpm. Slowly engage the tractor PTO clutch, or the feed roll and forage head drive of a self-propelled harvester. Once the harvester is in operation and no problems are noted, bring the engine rpm up to the recommended operating rpms. Operate the tractor at the proper PTO speed (540 or 1000 rpm), depending on the forage harvester drive requirement. Lower the forage head to the operating height. Then ease the harvester into the crop (Fig. 50).

Where difficult conditions require slow speed, shift to a lower gear and keep the engine at the rated operating speed so the harvester will functioning properly.

Fig. 51—Watch the Blower Spout Carefully to Avoid Waste

Except in an emergency, allow the machine to blow out the crop before you disengage the tractor PTO or harvester drive to avoid plugging the feed rolls, cutterhead, or blower.

OPERATING TIPS

Operate a harvester at a ground speed which uses its full capacity but does not overload the machine. Don't drop forage harvester wheels into holes or straddle ridges, particularly with flail choppers that will dig into the ground. Raise the forage head or flail rotor to safely pass over rocks and ridges.

At the end of the row or windrow, raise the forage head or flail before turning. Turn the blower spout as each turn is made to keep material flowing into the wagon or truck.

Some manufacturers make blower spouts that follow the wagon around corners.

FILL THE WAGON EVENLY

Control the wagon loading process by adjusting the spout and deflector cap to fill the wagon evenly from the rear to the front. Make maximum use of wagon or truck capacity by loading sides and corners too, not just the center. Check constantly to make sure the blower spout is positioned properly and that material is entering the wagon or truck in the right pattern (Fig. 51). If the wagon or truck does not have a roof, use the blower spout cap carefully so material doesn't blow out over the sides. When filling a truck, the truck driver usually has the responsibility of keeping pace with the harvester.

CHANGING WAGONS

When changing wagons, make the switch as quickly and safely as possible to maintain high field efficiency. While hitching wagons, never let anyone stand between the harvester and the wagon. Wait until the tractor or harvester has stopped before stepping between the machines to install the hitch pin.

CLEARING CUTTERHEAD

When you disengage a harvester drive let the cutterhead, blower, or flails run long enough to clear the chopped forage out of the machine. After the material is cleared out of the harvester, disengage the tractor PTO clutch or the harvester drive on self-propelled models. With the PTO disengaged the cutterhead, blower, and other components can free wheel to a stop, avoiding strain on the drive components.

If the harvester plugs, immediately disengage the PTO or drive clutch and stop forward travel. Always lower the forage head, stop the engine, and take the key before dismounting. Wait until all the parts come to a complete stop before inspecting, unplugging, or repairing the harvester.

FLAIL HARVESTER OPERATION

Some service may be necessary during field operation of flail harvesters. The rotor usually requires the most attention. If excessive vibration occurs, disengage the tractor PTO clutch immediately, wait until the rotor stops, then check for damaged or missing flails or other problems. Correct the problems as directed in the operator's manual.

On cut-and-throw flail harvesters, adjust the shear bar in the rotor housing as directed in the operator's manual.

If the chopper is equipped with cutting knives on the blower, keep the knife clearance adjusted as recommended to maintain cutting ability and avoid wasting power. Adjust the fan housing and paddles to maintain optimum blower capacity.

Unplugging a Flail Harvester

If a flail harvester plugs, disengage the tractor PTO, stop the engine, and wait for all moving parts to stop. Then pull the clogged material out the clean out openings. Always block up the rotor before attempting to work under the machine to avoid personal injury.

FORAGE HEAD OPERATION

A variety of forage heads may be used with most forage harvesters. Because makes differ, field adjustments and detailed operating instructions are beyond the scope of this book. Refer to the operator's manual for the harvester. However, some general field adjustments and operating practices are common to most units.

Windrow Pickup

Adjust the operating height as low as possible without having teeth dig into ground (Fig. 52). Set the height higher if the crop will grow back fast, and leave a little green. Lower the pickup teeth to pickup extremely light windrows or windrows that are settled or matted.

Operate teeth as high as possible to reduce the amount of foreign material entering the forage harvester. Choose the best operating height. Pick up the crop as completely as possible without damaging equipment.

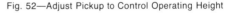

Fig. 52—Adjust Pickup to Control Operating Height

Direct-Cut or Mower Bar

Do not run the cutterbar any closer to the ground than necessary to get all the crop. Adjust the float-tension springs so the head will float, rather than drag over obstructions. Level the head from side to side. Open fields and establish cutting patterns the same way you would for mower conditioners and windrowers.

Row Crop and Stover Heads

In rocky fields and in high-ridged crops, keep the head high enough so the knife assembly clears rocks and ridges.

Ear Corn Snapper

Adjust ear corn heads to match individual field conditions. Snapping bars must be adjusted to stalk and ear size. Gathering chain speed can be adjusted to match ground speed on some heads.

Operate the head low enough to pull in stalks and for the snapper rolls to strip ears off the stalks. Check the operator's manual for details.

Flail Head

Keep the flails sharp and the rotor balanced for smooth cutting with minimum power. Raise or lower the rotor according to crop and field conditions, but never operate so low the flails strike the ground.

Fig. 53—Keep Transport Width as Narrow As Possible

TRANSPORT

Place the tongue of pulled harvesters in transport position and rotate the discharge spout to the rear-delivery position. If transporting a wagon behind the harvester, attach the wagon tongue near the centerline of the forage harvester so the wagon will follow directly behind the harvester (Fig. 53).

IMPORTANT: When transporting a forage harvester use a clearly visible SMV emblem and turn on the flashing warning lights so others will know what you are. The SMV emblem should be mounted on the rear of the harvester or wagon and 2 to 6 feet (.6 to 1.8 m) above the ground to provide proper light reflection.

Self-propelled harvesters may be transported under their own power or hauled on a truck unless restricted by local law.

SAFETY

Safety features are designed into harvesters.

Equipment should be operated by responsible people who know what they are doing.

Follow these safety practices, and safety signs in the tractor and harvester.

● Disengage all power, shut off the engine, and take the key before servicing a forage harvester. Wait for all moving parts to stop before unlatching doors or shields.

● Never stand under the discharge spout or in the path of the chopped forage while the harvester is operating.

● Keep safety shields in place when operating. Make sure rotating shields turn freely and the PTO shaft is locked securely.

● Use a wooden block to prevent the cutterhead from turning while knives are being adjusted (Fig. 54).

● Keep hands, feet, and clothing away from moving parts. Wear fairly tight, belted clothing. Loose jackets, shirts, and sleeves are likely to tangle in moving machinery.

● Unhitch wagons on level ground or parked across the slope so they don't roll.

● Only the operator rides on the tractor, harvester, or wagon, or on the operator's platform of self-propelled harvesters.

● Be sure everyone is clear of the harvester before starting the engine or engaging the clutch. People can be struck and injured by flying material, caught in moving parts, or run over.

● **Hydraulic warning page 334.**

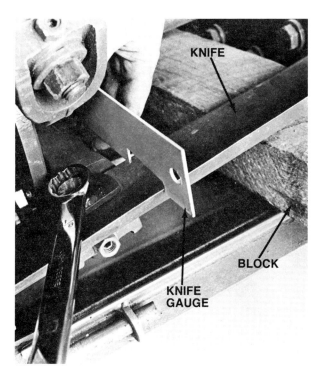

Fig. 54—Block Cutterhead When Adjusting Knives

• Be especially alert when operating on hillsides. A harvester or tractor can tip sideways. If a machine drops a wheel in a hole the machine can tip over in an instant.

• Keep tractors and self-propelled harvesters in gear when traveling downhill. Shift to a lower gear on steep downgrades.

• On 4-wheel drive harvesters, disengage the power rear wheel drive when operating on slick, icy roads. Refer to the operator's manual.

• Wear safety glasses when sharpening rotating knives. Avoid eye injury.

• Never smoke or have any open flame or sparks near when filling the fuel tank or servicing the fuel system.

• Keep engines clean to reduce the chance of fire. Keep a fully charged fire extinguisher on the tractor or harvester at all times. And be sure all operators know how to use the extinguisher.

• Refill the radiator when the engine is cold. To avoid being scalded when the radiator cap is removed from a pressurized cooling system, turn the cap slightly to the first stop so steam can escape through the overflow pipe. After all pressure is relieved, remove the cap.

• Before using booster batteries, read the instructions in the operator's manual. Be sure the cables are connected in proper sequence or the battery could explode.

MAINTENANCE

Most forage harvester maintenance involves the cutting components in the forage head, cutterhead and flails. Material should be cut cleanly, not "chewed" or torn apart. The rotating knives, shear bar, and recutter screen should be kept in good condition. Maintenance of cutting parts determines the cutting quality and the amount of power used. Dull, worn parts increase wear. The power requirement also increases fuel consumption. General cutterhead assembly maintenance is similar for most machines, but for specific adjustments refer to the harvester manual.

CAUTION: Escaping fluid under pressure can penetrate the skin causing serious injury. Relieve pressure before disconnecting hydraulic or other lines. Tighten all connections before applying pressure. Keep hands and body away from pinholes and nozzles which eject fluids under high pressure. Use a piece of cardboard or paper to search for leaks. Do not use your hand.

If ANY fluid is injected into the skin, it must be surgically removed within a few hours by a doctor familiar with this type injury or gangrene may result.

CAUTION: Do not feel for pinhole leaks. Escaping fluid under pressure can penetrate the skin causing injury. Relieve all hydraulic pressure before working on a pressurized hydraulic line or component.

STATIONARY KNIFE

Whether the shear bar has tungsten carbide on the cutting edge or can be turned to renew the cutting edge, it must be adjusted each time the rotating knives are sharpened. Always set the shear bar to the minimum clearance.

ROTATING KNIVES

The cutting edges of rotating cutterhead knives must be sharp. The closer they are adjusted to the shear bar, the longer the cutting edges will stay sharp. Rotating knives usually require sharpening at least once a day during heavy use.

Always torque the knife mounting bolts to the manufacturer's specifications to prevent damage.

KEEP FLAIL ROTOR IN BALANCE

If a new flail (knife) is installed, the flail 180 degrees opposite it on the rotor should also be replaced with a new flail to keep the rotor balanced. The second worn knife may, if its condition warrants, be used as a replacement when another equally-worn knife must be replaced.

Never operate a flail harvester with a flail missing. Vibration, resulting in metal fatigue and broken parts at almost any point in the machine, is caused by a missing flail.

Check flail sharpness and resharpen.

OTHER MAINTENANCE

Check and adjust fan-paddle clearance so chopped forage will be blown correctly.

Check the belts and chains for excessive wear and proper tension.

Keep knife sections tight and sharp on direct-cut heads.

Promptly repair or replace damaged or missing teeth on windrow pickups.

Keep gathering chains or belts and cutting knives sharp and adjusted on row crop and stover heads.

Keep the tires inflated.

Maintain the engine on self-propelled harvesters as recommended in the operator's manual (Fig. 56).

Fig. 56—Maintain Engines

STORAGE

Proper storage reduces weathering of rubber components, reduces rusting and paint deterioration, and improves resale value.

● Shelter the harvester in a dry building.

● Clean the harvester thoroughly inside and out. Trash and dirt draw moisture that causes rust.

● Paint places where the paint has worn off. Remove the chains and wash them in solvent. Dry the chains well and coat them with heavy oil.

● Block up the harvester to take the weight off the tires. Do not deflate tires. If the harvester is stored outdoors, cover the tires to protect them from sunlight, grease, and oil or store them in a dark, cool, dry place. Support the forage head with blocks to keep it off the ground and to relieve the weight on the hydraulic cylinders.

● Loosen the belts and wipe them clean with a good, non-flammable solvent.

● Prepare the engine, transmission, final drive, and hydraulic system on a self-propelled harvester for storage following instructions in the operator's manual. Add rust inhibitor to the transmission as recommended by the manufacturer.

● Lubricate the harvester completely. Grease the threads on adjusting bolts.

● List needed repairs and buy parts for the following season.

Keep these parts on hand:

- *Cutterhead knives*
- *Shear bar*
- *Chain links and splice links (some of each size used on the harvester)*
- *Reel teeth for direct-cut heads and windrow pickups*
- *Belts*
- *Fuel, air, and oil filters (self-propelled harvesters)*
- *Knife sections (row crop and direct-cut heads)*
- *Flails (flail harvesters and flail heads for other harvesters)*

TROUBLESHOOTING CHART

PROBLEM	POSSIBLE CAUSE	POSSIBLE REMEDY
This chart is designed to help locate probable causes, and help solve problems that occur during operation. See the operator's manual for specific adjustments.		
RAGGED CUT ENDS OR EXCESSIVE COB LENGTHS.	Dull cutterhead knives.	Sharpen knives.
	Dull shear bar (stationary knife).	Replace or turn shear bar.
	Excessive knife-to-shear bar clearance.	Adjust shear bar or rotate knives.
	Machine set for too long a cut.	Reduce length of cut.
	Not enough material in feed rolls for good control.	Pickup: Increase windrow size.
		Row crop or direct-cut heads: Increase ground speed.
	Cutting haylage or corn silage.	Install recutter screen (cut-and blow harvesters only).
RAGGED STUBBLE LEFT ON GROUND.	Improper knife register on row crop head.	Set knife register.
	Knife and guards in poor condition on direct-cut head.	Check and adjust guards or replace knife.
	Excessive ground speed.	Reduce ground speed.
	Knives not centered on row.	Reset hitch. Adjust or add wheel extensions. Drive more carefully.
	Head set too high.	Reduce operating height.
INSUFFICIENT "BLOWING POWER".	Excessive paddle-to-housing clearance.	Reset paddles or housing.
	Using too short cut for wet material.	Increase length-of-cut; or let crop dry more.
	Harvester not operating at proper speed.	Check tractor or harvester engine for proper rpm. Check drive belt tension.
EXCESSIVE POWER REQUIREMENT.	Dull cutterhead knives.	Sharpen or replace knives.
	Dull shear bar.	Replace or turn shear bar.
	Too much knife clearance.	Adjust stationary knife, and rotating knives if necessary.
	Length-of-cut too short.	Increase length of cut.

PROBLEM	POSSIBLE CAUSE	POSSIBLE REMEDY
KNIVES NOT BEING GROUND ON ONE END	Knives out of parallel with sharpening stone.	Move unground end of knife out to sharpening stone.
	Sharpening stone not properly seated in stone holder.	Reset stone.
	Stone broken.	Install new stone.
EXCESSIVE POWER REQUIRED WHEN USING RECUTTER SCREEN.	Knives dull.	Sharpen or replace worn knives.
	Excessive knife-to-screen clearance.	Set screen closer to knives.
	Excessive surface moisture on crop.	Use larger screen. Remove screen. Wait for crop to dry.
	Screen openings too small.	Use larger screen.
KNIVES HITTING RECUTTER SCREEN.	Screen not properly installed.	Reinstall screen.
	Deformed or damaged screen.	Model screen to correct shape or replace.
FAN AND CUTTERHEAD CLUTCH SLIPPING.	Clutch out of adjustment.	Adjust clutch.
	Clutch linkage out of adjustment.	Adjust linkage to permit full throwout bearing travel.
	Clutch linkage or carrier hanging up and not reaching over-center position.	Adjust linkage or correct carrier hang-up. Check for proper lubrication.
	Cutterhead drive belt slipping.	Check and adjust belt tension.
	Clutch parts badly worn.	See forage harvester dealer.
FAN AND CUTTERHEAD CLUTCH THROWOUT BEARING FAILURE.	Improper lubrication.	See forage harvester dealer.
		Provide proper lubrication in future.
EXCESSIVE VIBRATION OF KNIFE SHARPENING STONE.	Cutterhead speed too fast.	Reduce speed.
	Sharpening stone crank nut loose.	Tighten adjusting nut on crank.
	Stone worn enough that knives strike holder.	Install new stone.
	Too much crank pressure on on stone.	Reduce crank pressure.
KNIFE SHARPENING STONE HOLDER WON'T SLIDE FREELY.	Grease and dirt on shaft.	Clean shaft.
	Stone holder mechanism bent.	Straighten or replace damaged parts.
INSUFFICIENT DELIVERY FROM DISCHARGE SPOUT.	Hole in spout liner.	Replace liner.
	Excessive fan blade-to-housing clearance.	Reset fan blades and/or housing.
	Using too short cut for wet material	Increase length-of-cut, or let crop dry more.
	Harvester not operating at proper speed.	Check engine for proper rpm.
	Fan not properly installed.	See forage harvester dealer.

SUMMARY

Forage harvesters chop crops into short uniform lengths for storage in silos. Forage harvesters may be used for direct cutting and chopping of hay or row crops such as corn and sorghum. Forage harvesters can also be used to chop dry hay, but this is not a common practice.

Forage heads may be used to pick up windrows and harvest standing hay, row crops, stover, and ear corn.

Forage harvesters may be mounted, pulled, or self-propelled. Mounted harvesters are attached to the tractor 3-point hitch. Pulled harvesters are pulled by a tractor. Power to operate mounted and pulled harvesters is supplied by the tractor engine, through the PTO. Self-propelled forage harvesters are propelled by their own engine. The same engine supplies power for the forage harvester functions.

CHAPTER QUIZ

1. (Fill in the blanks.) Forage harvesters are usually classified as: Cut-and-_____, and Cut-and-_____.

2. List six forage heads.

3. What is the main function of a forage harvester?

4. What is the purpose of an SMV emblem?

5. Name two benefits of proper shear bar (stationary knife) adjustment.

6. What controls the rate of material flow to the cutterhead?

7. (True or false?) A forage harvester spout should be adjusted to fill trailing wagons from the front to the rear.

8. Name two ways to change the length-of-cut.

9. What forage harvester components require the most frequent inspection and maintenance?

10. (True or false?) Flails are rigidly mounted to the rotor shaft.

12
Self-Unloading Forage Wagons

Fig. 1—Self-Unloading Forage Boxes Fit Many Forage Harvesting Systems

Fig. 2—Unloading Forage

INTRODUCTION

Two kinds of self-unloading forage wagons are described in this chapter:

- **Forage boxes**
- **High-dump wagons**

The chapter is divided into two sections — one for each wagon.

SECTION 1: FORAGE BOXES

Self-unloading forage boxes have been developed for many uses in hay and forage harvesting and in feeding (Fig. 1). Forage boxes are mounted on a running gear or truck, and are used to harvest, transport, and feed:

- **Silage**
- **Haylage**
- **Green chop**
- **Ear corn**
- **Bales**

Forage boxes are often called bunk-feeder wagons because they are used in feeding silage and rations where feeding areas are widely separated.

Most forage boxes unload into a front chamber and discharge material out one side (Fig. 2).

Some boxes can unload from the rear. When a forage box is used to catch and haul bales from a bale ejector it must be able to unload from the rear to unload the bales. Rear unloading is also used to fill trench or bunker silos.

Forage boxes move material in three ways (Fig. 3):

- **Floor apron-to-cross-conveyor**
- **Floor apron-to-cross-auger**
- **Floor auger-to-cross-conveyor**

Most apron forage boxes may be used as front- or rear-unloading boxes. But auger-to-cross-conveyor boxes can only be used for front unloading materials that can be moved by auger.

FORAGE BOX COMPONENTS

Whether mounted on a running gear or truck, most forage boxes have (Fig. 4):

- **Chassis (running gear or truck)**
- **Box (sides, ends and floor)**
- **Beaters**
- **Floor conveyor**
- **Cross conveyor and extension**
- **Drives**
- **Controls**

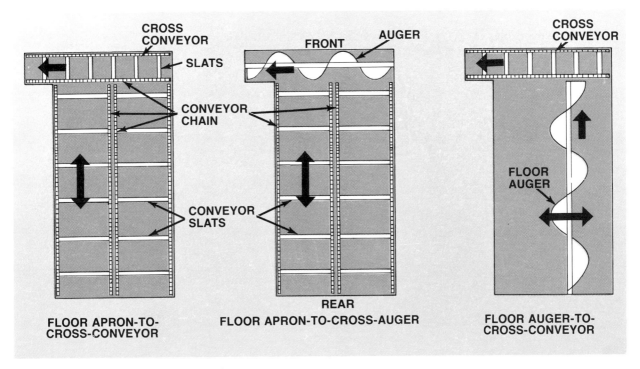

Fig. 3—Three Types of Forage Box Unloading Systems

Fig. 4—Forage Box Components

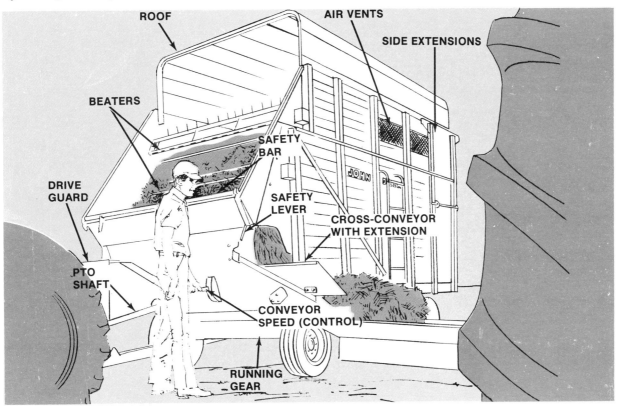

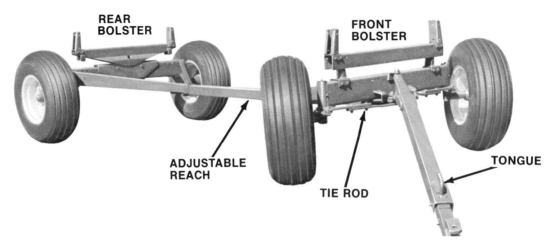

Fig. 5—Running Gear

CHASSIS (RUNNING GEAR)

The running gear has a frame, wheels, and tongue (Fig. 5). The running gear or truck must be strong enough to carry both the heavy forage box and a full load. Load size must be limited if running gear capacity is too small. (Calculation of load weights is discussed later in this chapter.) Some running gears use tandem rear axles or dual wheels to increase load-carrying capacity.

Auxiliary brakes are usually added to the running gear for safer stops and better control of heavy loads.

BOX CONSTRUCTION AND ATTACHMENTS

Box dimensions govern the volume of material which can be hauled by any forage box. Capacity may be increased on most forage boxes (for hauling lighter materials) by adding side extensions. If the wagon is used with a forage harvester, a roof may be added to help reduce forage losses

(Fig. 6). Box volume ranges from about 250 to 750 cubic feet (7 to 21 m³).

Box size and load capacity must be matched to the forage harvester used or the number of animals fed to avoid wasting time changing wagons, reloading, and traveling. If equipment is too large it ties up excessive capital. However, economic penalties of large equipment are usually lower than the potential losses from untimely operation caused by small equipment.

Forage box floors, walls, side extensions, and roofs are wood, steel, aluminum, or a combination. When a roof is used, slots or screen sections are usually provided in the sides so air can escape.

Many forage boxes have a rear door which is usually hinged at the top for unloading to the rear (Fig. 7). Rear doors are latched in the closed position and supported in the raised position to prevent accidental opening or closing. A spring-balanced rear door on some boxes makes opening and closing easy.

Fig. 6—Forage Box with Side Extensions and Roof

Fig. 7—Forage Box Rear Door

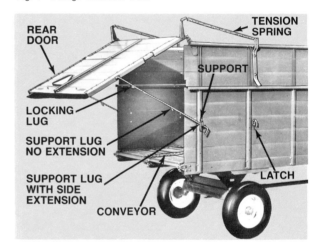

Fig. 8—Forage Box with Tilting Roof

On some models the front end of the box roof may be tilted upward to provide more clearance for filling, and lowered to reduce overall box height (Fig. 8).

BEATERS

Beaters, consisting of "tooth bars" on shafts, help unload forage. As the floor conveyor moves the load forward, the rotating beaters break up lumps. This rotating action helps feed the material evenly into the cross conveyor (Fig. 9).

Beaters may also help blend other materials with the forage. Concentrates, grains or preservatives are usually spread over the top of the load before starting to unload, or on the floor of the forage box before loading. Beater action during unloading blends the materials.

Most forage boxes have two beaters. When side extensions are added, a third beater is usually required.

FLOOR CONVEYOR

Material is moved forward to the forage box cross conveyor by a chain-and-slat system or an auger. On most boxes the chain-and-slat conveyor may be reversed for rear unloading (Fig. 10). On some boxes reversing is done by shifting a lever. On others the drive system must be changed. Chain-and-slat conveyors are most common.

Most chain-and-slat floor conveyors consist of four chains and two sets of slats (Fig. 10). A few boxes have three conveyor chains and full-width slats.

Some boxes are designed with an auger which moves from side to side while conveying material to the cross conveyor, instead of using chain-and-slats. Beaters are not required with auger unloading systems.

CROSS CONVEYOR

As material is moved to the front of the wagon, it drops into a cross conveyor which can be a belt, auger (Fig. 11), or a chain-and-slat system (Fig. 12). The cross conveyor carries material to the side of the box for unloading.

Extension conveyors may be added to some cross conveyors to make unloading into bunks or blowers easier (Fig. 13). The height of most extension conveyors may be adjusted for more convenient feeding or unloading.

DRIVE SYSTEMS

Forage boxes are powered by a tractor or truck PTO operating at 540 or 1000 rpm. Power is carried through shafts, chains, and sprockets to a ratchet system (Fig. 14) or a worm-gear system to drive the floor and cross conveyors and the beaters. Ratchet drives are common, but they produce shake and stress components.

Floor conveyor speed is adjustable so you can control the unloading rate. You can make small changes in unloading speed by varying engine speed.

Fig. 9—Rotating Beaters Smooth Material Flow

Fig. 10—Chain-and-Slat Floor Conveyor

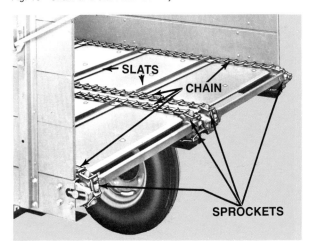

Fig. 11—Auger Cross Conveyor

Fig. 12—Chain-and-Slat Cross Conveyor

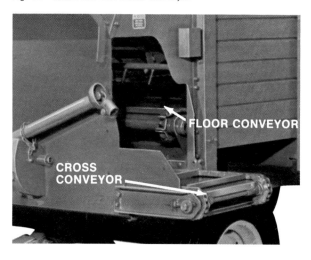

FLOOR CONVEYOR

CROSS CONVEYOR

Fig. 13—Chain-and-Slat Extension Conveyor

CONTROLS

The most common controls are:

- **Beater and floor conveyor control**
- **Safety clutch**

Beaters and the floor conveyor are controlled by the same lever or by separate levers (Fig. 15). Some rear-unloading boxes have a separate control lever for stopping the floor conveyor or changing unloading speed from the rear of the box.

Safety Clutches

Safety clutches are usually located on or above the front panel of the forage box (Fig. 16). If you move a lever or hit the cross bar, the beaters and floor conveyor stop.

Fig. 14—Typical Forage Box Drive System

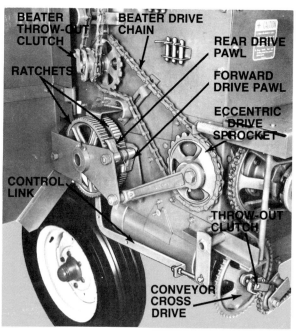

BEATER THROW-OUT CLUTCH

BEATER DRIVE CHAIN

REAR DRIVE PAWL

RATCHETS

FORWARD DRIVE PAWL

ECCENTRIC DRIVE SPROCKET

CONTROL LINK

THROW-OUT CLUTCH

CONVEYOR CROSS DRIVE

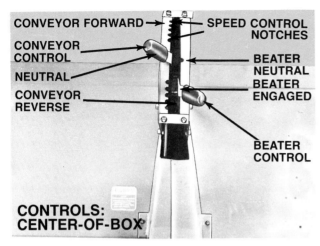
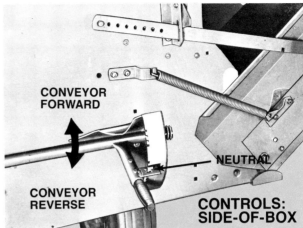

Fig. 15—Forage Box Controls

The safety clutch may also stop the cross conveyor. On most forage boxes, the cross conveyor operates continuously whenever the truck or tractor PTO is engaged.

FORAGE BOX CAPACITY

First, determine the maximum gross load you expect the running gear to carry. This is the weight of the forage box plus the weight of the material being transported (Fig. 17). This combined weight must not exceed the running gear capacity.

CALCULATING FORAGE WEIGHT

Although volume information is usually provided by the manufacturer, it can be calculated by using the following formula and inside dimensions of the forage box.

Width(W) × Length(L) × Depth(D) = Volume in cubic feet or (m³)

When forage box volume is known or calculated, determine the net weight of material the forage box can hold by using the approximate weight per cubic foot (m³) of different materials shown in *Table 1*. However, remember the weights for these materials may vary widely due to moisture content, length-of-cut and how tightly the material is packed.

For example, determine the weight of a forage box and the material:

Consider a forage box with a 6-ton (5.4 t) capacity for a diversified harvesting-feeding operation. The interior of the box measures 75 inches wide, 180 inches long, and 60 inches deep (1905 × 4572 × 1524 mm) (Fig. 18).

Fig. 16—Safety Clutch System

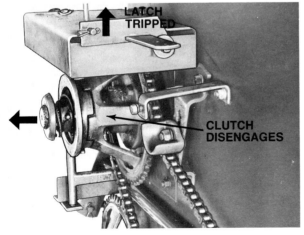
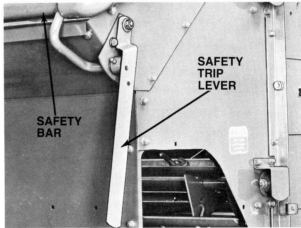

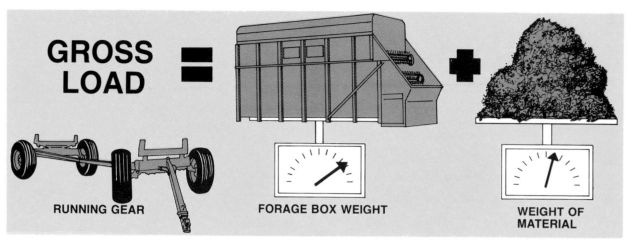

RUNNING GEAR   FORAGE BOX WEIGHT   WEIGHT OF MATERIAL

Fig. 17—Gross Load Equals Weight of the Forage Box Plus Weight of the Material Transported

TABLE 1		
Approximate weight of materials in pounds per cubic foot (kilograms per cubic meter)		
CROP	WEIGHT Per Cu. Ft.	WEIGHT Per Cu. Meter
Shelled Corn	45 lb.	(20)
Silage	26 lb.	(12)
Haylage	18 lb.	(8)
Chopped Dry Hay	12 lb.	(5)

If the box has a 6 ton (5.4 t) load limit, and a weight of 2,700 pounds (1,226 kg) (almost 1 1/2 tons) (1.3 t), it would require a running gear with 7 1/2 ton (6.8 t) capacity. However, to be safe, the box volume must be determined and the load

Fig. 18—Use Interior Box Dimensions to Calculate Volume and Capacity

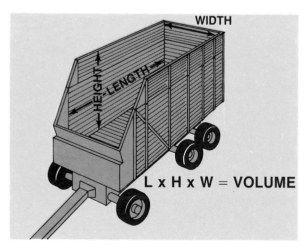

WIDTH

HEIGHT

LENGTH

L x H x W = VOLUME

weight calculated for different materials because not all forages weigh the same per cubic foot.

To find box capacity in English dimensions from the dimensions given earlier, use the volume formula and unit-factor system to convert inches into feet.

Volume (ft.³) = W × L × D (in feet)

$$= 75 \text{ in.} \times \frac{1 \text{ ft.}}{12 \text{ in.}} \times 180 \text{ in.} \times \frac{1 \text{ ft.}}{12 \text{ in.}} \times 60 \text{ in.} \times \frac{1 \text{ ft.}}{12 \text{ in.}}$$

$$= 6.25 \text{ ft.} \times 15 \text{ ft.} \times 5 \text{ ft.}$$

$$= 468.75 \text{ cubic feet (469 for easier figuring)}$$

Now use the volume and material weights from *Table 1* to determine the weight of a load of each type of material. Keep in mind that the forage box being considered has a load limit of 6 tons.

Haylage

First, take the weight in *Table 1* for haylage (18 lbs/cu. ft.), and find the weight of the crop if the full 469 cubic foot capacity is used.

$$\text{Total weight (tons)} = 469 \text{ cu. ft.} \times \frac{18 \text{ lbs.}}{\text{cu. ft.}} \times \frac{1 \text{ ton}}{2000 \text{ lbs.}}$$

$$= 4.22 \text{ tons (of haylage)}$$

So, if this particular box is used to transport haylage, the load weight will be well within the manufacturer's recommend limit.

Silage

But, what about a heavier material such as silage? As shown in *Table 1*, silage weighs about 26 pounds per cubic foot. So, total weight will be:

$$\text{Weight (tons)} = 469 \text{ cu. ft.} \times \frac{26 \text{ lbs}}{\text{cu. ft.}} \times \frac{1 \text{ ton}}{2000 \text{ lbs}}$$

$$= 6.1 \text{ tons (of silage)}$$

This is slightly more than the rated maximum capacity. So the box should not be completely filled with silage.

270

Shelled Corn

A full load of shelled corn would exceed the load limit of the forage box. (A full load of any material weighing more per cubic foot than silage will have a total weight of more than 6 tons.) To determine the amount of shelled corn (at 45 lbs/cu. ft. — (*Table 1*) that could be safely hauled, use the following formula to find out how much corn you can haul in the box.

$$\text{Depth} = \frac{\text{Maximum Weight Limit (lbs)}}{\text{W (ft.)} \times \text{L(ft.)} \times \text{Material density (lbs cu. ft.)}}$$

$$= \frac{6 \text{ tons} \times 2000 \text{ lbs/ton}}{6.25 \text{ ft.} \times 15 \text{ ft.} \times 45 \text{ lbs/cu. ft.}}$$

$$= \frac{12{,}000 \text{ lbs}}{4218.75 \text{ ft.}}$$

$$= 2.84 \text{ feet (of shelled corn)}$$

So, if shelled corn is hauled in this box, the box should not be filled more than 2.84 feet (about 2 ft. 10 in.) (Fig. 19).

Tire Rating

Tire rating is important when you match running gear to forage boxes. If tire capacity exceeds the capacity of the box and gear, fill the box to the maximum box and gear rating. But when tire capacity is less than the boxgear rating, the tire capacity determines the maximum load.

With heavy loads and adverse operating conditions using discarded tires on forage wagons is false economy. Tire failure during harvest could idle a forage harvester, blower, and a 2- or 3-man harvesting crew. During delays the moisture content of wilted crop can drop below acceptable limits for fermentation and storage. The resulting reduction in feed quality could be far more costly than a complete set of good wagon tires.

High capacity flotation tires with adequate rating for the *maximum* loads can reduce overall operating costs by reducing repairs and downtime and easing operation in soft fields.

FORAGE BOX PREPARATION

Learn the controls and operating procedures in the operator's manual before you operate a forage wagon.

TRACTOR PREPARATION

Tractor preparation before forage wagon operation can save time and improve efficiency.

1. Adjust wheel tread width for good stability and to match row spacings.

2. Adjust drawbar length and height for PTO operation. Pin drawbar parallel to the centerline of the PTO shaft.

3. Inspect tires and inflate to proper pressure.

4. Check the brakes. Loaded forage wagons can be very hard to stop on steep slopes.

5. Add front weights for stability, particularly when operating on hilly land. Add rear wheel weights for traction and braking.

Fig. 19—Density of Material Determines Filling Height of a Forage Box

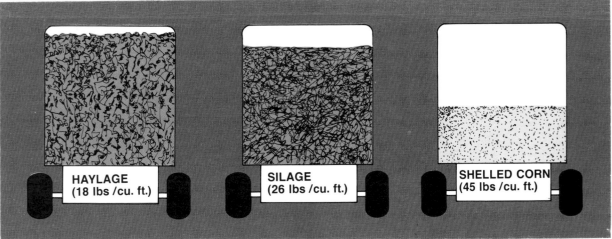

HAYLAGE
(18 lbs /cu. ft.)

SILAGE
(26 lbs /cu. ft.)

SHELLED CORN
(45 lbs /cu. ft.)

WAGON PREPARATION

A few extra moments spent preparing a forage box often saves time and effort later.

1. Determine the maximum weight. If the load weight exceeds box, running gear, or tire capacity, determine the maximum load which can be hauled without exceeding the limiting factor.

2. Inspect tires for cuts, breaks, or other damage, and inflate them to the recommended pressure (Fig. 20).

3. Lubricate the box and running gear, and grease wheel bearings as recommended in the operator's manual.

4. Set the wagon tongue length (if adjustable) to the proper position for PTO operation. Couple the wagon tongue to the tractor drawbar with a safety hitch pin and safety chain.

5. Clean the PTO shaft before connecting the PTO shaft to the tractor. Lock the universal joint firmly in place.

6. In cold weather, loosen frozen conveyor chains and slats *before* applying power to the drive train.

7. With the tractor engine at low throttle, engage the tractor PTO clutch and operate the forage box a short time to be sure that floor conveyor, beaters, and cross conveyor are functioning properly. A broken or malfunctioning floor conveyor could force you to unload several tons of forage by hand before repairs can be made.

FORAGE BOX OPERATION

Forage box operation is discussed in three phases:

- **Loading**
- **Unloading**
- **Transport**

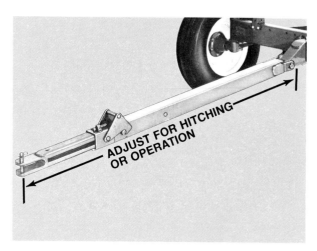

Fig. 21—Adjust Tongue Length for Safer Hitching

Operator training, experience, and attitude affect forage box efficiency and productivity.

LOADING FORAGE WAGONS

Before loading, couple the forage wagon to the forage harvester or baler. Back the tractor carefully into position. Put the tractor in PARK, shut off the engine, and take the key before dismounting. Insert the safety hitch pin. An adjustable, telescoping tongue is available for many forage wagons to make hookup easier (Fig. 21).

Fig. 20—Inflate Tires To Recommended Pressure

Fig. 22—Have Anyone Assisting with Hookup Stand Clear while Backing to the Wagon

If anyone is helping hitch the wagon, do not permit them to stand in front of the wagon while the tractor or forage harvester is backing or even in reverse gear (Fig. 22). Shut off the tractor engine, take the key and shift the transmission into park before hooking up the wagon.

Loading forage boxes properly depends almost entirely upon the operator's skill and effort in controlling the harvesting unit and filling spout or bale ejector. For easier filling and smoother unloading, load forage wagons from back to front (Fig. 23). Direct material into corners and along the sides as the box fills to keep the load balanced and for more efficient use of forage box capacity. Never exceed the capacity rating in the operator's manual. When turning, turn the delivery spout to keep the material directed into the box.

UNLOADING FORAGE WAGONS

Position the forage wagon at the blower or elevator properly (Fig. 24). After the wagon is positioned, follow these steps:

1. Stop the tractor engine.

2. Attach the wagon PTO shaft to the tractor PTO.

3. If the wagon is equipped with a folding cross conveyor extension, lower the extension and adjust the height.

4. When unloading into a blower, start the tractor or motor powering the blower and bring the blower up to operating speed. When unloading bales or forage into an elevator, start the elevator and adjust the speed.

5. Make certain the wagon control levers are in *neutral.*

The above procedures apply to all self-unloading forage boxes. To simplify explanations, other procedures are divided into two parts:

- Unloading from a cross conveyor

- Unloading from the rear

These two unloading procedures usually require changes in wagon operation.

Unloading from a Cross Conveyor

Here is the procedure for unloading from the cross conveyors of most forage wagons.

1. With the blower or elevator running, start the tractor engine and, at reduced throttle, engage the PTO clutch. This will start the cross conveyor and clear material that has fallen into the unloading chamber.

2. If the forage wagon is equipped with a separate beater control, engage it to clear material from around the beaters.

3. Place the floor conveyor control in operating position to start moving material forward. If there is a choice of conveyor speeds, select the speed best suited to the material

Fig. 24—Take Time to Position Forage Wagons Properly for Unloading

Fig. 23—Load Forage Boxes from Back to Front

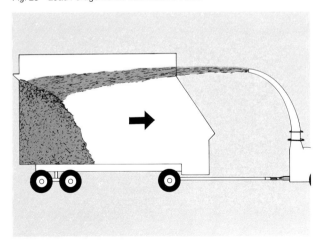

Fig. 25—Select Proper Floor Conveyor Speed

Fig. 26—Don't Hit the Bunk

being unloaded and the blower or elevator capacity (Fig. 25). Attempting to save time by overloading a blower or elevator usually requires much more time than normal operation because of the probability of plugging, equipment damage, and subsequent cleanout or repair. Adjust the tractor throttle setting to the correct unloading rate.

4. If the height of the cross-conveyor extension requires adjustment, disengage the PTO clutch and stop the tractor engine before adjusting.

5. Most auger extensions are kept at a fixed height. If the cross conveyor clogs, disengage the beaters and floor conveyor and place the control lever in neutral. On some forage boxes the floor conveyor can be shifted into reverse to relieve clogging. If this is necessary, reverse the conveyor *briefly* and wait for the blockage to clear. If beaters or the unloading chamber remain clogged, stop the tractor engine before attempting to unclog the wagon.

6. When the load is nearly off and thinly spread over the conveyor, shift the floor conveyor control to a higher speed and disengage the beaters, if possible, for faster cleanout.

7. After unloading, place the control levers in neutral and disengage the tractor PTO. Disconnect the wagon PTO shaft and place it in the transport position on the box. Raise the cross-conveyor extension, if used, and secure it in the transport position.

Unloading into a Feedbunk

When using a forage wagon for feeding follow this unloading procedure.

1. Drive to the feeding area and stop with the cross conveyor over the end of the feedbunk. Stop the tractor engine. Attach the wagon PTO shaft to the tractor PTO.

2. Lower the conveyor extension over the edge of the feedbunk and adjust the height. Keep the conveyor high enough so it doesn't hit the bunk during unloading.

3. Start the tractor engine, and at reduced throttle, engage the PTO clutch. Put the tractor in gear and move forward slowly as material begins to flow from the cross conveyor. Let the cross conveyor discharge most of the material already in the unloading chamber before you engage the beater drive to clear material from the beaters. Engage beater drive and then floor conveyor, if separate controls are provided.

4. Drive parallel to the bunk. Don't run into the bunk (Fig. 26). Adjust ground speed and speed of the floor conveyor to deliver forage into the bunk at a good rate.

5. When the wagon is empty, place the controls in neutral, disengage the PTO clutch, stop the engine, and raise the

cross-conveyor extension. Be cautious passing through gates. You could damage the cross conveyor or extension.

Unloading Forage Boxes From The Rear

In some situations, such as filling trench or bunker silos, it may be faster or more convenient to unload a forage wagon from the rear. On some boxes the floor conveyor may be reversed by shifting a lever or installing a conversion kit for the drive systems. If a conversion is required, follow directions in the operator's manual.

Before unloading a forage box from the rear:

1. Disengage the cross conveyor drive or clutch.

2. Disengage the beater drive or clutch.

3. Close the drive guard before operating the wagon.

4. Unlatch and raise the rear door (Fig. 27).

To unload:

1. Place the control levers in neutral.

2. Start the tractor engine, and at reduced throttle engage the PTO clutch.

3. Select a reverse speed suited for the operation, and begin unloading.

4. Set tractor engine rpm at a good unloading rate.

5. Continue to adjust the throttle and conveyor speed to get the best unloading rate.

6. You can speed up after the conveyor is nearly cleared.

Fig. 27—Unlatching the Rear Door

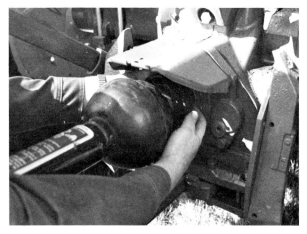

Fig. 28—Disconnect Powershaft and Secure in Transport Position

7. After unloading, place all controls in neutral and disengage the tractor PTO. Lower and latch the rear door, disconnect the PTO shaft and place the shaft in transport position.

TRANSPORT

Before transporting any forage wagon, follow these steps:

1. Make sure the safety hitch pin is locked in place.

2. Connect a safety chain.

3. Disconnect the powershaft from the tractor and secure it in the transport position (Fig. 28).

4. Lower and latch the rear door, if it has been opened.

5. Raise and secure the cross-conveyor extension, if it was lowered.

When transporting a forage wagon on a road or highway use a clearly visible SMV emblem and turn on the flashing warning lights. Check local governmental regulations regarding equipment transport and the display of emblems and lights.

Check and follow recommendations in the operator's manual regarding transport speed. One manufacturer recommends:

1. Avoid towing a loaded wagon faster than five miles per hour unless the wagon is equipped with brakes. Never exceed 20 miles per hour with a loaded or unloaded forage wagon.

2. Avoid driving a tractor and loaded forage wagon down a hill that is steeper than 15 degrees, unless the wagon is equipped with brakes.

MAINTENANCE

Operating adjustments vary among different forage boxes. The operator's manual is the best reference for forage box service.

Some common adjustments:

- *Floor conveyor chain and drive-chain tension*
- *Cross conveyor chain and drive-chain tension*
- *Beater drive-chain tension*
- *Main drive-chain tension*

Proper drive-chain tension is essential to smooth operation, reduced wear, and maximum parts life. Check all chains regularly and adjust the tension (Fig. 29):

Always stop the engine before making any adjustments.

Keep the safety clutch or throwout bar adjusted. See the operator's manual for specific settings.

Maintain correct clearance between augers and housings. Excessive clearance reduces capacity, especially in fine materials, and could cause plugging if forage wraps over edges of the auger. Insufficient clearance causes rapid auger and housing wear and stresses auger bearings.

Be alert for damaged, broken, or missing parts or signs of rapid parts wear. Make repairs and adjustments immediately so problems don't affect other parts of the wagon.

Follow the maintenance procedures outlined in the operator's manual and provide service at the recommended time.

Hydraulic warning page 334.

TROUBLESHOOTING

Troubleshooting procedures and problem areas vary for each forage wagon type and model. The following troubleshooting chart applies particularly to a box with chain-and-slat floor conveyor and cross-conveyor, and a ratchet conveyor drive.

Fig. 29—Keep Chains Tight

TROUBLESHOOTING CHART

PROBLEM	POSSIBLE CAUSE	POSSIBLE REMEDY
POWERSHAFT HALVES SEPARATE OR JAM WITH TRACTOR IN SLIGHT TURN.	Wagon gear has wrong length tongue.	Shorten or lengthen wagon tongue.
	Drawbar improperly positioned for PTO operating speed.	Adjust drawbar length for 540 or 1000 rpm operation.
APRON CONVEYOR AND BEATERS DO NOT OPERATE.	Safety-trip bar latch disengaged.	Reset safety-trip bar.
	Jaw clutch does not move freely.	Clean and grease.

PROBLEM	POSSIBLE CAUSE	POSSIBLE REMEDY
APRON CONVEYOR DOES NOT MOVE IN ACCORDANCE WITH CONTROL LEVER SETTING.	Ratchet-drive rate of feed improperly adjusted.	Adjust rate of feed.
APRON CONVEYOR DOES NOT OPERATE.	Control lever in neutral.	Place lever in desired forward or reverse notch.
	Feed or lock pawl broken.	Replace pawl(s).
APRON CONVEYOR DOES NOT MOVE TO REAR WITH LEVER IN REVERSE NOTCH.	Ratchet-drive rate of feed improperly adjusted.	Adjust rate of feed.
BEATERS WILL NOT STOP TURNING WHEN CONTROL LEVER IS IN NEUTRAL POSITION.	Clutch not completely disengaged.	Adjust clutch.
BEATERS WILL NOT OPERATE.	Clutch pin sheared.	Replace beater shear pins
	Cross conveyor over filled.	Engage clutch and unload cross conveyor.
	Beater clutch disengaged.	Engage clutch.
CROSS CONVEYOR WILL NOT OPERATE.	Cross-conveyor clutch disengaged.	Engage clutch.
	Clutch pin sheared.	Replace pin.
CROSS CONVEYOR IDLER ROLLERS DO NOT TURN FREELY.	Bearings improperly aligned.	Loosen bearing-retaining bolts until rollers turn freely; then tighten bolts.
BEATER AND APRON DRIVE WILL NOT DISENGAGE	Control failure or improper adjustment.	Repair or adjust as needed.
BEATER TEETH STRIKE FLOOR CONVEYOR DRIVE CHAIN WHEN UNLOADING FROM THE REAR.	Floor conveyor drive chain not properly adjusted.	Adjust floor conveyor drive chain.
EXCESSIVE NOISE IN THE RATCHET ASSEMBLY.	Ratchet out of adjustment.	Adjust ratchet.
FLOOR CONVEYOR DRIVE-CHAIN MALFUNCTIONS WHEN UNLOADING FROM THE REAR.	Floor conveyor drive chain too loose.	Be sure floor conveyor drive chain or properly tightened.

SAFETY

You can avoid accidents by observing safety. Read and follow the instructions in the operator's manual and on the decals on the forage wagon.

• Don't let people operate equipment if they don't know what they are doing.

• Wear relatively tight, belted clothing. Loose clothing catches in moving parts.

• Never enter a forage box or place your hands or feet near the beater while the engine is running or the forage wagon is operating.

• A safety-trip lever and bar are provided for the safety of the operator. *Know how to operate them.*

• When operating a forage wagon, always remain at the controls and alert until the operation is completed.

• Always lift the cross-conveyor extension by the handle, never by the conveyor slats.

• Disengage all drives, stop the engine and take the key before adjusting, lubricating, or cleaning a forage wagon.

• Keep guards and shields in place at all times while the machine is operating. Stop the machine, shut off the engine, and take the key before removing guards or shields.

• When replacing high-strength bolts or shear pins, do not substitute regular bolts.

• Be sure rotating PTO shaft shields turn freely.

• Two fully-loaded wagons at speeds recommended by the manufacturer.

• For safer stops with loads, equip the running gear with brakes, particularly for hill and road transport.

• Never drive the tractor and loaded wagon down a hill steeper than 15 degrees, unless the wagon is equipped with brakes.

SECTION 2:
HIGH-DUMP WAGONS

High-dump wagons came into widespread use with the introduction and acceptance of self-propelled hay cubers (Fig. 30). More recently, high-dump wagons with larger capacities and faster unloading cycles have been introduced for use with forage harvesters and similar machines (Fig. 31).

High-dump wagons offer two major advantages in field operations:

• Decrease the number of transport vehicles needed by quickly transferring material into higher-speed vehicles for road transport.

• Transfer hay or forage to trucks which cannot enter the field due to soft or rough ground conditions.

Like forage boxes, high-dump wagons may be used with a number of forage and grain crops. High-dump wagons are also used to harvest vegetables, sugar beets, and sweet corn.

DUMP-WAGON TYPES AND PURPOSES

High-dump wagons used for hay and forage harvesting may be divided into two categories:

• **Smaller, cuber**

• **Larger, forage harvester**

Fig. 30—Tandem-Axle, High-Dump Wagons Are Frequently Used with Field Cubers

SMALL DUMP WAGONS

High-dump wagons normally used with self-propelled cubers have an open top and tandem axles. This style of wagon usually has a low profile for easy loading with the cuber elevator and relatively low capacity.

LARGE DUMP WAGONS

Wagons used with forage harvesters differ from the smaller models in several ways. Most of them have:

- *Larger bin capacity*
- *Running gear instead of tandem wheels and hitch*
- *Hinged roof to help control chopped-forage losses during harvest*
- *Faster dumping cycle to save field time*

The hinged roof is usually removable.

COMPONENTS

Major high-dump wagon components:

- **Axles and main frame**
- **Bin**
- **Dumping mechanism**

These components all work together for efficient loading, transport, and unloading.

AXLES AND MAIN FRAME

The wagon axles and main frame support the bin. On some models, the frame design lets you add weight, such as concrete, to one side of the wagon to counterbalance the load when the bin is raised. When raising the bin, make sure the wagon is on nearly level ground. ·

Fig. 31—Some High-Dump Wagons Are Used with Self-Propelled Forage Harvesters

Fig. 32—Unloading is Easy

Fig. 33—Hinged Roof Swings Open to Dump

BINS

Bin size determines the capacity of a high-dump wagon. Capacity of most units ranges from about 4.5 to 9 tons (4 to 8 t).

High-dump wagon bins have sides sloping outward from the bottom to make it easier for material to slide out (Fig. 32).

Some bins may be equipped with a side extension which tilts outward as the bin is raised and helps direct material into the truck or trailer.

Many bins may be equipped with roofs, which have one stationary section and a hinged portion on the dumpside of the bin. Part of the roof may be screened to permit air from the forage harvester blower to escape without blowing away fine particles of leaves and stems. The roof is automatically unlatched and swung open as the bin is tipped to dump (Fig. 33).

DUMPING SYSTEMS

Two types of hydraulic dumping systems are used with high-dump wagons:

- **Lift-pivot-and-dump**
- **Stabilize-lift and pivot-and-dump**

The lift-pivot-and-dump system is frequently used on smaller dump-wagons with fixed axles and rigid frames. The cylinders lift, then pivot the bin to dump the contents.

Two lift cylinders, a flow-control valve, stabilizers, and hydraulic lines comprise the hydraulic system of dump wagons mounted on a running gear with pivoting front axle. Stabilizers are needed to "set" the front axle for unloading. The flow-control valve directs the flow of oil to the stabilizers first. When the stabilizers are positioned, oil is automatically diverted to the lift cylinders and the bin is raised and dumped.

One of the most important components in any hydraulic system is *clean hydraulic oil.* Always clean hydraulic couplings before connecting hoses and avoid getting dirt into the system when adding oil or changing filters.

If a high-dump wagon is towed and hydraulically operated by a tractor, cuber, or self-propelled forage harvester using a different type of hydraulic oil, all cylinders and lines on the wagon must be drained and refilled with the same type of oil in the towing vehicle.

Always follow hydraulic system maintenance and safety recommendations in the operator's manual.

DUMP-WAGON FUNCTIONING

Unloading action of high-dump wagons may be classified as:

- **Lift-and-pivot**
- **Direct pivot**

LIFT-AND-PIVOT UNLOADING

Shifting the hydraulic control lever on the tractor, cuber, or forage harvester actuates the dumping cycle.

Two dump cylinders extend to raise the bin and lifting frame up the tracks (Fig. 34). As the cylinders continue to extend after the frame reaches the top of the tracks, the bin is pivoted to dump the load. As the bin is rotated away from the lifting frame, bin latches automatically engage the top of each track. These latches prevent the raised bin and frame from moving back down the tracks before the bin returns to its normal upright position against the frame.

When the hydraulic control lever is moved in the opposite direction, lift cylinders retract and the bin pivots back against the frame. Bin latches are released automatically and the bin and frame roll down the tracks to the normal position on the main wagon frame.

DIRECT-PIVOT UNLOADING

The direct-pivot unloading cycle differs from the lift-and-pivot system two ways:

1. Stabilizers brace the front wagon axle.

2. The bin begins to pivot as soon as the cylinders start lifting.

The dumping cycle begins when the operator moves the hydraulic control lever on the towing vehicle. Hydraulic oil, controlled by the flow-control valve, is directed to the stabilizers on each side of the front axle. As pressure builds in the system, the stabilizer rams lower to stabilize the frame and front axle (Fig. 35).

When stabilizer rams are fully extended, the flow-control valve locks hydraulic oil in the stabilizers and diverts all flow to the hydraulic cylinders to continue the lifting process (Fig. 36).

As the bin is raised, the roof-locking latch unhooks allowing the roof to open. Tension on the roof springs helps open and close the roof when the bin is moved.

Reversing the hydraulic control lever lowers the bin.

When the bin is completely lowered, bin weight pushes in the stem of the flow-control valve, releases pressure in the stabilizers, and permits the front axle to pivot again.

Fig. 34—Bin and Lifting Frame Travel to Top of Tracks Before Bin Pivots With Lift and Pivot Unloading

DUMP-WAGON PREPARATION

Because of the great amount of weight transferred to one side of the wagon during the dumping process, preparing high-dump wagons for field operation is just as important as correct operation.

Fig. 35—Stabilizer Rams, Lowered Against the Front Axle, Support the Box Frame During Unloading

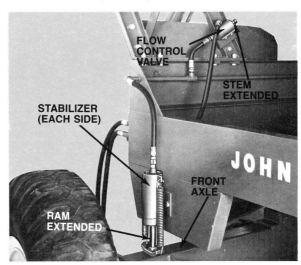

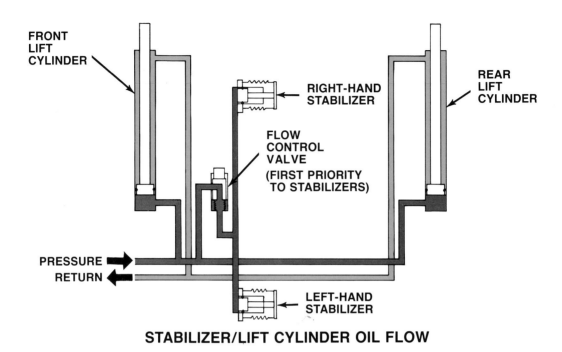

STABILIZER/LIFT CYLINDER OIL FLOW

Fig. 36—Hydraulic Oil Is Diverted to Cylinders for Lifting *After* Stabilizers Are Set

There are three tasks involved in preparing wagons for operation:

- *Preparing the towing vehicle*
- *Preparing the high-dump wagon*
- *Attaching to the towing vehicle*

PREPARING THE TOWING VEHICLE

Follow instructions in the operator's manual closely. Two important areas must be checked:

1. *Ballast, brakes, and tires.* To avoid injury or machine damage, the towing vehicle should be heavy enough to stop both itself and a loaded wagon within a safe distance. Extra ballast improves braking ability. Brakes must operate properly and provide safe, straight stops without grabbing or pulling to either side. Tires must be in good condition and properly inflated.

2. *Hydraulic system.* The towing vehicle hydraulic system must have adequate pump capacity and system pressure to operate the wagon. Check hydraulic fluid level and add oil if necessary. Oil in both the towing vehicle and the wagon hydraulic system must be the same. If it is not, drain the oil from wagon components and refill with the same type used in the towing vehicle.

Follow other preparation procedures outlined earlier for tractors towing forage boxes.

PREPARING THE HIGH-DUMP WAGON

For maximum stability, the tires opposite the dumping side of the wagon should be ¾ full of water-calcium chloride solution (Fig. 37). Calcium chloride in the water adds additional weight and prevents freezing.

On some high-dump wagons, frame compartments may be filled with concrete for additional counter-balancing weight.

Clean rust and crop residue off the inside of the bin so material can flow. If material sticks, spray the inside of the bin with one of the coatings available to provide a slick surface. Coatings contain graphite or Teflon and are usually available in hardware and implement stores.

Consult the operator's manual for preparation details and additional procedures.

Fig. 37—Ballast Tires and Frame

BOX IN DUMP POSITION

ATTACHING TO THE TOWING VEHICLE

Follow these steps to attach a high-dump wagon to a towing vehicle:

1. Adjust the wagon tongue to the right length.

2. Raise or lower the tongue of tandem-axle wagons with the hitch jack to match drawbar height of the towing vehicle.

3. Attach the wagon hitch to the drawbar or hitch plate of the towing vehicle with a safety hitch pin. Raise hitch or frame stands at the front and rear, if used.

4. Clean hose couplings and inspect all connections, lines, pipes, and hoses for damage. Use a piece of wood or cardboard — instead of hands — to search for leaks. Attach hydraulic hoses to remote outlets.

DUMP WAGON OPERATION

After connecting the hydraulic hoses bleed the trapped air out of the hydraulic system before loading the wagon. Slowly cycle the bin several times to force air from the system. Air can disrupt operation after the bin is loaded. Check the hydraulic fluid level in the towing vehicle after the air is removed from the wagon system and refill if needed.

Always fill the wagon uniformly. Blow forage to the back of the wagon first and allow the wagon to fill forward (Fig. 38). Hay cubes should load fairly level because of the center drop from the cuber elevator.

If a wagon is to be dumped when it is only partly filled, be sure it is evenly loaded from front to rear so the weight will be distributed during dumping.

UNLOADING HIGH-DUMP WAGONS

Position the truck or trailer directly beside the wagon. The type of material in the wagon affects the distance between the side of the truck and the wagon (Fig. 39). Heavier material slides faster and carries farther out from the wagon edge. So the truck should be positioned farther away from the wagon when dumping heavy material.

To minimize dumping time drive the truck up beside the wagon, and unload.

CAUTION: Keep the wagon on level ground so it doesn't turn over.

After the wagon and truck are positioned, raise the bin to dump the contents. When the bin is empty, lower the bin to the main wagon frame, and go back to harvesting.

TRANSPORT

Before transporting a high-dump wagon, be sure a clean and clearly visible SMV enblem (Fig. 40), reflectors, and the proper warning lights are on the wagon. Turn on the flashing lights to let others know what you are.

Check local regulations for specific requirements.

To reduce the danger of injury or equipment damage, be sure the towing vehicle can stop the wagon in a safe distance. Add wagon brakes if necessary.

Fig. 39—Position Truck to Reduce Spills

Fig. 38—Fill from Back to Front

Fig. 40—Display SMV Emblem

Always secure the hitch with a safety hitch pin or spring-locking pin, and use a safety chain.

Never transport a high-dump wagon unless the bin is lowered completely to the wagon frame.

When transporting a wagon behind a forage harvester or other vehicle with a hitch plate that is not centered, shift the wagon tongue to the offset position to keep the wagon as far to the right side of the roadway as possible.

STORAGE

High-dump wagons usually require storage preparation at the end of the season and at the beginning.

END OF SEASON

• If possible, store the wagon in a dry shelter.

• Clean the wagon thoroughly, inside and out. Repaint any places where paint is scratched or worn.

• Block up the wagon to remove the weight from tires. If tires cannot be stored inside, cover them to protect them from sunlight, dirt, and grease. If tires are removed, store them in a cool, dry, dark place. Do not deflate tires.

• Install dust caps on hydraulic hose couplings.

• List replacement parts needed for the next season and buy or order them early.

• Install replacement parts during the off-season — be ready to work without delay in the busy season.

BEGINNING OF SEASON

Carefully check the wagon when it is removed from storage. Help avoid costly breakdowns during the season by keeping the wagon in excellent condition.

• Replace wheels, if they were removed, and remove blocks from under wagon.

• Clean the wagon thoroughly, inside and out.

• Lubricate all points on the wagon as recommended in the operator's manual.

• Check tire pressure and inflate as recommended.

• Check and tighten all bolts to recommended torque.

• Check running gear tie-rod adjustment.

• Bleed hydraulic cylinders and lines.

• Check stabilizer operation, if used. Adjust flow-control valve if necessary.

SAFETY

To reduce accidents, follow safety rules. Insist they be followed by others working with machinery.

• Stand clear of the wagon when a towing vehicle is being backed into position for hitching, and when raising, dumping or lowering the bin.

• The bin should not be raised: near overhead power lines, if it isn't hitched to a towing vehicle, when the wagon is on uneven ground, or with a low or flat tire. Stabilizers (if used) must be lowered onto the front axle before the bin is raised and adequate ballast provided in the tires and frame opposite the dump side of the wagon.

• Leaving the bin raised for long periods of time could result in component failure and danger to bystanders or other equipment.

• Never service, lubricate, adjust or transport a wagon unless the bin is completely lowered onto the frame and the tractor engine is stopped.

• Maximum wagon speed should not exceed the manufacturer's recommendations.

• Always secure the hitch pin with a spring-locking pin or other safety device, and use a safety chain when towing a wagon on a road or highway.

• When transporting a wagon, center the wagon behind the towing vehicle, or shift the hitch to position the wagon as near the right side of the roadway as possible.

• Relieve pressure in valves and lines before disconnecting any hydraulic fittings. Before applying pressure to the hydraulic system, be sure all connections are tight and that lines, pipes, hoses, and components are not damaged or leaking. Fluid escaping from a small hole can be almost invisible. Use cardboard or wood — not hands — to locate suspected leaks. Escaping hydraulic fluid under pressure can penetrate the skin and cause serious injury or infection. Consult a doctor immediately if injured by escaping fluid.

Hydraulic warning page 334.

TROUBLESHOOTING CHART

PROBLEM	POSSIBLE CAUSE	POSSIBLE REMEDY
BIN DOES NOT RAISE PROPERLY.	Towing vehicle has inadequate hydraulic system pressure.	Use hydraulic system with recommended capacity.
	Towing vehicle hydraulic system low on fluid.	Add correct hydraulic fluid.
	Towing vehicle rpm too low.	Increase rpm.
	Wrong flow-control-valve setting.	Adjust flow-control valve.
	Dirty hydraulic filter.	Replace filter.
	Restricted hydraulic hoses.	Remove restriction or replace hoses. Bleed system.
	Hydraulic fluid not returning properly.	Check couplers and fittings. See your wagon dealer.
	Hydraulic fluid escaping from lines.	Check fittings and lines. Tighten or replace.
	Hydraulic fluid escaping from cylinders.	See your wagon dealer.
UNLOADING IMPROPERLY.	Dump cycle too slow.	Use hydraulic system with recommended capacity.
	Material in bin too moist.	Dump bin faster.
	Roof not opening properly.	Adjust spring tension.
	Dumping on uneven ground.	Always dump on level ground.
	Cylinders binding.	Load material evenly in bin.
	Towing vehicle has inadequate hydraulic system pressure.	Use hydraulic system with recommended capacity.
WAGON UNSTABLE WHEN UNLOADING.	Stabilizers not extending properly.	Adjust flow-control valve.
	Insufficient liquid ballast in tires.	Adjust ballast.
	Low or flat tire.	Repair tire. Inflate to correct pressure.
	Dumping on uneven ground.	Always dump on level ground.
	Unbalanced load.	Load bin evenly.
WAGON DOES NOT TOW PROPERLY.	Tie rods not adjusted properly.	Adjust tie rods.
	Wheel bearings not lubricated or adjusted properly.	Lubricate and/or adjust wheel bearings.
	Worn wheel bearing.	Replace bearing.
STABILIZERS DO NOT RETRACT.	Flow-control valve not adjusted properly.	Adjust valve.
STABILIZERS DO NOT REMAIN EXTENDED WHILE THE BIN CYCLES.	Damaged flow-control valve.	See your wagon dealer.

SUMMARY

Self-unloading forage wagons are versatile parts of many hay and forage harvesting systems. The two most commonly used wagons are:

- **Forage boxes**
- **High-dump wagons**

Forage box wagons are used for hay and forage crops.

High-dump wagons are used for hay and forage crops, as well as other materials. Their most common use is with hay cubers and pulled and self-propelled forage harvesters. High-dump wagons may be unloaded into trucks or trailers while still "in the row," to avoid loss of time in hooking and unhooking wagons.

Each type of wagon can fill important needs in hay and forage systems. Their application depends on forage-harvester capacity, transport distance, and versatility needed.

CHATPER QUIZ

1. (Fill in the blanks.) Two types of self-unloading wagons are _____ and _____.

2. List four or more different materials that are handled by forage boxes.

3. (True or false?) All forage boxes can be unloaded from the rear.

4. What are the functions of beaters in a forage box?

5. What factors determine the allowable gross load for safe operation of a particular forage box?

6. (True or false?) Forage boxes are powered by either a tractor or truck PTO.

7. (True or false?) High-dump wagons are used only for handling hay cubes?

8. (Fill in the blanks.) The capacity of high-dump wagons ranges from _____ to _____ tons.

9. What can be done to reduce the stopping distance of a forage wagon?

10. For safety and maximum stability, what measures can be taken to counterbalance a high-dump wagon?

13
Blowers

Fig. 1—Forage Blower Operating

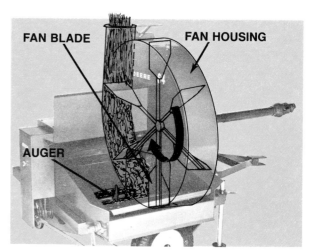

Fig. 2—Forage Blowers Throw Material

INTRODUCTION

Forage blowers are the machines most commonly used for placing chopped forage into storage structures (Fig. 1). They offer both convenience and capacity for efficient work. But any forage blower must have adequate capacity and must be used intelligently, safely, and effectively to avoid creating a "bottleneck" in a forage harvesting operation. The blower should keep up with the forage harvesting and transport operations.

As a general rule of thumb: **The capacity of a forage blower should be double the capacity of the forage harvester.** This generally will offset the time lost in transporting forage from the field.

BASIC FORAGE BLOWER OPERATION

Forage blowers are basically throwing devices with the "throwing" or propelling unit being a fan with paddles. Material enters the blower housing near the outer edge of the fan, is moved by centrifugal force to the end of the blower blades, and accelerated to the fan speed. When material reaches the blower spout it is thrown upward through the discharge pipe (Fig. 2).

The performance of a forage blower is influenced by the following factors:

- **Available power**
- **Fan speed**
- **Fan-blade tip clearance**
- **Type of material**
- **Delivery pipe size and arrangement**
- **Feed rate of the material**

For better understanding of these factors, let's discuss the functions of basic components involved in blower operation (Fig. 3).

BASIC COMPONENTS

Basic components of a forage-blower:

- **PTO shaft**
- **Drives**
- **Hopper and conveyor assembly**
- **Blower-housing assembly**
- **Blower pipe and attachments**
- **Recutter attachments**
- **Transport attachments**

Recutter attachments are not available for all blowers.

Power Source

A forage blower may be powered by a stationary engine, tractor, or an electric motor. Tractors are the most common power source.

Power required to run a blower is determined by fan speed, type of forage, and the rate and uniformity forage is fed into the blower.

The capacity of a blower depends on forage, moisture content, discharge height, fan speed, and power available.

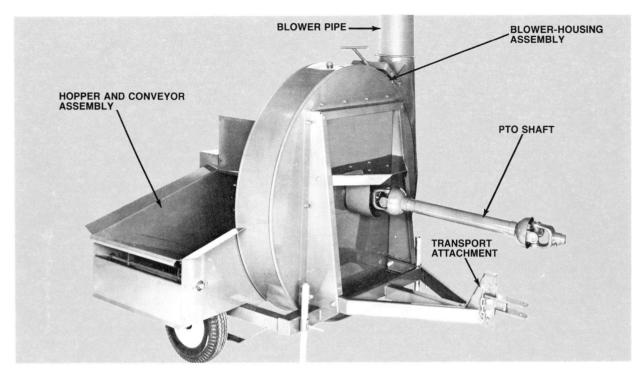

BLOWER PIPE →

BLOWER-HOUSING ASSEMBLY

HOPPER AND CONVEYOR ASSEMBLY

PTO SHAFT

TRANSPORT ATTACHMENT

Fig. 3—Forage Blower System

Some average blower capacities are (Fig. 4):

● *Corn or grass = 20 to 150 tons per hour*

● *Wilted forage = 20 to 70 tons per hour*

Fig. 4—Common Blower Capacities

Average power requirements are:

● *Corn or grass silage = 1 to 1.5 horsepower-hours per ton*

● *Wilted forage or haylage = 1 to 2 horsepower-hours per ton*

(See the specific operation manual for each machine for exact specifications).

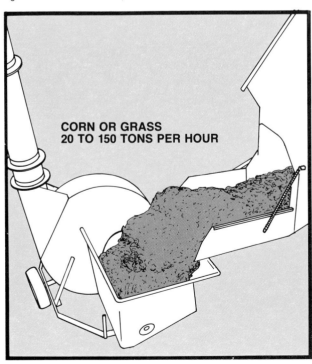

CORN OR GRASS
20 TO 150 TONS PER HOUR

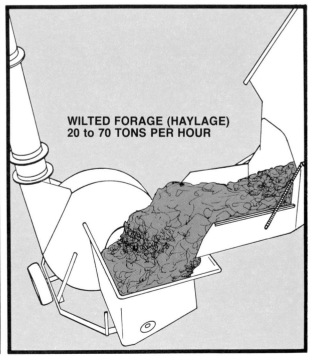

WILTED FORAGE (HAYLAGE)
20 to 70 TONS PER HOUR

The average tractor power required to operate a blower ranges from 20 to 80 horsepower (15 to 60 kw) or more, depending on blower capacity and other factors. However, heavy feed rates, high-capacity blowers, and the use of a recutter attachment may require much more than 80 horsepower

A good rule-of-thumb for estimating horsepower requirements is: Number of horsepower equals the height of the silo in feet (Fig. 5).

Drives

Either chain or belt drives are used to operate the fan, hopper, conveyor, or recutter. On most blowers, the fan is mounted directly on the tractor PTO shaft which provides a fan speed of 540 rpm.

Other blowers have an auxiliary chain and sprocket drive which can provide a range of fan speeds and use tractors with either 540 or 1,000 rpm PTO. This provides adaptability for silo height, available horsepower, and the type of crop being stored.

Hoppers

Hoppers on most forage blowers are of these types:

- **Pan-and-auger**
- **Conveyor-and-auger**
- **Rotating-pan**

The PAN-AND-AUGER hopper lets material fall directly to the auger (Fig. 6). On most pan-and-auger blowers the auger is about 3-feet long (1 m) and may be mounted at a 90° or 45° angle to the fan. On some blowers, a vibrating shaker pan in the bottom of the hopper smooths material flow to the auger and speeds unloading. The auger carries material to the opening in the fan housing where it is picked up by the fan.

The CONVEYOR-AND-AUGER hoppers use chains and slats or a belt on a level apron to carry material to the auger (Fig. 7). Conveyor-and-auger hoppers make it easier to unload low-discharge boxes or boxes which can only unload from the rear.

The conveyor is usually about 8 to 12 feet long (2.4 to 3.6 m). On most blowers the conveyor may be raised to vertical so a tractor and wagon can pass and then lowered so the wagon can be unloaded from the rear.

Most conveyor-and-auger systems can be shifted in or out of gear with a clutch lever on the blower.

ROTATING-PAN hoppers have a horizontal, rotating feed table which whirls material directly into the blower opening (Fig. 8). An adjustable baffle helps control the amount of material entering the blower and reduces the chances of plugging the blower.

Blower-Housing Assembly

The blower-housing assembly has three major parts:

- **Fan**
- **Housing**
- **Rim**

Fig. 5—Horsepower Equals Silo Height in Feet

Fig. 6—Pan-And-Auger Blower

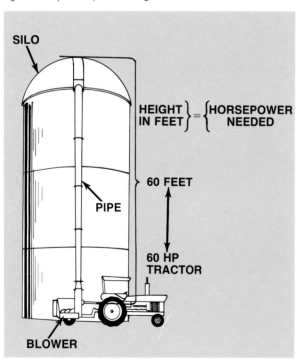

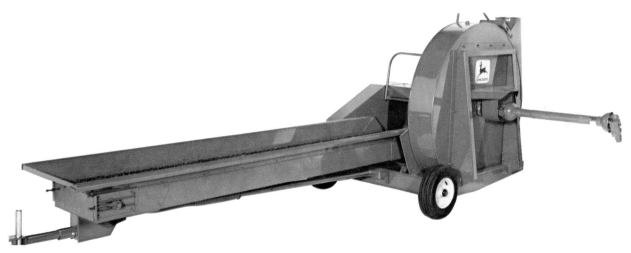

Fig. 7—Conveyor-And-Auger Hopper

Fig. 9—Blower Fan

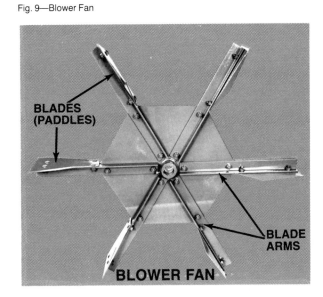

Most blower *fans* consist of a *flywheel* with four to six *paddles* (Fig. 9). Fan paddles are adjustable so you can set a close tolerance between the paddle tips and the fan housing for maximum blower efficiency.

The **fan housing** on many blowers includes **air vents** and a **water inlet**. Air vents relieve the vacuum which forms behind each paddle (Fig. 10). A water inlet is required when gummy forage, such as alfalfa haylage, is being handled. Addition of a small amount of water prevents gum buildup on blower parts and helps maintain capacity (Fig. 11).

The **throat,** which directs material into the blower pipe, is attached to the housing rim. The rim may be pivoted around the blower housing to get the best angle for the pipe (Fig. 12).

Fig. 8—Rotating Pan Hopper

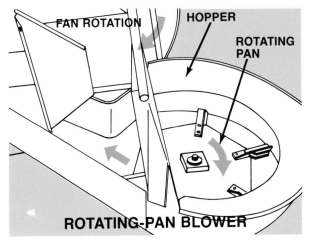

Fig. 10—Air Vents on Fan Housing

Fig. 11—Water Inlet on Fan Housing

A fan-blade cleaner is used in some blowers to keep the ends of the fan blades clean, and to keep material from building up between the blades and the housing (Fig. 13).

Blower Pipe and Attachments

Although some storage systems use a one piece blower pipe, in most cases a number of sections of blower pipe are assembled to fit the structure size. The pipe may be taken down and moved from one silo to another. However, many farmers find it more convenient to install blower pipe permanently on each silo and only move the blower.

The most common pipe diameter is 9 inches (229 mm). Pipe lengths may vary from 2 to 8 feet (.6 to 2.4 m). Telescoping pipe sections are also available which adjust from 2 to 8 feet (.6 to 2.4 m) long.

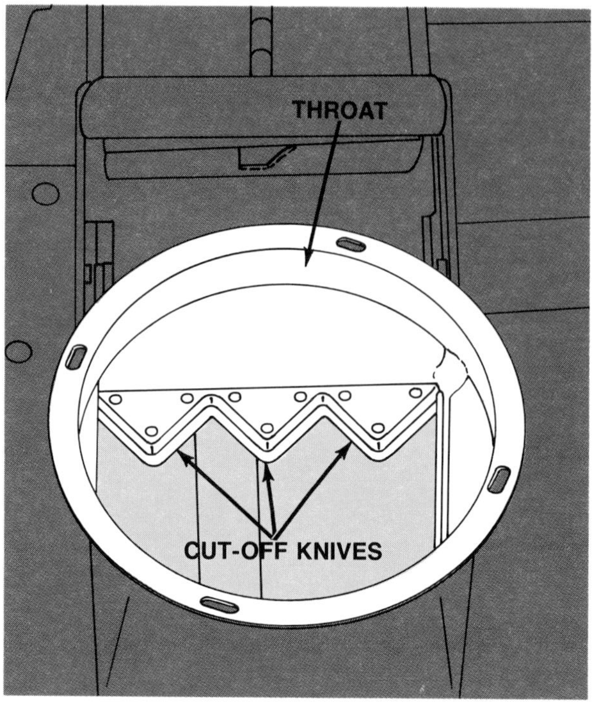

Fig. 13—Knives in Blower Throat Clean Paddle Ends

Use a combination of the longest pipes available to save time and reduce the number of joints, which can leak (Fig. 14).

Many attachments are available for blower pipe.

Blower pipe is available in several lengths and diameters to match blower and structure sizes (A-Fig. 15). A clamp on telescoping pipe lets you adjust and lock the pipe length. Attach telescoping pipe directly to the blower throat. Blower pipe is made of galvanized steel or PVC.

Fig. 12—Pivot Housing Band to Line Up with Blower Pipe

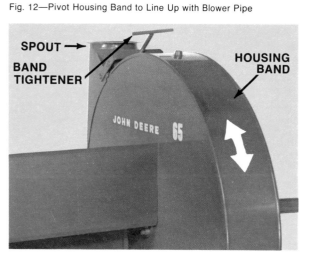

Fig. 14—Blower Pipe Arrangement for a 48-Foot (15 M) Silo

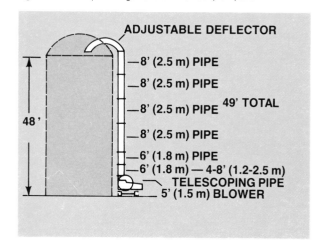

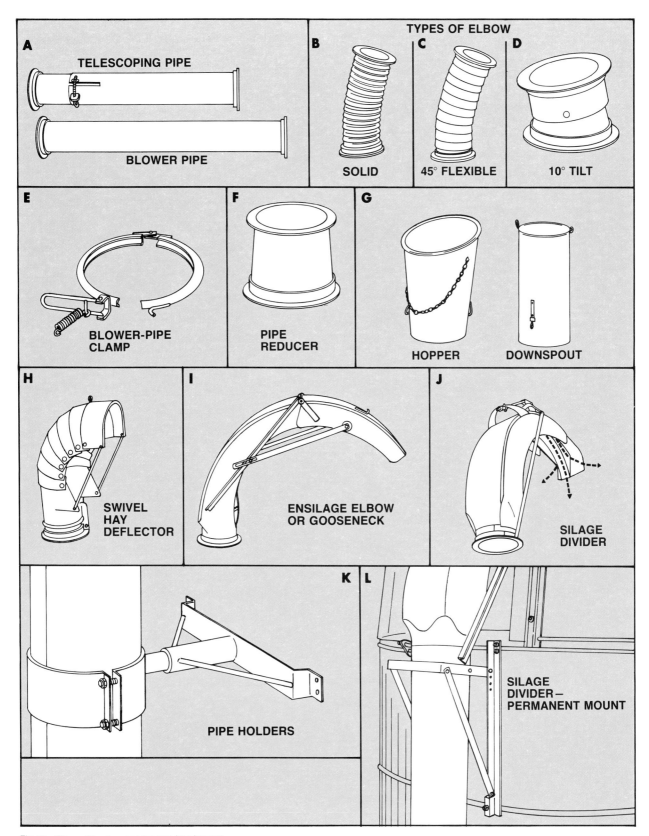

Fig. 15—Blower Pipe Accessories and Attachments

293

Solid elbows are used to change the direction material flows or to deflect material as it leaves the blower pipe (B-Fig. 15). Elbows are available in 22½ and 45 degree angle sections which may be used in series. The solid elbow is best without leaking badly for the discharge end of the pipe.

Flexible elbows can bend up to 45 degrees (C-Fig. 15). They are usually used at the discharge end of the pipe.

A **ten-degree tilt elbow** is attached directly to the blower discharge outlet to make it easier to align pipe and to level the blower faster (D-Fig. 15).

Blower-pipe clamps are a fast, convenient way of assembling pipe sections without bolting. Blower-pipe, flanges, and clamps must match so material flow won't be restricted (E-Fig. 15).

A **pipe reducer** cuts down the size of the blower outlet so you can use smaller diameter pipe (F-Fig. 15). Reducing pipe diameter generally increases the power requirement and decreases capacity.

A **distributor hopper** and **downspout sections** can be used to direct silage flow to any part of the silo to pack it uniformly (G-Fig. 15). More than three downspout sections in a line will usually cause plugging.

The rope controlled **swivel hay deflector** is an efficient means of directing the flow of dry, chopped hay into a barn, silo, or stack or to distribute chopped hay over driers (H-Fig. 15). A deflector can be installed on straight pipe or used with solid elbows.

An **ensilage elbow (or gooseneck)** (I-Fig. 15) can be adjusted to direct material flow to the center of a large-diameter silo or to control material flow when the silo is nearly filled.

The **silage divider** directs silage evenly through the silo and reduces build-up in the center so unloaders can work efficiently (J-Fig. 15). Dividers can be adjusted to silo diameter.

Pipe holders eliminate the dangerous job of setting up the blower pipe each time a silo is filled (K-Fig. 15). Pipe holders are bolted to the silo and pipe is left permanently installed. Blower pipe is not handled as often when pipe holders are used. So there is less chance of dents. Pipe holders hold pipe 6, 12, and 20 inches (152, 305, and 508 mm) from the silo. A short holder is used at the top and a longer holder at the bottom to provide clearance for the blower.

Silage Divider — Permanent Mount

Silage dividers are attached to the silo to direct silage flow evenly throughout the silo (L-Fig. 15).

Recutter Attachments

Some blowers are equipped with recutter attachments which chop material as it is fed into the blower. Recutters are used for feed processing more than forage handling so they will not be covered in detail in this book. However, recutters play an important part in some forage harvesting systems.

Fig. 16—A Recutter Cuts A Second Time for Better Packing

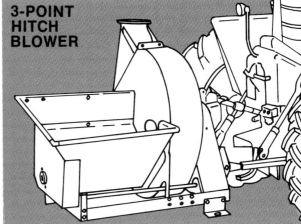

Fig. 17—Blower Transport Methods

For example, forage crops must be cut "fine" for the best packing and handling, but an extremely short cut could greatly reduce forage harvester capacity. An alternative solution is to cut reasonably short with a forage harvester and use a recutter on the blower to help balance the productivity of each machine (Fig. 16). Of course, using a recutter requires additional power. Most recutter-equipped blowers require at least an 80 horsepower (60 kw) tractor.

Recutter attachments have either:

• *Flywheel-attached hammers and knives or*

• *Cutting cylinder with replaceable screens*

A recutter may also be used to grind high-moisture ear corn for ear corn silage.

Transport Attachments and Stands

Most blowers come with transport attachments including wheels and hitch or 3-point hitch attachments (Fig. 17). Stands are also available to level and stabilize the blower during operation.

Steps to be covered in the proper operation and adjustment of forage blowers are:

• **Planning and preparation**

• **Preliminary settings and adjustments**

• **Operation**

• **Transport**

• **Safety**

PLANNING AND PREPARATION

Capacity is the most important consideration in selecting a blower for a forage harvesting system. An adequate power source must also be available.

Power, fan diameter and speed, and silo height are the important factors in blower selection. For example, according to a Michigan State University report, a 70 horsepower (52 kw) tractor can blow approximately 57 tons of corn silage per hour into a 70 foot (21 m) high silo. But the same size tractor could blow almost 70 tons per hour into a 60 foot (18 m) silo, and nearly 90 tons into a 50 foot (15 m) structure. Increasing fan diameter (with equal speed) increases blower "throwing" capacity because the paddle tips travel faster and throw material harder.

PRELIMINARY SETTINGS AND ADJUSTMENTS

Major activities that must be completed before operating a forage harvester:

• **Blower pipe installation**

• **Tractor preparation**

• **Blower preparation**

• **Blower placement**

BLOWER PIPE INSTALLATION

Calculate the length of blower pipe you need. Bolt or clamp the blower-pipe sections and the deflector together (Fig. 18). Keep in mind the following **basic principles**:

• Sharp bends reduce capacity and cause plugging. If elbows must be used, use large-radius elbows.

• Solid elbows are preferable to flexible elbows which may leak or flutter. Install elbows as close to the discharge end of the pipe as possible. Don't use an elbow at the blower.

• Bolt solid elbows together to hold alignment. Never use clamps.

• For wilted hay or very heavy material, set pipe as near

Fig. 18—Bolt or Clamp Pipe Sections Together Securely

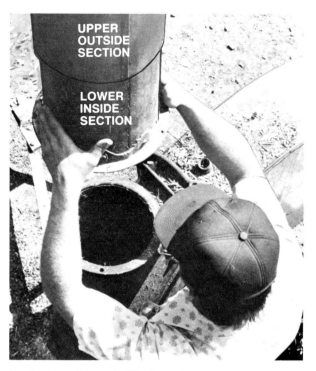

UPPER OUTSIDE SECTION

LOWER INSIDE SECTION

Fig. 19—Correct Telescoping Pipe Connection

vertical as possible to get the most capacity from the blower.

• Make sure there are no holes in the pipe or connections.

• Use the largest pipe and accessories specified for a blower.

• Any variation in pipe size or dents that create ridges may set up turbulence and reduce capacity. Avoid constrictions. Never use an 8-inch (203 mm) elbow with 9-inch (228 mm) pipe. Always attach the smaller (inside) end of telescoping pipe to the blower so that material flows from the smaller end *into* the larger (outside) pipe (Fig. 19).

• Do not use dented or bent pipe.

• Always provide approximately 8 to 10 inches (203 to 254 mm) minimum clearance from the open bottom of gooseneck or ensilage elbows to the top edge of the silo. If you don't, turbulence in the silo and back-pressure may cause plugging.

• Be sure telescoping pipe and flexible elbows are installed with the right end up. The small end must feed into the large end.

ATTACHING BLOWER PIPE TO A SILO

Bolt or clamp the blower pipe and elbows together on the ground. Assemble the shorter sections of pipe at the bottom so the final length of all pipe can be changed easily. Don't use several short lengths of pipe. Use a telescoping section, which has a 12 to 36 inch (305 to 914 mm) adjustment.

IMPORTANT: If the blower pipe is attached with clamps, use the proper size clamps and inspect the clamps frequently for wear and damage.

Raise the pipe by securely attaching a strong rope and pulley to the top of the silo. Fasten one end of the rope to the center of the pipe (Fig. 20). Place a half-hitch around the pipe approximately 8 feet (2.4 m) from the top. Then raise the pipe into position. An adjustable fan housing band on the blower will let you connect the pipe at the necessary angle to reach the silo. Don't let the pipe bang on the silo and dent.

CAUTION: Never stand under the blower pipe while it is being raised.

After the pipe is in position, secure the rope to the blower frame or close to the bottom of the silo until the pipe is attached to the blower. Fasten the upper end of the pipe securely to the silo. The pipe must be set as nearly vertical as possible to reduce friction between forage and pipe.

Fig. 20—Tie Rope Securely Before Raising Pipe

TRACTOR PREPARATION

Adjust the tractor drawbar for PTO operation and pin it in the proper position. Be sure the tractor is tuned for optimum fuel consumption and power output, and make certain the brake lock or transmission park lock will hold the tractor in a fixed position while running the blower.

BLOWER PREPARATION

Before setting up the blower, inspect the entire machine and service it as recommended in the operator's manual.

● *Check and replace damaged or badly worn drive belts or chains. Check and adjust belt and chain tension.*

● *Lubricate the blower.*

● *Check tire condition and inflate to the recommended pressure.*

● *Check for loose bolts and nuts and torque them to specification.*

● *If major moving parts have been replaced, run-in the blower for a short period and check for hot bearings, improper assembly, or other problems.*

Check Fan Blade Clearance

To avoid blower damage and rapid wear, the tips of fan blades must not strike the fan housing. Wide clearance between paddles and housing lets some forage wrap over the blade ends and be carried around again by the fan. This reduces fan capacity and rapidly increases the power requirement.

Adjust the paddles as recommended in the operator's manual (Fig. 21). Paddle clearance is usually 1/16 to 3/16 inch (1.5 to 5 mm). For a rule of thumb, adjust the paddles to clear a dime but drag a nickel placed in the bottom of the fan housing. After adjusting the paddles, turn the fan by hand for one or more revolutions to be certain all the paddles clear the housing. **Always retighten bolts to recommended torque.**

SETTING UP THE BLOWER

After the blower pipe is installed, set up the blower:

1. Position the blower with the discharge spout next to the barn or silo and directly under the blower pipe (Fig. 22). Always position the blower and pipe so that wagons and trucks can be *driven* forward to the blower for unloading. Backing into unloading position is more difficult and can be time consuming.

2. Place the blower so the pipe will be nearly vertical to reduce friction.

3. Level the blower by following one or more of these procedures.

(a) Reposition the transport wheels on the blower frame.

(b) Remove transport wheels and support the blower on the frame and leveling stands. (Check hopper height requirements — next page.)

(c) Dig shallow holes for the wheels or block up under the wheels or frame. Be sure blocks are solid and cannot tip or collapse during operation.

(d) Keep the blower tongue attached to the tractor drawbar, and adjust the hitch to level the blower, front-to-rear.

Fig. 21—Adjust Fan Blade Clearance for Maximum Blower Efficiency

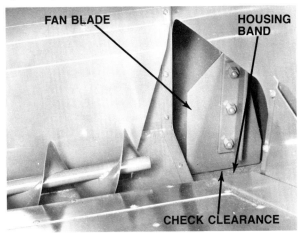

FAN BLADE

HOUSING BAND

CHECK CLEARANCE

Fig. 22—Line Up Blower And Pipe Around the Blower Housing

(e) Level blowers mounted on 3-point hitches by adjusting the support stands before removing blower from the tractor.

4. After the blower is leveled, lower all stabilizing stands to support the blower during operation.

5. Set blower hopper height to accommodate the height of unloading wagons and trucks. On some blowers, wheels must be adjusted or removed to reduce hopper height (Fig. 23). To save time, check the wagons before you level blower.

Fig. 23—Adjust Hopper Height by Moving the Wheels

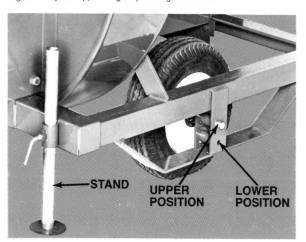

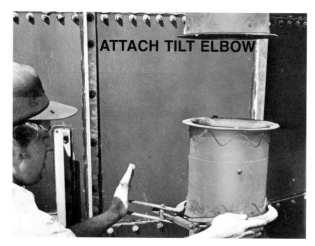

Fig. 24—Attach Tilt Elbow to Blower

6. After resetting wheel height, grease the axle sockets so the axles don't rust in place. Set the axles in the lowest frame position so the ground clearance is maximum.

7. Connect the tilt elbow section to the blower spout. Tilt it to line up with the blower pipe (Fig. 24).

8. Pivot the fan housing band around the blower housing so material is blown straight into the pipe (Fig. 25). An extremely low pipe angle may reduce capacity with some types of heavy material or wilted hay because of added friction on the lower side of the pipe.

Fig. 25—Line Up Spout And Blower Pipe

9. Retighten the clamp after adjusting the fan housing band.

CAUTION: After adjusting the band, make sure the fan housing side plates are seated in the grooves in the blower band.

10. Couple the blower pipe to the blower by sliding down the lower telescoping pipe section until it lines up with the tilt elbow and bolt or clamp the pieces together (Fig. 26).

11. Connect the blower PTO shaft to the tractor and blower. Keep trailing blowers hitched to the tractor drawbar. Fasten a safety chain between the tractor and frame of 3-point hitch mounted blowers so the PTO shaft won't separate during operation.

12. Keep the tractor centerline, PTO shaft, and blower shaft directly in line and the tractor as nearly level as possible so the PTO doesn't misalign. PTO alignment reduces noise and vibration and makes the bearings and universal joints last longer.

BLOWER OPERATION

Power flow from the tractor to the blower must be smooth and even. Untuned tractors and slow-acting governors that permit excessive speed variation damage the PTO and shear bolts.

Fig. 26—Line Up Telescoping Pipe and Fasten to Blower

FAN SPEED

Most blowers operate at 540 or 1,000 rpm. Check the tractor to see that it is operating at the recommended speed and that the speed does not drop below the recommended level when the blower is operating under load.

STARTING AND STOPPING

Connect the blower hitch to the drawbar and set the tractor brakes. Block the wheels to secure the tractor. With the engine at low throttle, engage the PTO clutch slowly to make sure the blower turns freely. Open the throttle and bring the blower up to operating speed.

To stop the blower, allow enough time for the remaining crop to clear the fan and blower pipe before disengaging the tractor PTO clutch.

BLOWING STICKY HAYLAGE

There is a water line coupling welded to the fan housing. Water dissolves the gum deposits left by sticky haylage. The correct amount of water can be determined by checking the fan and inside the blower housing between loads. If gum deposits are present, increase the amount of water with each load until the gum is gone. If there is no gum, try reducing the water slightly.

Install a shut-off valve on the water inlet and couple a garden hose to the valve. Arrange the hose so you can't trip over it.

When water is added, start the blower first. Then add water when the crop is being fed into the blower.

UNLOADING INTO BLOWER

After the blower is started and running properly, begin unloading material into the hopper or conveyor. Start at a low rate and gradually increase the flow (Fig. 27).

A smooth, steady stream of forage into the blower is what you want. **Unload into the top of the vibrating shaker or pan** so the vibrating pan has the maximum amount of time to shake apart wads.

Stay close to the blower during unloading. Observe blower and wagon operation. Excessive amounts of forage can plug any blower. But plugging can usually be avoided by constantly watching the unloading procedure and adjusting material flow when necessary.

Fig. 27—Start Unloading Slowly

Fig. 28—Correct Blower Transporting Position

STOPPING OPERATION

When the wagon or truck is unloaded, shut off the water and disengage the PTO clutch first so the blower will freewheel to a stop. Then decrease the throttle setting.

CAUTION: Shut off power to the blower between loads so there is no hazard to people and less wear on the machine.

TRANSPORT

Blowers are usually transported:

● *On transport wheels*

● *On the tractor 3-point hitch*

For long moves, load the blower on a truck, wagon, or trailer. The small wheels and high pressure tires on blowers can cause a very rough ride for the blower.

● Before transport, place the PTO shaft in the hopper or other safe place (Fig. 29).

● On some blowers the hitch stand can be raised and locked into transport position with a positioning rod and spring locking pin.

● If the blower has a hinged conveyor, raise and lock it securely in the transport position.

● Reinstall the transport wheels if they were removed for operation or shift wheels to the lower axle positions for more clearance.

● Raise all stands and secure them in the transport position (Fig. 28).

● Hitch blower to the tractor drawbar or 3-point hitch.

● Always use a clearly visible SMV emblem and turn on the flashing lights to warn others.

SAFETY

Operating a forage blower is one of the most dangerous jobs on a farm. One operator usually controls two machines at the time time — the blower and an unloading wagon or truck — and is surrounded by PTO shafts, conveyors, auger or rotating table, and the blower flywheel (Fig. 29). Never let yourself be "hurried" into an accident. Take time for safe operation.

● Use strong rope and special care to put up the blower pipe. Be sure knots are safely tied and the pulley securely fastened at the top of the silo.

● Be sure shields, guards, and safety screens are in place and in working order before starting a blower.

● Make sure blower pipes are securely attached to the silo and to the blower before starting the blower.

● To reduce the danger of falling, keep silo ladders in good condition and avoid climbing when shoes are wet and muddy.

● **NEVER STEP OVER A PTO SHAFT.**

● **NEVER** climb over or around a blower hopper or wagon blower conveyor when they are running. Trying to save a few steps by taking chances can be disastrous. The polishing action of forage on metal makes hoppers and conveyors as slippery as glass.

● Never use your hands and feet to force material into the blower. Never use sticks or tools for this purpose. They will either be caught and pull you into the blower, or violently ejected back into you.

● If material bridges and refuses to flow into the blower, **STOP** the blower and remove the blockage.

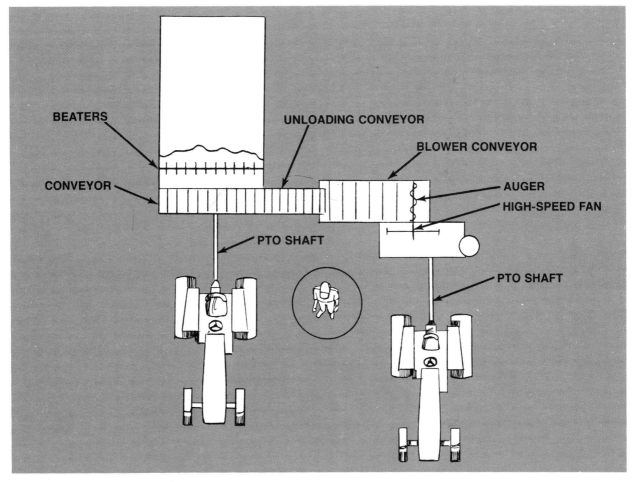

Fig. 29—Danger Points in Blower Operation

CAUTION: Wait until the auger and fan have completely stopped before reaching into the hopper.

● Never run the blower faster than the maximum speed specified by the manufacturer. Be sure the tractor PTO speed (either 540 ro 1000 rpm) matches the speed required by the blower.

Before cleaning, lubricating, and adjusting the blower:

● **Disengage all power.**

● **Stop the tractor engine and take the key.**

● **Wait for the blower to stop rotating.**

> *CAUTION:* **Nitrogen dioxide, commonly called silo gas, is extremely poisonous and *may* be produced during the fermentation of silage. Silo gas is heavier than air, has a bleach-like odor and yellow-brown color. Inhalation of amounts even too small to smell or see can cause serious lung irritation and injury.**
>
> **Symptoms are throat irritation, coughing, and chest pains. If more than a few whiffs are inhaled, violent coughing and asthma may occur. Death may come quickly if large amounts of the gas are inhaled.**
>
> **During silo filling be alert for bleach-like odors and yellowish-brown fumes in or near the silo, particularly in the morning after filling the previous day. The gas is heavier than air and will collect in the silo as silage settles below door level, or flow down the silo chute into feedrooms or low areas near the silo base.**
>
> **The greatest danger is within 12 to 60 hours after silo filling, but the gas may be present for several weeks. After filling has stopped, enter the silo only when absolutely necessary, especially the first day or two after filling. Never enter a newly filled silo alone.**
>
> **If anyone *must* enter the silo, operate the silage blower for at least 15 to 20 minutes before going in. If any coughing or throat irritation is experienced, get out of the silo immediately, and consult a doctor. Recovery may appear to be fast followed within a few hours by severe illness due to lung damage.**

Fig. 30—Lubricate and Service the Blower

MAINTENANCE

Proper blower maintenance can help increase capacity, reduce power requirement, extend blower life, and make blower operation easier and safer.

• Keep all drive chains and belts tensioned correctly as recommended by the manufacturer.

• Keep the fan blade clearance adjusted for optimum blower efficiency.

• Replace or repair damaged parts.

• Don't let gum buildup inside the blower. Inject water on the blades.

• Protect blower pipe from dents and bends. Damaged pipe reduces capacity.

• Replace or repair damaged parts promptly.

• Follow the recommendations in the operator's manual for lubrication and service (Fig. 30).

STORAGE

To store a blower, follow these suggestions:

• Shelter the blower in a dry place.

• Clean the blower thoroughly, inside and out. Trash and dirt draw moisture and encourage rust.

• Lubricate the blower according to the instructions in the operator's manual. Coat exposed working parts with grease or rust preventative.

• Paint where paint has worn.

• Remove the chains and wash them in solvent. Dry and coat them with a heavy oil.

• On trailing blowers, block up the frame to take the weight off the tires. Do not deflate the tires. If the blower is stored outside, cover the tires for protection from sunlight, dirt, and grease.

AFTER STORAGE

To prepare the blower for use after storage:

• Remove the heavy oil from chains.

• Lubricate the blower as recommended in the manual.

• Check air pressure in the tires.

• Tighten loose bolts, nuts, and set screws.

• If any major moving parts have been replaced, run them in by operating the blower for a few minutes without forage.

TROUBLESHOOTING

Most blower operating problems are caused by improper operation and maintenance, or the incorrect assembly of blower and pipe. This chart includes some probable causes and remedies for blower troubles.

TROUBLESHOOTING CHART

PROBLEM	POSSIBLE CAUSE	POSSIBLE REMEDY
BLOWER PIPE CLOGGED.	Tractor engine speed too low.	Adjust engine speed.
	Pipe or elbows installed upside down.	The small end of telescoping pipe or flexible elbows must feed into the large end.
	Blowing gummy material.	Flush the blower with a little water or use the water inlet to add water as forage is unloaded.
	Faulty tractor.	Repair tractor or use tractor with correct PTO speed.

PROBLEM	POSSIBLE CAUSE	POSSIBLE REMEDY
	Too many elbows.	Reduce quantity of elbows used.
	Not using standard pipe.	Use pipe specified for this blower.
	Using dented or bent pipe.	Straighten or replace damaged pipe sections.
BOLTS SHEAR EXCESSIVELY.	Tractor not operating properly.	Repair tractor.
	Using improper shear bolts.	Use only recommended shear bolts.
PTO DAMAGE.	PTO not in alignment.	Align PTO.
	Shear bolts too loose.	Adjust shear bolt tension.
	Tractor not operating properly.	Repair tractor.
FAN STRIKES HOUSING.	Fan blades out of adjustment.	Examine fan to see where it strikes. Adjust fan in housing to clear all points.
FALLOUT FROM CENTER-FILL ELBOW.	Fan rpm too low.	Use recommended rpm.
	Insufficient power for required volume.	Use recommended tractor size.
	Gummy pipe.	Clean pipe.

SUMMARY

Blowers are useful in chopped-forage systems. Match the power source, blower, and silo height to provide adequate capacity to keep up with the forage harvester.

Use a blower with twice the capacity of the forage harvester. This will allow for forage transport time from field to blower and other reasonable delays.

Proper blower selection, operation, and maintenance strengthens the forage system. However, blower operation can be only as safe as the operator controlling the system. Do not rush around the blower and never attempt to increase capacity by overloading equipment or increasing speed above recommended limits. Keep shields in place and don't let anyone run the equipment who doesn't know what they are doing.

Never sacrifice safety for speed.

CHAPTER QUIZ

1. (True or false?) The capacity of the blower should be double the capacity of the forage harvester.

2. List four factors that influence the performance of a forage blower.

3. What is a good rule-of-thumb for estimating tractor size needed to power a blower for filling a silo.

4. Why is there an air vent in the fan housing?

5. Why is there a water inlet in the fan housing?

6. (True of false?) The usual diameter of blower pipes and attachments is 12 inches (305 mm).

7. Why is it important to stay near the blower while forage is being unloaded into the blower hopper?

8. Why is adjustment of fan blade clearance important?

9. (True or false?) Blower capacity and efficiency are greatest when blower pipe is set at a 15 degree or greater angle.

14
Selecting Equipment

PRODUCT SELECTION

Hay and forage producers cannot get top profits or make quality livestock feed unless they use the right harvesting system for their conditions.

Choosing a system is not a simple task. Each decision must be based on thoughtful answers to many questions (Fig. 1). Many factors must be considered simultaneously.

Of course, no harvesting system can meet the needs of all farms because there are too many variables. But each manager can choose, and adapt parts from a wide variety of systems to provide the best program for his particular operation.

Systems and equipment chosen should use farm resources to the best advantage and fit in with overall farm objectives.

Perhaps the first and most important decision to make is: Will the crop be used on the farm or sold? Then consider product adaptability to the operation, and choose (Fig. 2):

- **Hay**
- **Silage**
- **Haylage**
- **Stover**

Answers to these considerations are fundamental, and limit the choices of harvesting systems suitable for a particular operation.

TYPE OF PRODUCT

Here are a few pros and cons of forage products.

Hay Versus Silage or Haylage

Haymaking requires lower investment in equipment and storage and handling facilities than silage or haylage. It is also more convenient for feeding at scattered locations. Surplus hay is usually easier to sell than extra silage or haylage. Conventional bales are particularly easy to market.

Hay generally requires more labor per ton of dry matter than silage or haylage and has higher storage losses. In most situations there is also more waste when feeding hay.

Silage and haylage are usually more palatable than hay, which results in less waste during feeding. It is easy to completely mechanize the harvest, storage, and feeding of haylage and silage, and both can be mixed with concentrates for complete rations.

Because silage and haylage are harvested with higher moisture content, there is less leaf loss than with hay. Both products can be harvested during damp weather when haymaking would be impossible without artificial drying, and they require less labor per ton of dry matter.

Fig. 1—Many Factors Must Be Evaluated to Select Hay Harvesting Equipment

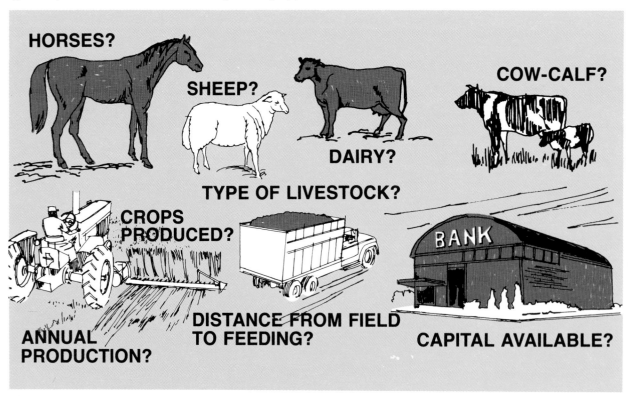

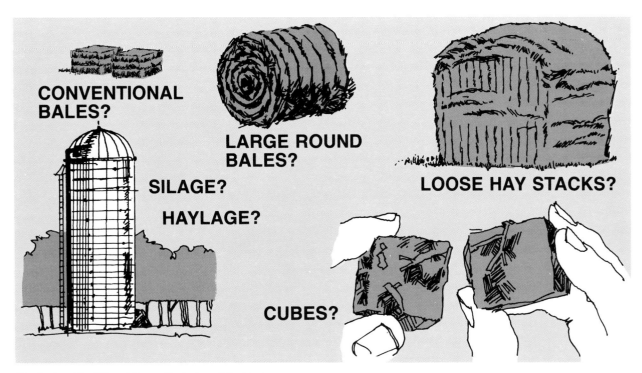

Fig. 2—Consider Different Forage Products and Packages

Silage and haylage require high investment in harvesting, storing, and feeding equipment and facilities if the complete process is mechanized. Surplus haylage and silage are not easy to market. Both are perishable products requiring good management for harvesting, storing, and feeding. Storage losses can be high if forage is not cut properly and packed in the silo and if the structure is not well sealed. Large air pockets or leaks in the silo can cause spoilage.

Hay-Crop Silage or Haylage?

High-moisture silage may be direct-cut to save time and equipment costs (Fig. 3), or windrowed and permitted to wilt. Higher moisture content when forage is chopped means less waiting time between cutting and chopping.

However, direct-cut silage is apt to have high seepage and nutrient losses during storage. It requires handling many extra tons of water during harvesting, storing and feeding.

Good haylage is palatable and may increase consumption per animal, which could result in higher milk production or added weight gain. There are fewer tons of material to handle, store, and feed compared to silage. And meat or milk production per acre is often higher with haylage than with other kinds of forage.

Haylage must be windrowed before chopping, which requires extra labor and added equipment costs. A longer

Fig. 3—Direct-Cutting High-Moisture Silage

time is required between windrowing and chopping compared to silage, which increases the possibility of weather damage. Haylage must be cut fine and carefully packed so air is excluded to get proper fermentation. If haylage is stored too dry it may heat and spoil instead of fermenting. If combined with air in the structure, dry haylage may become hot enough to burn.

Cubes

Cubes require the lowest volume of any current hay packages for transport and storage. They can be mixed with concentrates for complete rations, and handling and feeding cubes is easily mechanized (Fig. 4). Labor requirement per ton for harvesting, storing, and feeding cubes is low.

Cubing requires high equipment investment, high annual volume, and high horsepower input. Field cubing is limited to areas where hay can dry in the windrow to 10 or 12 percent moisture content. Unless special binding materials are mixed with the forage, the crop must be all legume or have less than 11 percent grass mixed with the legume.

Stover

Stover is low-cost maintenance forage for brood cows and growing stock. More roughage can be harvested per acre with a round baler or stack wagon than grazing animals would pick up. Stover can be harvested and fed from fields without fences or water where grazing would be impossible. It can be used for feed or bedding and helps spread equipment costs over more acres. Harvesting stover lets farmers keep more animals on an acreage.

Stover has low food value and must be supplemented properly to maintain adequate animal health. Sometimes it is difficult to hold stover packages together, especially during transport or soon after packaging.

MACHINE AND SYSTEM SELECTION

Correct machine selection can make a system work.

PICKING THE RIGHT MACHINE

Each piece of equipment must match the rest of the system for efficient operation. Making the best choice involves a comparison of favorable and unfavorable points of each machine. Look at each piece of equipment individually and in terms of the system selection factors listed later.

Mower or Mower-Conditioner?

Mowers have lower first cost, and normally are economical for smaller acreages. They can be used for cutting weeds, mowing around buildings, along roads, etc. Field capacity of mowers is lower, and if hay is conditioned, a special hitch must be used or conditioning must be done in a separate operation.

Mower-conditioners combine cutting and conditioning into a single, fast operation for faster drying (Fig. 5). This means less exposure of the crop to weather. Mower-conditioners are more maneuverable than mowers with separate conditioners, and can save the cost of separate conditioners and raking operations.

Mower-Conditioner or Self-Propelled Windrower?

Tractor drawn mower-conditioners and windrowers have lower first cost than self-propelled models and generally require less upkeep due to the lack of an engine and drive train. Mower-conditioners are smaller and have lower capacity than self-propelled windrowers, and always knock down some crop on the first round when opening a field.

Fig. 5—Mower-Conditioners Fit Some Systems Better Than Mowers

Fig. 4—Cube Handling is Easily Mechanized

Self-propelled windrowers have higher capacity than pulled mower-conditioners, are more maneuverable, and release a tractor for other work. They can open fields or start at one edge and work across the field without running over uncut crop. First cost of self-propelled machines is higher than pulled models, and upkeep is more expensive.

Conventional Balers and "Square" Bales

Conventional "square" (actually rectangular) bales are the most economical package for small hay volumes. Custom operation is available for very small acreages which cannot justify baler ownership. Bales can be stacked, hauled, and stored in a small space, compared to round bales and loose hay stacks. It is easy to control the feeding rate to small herds by limiting the number of bales at each feeding. Surplus square bales can be easily marketed and transported.

Conventional bales require large amounts of hand labor or expensive equipment for mechanical handling from field to storage. High annual volumes are required to economically justify an automatic bale wagon — the most widely used mechanical bale handling system. Conventional bales must be stored under a roof or covered with waterproof material or they will spoil.

Round Bales or Stacks?

Large round bales and loose hay stack wagons permit one-man operation from field to feeding, compared to three or four men required for conventional baling. They have comparable operating costs per ton at lower volumes and compete favorably with conventional bales at annual volumes of about 75 tons (68 t) or more. Package shape permits outside storage with little storage loss. The economic loss from outside storage of round bales and stacks is low compared to the cost of providing storage facilities for conventional bales. Round balers and stack wagons can be used to harvest stover for winter feed or bedding (Fig. 6).

Fig. 6—Spread Equipment Use By Harvesting Stover and Hay

Because of package shape and density, it is considered impractical to transport round bales or loose hay stacks for long distances. Without controlled feeding, waste may be excessive, particularly if animals are given free access to all bales or stacks in a field at the same time. Bales and stacks are too large for small herds and hay may be picked over and become unpalatable before it is consumed, even if placed in a manger or feed rack. Large round bales are a safety problem if they roll on a slope, or when lifted high on a front-end loader.

EVALUATING HARVESTING SYSTEMS

Some additional factors to consider, whether expanding or modifying a current harvesting system, or selecting a new one:

- Climate
- Type of crop and possible harvesting methods
- Crop acreage and yield
- Availability of a market for entire crop or surplus not fed on farm
- Type of livestock and feeding method
- Capacity of equipment
- Dependability of available equipment
- Effect of harvesting timeliness on quality
- Operating costs per ton fed or sold
- Labor requirement
- Availability and cost of labor
- Operator skills required for successful operation
- Management requirements
- Management abilities and desires
- Availability of investment capital
- Ability of new equipment to work with present equipment
- Usability of storage structures
- Suitability of system to the rest of the farming enterprise
- Flexibility of system to harvest crop residues
- Transportation from field to storage or feeding area or point of sale
- Dependability of dealer service and parts availability
- Distance to nearest dealer or service outlet

Many of these factors are interrelated and must be considered together in choosing or evaluating a particular system. Here are some reasons each of these factors must be considered. Additional factors may affect individual operations.

Climate affects the type of crops which can be produced, the time available for harvest, and the possibility of weather damage (Fig. 7) to the crop or interruption of harvest.

Fig. 7—Climate Affects Quality of Crop and Timeliness of Harvest

Fig. 8—Maximum Feeding Efficiency?

Type of crop (grass, legumes, row crops) dictates the *harvest methods.* Corn and sorghum may be harvested as silage or stover, but are not adapted for hay production.

Ownership of harvesting equipment is normally not economical for very small *crop acreage and yield.* Heavy yields of some grasses and legumes may require harvesting as silage because of the long curing time in the field required for hay production and the danger of weather damage.

Will the hay or forage be fed to dairy cows, beef cows, fattening cattle, sheep, or horses? Silage feeding may be impractical for beef cattle kept in open pastures all year. Similarly, feeding loose hay stacks would be difficult to impossible in a stanchioned milking barn. So, the harvesting system must complement the *livestock and feeding method* for maximum efficiency of the feeding system and overall hay or forage use (Fig. 8).

Before purchase, check on the *capacity of the equipment.* Can it complete operations on time without sacrificing crop quality? Is it too big? How about *dependability?* If constant repairs are required, capacity drops, operations may be delayed, and quality gets bad.

What is the *effect of harvesting timeliness on the quality* of a particular crop? Most hay crops should be cut in early bloom stages for optimum nutrient yield and quality. Delayed harvesting may produce more tonnage per acre, but actually fewer nutrients. If silage or haylage is harvested too dry it won't pack well and the danger of spoilage increases. Storing silage too wet increases seepage and nutrient loss.

When planning, consider *equipment operating costs per ton fed or sold,* not just the cost per acre or total annual operating costs. Look too at *labor requirement* plus the *availability and cost of labor* in the area (Fig. 9). Harvesting silage and conventional bales requires three or four men for efficient operation. Round balers and stack wagons require only one man. In some areas, labor may not be available at any price for manhandling bales, but might be available for driving a tractor or operating a forage blower.

Consider the *operator skills required for successful operation.* Be sure training time and facilities are available, especially for hired or part-time labor which may require more training. *Management requirements* range from harvesting stover after grain harvest to careful determination of moisture content, addition of proper amounts of water, and careful adjustment of hay cubers. *Management ability* and desire must be present for any system to operate efficiently. If a manager doesn't understand a system, or doesn't make the system perform properly, chances of successful operation are very small.

Availability of investment capital may determine the system size and capacity as well as the type of system. Chopped forage systems and cubers require far more capital than conventional baled hay, round bale, or loose stacked hay systems. Attempting to stretch severely limited capital may encourage a tendency to neglect maintenance and repairs which eventually increases system operating costs and reduces equipment capacity and service life.

New equipment must have the ability to work with equipment, unless an entirely new system is being developed. A new self-propelled wagon would be out of place with an older 7-foot (2.1 m) mower trailing a conditioner and conventional baler. So would 3-ton (2.7 t) forage boxes and running gear with a new self-propelled forage harvester.

Fig. 9—Is Labor Available And Inexpensive?

If you want a particular storage and feeding system, plan harvesting systems to *use present storage structures.* If you are considering an automatic bale wagon, storage facilities must have adequate vertical clearance. If structures limit expansion it may be more economical to change the structures.

A new *forage harvesting system must match the whole farming enterprise.* Avoid forcing competition between forage harvesting and other operations. Increase equipment use by including *flexibility in the system to harvest crop residues.*

Keep loading, unloading, and handling of hay or forage to a minimum by planning *transportation from field to storage, feeding place, or point of sale* BEFORE selecting harvesting equipment. Is special hauling or handling equipment needed?

Look carefully at the *dependability of dealer service and parts availability* of all system components before changing equipment. Parts availability and dealer product knowledge could be problems with equipment not common in your area. Determine also the *distance to the nearest dealer or service outlet* for parts and repair service. A slightly less desirable machine or system, with strong support from a nearby dealer, could be a better alternative than buying the best equipment from a far-away source. Before accepting "the lowest price around," be sure the dealer is able and willing to provide adequate service after the sale.

The importance of each of these factors varies, depending on available resources and conditions. For example, family farms are frequently short on labor so they usually need low-labor systems. Commercial hay or forage growers may want systems with the highest possible capacity. However, for all operations, the greatest emphasis should be placed on managerial abilities. What are the goals of the operation? Without proper management, no system can be profitable, nor is it likely to yield a high-quality product.

BASIC HARVESTING SYSTEMS

No single piece of harvesting equipment can economically harvest a standing crop and place it in storage. Consequently, two or more machines must work together to harvest forage. Such a pair or group of machines is referred to as a "harvesting system." An efficient system harvests the crop properly and also permits each component to operate at full capacity. If machines do not complement each other, the system has poor field efficiency. Poor field efficiency increases costs and can lower the quality of forage. To maintain maximum efficiency, the harvesting system should be updated as new and more efficient harvesting equipment becomes available.

COMPARING HARVEST SYSTEMS

Harvest systems for hay, silage, and haylage are shown in the following diagrams and descriptions. These systems are well matched to allow good field efficiency for each machine. Included with the diagrams are annual system use and labor requirements per ton of forage from standing crop to storage. Labor requirements are based on the actual labor required to harvest and handle the forage but do not include the additional time required for proper system management and feeding. For uniformity, labor requirements are based on a hauling distance of one mile.

HAY HARVESTING SYSTEMS

SYSTEM 1, WAGON CHUTE LOADING CONVENTIONAL BALES

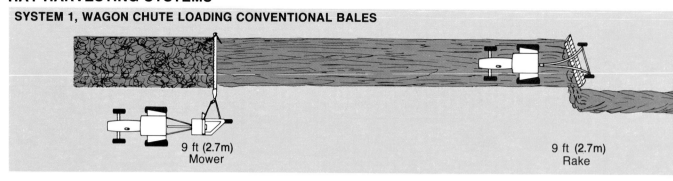

9 ft (2.7m)
Mower

9 ft (2.7m)
Rake

SYSTEM 2, EJECTOR LOADING CONVENTIONAL BALES

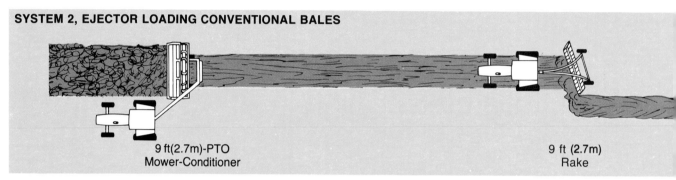

9 ft(2.7m)-PTO
Mower-Conditioner

9 ft (2.7m)
Rake

SYSTEM 3, HAND LOADING CONVENTIONAL BALES

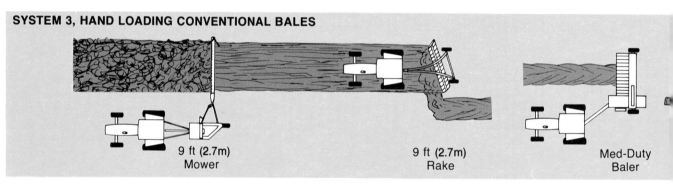

9 ft (2.7m)
Mower

9 ft (2.7m)
Rake

Med-Duty
Baler

SYSTEM 4, HAND LOADING CONVENTIONAL BALES

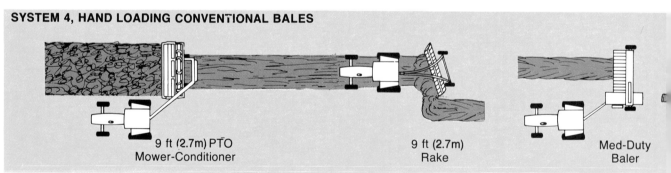

9 ft (2.7m) PTO
Mower-Conditioner

9 ft (2.7m)
Rake

Med-Duty
Baler

Systems 1, 2, 3, and 4

Systems 1, 2, 3, and 4 are the hay systems frequently used on smaller farms that feed all or most of the hay produced. Systems 1 and 3 may include a conditioner to help produce higher-quality hay (with an increase in labor per ton, see Table 1). Systems 1 and 2 are being replaced in some areas by round balers and stack wagons to reduce labor requirements. The use of Systems 3 and 4 is decreasing because laborers and custom haulers are becoming difficult to employ. With such a high labor requirement, expansion is limited, and excellent management is needed to harvest the highest-quality hay. However, these systems are well matched to many farms. They provide economical methods for harvesting hay and permit the sale of excess hay not fed on the farm.

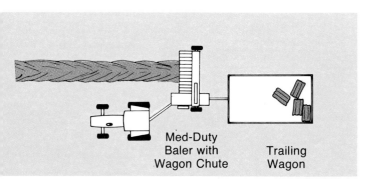

Annual Capacity Range	Labor Requirement (Field to Storage)
Tons/yr (t)	Man-hrs/ton (t)

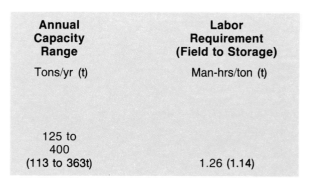

Med-Duty Baler with Wagon Chute — **Trailing Wagon**

125 to 400 (113 to 363t)	1.26 (1.14)

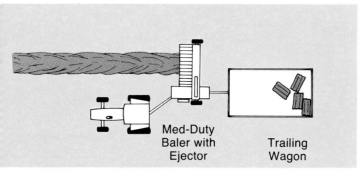

Med-Duty Baler with Ejector — **Trailing Wagon**

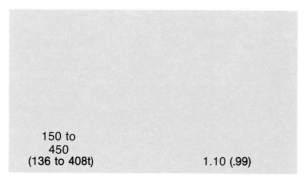

150 to 450 (136 to 408t)	1.10 (.99)

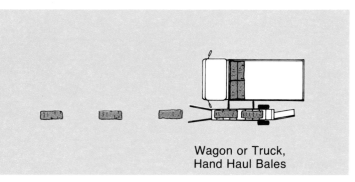

Wagon or Truck, Hand Haul Bales

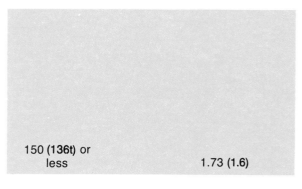

150 (136t) or less	1.73 (1.6)

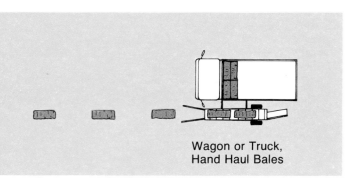

Wagon or Truck, Hand Haul Bales

125 to 400 (113 to 363t)	1.70 (1.5)

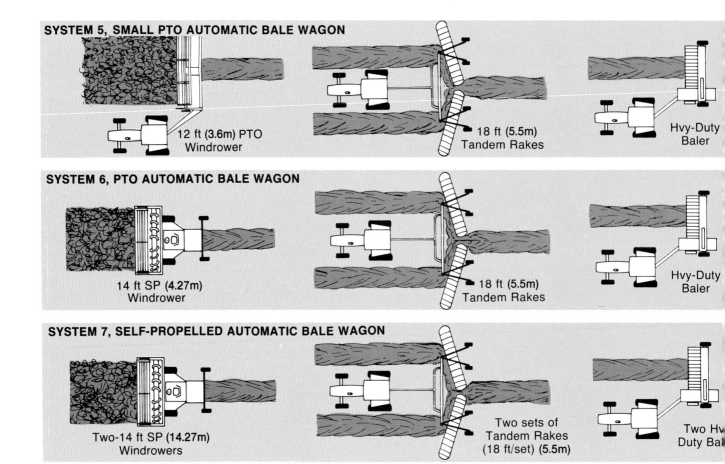

SYSTEM 5, SMALL PTO AUTOMATIC BALE WAGON

12 ft (3.6m) PTO Windrower

18 ft (5.5m) Tandem Rakes

Hvy-Duty Baler

SYSTEM 6, PTO AUTOMATIC BALE WAGON

14 ft SP (4.27m) Windrower

18 ft (5.5m) Tandem Rakes

Hvy-Duty Baler

SYSTEM 7, SELF-PROPELLED AUTOMATIC BALE WAGON

Two-14 ft SP (14.27m) Windrowers

Two sets of Tandem Rakes (18 ft/set) (5.5m)

Two Hvy Duty Ba

Systems 5, 6, and 7

Systems 5, 6, and 7 replace the 3-man bale-hauling crew in Systems 3 and 4 with an automatic bale wagon and one skilled operator. A cost analysis comparing System 4 with the automatic bale wagon systems shows breakeven annual tonnages of approximately 200, 350, and 800 tons (181, 317, and 725 t) for the 55 bale PTO wagon, 104 bale

PTO wagon, and 160 bale self-propelled wagon systems respectively. Increased use of these systems beyond the annual breakeven tonnage provides cost savings over System 4.

The use of automatic bale wagon systems is limited because of the large breakeven annual tonnages. However, substantial labor reduction can lead to increased production and provide an opportunity to acquire custom bale

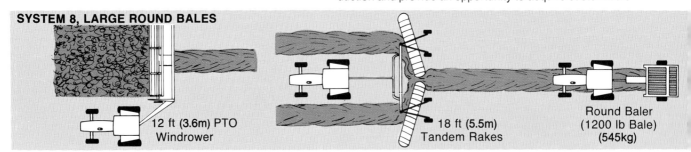

SYSTEM 8, LARGE ROUND BALES

12 ft (3.6m) PTO Windrower

18 ft (5.5m) Tandem Rakes

Round Baler (1200 lb Bale) (545kg)

System 8

The cost of owning and operating a round baler, System 8, compares favorably with systems 1, 2, 3, and 4. Cost comparisons show that the breakeven annual production to justify ownership of a round baler system is about 75 tons (68 t) per year.

One-man haying is feasible with a round baler system because bales are produced mechanically and can be moved and fed with a fork attachment on the 3-point hitch or front-end loader of a tractor. With this system, hand labor is eliminated; however, a mechanical device is always needed to move the bales. Due to their round shape, the bales are weather-resistant and require no special storage

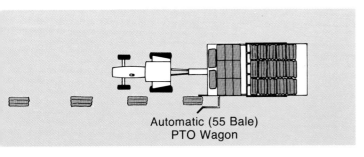

Automatic (55 Bale)
PTO Wagon

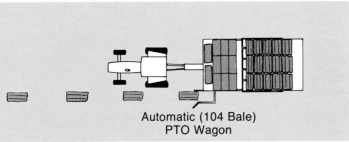

Automatic (104 Bale)
PTO Wagon

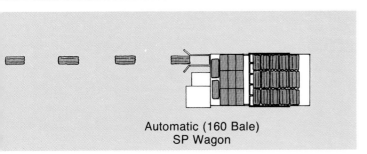

Automatic (160 Bale)
SP Wagon

Annual Capacity Range	Labor Requirement (Field-to-Storage)
Tons/yr (t)	Man-hrs/ton (t)
200 to 500 (181 to 453t)	0.63 (.57)
350 to 800 (317 to 725t)	0.54 (.48)
800 to 2,000 (725 to 1814t)	0.48 (.43)

hauling and stacking in some areas. High capacity in the hauling and stacking operation can also increase hay quality by reducing chances of weather damage in the field. This high quality can be preserved when bales are properly stored. However, special storage structures are required to accept the bale wagon during unloading.

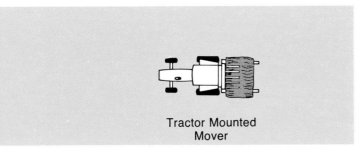

Tractor Mounted
Mover

75 to 600 (68 to 544t)	0.83 (.75)

cover. Since round bales do not stack efficiently, long-distance transportation is expensive. Also, without proper control, feeding losses may be excessive, which can reduce the cost savings realized from the baling and storing operations.

SYSTEM 9, 1-TON (.9t) STACKS

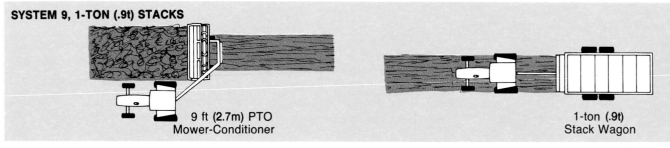

9 ft (2.7m) PTO
Mower-Conditioner

1-ton (.9t)
Stack Wagon

SYSTEM 10, 3-TON (2.7t) STACKS

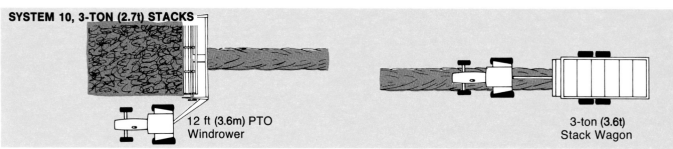

12 ft (3.6m) PTO
Windrower

3-ton (3.6t)
Stack Wagon

SYSTEM 11, 6-TON (5.4t) STACKS

14 ft (4.3m) SP
Windrower

6-ton (4.3t)
Stack Wagon

Systems 9, 10, and 11

Loose hay stack wagons, Systems 9, 10, and 11, are used on farms and ranches and commercial hay farms near markets. The breakeven annual tonnages, compared to Systems 1, 2, 3, and 4, for 1, 3, and 6 ton (.9, 33.6, and 4.3 t) loose hay stack wagon systems are about 75, 150, and 300 tons, (68, 136, and 272 t) respectively.

In addition to reduced harvesting costs, stack wagons save labor and make one-man haying possible. Stack wagons can stack a wide variety of materials: alfalfa, grass hay, straw, and even corn and milo stover. Stacks properly formed with a stack wagon resist weather so they can be stored outside without covering. No special management techniques are required, but operator experience will result in better stack shape and hay quality. Movers are needed

SYSTEM 12, CUBES

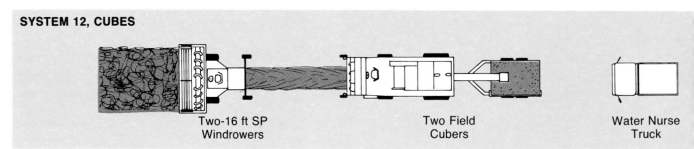

Two-16 ft SP
Windrowers

Two Field
Cubers

Water Nurse
Truck

System 12

Field cubing, System 12, is not widely used because of climate and crop restrictions. A cost analysis reveals that cubing of less than 1,000 tons (.907 t) per year per cuber is not economically justified. Therefore, field cubing is best suited to commercial alfalfa growers in a dry climate. The

high-density cubes require less storage space, receive a premium on the market, and are easy to handle, transport, and feed. A field-cubing system, to be operated successfully, requires an outstanding manager.

	Annual Capacity Range	Labor Requirement (Field-to-Storage)
	Tons/yr	Man-hrs/ton (t)

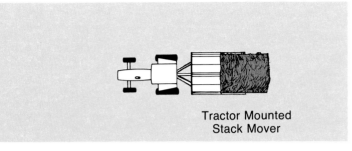

Tractor Mounted
Stack Mover

75 to 400
(68 to 363t)

0.84 (.76)

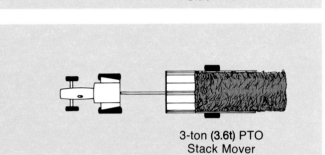

3-ton (3.6t) PTO
Stack Mover

150 to 700
(136 to 635t)

0.55 (.50)

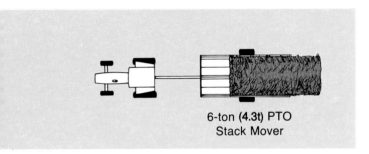

6-ton (4.3t) PTO
Stack Mover

300 to 1,000
(272 to 907t)

0.41 (.37)

to handle loose-hay stacks, but stacks are frequently unloaded near the edge of the field during stacking and are not moved until feeding. This permits more efficient use of labor, and eases scheduling problems during harvest. Proper control of feeding can eliminate excessive waste.

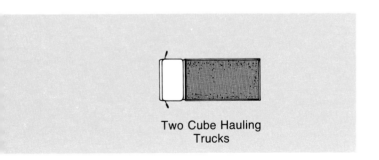

Two Cube Hauling
Trucks

2,000 to 10,000
(1814 to 9070t)

0.69 (.63)

317

SILAGE HARVESTING SYSTEMS

SYSTEM 13, SILAGE

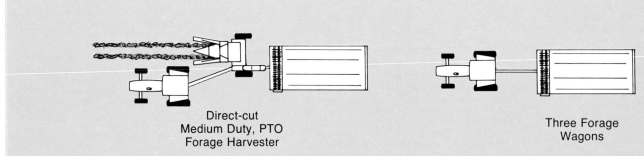

Direct-cut
Medium Duty, PTO
Forage Harvester

Three Forage
Wagons

SYSTEM 14, SILAGE

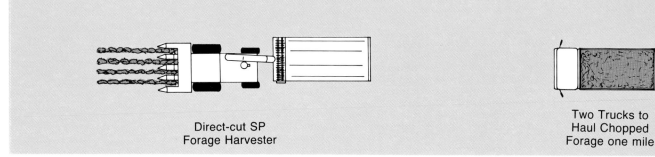

Direct-cut SP
Forage Harvester

Two Trucks to
Haul Chopped
Forage one mile

Systems 13 and 14

Direct-cut silage operations are the most labor-efficient methods of harvesting forage. However, a large investment in equipment and storage units discourages many potential silage producers.

System 13 is the most common silage-harvesting system used today. This system allows the smaller producer to own equipment, but it has sufficient capacity for larger operations. The breakeven tonnage to justify ownership is difficult to establish, because the entire harvesting system seldom is used to harvest less than 325 tons (322 t) of silage per year. Harvest requires three men — one to operate the forage harvester, one to transport forage wagons, and one to operate the forage blower.

System 14 is a higher-capacity, more expensive silage-harvesting system. Self-propelled forage harvesters are suited for larger operations, and are used for custom work. Normal annual output from a self-propelled forage harvester is from 2,000 to 10,000 tons (1814 to 9070 t). Since

SYSTEM 15, SILAGE

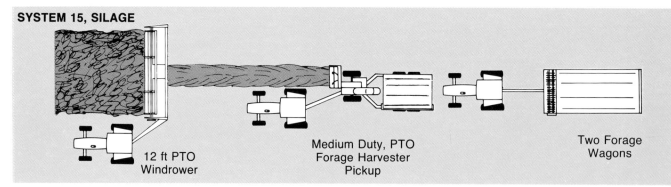

12 ft PTO
Windrower

Medium Duty, PTO
Forage Harvester
Pickup

Two Forage
Wagons

System 15

System 15 is a wilted-silage harvesting operation. The windrowing operation reduces the overall harvesting labor efficiency compared to Systems 13 and 14. Chopping capacity of the forage harvester is reduced with System 15, primarily because the per acre yield of most grasses, cereal grain crops, and legumes is lower than that of corn or forage sorghums. However, wilted-silage harvesting operations are used to remove excess moisture from a high-moisture crop before ensiling. Excess moisture in silage increases seepage loss during storage and causes silage to be soggy, sour, and unpalatable. Minimum annual tonnage to justify equipment for the wilted-silage operation of System 15 is typically 500 tons (454 t) of silage or the equivalent of 200 tons (181 t) of hay.

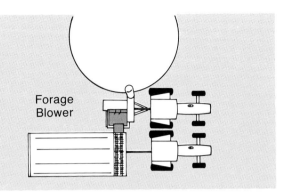

Forage Blower

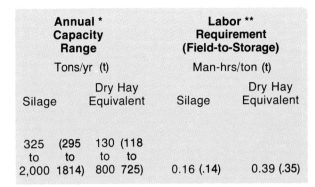

Annual * Capacity Range Tons/yr (t)		Labor ** Requirement (Field-to-Storage) Man-hrs/ton (t)	
Silage	Dry Hay Equivalent	Silage	Dry Hay Equivalent
325 to 2,000 (295 to 1814)	130 to 800 (118 to 725)	0.16 (.14)	0.39 (.35)

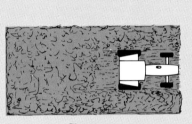

Tractor to Pack Silo

2,000 to 10,000 (1814 to 9070)	800 to 4,000 (725 to 3628)	0.10 (.90)	0.24 (.21)

this system has more capacity, additional labor is required to keep it operating at highest efficiency. At least four men are used with most self-propelled, direct-cut, silage harvesting operations. The additional labor is needed to haul green chopped forage from the field to the silo. But even with extra manpower, the labor efficiency of System 14 is greater compared to System 13 because of the increased harvesting capacity.

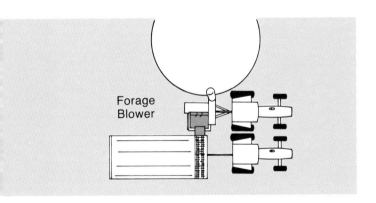

Forage Blower

500 to 1,200 (453 to 1088)	200 to 480 (181 to 435)	0.22 (.19)	0.54 (.49)

* Capacity ranges are based on silage at 50% moisture content. Capacity ranges are given for haylage and also converted to equivalent dry matter at 20% moisture to provide comparison with hay equipment.

** Labor requirements are shown for haylage and for equivalent dry matter with 20% moisture content to provide comparison with hay equipment.

HAYLAGE HARVESTING SYSTEMS

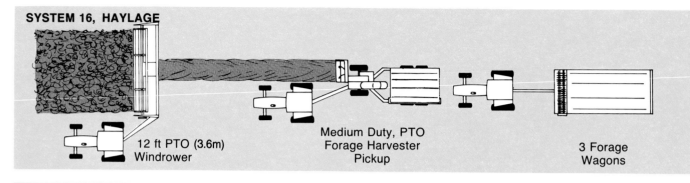

SYSTEM 16, HAYLAGE

12 ft PTO (3.6m)
Windrower

Medium Duty, PTO
Forage Harvester
Pickup

3 Forage
Wagons

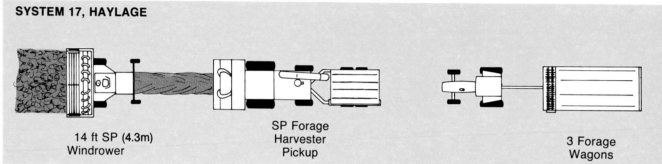

SYSTEM 17, HAYLAGE

14 ft SP (4.3m)
Windrower

SP Forage
Harvester
Pickup

3 Forage
Wagons

Systems 16 and 17

Systems 16 and 17 are haylage-harvesting systems. These harvest systems are similar to System 15 because of the windrowing and wilting operation. Annual tonnage required to justify ownership of these harvest systems also depends on the storing and feeding system. However, System 16 (PTO-driven forage harvester) and System 17 (self-propelled forage harvester) are seldom used to harvest less than 350 and 1,000 tons (317 and 907 t) of haylage per year, respectively. Three laborers are needed during harvest for an efficient operation.

MACHINE CAPACITY AND LABOR REQUIREMENT

Tables 1 and 2 list the field capacity and labor requirement for machines. The capacities presented in these tables are based on United States data. The observations were made over a wide range of field conditions, operator skills, and equipment conditions. A specific operation may have a higher or lower field capacity. In most cases the individual machine operations will be within 25 percent of the listed value.

TABLE 1

Information in Table 1 (p. 322) is based on an average production of one ton of hay per acre. Haul distances are one mile unless otherwise stated. Capacities are based on 80 percent field efficiency. This provides reasonable time for lubrication and refueling, minor repairs, lost time for turning, and so forth.

If ground speed and windrow size are adjusted to maintain equipment operation at full capacity at all times, an increase or decrease in yield per acre will not affect the labor requirement per ton or the capacity per hour. The labor and capacity per *acre* will vary with yield changes, however.

TABLE 2

Direct-cut silage operation capacities in Table 2 (p. 323) are based on production of 10 tons per acre (18 t per ha) (Fig. 10). Pickup operation capacities are based on an average yield equal to one ton of hay per acre. Haul distances are one mile unless otherwise stated. If equipment is operating at full capacity, a higher yield per acre will not affect hourly capacity or labor per ton.

Forage harvester capacities are based on a field efficiency of 65 percent because forage harvesters are more complex than hay harvesting machines and require more time for maintenance. This efficiency rating allows time for lubrication and fueling, wagon changes, knife sharpening, minor repairs and maintenance, lost time for turning, and so forth.

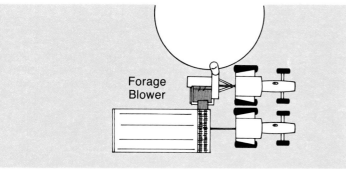

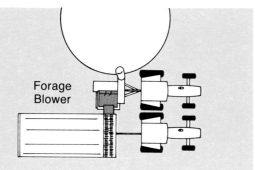

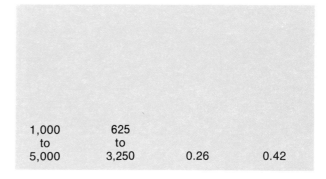

Annual * Capacity Range Tons/yr (t)		Labor ** Requirement (Field-to-Storage) Man-hrs/ton (t)	
Haylage	Dry Hay Equivalent	Haylage	Dry Hay Equivalent
350 (317 to to 1,000 907)	220 (199 to to 625 567)	0.43 (0.39)	0.68 (0.62)
1,000 to 5,000	625 to 3,250	0.26	0.42

* Capacity ranges are based on silage at 50% moisture content. Capacity ranges are given for haylage and also converted to equivalent dry matter with 20% moisture content to provide comparison with hay equipment.

**Labor requirements are shown for haylage and for equivalent dry matter with 20% moisture content to provide comparisonwith hay equipment.

Fig. 10—Direct Cut Silage Operation

USING THE TABLES

Data in the tables may be used to estimate and compare labor requirements for harvesting systems. For example, System 3 has a 9 foot mower, 9 foot rake, medium-duty baler, and a hand-hauling crew. From Table 1, labor requirements for each operation are:

Machine	Labor Requirement (man-hrs/ton) (t)	
Mower, 9-foot (2.7 m)	0.27	(0.24)
Rake, 9-foot (2.7 m)	0.19	(0.17)
Baler, medium-duty	0.16	(0.14)
Bales, hauling	1.11	(1.00)
TOTAL	1.73	(1.55)

The labor required to take one ton of hay from the standing crop to storage is 1.73 man-hours per ton (1.5/t); so 173 hours would be required to harvest and store 100 tons (90 t) of hay with this system. Additional time would be required for feeding.

DIRECT-CUT FORAGE HARVESTER

TABLE 1

TABLE 1
FIELD CAPACITY AND LABOR REQUIREMENT
FOR HAY-HARVESTING EQUIPMENT

Machine	Capacity tons/hr		Labor Requirement man-hrs/ton	
Bale mover, round—tractor-mounted				
Haul to storage	2.5	(2.8)	0.40	(.36)
Haul to feed	3.0	(3.3)	0.33	(.30)
Bale mover, round—truck-towed				
(5 bales per load)				
1-mile haul one-way (1.6 km)	11.5	(12.7)	0.09	(.08)
5-mile haul one-way (8 km)	6.5	(7.2)	0.15	(.14)
10-mile haul one-way (16 km)	3.7	(4.1)	0.27	(.24)
Bale wagon, automatic—55B, PTO	5.0	(5.5)	0.20	(.18)
Bale wagon, automatic—104B, PTO	8.0	(8.8)	0.13	(.12)
Bale wagon, automatic—160B, SP	13.7	(0.00)	0.07	(.06)
Baler, medium-duty—ejector or wagon chute	6.8	(7.5)	0.16	(.14)
Baler, medium-duty—bales on ground	6.4	(7.0)	0.16	(.14)
Baler, heavy-duty	8.0	(8.8)	0.13	(.12)
Baler, round—1200-lb. bale	7.5	(8.3)	0.13	(.12)
Bale, round—2000-lb. bale	8.5	(9.4)	0.12	(.11)
Bales, haul—3 men w/truck	2.7	(3.0)	1.11	(1)
Conditioner—7-ft. (2.1 m)	2.9	(3.2)	0.34	(.30)
Conditioner—9-ft. (2.7 m)	3.7	(4.1)	.027	(.24)
Cuber, field	4.0	(4.4)	0.25	(.22)
Cubes, haul—truck	4.0	(4.4)	0.25	(.22)
Cubes, water nurse truck	—	—	0.06	(.05)
Mower—7 ft. (2.1 m)	2.9	(3.1)	0.34	(.30)
Mower—9 ft. (2.7 m)	3.7	(4.1)	0.27	(.24)
Mower-conditioner—9 ft. (2.7 m), PTO	4.1	(4.5)	0.24	(.22)
Rake, single—9-ft. (2.7 m)	5.2	(5.7)	0.19	(.17)
Rake, tandem—18-ft. (5.5 m)	10.0	(11.0)	0.10	(.09)
Stack wagon—1-ton (.9 t)	5.0	(5.5)	0.20	(.18)
Stack wagon—3-ton (2.7 t)	6.5	(?.?)	0.15	(.14)
Stack wagon—6-ton (5.4 t)	7.5	(8.3)	0.13	(.12)
Stack wagon—8-ton (7.2 t)	8.0	(8.8)	0.13	(.12)
Stack mover—1-ton (.9 t)	2.5	(2.8)	0.40	(.36)
Stack mover—3-ton (2.7 t)	5.0	(5.5)	0.20	(.18)
Stack mover—6-ton, farm (5.4 t)	10.0	(11.0)	0.10	(.09)
Stack mover—8-ton (7.2 t)	15.0	(16.5)	0.07	(.06)
Stack mover—6 ton, highway (5.4 t)		(16.5)		
5-mile haul (8 km), one-way	15.0	(7.7)	0.07	(.06)
10-mile haul (16 km), one-way	7.0	(3.6)	0.14	(.13)
25-mile (40 km), one-way	3.3	(?.?)	0.30	(.27)
Windrower—12-ft. (3.5 m), PTO	4.9	(5.4)	0.20	(.18)
Windrower—14-ft. (4.2 m), SP	5.7	(6.3)	0.18	(.16)
Windrower—16-ft. (4.8 m), SP	8.0	(8.8)	0.13	(.12)

FEEDING TIME

Labor, health and age of the operator, and the number, type, and size of livestock affect the choice of hay and forage feeding methods and harvesting systems.

About one man-hour per ton (.9 man-hour per .9 t) is required for handfeeding conventional square bales, compared to about 0.33 man-hours per ton (.29/t) for large, round bales. Purdue University scientists estimate that feeding conventional bales to 50 cows requires an average of one hour per day, compared to about an hour per week to mechanically feed large round bales to the same size

TABLE 2 FIELD CAPACITY AND LABOR REQUIREMENT FOR FORAGE HARVESTING EQUIPMENT					
Machine	**Capacity *** tons/hr		**Labor Requirement **** man-hrs/ton		
68% Moisture Content	Silage	Dry Hay Equivalent	Silage	Dry Hay Equivalent	
Blower	25.0 (27.5)	10.0 (11.0)	0.04 (.04)	0.10 (.09)	
Harvester, direct-cut; small, PTO	12.0 (13.2)	4.8 (5.3)	0.08 (.07)	0.21 (.19)	
Harvester, direct-cut; medium, PTO	20.0 (22.0)	8.0 (8.8)	0.05 (.05)	0.13 (.12)	
Harvester, direct-cut; large, PTO	24.0 (26.4)	9.6 (10.6)	0.04 (.04)	0.10 (.09)	
Harvester, direct-cut; SP	40.0 (44.0)	16.0 (17.6)	0.02 (.02)	0.06 (.05)	
Harvester, pickup; medium, PTO	15.0 (16.5)	6.0 (6.6)	0.07 (.06)	0.17 (.15)	
Tractor; packing horizontal silo	40.0 (44.0)	16.0 (17.6)	0.02 (.02)	0.06 (.05)	
Truck; hauling chopped forage					
1 mile (1.6 km), one way	20.0 (22.0)	8.0 (8.8)	0.05 (.05)	0.13 (.12)	
5 mile (8 km), one way	16.0 (17.6)	6.4 (7.0)	0.06 (.05)	0.16 (.05)	
Wagon; hauling chopped forage					
3 wagons per man	8.3 (9.1)	3.3 (3.6)	0.04 (.04)	0.10 (.09)	
50% Moisture Content	Haylage	Dry Hay Equivalent	Haylage	Dry Hay Equivalent	
Blower	20.0 (22.0)	12.5 (13.8)	0.05 (.05)	0.08 (.07)	
Harvester, pickup; medium, PTO	10.0 (11.0)	6.3 (6.9)	0.10 (.09)	0.16 (.15)	
Harvester, pickup; SP	20.0 (22.0)	12.5 (13.8)	0.05 (.05)	0.08 (.07)	
Wagon, forage; hauling chopped forage;					
3 wagons per man	6.7 (7.4)	4.2 (4.6)	0.05 (.05)	0.08 (.07)	

* Capacities are based on moisture contents of either 68 or 50 percent as noted in the table. To provide a comparison with hay equipment, capacities have been converted to tons per hour of equivalent dry matter with 20 percent moisture content. That is, 25 tons of silage with 68 percent moisture content has the same amount of dry matter as 10 tons of hay with 20 percent moisture content.

** Labor requirements are shown for silage and haylage and for equivalent dry matter with 20 percent moisture content to provide comparison with hay equipment.

herd. Required feeding time may be increased or decreased by distance from storage to feeding area.

Feeding loose hay stacks on the farm requires an average of 0.4 man-hour per ton (.36/t) for 1-ton (1/t) stacks, 0.2 man-hour (.018/t) for 3-ton (2.7 t) stacks, and approximately 0.1 man-hour per ton (.9/t) for 6-ton (5.4 t) stacks.

Most silage and cube feeding systems are mechanized and require supervision and equipment control, more than actual labor, so feeding time can vary widely (Fig. 11). Time required per ton to feed silage from a trench or bunker silo also varies widely due to variations in equipment and methods — front-end loader direct to bunk; front-end loader to forage box and then to the bunk; or special silage loader to forage box.

If labor is plentiful, capital is short and herd size is small — conventional bales are probably the best choice. If operator age or health limits activity, round bales or loose hay stacks can be the best choice, even for relatively small herds. Dairy herds usually are fed large amounts of silage, and small amounts of hay.

SUMMARY

Hay and forage harvesting systems are available to the commercial producer and the livestock operator. The pri-

Fig. 11—Mechanized Cube Feeding System

Fig. 12—Select a System That Contributes to the Overall Operation

mary goals of each producer are to increase profits and reduce the costs of harvesting and handling forage. The profit margin in producing, harvesting, and handling forage is not very great. Therefore, a harvesting system must be used that contributes most to the overall operation (Fig. 12). The system selected must cut losses, through harvest timeliness, without increasing costs above an acceptable level. However, before any hay or forage harvesting system is selected, managerial abilities must be analyzed.

Information on hay and forage harvesting systems selection has been presented. However, further evaluation is needed to match a system to a particular farm. Picking a harvesting system is a difficult task. Matching equipment within a system to get high efficiency is even more difficult. Get more detailed information on matching and selecting equipment from the Fundamentals of Machine Operation Manual: Machinery Management.

CHAPTER QUIZ

1. (True or false?) Managerial capabilities must be evaluated when selecting a hay- or forage-harvesting system.

2. Explain why the automatic bale wagon systems reduce labor required to haul and store bales.

3. Typical labor requirement to harvest and store hay with a round baler system is 0.83 man-hours per ton. How many man-hours would be required with this system to harvest and store 150 tons of hay?

4. (True or false?) Loose hay stack wagon systems have good labor efficiency and make a one-man haying system feasible.

5. List three reasons why field-cubing is not widely used.

6. (True or false?) Direct-cut silage harvesting operations are not efficient labor systems because at least three laborers are required during harvesting.

7. (Fill in the blank.) A haylage harvesting operation requires considerably more labor per ton than a direct-cut silage operation primarily because of the _____ _____ operation.

8. How many man-hours would be required to windrow, stack, and move 150 tons of hay using a 12-foot windrower, 3-ton stack wagon, and a 3-ton stack mover? (See Table 1.)

Appendix

SUGGESTED READING

TEXTS

Machines for Power Farming; Stone, Archie A. and Gulvin, Harold E.; Wiley, New York, 1957.

Principles of Farm Machinery; second edition; Kepner, R. A.; Bainer, Roy and Barger, E.L.; AVI Publishing Company, Westport, Connecticut, 1972.

Farm Machinery and Equipment; fifth edition; Smith, Harris P.; McGraw-Hill, New York, 1964.

Yearbook of Agriculture, 1960: *Power to Produce*; United States Department of Agriculture, Washington, D.C.

Farm Power and Machinery Management; sixth edition; Hunt, Donnell R.; Iowa State University Press, Ames, Iowa, 1973.

Fundamentals of Machine Operation: Preventive Maintenance; John Deere Service Publications, Dept. F., John Deere Road, Moline, Illinois 61265.

Fundamentals of Machine Operation: Agricultural Machine Safety; John Deere Service Publications, Dept. F., John Deere Road, Moline, Illinois 61265.

Fundamentals of Machine Operation: Tractors; John Deere Service Publications, Dept. F., John Deere Road, Moline, Illinois 61265.

Fundamentals of Machine Operation: Machinery Management; John Deere Service Publications, Dept. F., John Deere Road, Moline, Illinois 61265.

VISUALS

Hay and Forage Harvesting Slide Set (FMO 142S). 35 mm. Color. Matching set of 160 slides for illustrations in FMO *Hay and Forage* text. John Deere Service Publications, Dept. F., John Deere Road, Moline, Illinois 61265.

TEACHER'S GUIDE AND STUDENT WORKBOOK

FMO Hay & Forage Harvesting Teacher's Guide (FMO-145T). Activities, exercises and transparency masters based on text. Student Workbook (FMO-146W). Study questions. John Deere Service Training, Dept. F, John Deere Road, Moline, Illinois 61265.

USEFUL INFORMATION

The following tables and charts are designed to serve as a quick reference to useful information related to hay and forage harvesting.

Where needed, examples are provided as to how to use this information.

WEIGHTS AND MEASURES

The following two charts show conversions of weights and measures from **U.S. systems** to **metric** and vice versa.

WEIGHTS AND MEASURES—U.S. TO METRIC

U.S. System			Metric Equivalent
LENGTH			
Unit	*Abbreviation*	*Equivalents In Other Units*	
Mile	mi	5280 feet, 320 rods, 1760 yards	1.609 kilometers
Rod	rd	5.50 yards, 16.5 feet	5.029 meters
Yard	yd	3 feet, 36 inches	0.914 meters
Foot	ft. or ′	12 inches, 0.333 yards	30.480 centimeters
Inch	in or ″	0.083 feet, 0.027 yards	2.540 centimeters
AREA			
Unit	*Abbreviation*	*Equivalents In Other Units*	
Square Mile	sq mi or m^2	640 acres, 102,400 square rods	2.590 square kilometers
Acre	A	4840 square yards, 43,560 square feet	0.405 hectares, 4047 square meters
Square Rod	sq rd or rd^2	30.25 square yards, 0.006 acres	25.293 square meters
Square Yard	sq yd or yd^2	1296 square inches, 9 square feet	0.836 square meters
Square Foot	sq ft or ft^2	144 square inches, 0.111 square yards	0.093 square meters
Square Inch	sq in or in^2	0.007 square feet, 0.00077 square yards	6.451 square centimeters
VOLUME			
Unit	*Abbreviation*	*Equivalents In Other Units*	
Cubic Yard	cu yd or yd^3	27 cubic feet, 46,656 cubic inches	0.765 cubic meters
Cubic Foot	cu ft or ft^3	1728 cubic inches, 0.0370 cubic yards	0.028 cubic meters
Cubic Inch	cu in or in^3	0.00058 cubic feet, 0.000021 cubic yards	16.387 cubic centimeters
CAPACITY			
Unit	*Abbreviation*	*U.S. Liquid Measure*	
Gallon	gal	4 quarts (231 cubic inches)	3.785 liters
Quart	qt	2 pints (57.75 cubic inches)	0.946 liters
Pint	pt	4 gills (28.875 cubic inches)	0.473 liters
Gill	gi	4 fluidounces (7.218 cubic inches)	118.291 milliliters
Fluidounce	fl oz	8 fluidrams (1.804 cubic inches)	29.573 milliliters
Fluidram	fl dr	60 minims (0.225 cubic inches)	3.696 milliliters
Minim	min	1/60 fluidram (0.003759 cubic inches)	0.061610 milliliters
		U.S. Dry Measure	
Bushel	bu	4 pecks (2150.42 cubic inches)	35.238 liters
Peck	pk	8 quarts (537.605 cubic inches)	8.809 liters
Quart	qt	2 pints (67.200 cubic inches)	1.101 liters
Pint	pt	½ quart (33.600 cubic inches)	0.550 liters
MASS AND WEIGHT			
Unit	*Abbreviation*	*Equivalents In Other Units*	
Ton	tn (seldom used)		
short ton		20 short hundredweight, 2000 pounds	0.907 metric tons
long ton		20 long hundredweight, 2240 pounds	1.016 metric tons
Hundredweight	cwt		
short hundredweight		100 pounds, 0.05 short tons	45.359 kilograms
long hundredweight		112 pounds, 0.05 long tons	50.802 kilograms
Pound	lb or lb av also #	16 ounces, 7000 grains	0.453 kilograms
Ounce	oz or oz av	16 drams, 437.5 grains	28.349 grams
Dram	dr or dr av	27.343 grains, 0.0625 ounces	1.771 grams
Grain	gr	0.036 drams, 0.002285 ounces	0.0648 grams

WEIGHTS AND MEASURES—METRIC TO U.S.

Metric System			U.S. Equivalent		
LENGTH					
Unit	*Abbreviation*	*Number of Meters*			
Kilometer	km	1,000	0.62 mile		
Hectometer	hm	100	109.36 yards		
Decameter	dkm	10	32.81 feet		
Meter	m	1	39.37 inches		
Decimeter	dm	0.1	3.94 inches		
Centimeter	cm	0.01	0.39 inch		
Millimeter	mm	0.001	0.04 inch		
AREA					
Unit	*Abbreviation*	*Number of Square Meters*			
Square Kilometer	sq km or km²	1,000,000	0.3861 square mile		
Hectare	ha	10,000	2.47 acres		
Are	a	100	119.60 square yards		
Centare	ca	1	10.76 square feet		
Square Centimeter	sq cm or cm²	0.0001	0.155 square inch		
VOLUME					
Unit	*Abbreviation*	*Number of Cubic Meters*			
Stere	s	1	1.31 cubic yards		
Decistere	ds	0.10	3.53 cubic feet		
Cubic Centimeter	cu cm or cm³ also cc	0.000001	0.061 cubic inch		
CAPACITY					
Unit	*Abbreviation*	*Number of Liters*	*Cubic*	*Dry*	*Liquid*
Kiloliter	kl	1,000	1.31 cubic yards		
Hectoliter	hl	100	3.53 cubic feet	2.84 bushels	
Decaliter	dkl	10	0.35 cubic foot	1.14 pecks	2.64 gallons
Liter	l	1	61.02 cubic inches	0.908 quart	1.057 quarts
Deciliter	dl	0.10	6.1 cubic inches	0.18 pint	0.21 pint
Centiliter	cl	0.01	0.6 cubic inch		0.338 fluidounce
Milliliter	ml	0.001	0.06 cubic inch		0.27 fluidram
MASS AND WEIGHT					
Unit	*Abbreviation*	*Number of Grams*			
Metric Ton	MT or t	1,000,000	1.1 tons		
Quintal	q	100,000	220.46 pounds		
Kilogram	kg	1,000	2.2046 pounds		
Hectogram	hg	100	3.527 ounces		
Decagram	dkg	10	0.353 ounce		
Gram	g or gm	1	0.035 ounce		
Decigram	dg	0.10	1.543 grains		
Centigram	cg	0.01	0.154 grain		
Milligram	mg	0.001	0.015 grain		

ACREAGE PER MILE OF VARIOUS WIDTHS

Width	Acres
1 foot	0.121
5 feet	0.605
8 feet	0.968
10 feet	1.21
12 feet	1.452
14 feet	1.694
15 feet	1.815
16 feet	1.936
18 feet	2.178
20 feet	2.42
24 feet	2.904
25 feet	3.025

ACRES-PER-HOUR CHART

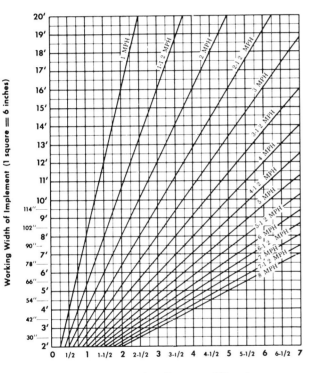

EXAMPLE: (Using a 3-bottom, 14-inch plow cutting 42 inches, traveling at 3¼ mph.) Find 42 inches in the left-hand column. Follow the line at 42 to the right to a point midway between the diagonal lines marked 3 mph and 3½ mph. From this point, follow nearest vertical line to bottom of chart. Note acreage per hour is slightly less than 1½.

HOW TO DETERMINE FIELD SPEED

To determine how fast you are operating hay and forage equipment in the field, estimate speed as follows:

1. Mark off a distance of 176 feet in the field.

2. Drive the measured distance at the speed you would normally operate that machine.

3. Check the number of seconds required to drive between the markers with a stop watch or watch with a sweep second hand.

4. Divide the time in seconds into 120 for speed in miles per hour (mph).

5. Adjust the operating speed, if necessary, to the recommended speed for that equipment.

The chart below lists the time in seconds for speeds up to 8 miles per hour.

FIELD SPEEDS	
Time To Drive 176 Feet	Speed
120 seconds	1 mph
60 seconds	2 mph
40 seconds	3 mph
30 seconds	4 mph
24 seconds	5 mph
20 seconds	6 mph
17 seconds	7 mph
15 seconds	8 mph

DIRECTIONS: In the left-hand column, find the line representing the working width of your equipment. Follow the line to the right until it reaches the diagonal line representing your speed of travel. From this point, follow the nearest vertical line directly to the bottom of the chart and estimate the acres per hour from the nearest figure. Note: If your equipment is wider than 20 feet, or the horizontal and diagonal lines do not meet on the chart, make your estimate using half (or one-fourth) the working width and multiplying the result by two (or four, whichever is applicable).

APPROXIMATE DRY MATTER CAPACITY OF SILOS

Depth of Settled Silage, ft	Silo Diameter, ft										
	10'	12'	14'	16'	18'	20'	22'	24'	26'	28'	30'
	TONS of dry matter										
20'	8	12	16	21	27	33	40	47	56	65	74
22	9	14	19	24	30	38	48	54	64	74	85
24	11	15	21	27	34	43	52	61	72	83	96
26	12	17	23	30	38	48	58	68	81	94	107
28	13	19	26	35	44	53	64	76	90	104	119
30	15	21	29	38	47	59	71	84	99	115	132
32'	16	23	32	41	52	65	78	93	109	127	145
34	18	25	34	45	57	70	85	101	119	137	158
36	19	28	37	48	62	76	92	109	129	150	172
38	21	30	41	53	67	82	100	118	139	161	185
40	22	32	44	57	72	89	107	127	150	173	199
42'		34	47	61	77	95	115	137	161	186	214
44		37	50	65	82	102	123	146	172	200	229
46		39	53	69	88	108	131	155	183	212	244
48		42	56	74	93	115	140	166	195	226	260
50		44	60	78	99	122	148	175	206	239	274
52'			64	83	105	129	157	186	219	254	291
54			67	88	111	137	165	197	231	267	306
56			71	93	117	144	174	207	243	282	324
58			74	98	123	151	183	218	261	297	339
60			78	102	129	159	192	228	273	309	357
62'					135	167	201	239	287	324	374
64					142	174	210	250	301	339	391
66					149	182	219	260	314	354	407
68					155	190	228	271	328	369	424
70					162	198	237	282	342	384	441
72'								293	356	400	458
74								305	371	415	476
76								316	385	431	493
78								328	400	446	511
80								339	414	462	528

Silage dry matter (%) = 100 − % moisture content of silage.

To estimate tons of conventional silage (approximately 30-35% dry matter; 65-70% moisture content) multiply dry matter capacity by 3.

For silage with different moisture content:

Estimated tons of silage =

100 x Tons of dry matter

Estimated % dry matter in silage

Source: Midwest Plan Service, Iowa State University, Ames, Iowa.

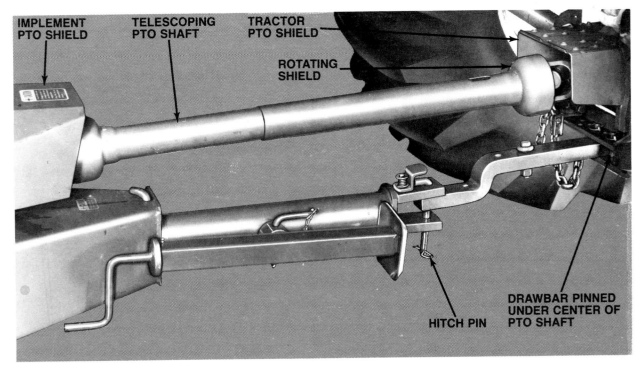

IMPLEMENT PTO SHIELD

TELESCOPING PTO SHAFT

TRACTOR PTO SHIELD

ROTATING SHIELD

DRAWBAR PINNED UNDER CENTER OF PTO SHAFT

HITCH PIN

Fig. 1—Adjust Tractor Drawbar

DRAWBAR AND PTO POSITIONING

Most current tractors and PTO driven implements are designed to conform to ASAE-SAE PTO standards for proper operation and to permit interchangeability of tractors and implements of different makes. *Always be sure the tractor PTO speed (540 or 1000 rpm) matches the speed required by the implement.*

For tractors and equipment that meet the standard dimensions (Fig. 1):

● Align the drawbar hitch pin hole vertically with the centerline of the tractor PTO shaft and pin the drawbar securely in place.

● Adjust drawbar length to provide 14 inches (540 rpm PTO) or 16 inches (1000 rpm PTO) from the end of the tractor PTO shaft to the center of the drawbar hitch pin hole. Most current tractors have holes properly placed in the drawbar to provide the correct settings.

● Adjust drawbar height to within 13 to 17 inches (15 inches preferred) from the ground to the top of the drawbar at the hitch pin hole. Be sure tires are properly inflated before measuring.

● Adjust distance between the top of the tractor drawbar and centerline of PTO shaft to between 6 and 12 inches (8 inches preferred). Adjust PTO shaft support bracket on the implement if necessary.

● Be certain the telescoping PTO shaft is locked firmly to the tractor and implement PTO shafts to prevent accidental disconnection during operation.

● Keep all PTO shields in place and be sure rotating shields are free to turn.

● Avoid raising or lowering 3-point hitch-mounted, PTO-driven implements far enough to disengage telescoping PTO shaft sections during operation.

● Always use a safety hitch pin and be sure pin is locked securely in position to prevent accidental uncoupling of the implement during operation.

● *Always follow instructions in the equipment operator's manual for specific hitching recommendations.*

FIRE PREVENTION

Dry hay and forage burns rapidly. Spontaneous combustion can occur when large amounts of wet hay are stored in a barn or large stack. Even haylage and dry silage will burn from spontaneous combustion if the structure is not tightly sealed or if material is not well packed. Don't leave air pockets in silage and haylage during silo filling.

Fires can be started by faulty electrical wiring in hay barns or by careless use of matches near hay. Avoid fires and flammable materials by careful use of welders, lights, and power tools.

Keep grass and weeds mowed around hay storage buildings and stack yards to prevent the spread of grass fires into stored hay. If large numbers of stacks or bales are stored in a single place, leave occasional "fire lanes" or alleys between stacks or bales to slow fire spread in case it should get started, and to provide better access to hay for feeding.

Faulty exhaust systems and electrical wiring on tractors and self-propelled equipment touch off fires in hayfields and storage places every year. Many fires are started during careless refueling and when engine fuel systems leak.

Leaking hydraulic and brake fluids can be ignited if they contact hot spots. Friction from hay or forage wrapped around moving machinery parts can generate enough heat to start a fire.

"Good housekeeping" around hay storage areas, careful equipment operation, maintenance of buildings and equipment, and fire extinguishers on equipment and in each building are the best fire insurance policies available.

CAUTION: Escaping fluid under pressure can penetrate the skin causing serious injury. Relieve pressure before disconnecting hydraulic or other lines. Tighten all connections before applying pressure. Keep hands and body away from pinholes and nozzles which eject fluids under high pressure. Use a piece of cardboard or paper to search for leaks. Do not use your hand.

If ANY fluid is injected into the skin, it must be surgically removed within a few hours by a doctor familiar with this type injury or gangrene may result.

CAUTION: Do not feel for pinhole leaks. Escaping fluid under pressure can penetrate the skin causing injury. Relieve all hydraulic pressure before working on a pressurized hydraulic line or component.

GLOSSARY

AIR-PACK STACKER—Loose-hay stack wagon which blows chopped hay into the wagon with sufficient force that mechanical compacting is not required.

AUTOMATIC BALE WAGON—Machine which mechanically lifts bales from the ground and stacks them on the wagon bed. When loaded, the bed can be tilted and the entire load removed in a single stack. Bale wagons may be tractor-drawn or self-propelled.

BALANCED-HEAD KNIFE DRIVE—Specially-designed cutterbar knife drive which reduces vibration caused by reciprocating knife action.

BALE—Forage compressed into a rectangular or cylindrical package to increase density for easier handling, transport or feeding.

BALE ACCUMULATOR—A trailing attachment for conventional balers which collects and automatically unloads about 8 to 12 bales which can then be loaded on a wagon or truck by a tractor front-end loader with a special fork attachment.

BALE EJECTOR—An attachment for conventional balers which throws bales into a trailing wagon to eliminate hand loading or intermediate handling between baling and transport to storage.

BALE MOVER—Device for mechanically moving large round bales. It may be attached to a tractor 3-point hitch or front-end loader; mounted in a pickup truck bed; or trailed behind a tractor or truck.

BALER—Machine used to compress hay into bales. **Conventional balers** use a reciprocating plunger to press forage into a rectangular bale chamber to form bales which may be tied with two or three wires or twines. **Round balers** roll windrows either on the ground or in a cylindrical bale chamber to form bales weighing 1000 to 3000 pounds. Round bales may be tied with twine, or left untied, depending upon baler design and anticipated handling and feeding needs.

BALER TIMING—Synchronizing the operation of plungerhead, feeder teeth and needle drive to prevent needles from entering the bale chamber at the wrong time, or the plunger from striking feeder teeth.

BARN CURING—Artificial drying of hay with natural or heated air, usually to reduce exposure time in the field and possible weather damage.

CONDITIONER—Machine which crushes or cracks plant stems soon after they are cut to hasten drying.

CRIMPER ROLLS—Corrugated rolls on a hay conditioner which break forage stems at specific intervals to hasten drying.

CRUSHER ROLLS—Smooth conditioner rolls which crush plant stems to hasten drying.

CUBES—Small, high-density hay packages, usually about 1¼ inches square and 2 to 3 inches long.

CUT-AND-BLOW HARVESTER—Forage harvester which uses a cutterhead to chop material and a separate fan or blower to convey chopped material to a wagon or truck.

CUT-AND-THROW HARVESTER—Forage harvester which cuts forage and throws it into a wagon or truck in a single operation.

CUTTERBAR—Cutting device with a reciprocating knife having triangular blades or sections to cut standing crops.

CUTTERBAR LEAD—Setting the outer end of a mower cutterbar forward so that the cutterbar is perpendicular to the direction of travel during mower operation.

CUTTERHEAD—Rotating drum or flywheel in a forage harvester which supports the knives.

DEHYDRATION—Heating of hay to remove moisture. Economical only for high-value, high-quality crops such as alfalfa which will be incorporated into special livestock rations.

DIRECT-CUT SILAGE—Plants cut and chopped for silage in a single operation.

DRY MATTER CONTENT—Percent of total product weight which is not water. Dry matter content equals 100 minus percent moisture content.

FEED ROLLS—Pairs of rolls directly in front of a forage harvester cutterhead which regulate material flow to the cutterhead. Adjusting feed roll speed regulates length-of-cut.

FERMENTATION—The chemical change occurring in silage and haylage during storage.

FIELD CUBER—Machine used to produce cubes directly from windrowed hay.

FIELD CURING—Permitting hay or forage to dry naturally in a swath or windrow prior to chopping or packaging.

FLAIL—Cutting device with swinging knives or blades on a rotating horizontal shaft. Material is usually cut into several pieces as it is struck by succeeding flails and carried from standing position to the discharge point. Flails are used in different machine configurations to mow plants, chop forage, or as pickup units for forage harvesters and stack wagons.

FORAGE BLOWER—A fan-type conveyor used for placing chopped forage into storage structures.

FORAGE BOX—Self-unloading wagon box for handling silage, haylage, green chop, ear corn, mixed rations, and in some cases, bales. Most forage boxes unload either through a front cross conveyor or a rear door.

FORAGE HARVESTER—Machine which chops hay or forage into short lengths for easy storage or handling. With different header attachments they can cut standing crops, pick up windrows, snap ear corn or gather stover.

HARVESTING SYSTEM—A pair or group of machines used together to harvest hay or forage. An efficient system requires careful selection of individual machines so that each can work at full capacity.

HAY—Dried grass or legumes harvested and stored for livestock feed.

HAYLAGE—Low-moisture silage, with usually about 40 to 50 percent moisture content.

HIGH-DUMP WAGON—Wagon used to haul forage and other products which are unloaded by hydraulically raising and tipping the box to one side to empty the entire load at one time.

KNIFE GUARDS—Finger-line projections on a cutterbar which protect the knife from solid objects, provide a stationary shearing edge to oppose reciprocating knife action, and divide plants and guide them into the knife.

KNIFE REGISTER—Adjustment of a reciprocating knife so sections are equal distance from the centerline of the guards at each end of the cutting stroke.

KNIFE SECTIONS—Replaceable blades on a cutterbar knife.

KNIFE STROKE—Distance traveled by a reciprocating cutterbar knife. Stroke may be less than, equal to, or greater than guard spacing, depending upon mower design.

KNOTTER—Device which automatically holds and ties wire around a bale when the bale reaches the proper size.

LEDGER PLATES—Replaceable cutting edge of knife guards.

LENGTH-OF-CUT—Theoretical length of forage pieces if material was all fed straight into a forage harvester cutterhead—the distance feed rolls move material between knife cuts.

MECHANICAL-PRESS STACKER—Loose hay stack wagon which compresses hay or forage by mechanically or hydraulically forcing the wagon roof down against the load.

MOISTURE CONTENT—Percent of total product weight which is water. Moisture content equals 100 minus percent dry matter content of the product.

MOWER—Machine used to cut standing vegetation.

MOWER-CONDITIONER—Combination mower and conditioner which has conditioning rolls approximately the same length as the cutterbar.

NEEDLES—Slender, curved points which carry twine or wire from under the bale chamber to the knotter or twister when a bale reaches proper size.

PICKUP—Rotating drum-type mechanism with flexible teeth for lifting and conveying a windrow from the ground to a baler, forage harvester or other machine.

PITMAN—Device which converts rotary motion to reciprocating motion to drive a reciprocating cutterbar knife.

RAKE—Machine for windrowing swathed hay or forage, or to combine windrows for more efficient operation of harvesting machines. Also used to turn wet windrows for faster drying.

RECUTTER SCREEN—Curved plate with holes of various shapes and sizes which fits behind the cutterhead of some cut-and-blow harvesters to provide shorter length-of-cut.

RUNNING GEAR—The wagon; or frame, wheels and tongue, on which self-unloading forage boxes or other type boxes are mounted.

SHEAR BAR—Stationary knife in a forage harvester.

SIDE-DELIVERY RAKE—Rake with toothed parallel bars or wheels to roll plants to one side of the machine to form a windrow.

SILAGE—Green forage converted to animal feed through fermentation. Normal moisture content is 65 to 70 percent.

SILO—Structure for storing silage or haylage—may be a vertical cylinder, or a horizontal trench or bunker.

STACK MOVER—Machine for mechanically moving loose hay stacks. Movers for small stacks may be mounted on a tractor 3-point hitch, or attached to hitch draft links and be partially supported by caster wheels on each side. Larger stack movers are usually towed by tractors, and some are mounted on trucks.

STACK WAGON—Machine used to build stacks of loose hay or stover. Material may be picked up from a windrow by the stack wagon, or blown into the wagon by a forage harvester.

STACKER—Machine for stacking loose hay or forage.

STACKYARD—Outside storage area for large round bales or loose hay stacks.

STATIONARY CUBER—Machine used to form cubes of hay or forage gathered by a forage harvester, conventional baler, round baler, or loose hay stack wagon. Complete-ration cubes may be made by mixing concentrates and binders with the forage.

STOVER—Crop residue—usually corn or sorghum—left after grain is harvested.

SWATH—Cut forage or hay before windrowing.

TWISTER—Device which holds and twists together the ends of each wire on a bale.

WAGON CHUTE—Attachment for conventional balers which conveys bales onto a trailing wagon where they are stacked by hand by one or more men.

WILTED SILAGE—Forage cut and partially field-cured to reduce moisture content before chopping for silage.

WINDROW—Row of hay or forage formed by a rake, mower-conditioner or windrower to be picked up later by a harvesting machine.

WINDROWER—Machine for cutting forage or grain in which material is carried to the center of the table or platform by an auger or conveyor belts and fed into a narrow conditioner or dropped onto the ground.

INDEX